A BRIEF HISTORY OF

MODERN
WARFARE

RICHARD CONNAUGHTON

Constable & Robinson Ltd
3 The Lanchesters
162 Fulham Palace Road
London W6 9ER
www.constablerobinson.com

First published in the UK by Robinson,
an imprint of Constable & Robinson, 2008

A copy of the British Library Cataloguing in Publication
Data is available from the British Library

UK ISBN 978-1-84529-850-0

1 3 5 7 9 10 8 6 4 2

First published in the United States in 2008 by Running Press Book Publishers

9 8 7 6 5 4 3 2 1
Digit on the right indicates the number of this printing

US Library of Congress number: 2007936640
US ISBN 9780762433919

Running Press Book Publishers
2300 Chestnut Street
Philadelphia, PA 19103-4371

Visit us on the web!

www.runningpress.com

Printed and bound in the EU

RICHARD CONNAUGHTON, educated at the Duke of York's Dover, the Royal Military Academy Sandhurst and St John's Cambridge, served as a professional soldier for over thirty years. He took early voluntary retirement in the rank of Colonel as Head of the British Army's Defence Studies. He writes in the fields of politics, international relations and history, with particular reference to military intervention.

Also by Richard Connaughton

Rising Sun and Tumbling Bear: Russia's War with Japan

*The Republic of the Ushakovka: Admiral Kolchak
and the Allied Intervention in Siberia 1918–1920*

Military Intervention in the 1990s: A New Logic for War

Shrouded Secrets: Japan's War on Mainland Australia 1942–1944

Celebration of Victory: V-E Day 1945

The Nature of Future Conflict

Descent into Chaos: The Doomed Expedition into Low's Gully

The Battle for Manila (with John Pimlott and Duncan Anderson)

MacArthur and Defeat in the Philippines

Military Intervention and Peacekeeping: the Reality

Omai: The Prince Who Never Was

Other titles in the *Brief History* series

A Brief Guide to Charles Darwin   Cyril Aydon

A Brief Guide to the End of Oil   Paul Middleton

A Brief Guide to Global Warming   Jessica Wilson & Stephen Law

A Brief Guide to the Greek Myths   Stephen Kershaw

A Brief Guide to Islam   Paul Grieve

A Brief History of 1917   Roy Bainton

A Brief History of the Birth of the Nazis   Nigel H. Jones

A Brief History of British Kings and Queens   Mike Ashley

A Brief History of Christianity   Bamber Gascoigne

A Brief History of the Crusades   Geoffrey Hindley

A Brief History of the Druids   Peter Berresford Ellis

A Brief History of the Dynasties of China   Bamber Gascoigne

A Brief History of the End of the World   Simon Pearson

A Brief History of the Future   Oona Strathern

A Brief History of Globalization   Alex MacGillivray

A Brief History of Infinity   Brian Clegg

A Brief History of the Magna Carta   Geoffrey Hindley

A Brief History of Medieval Warfare   Peter Reid

A Brief History of the Middle East   Christopher Catherwood

A Brief History of Misogyny   J. Holland

A Brief History of the Normans   François Neveux

A Brief History of the Private Lives of the Roman Emperors   Anthony Blond

A Brief History of Science   Thomas Crump

A Brief History of Secret Societies   David V. Barrett

A Brief History of Stonehenge   Aubrey Burl

A Brief History of the Wars of the Roses   Desmond Seward

Dedicated to those who helped

CONTENTS

List of Illustrations and Maps   ix

 1 Introduction   1
 2 Goose Green 1982   29
 3 Grenada 1983   77
 4 The Iraq Conflict 1990–1991   123
 5 Mogadishu 1992–1993   161
 6 Gorazde 1995   203
 7 Operation Barras – Sierra Leone 2000   250
 8 The Battles for Fallujah 2003–2004   292
 9 Helmand 2006–2007   341
10 Reflection   384

    List of Abbreviations   399
    Notes   403
    Select Bibliography   435
    Index   439

ILLUSTRATIONS AND MAPS

Illustrations

Argentinean Prisoners at Goose Green. (*2 Para*)

Lieutenant-Colonel H. Jones, VC. (*The Defence Picture Library*)

Sir Paul Scoon, Maurice Bishop and Bernard Coard. (*Sir Paul Scoon*)

Richmond Hill Prison, the objective of Delta Force. (*A.R.G. Connaughton*)

St George's with Fort George. (*A.R.G. Connaughton*)

The Mitla Pass. (*Lieutenant-Colonel Alistair Mack*)

Brigadier Cordingley's press briefing on 28 November 1990. (*Patrick Cordingley*)

The British Army Challenger main battle tank. (*Patrick Cordingley*)

The Army MH-60K Special Operations Blackhawk. (*Department of Defense*)

Mike Durant's Super 64 helicopter over Mogadishu, 3 October 1993. (*Department of Defense*)

Lieutenant-Colonel Jonathon Riley with Lieutenant-General Rupert Smith. (*Jonathon Riley*)

Alpha and Bravo bridges, Gorazde, as seen from Observation Post 2. (*Jonathon Riley*)

Observation Post 2 from the rear. (*Jonathon Riley*)

The British Army's 'technical' Land Rover carrying a 12.7-mm (0.5-inch) Browning in a Weapons Mounted Installation Kit. (*Permanent Joint Headquarters*)

West Side Boys reporting to Benguema Camp to join the Sierra Leone Army. (*R.M. Connaughton*)

A confirmed insurgent stronghold goes up in smoke after a strategic aerial strike, 10 November 2004. (*Department of Defense; Lance-Corporal Joel A. Chaverri, United States Marine Corps*)

Howitzer gun crew of 4th Battalion, 14th Marine Corps shelling enemy positions inside Fallujah. (*Department of Defense*)

American soldiers entering a building in Fallujah, 12 November 2004. (*Department of Defense*)

Two members of a rescue team to locate Lance-Corporal Mathew Ford on board an Apache WAH-64 attack helicopter returning to Helmand. (*Royal Marines*)

Captain Mackenzie-Green, M Company, 42 Commando RM, sends a situation report in an operation to clear buildings used by the Taliban. (*Royal Marines*)

Lieutenant-Colonel M.J. Holmes RM giving orders to 42 Commando RM Group for Operation Silver, 6 April 2007. (*42 Commando Royal Marines*)

Maps

The Battles of Darwin and Goose Green   49

Operation Urgent Fury, Grenada   92

The Left Hook through Iraq   148

The Conflict in Mogadishu, 3 October 1993   184

The Former Yugoslavia, 1995   204

Operation Barras, Magbeni and Gberi Bana   280

Fallujah Phase 2   316

Helmand Province   351

1

Introduction

'The battles worthy of study and worthy of the
battle honours are not the bloody ones; they are the
ones that yield victory with few casualties.'

Rarely have war books been more popular. Images of conflict, often in remote places, are on our television screens on a daily basis yet the public is often uninformed as to what is happening and why British and American troops are there. This book fills that void and answers these questions by way of eight stories spanning a quarter of a century of conflict. The book goes somewhat further than the arbitrary selection of battles in so far as it cherry picks those that are among the greatest. The greatness of any battle is determined not by its size or by the numbers involved but rather by its influence upon future events. A battle is a constituent part in a war, there being one or more battles in a war. The Gulf conflict 1990–1 came close to being a one-battle war.

In May 1943, Sir Francis Tuker of the 8th Army wrote: 'The battles worthy of study and worthy of the battle honours are not the bloody ones; they are the ones that yield victory with few casualties. It is the approach that determines the outcome.' This is equally true of the high level of decision-making as it is of the lower level.

The eight stories in this book describe: Goose Green, the first battle of the Falklands conflict, 1982; the invasion of the island of Grenada, a member of the British Commonwealth, by the United States in 1983; the liberation of Kuwait,

1990–1; the battle for Mogadishu, 1992–3; the battle for
Gorazde in Bosnia, 1995; the rescue mission Operation Barras,
Sierra Leone, 2000; the battles for Fallujah, Iraq, 2003–4; and
the battles for Helmand Province, Afghanistan, 2006–7. Simply
describing these examples of modern warfare did not go far
enough, however. Certainly, while in the process of describing
the transition from Cold War to Hot War, issues arose that
needed to be recorded: changes in the type of conflict post-
Cold War, changes in technology and their impact upon
warfighting, the role and function of the United Nations (UN)
and NATO, an evaluation of the concept of peacekeeping,
public perceptions of the armed forces over a quarter of a
century and – that which does not change – the warrior and
the family unit to which he belongs and in which he fights.
This book is about the peculiarities, specifics and meaning of
these conflicts, following through the themes and threads.

Carl von Clausewitz (1780–1831) is remembered for his
posthumously published *Vom Kriege* (*On War*), in which he
wrote that war was an extension of politics by other means,
the civilian control of the military in democratic states being
a given. Mao Zedong, in his work *On Guerrilla Warfare*,
recognized that political and military affairs were not identical
but that 'it is impossible to isolate one from the other'. There
are two points to be drawn from that assertion. First, battles
come with a political wrapper, meaning they cannot be
properly understood without setting them in their political
context – a consideration that is secondary to describing the
action of soldiers on the ground. Second is our need to
understand what is meant by *war*.

We know that war is a military conflict between two or more
states or by groups within those states. War may be unlimited
or limited – what Clausewitz described as 'an act of force to
compel our enemy to do our will'.[1] Some theorists argue against

the use of the word 'war', preferring the term 'armed conflict'. There is some justification here. It would be wrong for example to describe the present counter-insurgency operation in Afghanistan as 'war'. Having said that, the term *war* will continue to be used as a form of shorthand for *armed conflict*.

The decision to commit the military to armed conflict is that of the leader of the Government, as advised by legal and military representatives and carried through a nation's Parliament. The essence of the decision-making process is formulated around the consideration of recognizable factors such as: whom can we send? Is there a vital national interest or moral obligation to intervene? Is there a real threat to international peace, security, the rule of law and humanitarianism? Is there a shared common aim? Can the proposed mission succeed? How is success to be defined? Can the conclusion – the end game – be envisaged, and do we have an exit strategy? In which case, how is failure to be defined? And, finally, who pays?

Armed conflict is subject to international law, which is to be found for the most part in the UN Charter. International law represents the rules of the game, to be obeyed by members of the UN. As in any game, fouls will be committed. Under Chapter I, Article 2(4) of the 1945 UN Charter, war is illegal except when expressly authorized by the Security Council, something which happened in the 1990–1 Middle East conflict but not in 2003. The only exception is the right of individual or collective self-defence under Chapter VII, Article 51 which, once taken, is to be reported to the Security Council. The United States' argument in support of preventive self-defence is that UN Charter law does not recognize the development and effects of modern weaponry.

More down to earth, at the face of battle, often in the heat of conflict, there is the question of calling the military to account for alleged war crimes. Whether the writ of the International Criminal Court (ICC) in The Hague applies to a particular state's nationals depends whether the court has been recognized by that state. The UK recognizes the ICC; the USA does not. The zeal with which the Blair Government prosecuted the British military is claimed by many to have been a double standard. There is criticism at the way those prosecutions were initiated by former Attorney General Lord Goldsmith who appears, prior to the war, to have confused his legal and political responsibilities. Having at first insisted that a second resolution was required from the Security Council prior to the 2003 invasion of Iraq, the situation inexplicably changed when he assured the Government that the state's participation in the war would be legal without the second resolution. The truth of what happened here will become clear in the inevitable British inquiry into the Iraq war.

One of Sir Robert Thompson's basic principles of counter-insurgency relating to the Malaya emergency and published in 1966[2] required the Government to function in accordance with the law. Although, in some circumstances, a reasonable argument can be made that in today's fast-moving world some international law is either obsolete or obsolescent, this is not an excuse to fashion the law to suit desired circumstances. The situation of the internees of Guantánamo Bay, whose treatment defies the description 'legal', is a case in point. Whether the Administration's fear of these individuals is real or imagined, the continuing incarceration of internees is hardly the best way to prosecute the so-called global War on Terror. Thompson wrote:

> There is a very strong temptation in dealing both with terrorism and with guerrilla actions for government forces to act outside the law, the excuses being that the processes of law are too

cumbersome, that the normal safeguards in the law for individuals are not designed for an insurgency and that a terrorist deserves to be treated as an outlaw.[3]

Thompson's thoughts, proven in Malaya, were applied too late in both Vietnam and Iraq. There is, however, evidence of the application of Thompson's thinking in Afghanistan. The basic principles, and they are so basic it is almost unbelievable that they were not applied as a matter of course, include:

First Principle – the government must have a clear political aim.

Second Principle – operate within the law.

Third Principle – the government must have an overall plan.

Fourth Principle – the government must give priority to defeating the political subversion, not the guerrillas.

Fifth Principle – in the guerrilla phase of an insurgency, a government must secure its base first.

There is an undeniable case to be made that the Malaya experience has little to compare with Vietnam or Iraq. In Malaya, the counter-insurgency was blessed by being easily contained, but principles and qualities should be applied according to the principle 'if the cap fits, wear it'. It comes down to having not one plan but also a plan B and desirably a plan C. Thompson identified as his three indispensable qualities in counter-insurgency, patience, determination and an offensive spirit, 'but the last should be tempered with discretion and should never be used to justify operations which are merely reckless or just plain stupid'.[4] There is a strong resonance here of the counter-insurgency in Afghanistan.

The 1945 Charter rectified a shortcoming in the earlier League of Nations by making provision in Chapter VII for enforcement action. Enabling resolutions from the Security Council will invariably authorize the use of 'all necessary means'. The permanent members of the UN Security Council – China, France, Great Britain, the Soviet Union and the United States, who gave themselves the power of veto within the Council – had been the victorious alliance united in war, not in peace. According to Brian Urquhart, 'The Charter assumed with a stunning lack of political realism, that they would stay united in supervising, and if necessary enforcing world peace.'[5]

The Cold War hobbled the UN's ability to exert enforcement measures in an increasingly bipolar world. As a consequence, peacekeeping, for which there is no provision in the UN Charter, found refuge under Chapter VI, the Pacific Settlement of Disputes. As will be seen in the chapters on Mogadishu and Gorazde, there is wide scope for confusion at the junction of Chapters VI and VII. As a rule, peacekeepers initially were not drawn from among the Security Council's permanent members and they confined the use of lethal force to self-defence. There were two implicit understandings: peacekeepers acted impartially at all times and their presence required the consent of the parties to the dispute. The chapter on Gorazde will reveal that peacekeeping – or peace support – cannot be conducted in environments where there is no peace to be kept.

Military skills or high standards of professionalism among peacekeepers were not as important as their patience and non-threatening presence. The aim was to hold the line until a political solution could be found to resolve the problem. *Sponsored* operations are one of two types of UN military operations which are commanded and controlled in-house from what is now known as the Department of Peacekeeping Operations (DPKO). The UN Force in Cyprus (UNFICYP), established in 1974, is one such example and is still in place. Chapter VI peacekeeping first became compromised in the Congo, where peacekeepers were engaged to coerce Katanga back under Congolese national authority. From that point, the obligatory abstention from the use of weapons other than in self-defence – in the increasing number of environments where the settlement of disputes by armed force had become the norm – became progressively more difficult to sustain. In circumstances where traditional peacekeepers found themselves in hostile, complicated environments and where the military of the states in dispute enjoyed a higher level of military skill and competence than they did themselves, the concept of traditional Chapter VI peacekeeping came under extreme pressure.

The DPKO is the operational arm of the UN Secretary-General, responsible for the day-to-day management of operations. National contingents were under a tenuous form of command under the UN's nominated commander. The federal nature of the force and the loosest of command arrangements reflected the fact that national commanders invariably consulted their own governments when anything other than the most routine operations was contemplated.

The second type of UN operation, which is far more prevalent, is the *sanctioned* operation, whereby a framework state is authorized by the UN to command and control an operation, supported by lesser states. This was demonstrated in the Iraq Conflict 1990–1. Alternatively, an organization such as NATO can be authorized to lead a military operation.

Such an example can be seen in Afghanistan. NATO in Afghanistan, commanding thirty-seven separate states, contained so many fissures that the question was not whether the enterprise would implode but when. NATO has been unable to act with clarity and purpose since the Warsaw Pact ceased to be the focus of everything it did or represented. The United States has consistently been the framework state, operating in her own interest on behalf of the UN. Occasionally there will be a fig-leaf when the USA operates under the cover of NATO.

States enter into armed conflict generally for reasons either of interest or conscience. Those conflicts sub-divide into either conflicts of obligation or conflicts of choice. A conflict of obligation might be justified by the presence of a vital national interest. For the Americans, the Iraq conflict in 2003 was a conflict of choice presented by the President as a conflict of obligation. Conflicts of obligation are restrained only by extreme considerations such as a financial crisis emerging in the Treasury or by domestic public protest crying 'enough'. Otherwise, bills are paid and casualties accepted as a constituent part of the obligation.

The rationale behind a conflict of choice is completely different and goes some way towards explaining why states in the Iraq coalition progressively withdrew. Conflicts of choice are characterized by low risk, low cost and short duration, precisely the same factors which appear to foretell an adverse influence upon NATO's Afghanistan operation. Technically, conflicts of obligation and conflicts of choice are mutually unsustainable. States participating in conflicts of choice will invariably be casualty-averse, budget-conscious and with an eye on the clock. The contradiction implicit in America's announcement of a surge of reinforcements into Iraq at the same time as the UK moved towards withdrawal was not lost on observers. Yet what was being witnessed was the proper enactment of the relationship between states engaged, on the one hand, in a conflict of obligation and on the other, a conflict of choice. The operational reality was that a military presence was still required in the south, in Basra. That presence could have been either American or British but, whoever it was, the presence remained vital. The 300-mile (483-kilometre) American southern supply route, regularly targeted with roadside bombs and grenades, runs from Kuwait City through Basra to Baghdad.

These same principles apply to NATO's operations in Afghanistan where the organization no longer has a Warsaw Pact to keep itself up to the mark and where an overzealous expansion renders consensus virtually impossible. The United States' justification for her obligatory presence in NATO in Afghanistan can be traced directly back to the events of 9/11 and the association with Afghanistan. That consideration does not apply to the other thirty-six members in the Afghanistan coalition, for whom to a greater or lesser degree the laws of the war of choice apply – that is, low risk, low cost and short duration. The applicability of the different considerations relative to wars of obligation and wars of choice are equally the same in both UN and NATO operations. Lesser states are bound to opt out over a period of time.

Goose Green became the first battle of the Falklands Campaign, 1982, in which Britain sought to eject Argentine forces from the British islands following the Argentine invasion. The task fell to the 2nd Battalion The Parachute Regiment. The men of that battalion defeated a larger force in defended positions by dint of willpower, courage and resourcefulness drawn from the spirit of a regimental family to which they all proudly belonged. They achieved their victory despite having been substantially undermanned and severely under-resourced, shortcomings which this book will revisit in respect of Iraq post-2003 and Afghanistan post-2006. Goose Green is a good fit to the theme that the greatness of any battle is determined not by its size or by the numbers involved but rather by its effect and influence upon future events. Goose Green had to be won to set the standard for the battles which followed elsewhere in the Falkland Islands. Self-determination was restored to the inhabitants, national self-belief was enormously boosted and Margaret Thatcher's Conservatives were returned to power.

The American battle for Grenada is often referred to as America's Falklands yet the dissimilarities are greater than the similarities. While both states were obliged to travel great distances to reach their battlefields, the groups of islands had little in common – the Falklands is cold and barren, Grenada tropical and lush. Both were conflicts of the Cold War era but that consideration effectively related only to Grenada. The Americans were well resourced, had a surfeit of manpower and revealed an urgent requirement to improve joint operations for the future. Both the British and Americans had similar approaches to a perennial problem – press relations and the media insistence that the public 'had a right to know'. Campaigning on islands helped control the media but, once admitted to the sweeping expanse of open deserts, media representatives arrived in their hundreds. Most reluctantly accepted the pool system that emerged as a solution to the enormous international interest in conflicts such as these. A number of journalists insisted on maintaining their independence. A number lost their lives as a consequence.

The Falklands and Grenada were both far distant from NATO and the Warsaw Pact's self-selecting battlefield of Western Europe's Central Region. The reality is that military budgets, equipment, manpower, tactics and doctrine were almost entirely devoted there to what is known as conventional warfare. The aim of both sides was to achieve a balance of terror so that the effect of going to war would be so terrible as to act as a deterrent. Both sides had arsenals of nuclear, biological and chemical weapons promising mutually assured destruction. They also had corps of armoured vehicles standing by to fight a war neither side wanted.

While NATO and the Warsaw Pact faced each other in the phoney war in the Central Region, a number of the constituent states were invariably off elsewhere fighting low-intensity conflicts. Britain's armed forces have been consistently on operations since 1945, and 16,000 men have died. There is a valid justification for the British Army to have trained for the high-intensity conflict of NATO's Central Region in that they had the ability to switch to lower-intensity conflict without major retraining. This is less applicable to America's armed forces which have only recently, with the introduction of a new counter-insurgency doctrine in Iraq, considered the inevitability of a culture change. The reverse cycle, focusing upon low-intensity conflict, with the expectation of being able to fight at higher levels of conflict, does not work.

Military thinking for specific operations is enshrined in doctrine – not that commanders feel obliged to follow doctrine. What doctrine does is 'to establish the framework of understanding of the approach to warfare in order to provide the foundation for its practicable application'.[6] The British have an intuitive approach to armed conflict while the Americans give relatively more credence to doctrine. However, when the Americans completed their conventional phase in Iraq, 2003, they outran their doctrine. The Third (US) Division, assigned to the battle for Fallujah in the Phase IV rebuilding phase, based its pre-operational training on conventional war. There have long been debates and argument on this issue in the US, an intellectual muddle between fighting and winning the nation's conventional wars and Military Operations Other Than War (MOOTW). The representation of the conventional phase of big army, big war, went as far as the removal of Saddam's statue. MOOTW did not click in. The Americans were stunningly unprepared for the post-conflict phase, including the insurgency. The question to be answered was, should the military keep faith with conventional warfighting, arguably fighting the last war, thereby ring-fencing the defence budget, or be prepared to fight small wars? Politicians wanted both, the military leadership the former and the mid to lower ranks of the officer corps the latter.[7]

At the start of the twentieth century, Britain's defence was founded upon the pre-eminence of the Royal Navy. A Frenchman remarked at the time, what a pity it was that the Royal Navy did not run on wheels. It was therefore the lot of the British Army to be the poor relation with limited expectations, tailored to fight small wars to achieve ambitious targets at low cost. By comparison, America's Army had an entirely different philosophical rationale. From its earliest beginnings, the function of the army was to preserve the integrity of the state, confronting any challenges to its survival with uncompromising violence. The British Army therefore evolved as an instrument of low-intensity conflict while America, not content with anything less than the total annihilation of any enemy contemplating treading on her, became wedded almost exclusively to the idea of conventional war.

Two world wars had an understandable effect upon British thinking to the extent that by the time we come to the Cold War, we find a British armoured corps of three armoured divisions and one infantry division dedicated to NATO's

Central Region. Undeniably, therefore, the British were also committed to conventional war, but what we had here was the quintessential Potemkin Village, a corps under-resourced and poorly equipped. Successive governments had so managed the British Army that its conventional warfighting capability had become severely constrained. Its confident participation in low-intensity conflict also became progressively less certain, particularly when a rule book change found the British Army in new circumstances with inadequate equipment.

When the British and American armed forces are put together there is an inevitable mismatch. Certainly, London's policy is to maintain proximity with Washington to the extent that the good though small British Army was once described by historian Correlli Barnet as America's warrior satellite. There is invariably a misalignment in the thinking between the world's superpower and any lesser state, no matter how well motivated that state may be to enter into such an alliance. The superpower is far more likely to see a crisis as a threat to her vital interest, a challenge to her pre-eminent position if you like, than a lesser state is ever likely to. America's conflicts of apparent obligation need not necessarily translate as anything more than a conflict of choice elsewhere. In circumstances where lesser states support America as a statement of solidarity, that solidarity comes with its own use-by date. One worrying trend in emergent asymmetric conflict is a potential American enemy's realization that America can be goaded into taking offensive action. Earlier in this chapter we quoted Thompson, that the offensive spirit 'should be tempered with discretion and should never be used to justify operations which are merely reckless or just plain stupid'.

In December 1988, the Soviet Union's Mikhail Gorbachev announced the withdrawal of Soviet forces from Eastern Europe and, as a consequence, the Warsaw Pact which had kept the whole together collapsed. The reverberations of self-determination sent tremors through a Soviet Union dividing into separate states, thereby confirming the end of the Cold War. Security organizations do not normally survive the demise of the organization they were created to confront. NATO, however, did not collapse but began a long-term process of adding former eastern bloc states to its ranks. Enlargement weakened it by generating a multitude of interests to accommodate. The USA owns NATO and continues to pay her dues because NATO provides a means of leverage in Europe, however: 'US policy in Europe aims not only to counter others' bids for hegemony, but to perpetuate America's own supremacy on the continent.'[8] As America experiences a relative loss of power, so NATO becomes ever more important to Washington as a reasonably pliant collective security oganization through which she can pursue her own foreign policy goals, particularly the global war on terrorism.

Towards the end of the Cold War, high technology had developed to such a degree that smart weapons could be deployed to cover ground in such a way as to permit the reduction of significant numbers of men with bayonets. The money saved by reducing manpower could be transferred to fund the new technology. Once the end of the Cold War had been confirmed, the allies moved quickly to extract their peace dividends. The US Army, for example, saw itself reduced to 60 per cent of its 1990s strength, from eighteen to ten divisions. When the Northern Ireland troubles ended, the British took a special manpower dividend. While the theory may have been sound at the time, the move from Cold War to Hot War means more manpower is required for the additional tasks being accepted. Battlefield technology has not become redundant but is an essential component in sustaining forces invariably too small to achieve the given tasks without technological support.

The 1990–1 liberation of Kuwait from Iraqi occupation appeared to many to herald a new dawn in international security cooperation, with states demonstrating the level of collegiality as imagined by the drafters of the 1941 Atlantic Charter. The Security Council legitimized conflict against Iraq and the long-held observance of the sovereignty of a state's territory passed into history. The important matter of legality did not proceed without disagreement between the United States and the United Kingdom. In view of the positions adopted in the legal preparation for the revisitation of Iraq in 2003, the national positions taken in 1990 may not have been entirely what might have been expected. In 1990 it was Margaret Thatcher who attempted to wean the USA away from seeking prior authorization for the use of force from the Security Council, relying instead on Article 51. She attempted to sway Secretary of State Baker but did not succeed. 'He said the UN authority was crucial to sustain the support of American public opinion for military action.'[9] What is relevant is both states' attempts to find legitimacy to justify their intended actions.

The United States was duly appointed the framework state for the Kuwait operation, joined by lesser states. It conducted a brilliant 100-hour blitzkrieg, forcing Iraq out of Kuwait, as described in Chapter 4. No Arab states entered Iraqi territory but states harbouring reservations or having insufficient capability had deep pockets to ensure that warrior states were adequately compensated for their trouble.

The reason why the Chapter VII Kuwait intervention was not likely to create a precedent is explained in Chapter 4. Understandably there were those impressed by the perfection of the operation who desired to preserve the mechanics for posterity. The British came forward as the unlikely scribes of a new doctrine which they called 'Wider Peacekeeping', notwithstanding the fact that the foray into Iraq had not been a Chapter VI peacekeeping operation. There had been no intellectual investment, merely a collecting of the thoughts of peace professionals. Sir Brian Urquhart, former UN Under Secretary-General, Special Political Affairs, found the document misleading. 'It is dangerous nonsense.'[10] In a rare example of military paranoia, the sponsors brooked no voices of opposition either from within or without their own community. Common sense eventually prevailed and Wider Peacekeeping simply disappeared.

The results of the first Iraq conflict were not entirely propitious. America's enemies now knew for certain that the only possible way she could be defeated would be through asymmetrical means, the emphasis placed upon psychology rather than upon raw power. The operation proved to be a high water mark for Britain. What was seen here was the negative result of producing a strategy out of the funds made available rather than producing the desired strategy and funding it accordingly. Concepts such as 'front line first' were bound to have negative influences. The deployment of a small, two-brigade, British division to the Middle East, possibly the last occasion an armoured British division proper would be seen on operations, effectively stripped out the parent 1st British Corps of many of its resources, leaving it exposed as a Potemkin Village. There had been a stunning victory but one which also had a profound effect and influence upon future events. Among the lessons learned was that a future attack upon Iraq would be 'do-able'.

Mogadishu was a tragedy in 1992–3: it is no less a tragedy today when it has become a pawn in the global War on Terror. There were three separate missions, commencing with a Chapter VI humanitarian mission to bring relief to a suffering people. The UN tried, yet the environment in which they operated, and those who lived in that environment, proved to be utterly uncompromising. The whole concept of peacekeeping was tested and proved unequal to the challenge. The Americans came, brought firepower and muscle and, with the encouragement of the UN Secretary-General, chose sides. They forfeited any pretence of impartiality and never gained control in a taxing urban environment. The enabling UN resolution was upgraded to Chapter VII but the truth was that there was no real understanding of what fighting in an urban environment involved. With the world becoming increasingly urbanized, this form of conflict is predicted to increase.

Mogadishu differs from Fallujah in that the former was fought among the entire population of southern Mogadishu whereas Fallujah was virtually empty of all but the combatants. The entry of foreign troops into Mogadishu became a challenge to Aideed's tribe to oust the uninvited, the unwanted, and to punish them so that they would not contemplate a return. That is what happened. Had that lesson been properly learned, there would have been neither an Iraq nor an Afghanistan because strategists would have realized that it is the presence of foreign troops, especially in Muslim countries, which transforms these conflicts into wars of liberation against foreign occupation.

There was distrust between the US and the UN, the former regarding the latter with a high degree of contempt. The multiplicity of lines of command and control spread confusion. The intended state of confidentiality imposed by the Americans worked against them when the UN was called to the rescue. The UN had no idea of the nature of the operation or where precisely it was being played out in the streets of southern Mogadishu. Although the US and the UN were on the same side, they failed to work together. The same was seen in Bosnia between the UN, the US and NATO, and in Fallujah, immediately before the first battle, there was almost a 'corporate breakdown in the relationship between the Americans and British in Baghdad'.[11]

The overreaction to the sight of the body of a dead American airman being abused in a Mogadishu street was to be repeated after the murder of four contractors became the justification for the first battle of Fallujah. In Mogadishu, the mission was successfully achieved in so far as Aideed's men had been brought in for interrogation, but there was a price to be paid: someone had to be identified to shoulder the blame for the fiasco. President Clinton's placing the blame on the UN was immoral. The result of Mogadishu was US and presidential casualty-aversion. No Americans were available for a timely intervention into Rwanda, 1994. The effect of the refusal to make American ground forces available for the Bosnia crisis raises the interesting hypothetical question: if American ground forces had been available, what effect would that have had upon American policy there?

Chapter 6, Gorazde, examines the events in one of the so-called 'Bosnian Safe Areas'. The British battalion there had an impossible mission. The effect of the escape of the British battalion from Gorazde was, first, to give the green light for NATO operations against Bosnia's Serbs, ending in the Dayton Peace Settlement and, second, to emphasize the reality that UN peacekeeping operations cannot be conducted in environments where there is no peace to be kept. Britain learnt her lesson. When she went into Sierra Leone, as described in Chapter 7, she did so independently of the UN force there.

With a question mark over the efficacy of UN operations,

it is opportune to glance at NATO's performance in Kosovo, which came as a postscript to the Bosnian conflict as concluded by the Dayton Peace Settlement. President Clinton examined the problem of Kosovo with its 90 per cent Albanian population subservient to a Serb minority. Self-determination for the Albanians could be achieved only through a land campaign, in which NATO reflected America's casualty-aversion. The UN, which had so patently suffered military failure in Bosnia, was not a candidate for intervention in Kosovo. Clinton weighed the balance between his reluctance to commit his ground forces and his insistence that NATO must be seen to succeed. The former commander of the UN Protection Force (UNPROFOR) in Bosnia, General Rose wrote, 'For if NATO is not prepared to accept a risk to its soldiers in either peace support operations or war, then it is militarily useless.'[12] To Clinton, the sentiment that NATO must succeed was the stronger of the two and accordingly he approved a ground offensive into Kosovo to commence on 13 September 1999.

I do not intend to analyse the Kosovo campaign in detail, only to examine the modus operandi of the NATO force under command of the American General Wesley Clark. The referral of military matters by national commanders back to their capitals for endorsement is not confined to peacekeeping. Clark described how 'NATO commands were like puppets, with two or six or sometimes dozens of strings being pulled from behind the scenes by the nations themselves, regardless of the formalistic commitment of forces . . . All UN and NATO forces were in fact national forces.'[13] General Clark may have had in mind the order he gave the British General Mike Jackson to confront a Russian column in Kosovo. Jackson refused, saying 'I have no intention of starting the Third World War'.[14] There is no reason to believe the situation

with regard to NATO's position in Afghanistan is any different. In fact, the suggestion is that it is worse.

The observant should have noticed that NATO had strayed
out of its area of operations. French Foreign Minister Hubert
Védrine took the contrary view that Bosnia and Kosovo were
'on the immediate periphery of NATO and clearly not out-
of-area'.[15] The Administration's representatives considered
Kosovo an ideal opportunity to prove to those in Congress
that NATO has to 'go out of area or out of business', and that
NATO did have continuing relevance and utility into the
new millennium. Taking NATO as far as Afghanistan
exaggerated that point. The truth is that, compared with the
Gulf conflict's successful ad hoc coalition, NATO's alliance
in Kosovo proved to be brittle and often dysfunctional.

UN Security Council Resolution 1270 of 22 October
1999, providing for the creation of the United Nations
Mission in Sierra Leone (UNAMSIL), was clear evidence
that failure in such areas as Bosnia was not going to diminish
the UN's aspiration to continue the peacekeeping tradition.
Resolution 1270 was somewhat anomalous in that it was
mandated by reference to Chapter VII although its conditions were pacific and might have been thought applicable
to a Chapter VI peacekeeping force. The forces attracted
to its policing were essentially African and Asian troops of
a standard required to monitor a peacekeeping agreement where
the consent of both parties – the Sierra Leone Government
and the Revolutionary United Front (RUF) – was in place.
In Sierra Leone the insurgents, the RUF, were stronger and
more determined than the UN. During the settling-in period,
the RUF inflicted significant reverses upon the UN. Large
numbers were taken hostage, some were killed and others
had to be rescued by the Indian Army. The UN's internal
command arrangements were hopeless, largely because of

different understandings of the meaning of operational effectiveness. The better-trained Indians and Nigerians were exceptions to this rule yet the former withdrew from UNAMSIL, citing irreconcilable differences with Nigeria, which led UNAMSIL.

The RUF's reneging on the Lomé agreement and advance on Freetown, capital of Sierra Leone, led to the British conducting two rapid reaction operations: the first, Operation Palliser, to halt the advance of the RUF; and the second, Operation Barras, a consequence of Palliser when members of a British training team became the hostages of a volatile group of insurgents, the West Side Boys. Both operations illustrated the enactment of the glass of water strategy, whereby speed of deployment enabled the initial sparks of the crisis to be doused before the problem became an inferno requiring the attention of a large fire brigade. Paras and Marines, the most appropriate forces for these operations, enjoyed a self-sufficiency with which to conduct them. Britain did not join UNAMSIL, in part because of the differing operational standards – 'the African battalions adjust to doing nothing very easily'[16] – and the essential requirement to maintain operational security. The Falklands was thought to have been Britain's last opportunity to conduct operations unilaterally, yet victory there would have been far more difficult had it not been for American logistical support. The Sierra Leone interventions were better examples of unilateral action.

Operation Barras, the rescue of hostages from the West Side Boys insurgents, could in some respects be thought of as a rural version of the capture of wanted men in urban southern Mogadishu and the unforeseen requirement to rescue Delta Force and Rangers committed to that operation. Both missions were a success, Barras more so. It had been a brilliant operation, from planning through to the execution phase, together with all the lines of support which were put in place to ensure the hostages were safely rescued. Beyond the operation and its immediate aftermath, there was a set of wider implications. From a military perspective, lessons will have been learned concerning the application of force in the form of a surgical strike on an operation where time and space were severely constrained. Then there was the follow-on political impact of such a stunning success on the fragile situation in Sierra Leone, in the region and wider Africa.[17]

Operation Barras emphasized the difference between quality and quantity. Greatness in terms of effect was not prejudiced by the relatively small size of the operation. Barras was a lesson to the UN of what a small number of well-trained, determined men were capable of achieving. It laid down the standard. The impact Barras had upon the international community's image of Britain's armed forces approached the levels reached after Goose Green and the Falklands Campaign. While military success is fine, however, the final solution has to be of a political nature and in that respect Sierra Leone still has a long way to go. That is not the only consideration to qualify the success of Barras. The operation emboldened the messianic Prime Minister Blair to seek out further successes in Iraq and Afghanistan.

The intention to present a logical, structured argument on how conflict has changed since 1982 comes to a halt in Iraq, 2003. The splendid conventional phase, a veritable blitzkrieg, emphasized how environment can impact upon success or failure. For example, smart bombs came into their element in the desert of Arabia whereas they had been a relative failure in the damp, cloying, misty climate of the Balkans. Failure came to the allies in Iraq at a time when Washington believed the mission had been accomplished. Whether defeat has been snatched from the jaws of victory remains to be seen. The insurgency which followed, of which the battles for Fallujah were part, was attributable to the Pentagon believing émigrés' assurances that the military would be greeted as victors, the failure of the belligerent occupants to compensate *immediately* for the absence of the government which they had removed, the failure of the Americans and British to have a sufficiency of forces in place to manage the Phase IV post-Conflict Resolution, and the failure of the Americans to comprehend that the insurgency which followed the accomplishment of the mission was a new phase of warfare requiring different tactics and a change of mindset.

The Pentagon plan to defeat Iraq ended before Phase IV, post-Conflict Resolution, because Secretary of Defense Rumsfeld had taken as gospel the assertion of the Iraqi émigré Ahmad Chalabi that the American forces would be greeted with open arms. That did not happen, but in such conflicts there is invariably a honeymoon period where those indignant at the presence of an occupying force are capable of being swayed if the invader indicates an intention to go some way with reconstruction towards meeting their expectations. The results arising from the disassembling of the machinery of government and the heavy-handed treatment of the Iraqis are measurements of the depth of cluelessness of what was to be achieved and how. There were, as is almost inevitable, insufficient troops available. Among those tasks which should have been obvious as requiring attention were the National Museum, full of relics of this the cradle of civilization, and ammunition depots burgeoning with thousands of tons of high explosives readily available and capable of sustaining insurgency for decades. The available military were directed to defend the Oil Ministry.

What exacerbated the magnitude of this conflict and led to a long, bloody, bitter phase of combat was the failure of President George W. Bush to understand that the impact of his cavalier dismissal of the importance of Thompson's second principle, to operate within the law, magnified as a consequence Islamic opposition to the invasion. There is the quite different question how it came about that Britain, who has experience of these matters, acquiesced in meekly following a bad plan and a bad idea.

Margaret Thatcher had told Prime Minister Blair to stay close to the Americans: his friend, the influential former President Clinton, advised him to stay close to Bush. British foreign policy therefore came to be directed from the White House, effectively bringing to an end governance by the War Cabinet. Writing of the Blair–Bush relationship, one Washington observer, Kendall Myers, wrote: 'It was a done deal. From the beginning, it was a one-sided relationship that was entered into with open eyes . . . there was no payback, no sense of reciprocity.'[18] This meant that Britain was seen to be behaving as a partner to the superpower and not simply as an independent, medium power with limited means.

The hands-on man in Baghdad after the 2003 victory was the coalition Provisional Authority Administrator, L. Paul 'Jerry' Bremer. His decisions had a profoundly destabilizing effect throughout Iraq but particularly in the Sunni Anbar Province in which lies Fallujah. His short-termed predecessor, Lieutenant-General Jay Garner, said his successor made three profound mistakes within days of his arrival: disbanding the Iraqi Army, de-Ba'athification and disbanding the Iraqi governing group. The influence of these measures was particularly profound on Fallujah. The Iraqi military had not performed at all well against the Americans but in their own familiar cities they were different people. The de-Ba'athification and disbanding of the governing group had a disproportionately negative influence on Fallujah because of the disproportionate number of government administrators living in that city.

The marginalized Geoff Hoon, Secretary of State for Defence, said Britain would have had a different approach. His ideas and influence were not sought. 'Firstly, we would not have disbanded the Iraqi Army. We were very concerned in the final stages of the conflict that the Iraqi Army was a force for stability in Iraq and I think we would have preferred for that army to remain intact.' Instead, many of the redundant soldiery took up arms against the coalition. 'I don't think we would have pursued the de-Ba'athification policy in the same way. We understood from perhaps experience in Europe that quite a lot were Ba'athists because they had to be if they wanted to be teachers or administrators and they weren't necessarily committed to Saddam Hussein.'[19] The chaos which followed the removal of Iraq's administrators should not have been unexpected. Nor should the strengthening of the insurgency by Iraqis who would otherwise not have been militant had it not been patently apparent to them that their country had been better under Saddam Hussein than under the occupiers. The importance of the second battle of Fallujah lies in it being a tipping point, heralding change of heart among formerly ambivalent local Sunni sheikhs who gave al-Qa'eda orders to leave Anbar Province, thus creating the first welcome signs that the tide might be turning.

The bane of coalition life in Iraq became the Improvised Explosive Device (IED), a simple device involving wiring-up artillery shells, hundreds of thousands of which were left as plunder in abandoned ammunition depots. The coalition main battle tanks were relatively well protected from the effects of IEDs but, making the point that technology is not a one-way street, the Iranians introduced hollow-charge devices for disabling tanks. These were far from improvisations. More-over, they exported their success with these devices from Iraq into Afghanistan. Another successful asymmetric device is the suicide bomber. Large numbers of potential martyrs have been trained in terrorist camps. That there are so many Islamists prepared to die for their cause will continue to wreak havoc both in conflict and non-conflict environments. There are no guarantees that serious attention paid to resolving these causes will not generate new, different causes. Nevertheless, there is merit in making the investment.

There should be a golden rule that every would-be interventionist must learn what history tells him or her of the area in which he or she is interested. The Americans in Mogadishu could have learned from Britain's earlier experiences in Somalia. A State Department analyst expressed the view that for the want of reading a book on the last British invasion of Iraq in the 1920s, 'he might have hesitated'.[20] Specifically, in Iraq 1919–20 there was unrest in Mesopotamia following the British occupation after the First World War. Insurrections in 1920 in Mesopotamia and in 1922–4 in Kurdistan could not have given a clearer picture of a people resenting foreign occupation. The British fought three wars in Afghanistan, as described in Chapter 8.

Had those in the British Task Force in the Falklands in 1982 or those Americans sent to Grenada in 1983 been told that NATO would be commanding a military operation in Afghanistan in 2006, such a thought would have been beyond their imagination. The US had been keen to find a role for NATO and, as improbable as it might seem, Afghanistan had to do. Washington recognized that NATO could not be seen to fail in Afghanistan, for to do so would seriously undermine the logic of persevering with a relic of the Cold War. The signs of success, however, are not propitious.

In 2006, during a visit to Afghanistan of Britain's then Secretary of State for Defence John Reid, he announced, 'We would be perfectly happy to leave in three years and without firing one shot because our job is to protect the reconstruction.'[21] Apparently, there was an idea to deploy 3 Para Group as an 'ink spot', or governance zone, to provide the essential security to allow reconstruction to develop in one place, to prove itself so that the Afghanis would wish to embrace what they had seen elsewhere. Unfortunately, that did not happen. 3 Para's enforced deployment resembled an ink spray rather than an ink spot. Involvement in the reconstruction process remained an aspiration because the representative of Britain's Department of International Development (DfID) allegedly refused to be seen associating with the military. Health and Safety issues also intervened to prevent governmental and non-governmental organizations providing humanitarian assistance to local people. The Taliban therefore succeeded in preventing the humanitarian organizations providing support where needed.

Britain first committed a capped Light Brigade to Afghanistan, comprising just one reinforced battle group – that is a battalion with support and service increments. There was a time when strategic military estimates were made to validate operational deployments. With a large element of the British armed forces still stuck in Iraq, it would not have seemed the best of times to volunteer for another quagmire in Afghanistan. There is no military experience within the Government, however. The decision-makers are entirely dependent upon the advice of the service Chiefs. That does not mean that the politician has to accept the military advice but, when a militarily nonsensical action is taken, the first questions should be put to the Chiefs of Staff.

The numerically inadequate British Task Force was obliged

to draw on American air support buttressed by RAF Harriers as force multipliers, to compensate for having insufficient troops for the assigned task. This was a risky option with the potential to generate fratricide and also collateral damage to Afghan non-combatants, the latter of which was only too easily exploited to their advantage by the Taliban.

The above short review of the issues relating to the battles to be examined in this book illustrates that what we have here is a cat's cradle of combat and political issues. The conflicts in Iraq and Afghanistan are yet to conclude and therefore cannot be fully assessed. How these conflicts measure up remains to be seen.[22]

2

Goose Green
1982

'Sunray is down'

At the end of the Falklands war, Field Marshal Lord Bramall, then Chief of the General Staff, recalled receiving a letter from a distinguished predecessor, Field Marshal Lord Harding of Petherton.[1] Lord Harding had explained that the Falklands victory had reminded him of a sentence from one of Winston Churchill's wartime speeches: 'All the great struggles in history have been won by superior willpower wresting victory in face of odds or upon the narrowest of margins.' To that, Lord Harding had added his own commentary:

> And it seems to me that the greatest single factor in the Falklands campaign was that all ranks of all three Services had the will to take the risks, the will to overcome the obstacles, the will to face the dangers, and the will, if need be, to make the final sacrifice – the will to decide and the will to win, the indomitable spirit of the warrior, fully supported by the same spirit in the Prime Minister, the Government and the public.

The Prime Minister at the time of the Falklands Conflict, Margaret Thatcher, wrote:

> The significance of the Falklands War was enormous, both for Britain's self-confidence and for our standing in the world. Since

the Suez fiasco in 1956, British foreign policy had been one long retreat. The tacit assumption made by British and foreign governments alike was that our world role was doomed steadily to diminish. We had come to be seen by both friends and enemies as a nation which lacked the *will* and the capability to defend its interests in peace, let alone in war. Victory in the Falklands changed that.[2]

The way forward was led by an under-resourced Parachute battalion which won the first land battle of the conflict, Goose Green, a battle which had to be won to set the standard for the battles which followed. Willpower, therefore, was one of the most potent elements that contributed to British success in the Falklands.

On 1 April 1982, Rex Hunt, Governor of the Falkland Islands, was at home in the islands' capital, Stanley, when a flash signal from London arrived containing news (attributable to apparently reliable sources), that 'an Argentine Task Force will gather off Cape Pembroke early tomorrow morning 2 April'. The news shattered the tranquillity of the small South Atlantic island and set in train an extraordinary chain of events.

The Falkland Islands, British sovereign territory, cover 4,700 square miles (12,173 square kilometres), the equivalent of Cornwall, Devon and Dorset combined or the state of Connecticut. The group lies approximately 400 miles (644 kilometres) due east of Argentina and 8,000 miles (12,875 kilometres) from Britain. The then civilian population numbered approximately two thousand, mostly of British stock, successors to their forebears who first populated the islands in 1833. There has been a continuous British presence there ever since. Before then, the Falklands belonged to Argentina.

On 2 April 1982, following signs of intensive military preparation, the Argentinians invaded the Falklands. Stanley fell to an Argentine marine landing force comprising an amphibious commando company, a platoon from C Company 25 Infantry Regiment with artillery support. Shortly after Stanley was taken, the 9th Brigade dispersed over the surrounding islands. The next day South Georgia, a dependency of the Falkland Islands, fell to the Argentinians.

The contents of the signal sent to Rex Hunt had been disseminated to ministers in London the previous day.[3] The Secretary of State for Defence, John Nott, hurried to the House of Commons where he briefed Prime Minister Margaret Thatcher. 'I just say it was the worst moment of my life,' she said.[4] Her staff immediately convened a meeting in the House to discuss the next step.

The First Sea Lord, Admiral Sir Henry Leach, had spent 31 March visiting a weapons establishment at Portsmouth. At 6 p.m., still in uniform, he called in to his office at the Ministry of Defence, Whitehall, to hear the latest news of an apparent Argentine mobilization. He read two separate, contradictory briefs produced for Nott. One said 'further naval deployments were unnecessary and undesirable'. Unable to reconcile the facts with the advice, he became extremely annoyed. The Argentine initiative represented 'a clear imminent threat to a British overseas territory – what the hell was the point in having a Navy if it was not used for this sort of thing?'[5] Taking time to change into a suit, he went off in search of Nott.

John Nott had been appointed Secretary of State for Defence for the express purpose of bringing the defence programme into line with what could then be afforded. The First Sea Lord believed Nott to be anti-Navy, yet the facts do not support such an opinion. The Royal Navy had a high profile, enjoying a pre-eminent position in British defence priorities, the first of which was the nuclear deterrent founded upon Royal Navy Trident nuclear submarines. This role came as something of a mixed blessing for previously, when the deterrent was provided by the RAF, it was funded separately. Nott decided that Trident would be paid for out of Navy money, which is why it was now short of funds.[6] The 1981 Defence Review had proposed reducing the active frigate/destroyer fleet to forty-two ships with eight in reserve. The carrier *Invincible* was to be sold to Australia. The two assault ships (LPDs), *Fearless* and *Intrepid*, were scheduled for decommissioning.

When Leach entered the House of Commons conference room, Mrs Thatcher smiled, inviting him to join the anxious-looking group assembled to respond to the news. 'Could we', she asked him, 'really recapture the islands if they were invaded?' 'Yes, we could,' he replied, 'and in my judgement we should. Because if we do not . . . in another few months we shall be living in a different country whose word counts for little.' He went on, 'although prevention of an Argentine occupation of the Falklands is impossible, its repossession is possible.' He told the Prime Minister that a Task Force could be 'ready to leave in forty-eight hours'[7] and would reach the Falkland Islands in three weeks. Mrs Thatcher had an idea the voyage would take no more than three days.

Leach said that whatever had to be done must not be half-hearted. Nott did not hide his scepticism but Leach was among political animals whose ways he knew well. He recognized the attraction of publicizing a masterstroke follow-ing the announcement in the House on 3 April of the Argentine invasion. There were no doubts in the Prime Minister's mind that recovering the Falkland Islands, a vital national interest, would entail a war of obligation, for which the British public would not be casualty-averse.

The first-line assets then available to the Royal Navy were impressive. 3 Commando Brigade comprised 40, 42 and 45 Commando. They would need reinforcement by two Army battalions to form a first echelon. Their two assault ships, *Fearless* and *Intrepid*, were available. The Royal Fleet Auxiliary manned the landing ships logistic while the balance of the requirement, essentially passenger ships, would be ships taken up from the trade (STUFT), notably the P&O liner SS *Canberra*. The warships divided into two Task Forces commanded by Admiral Fieldhouse. Task Force 317 consisted of the two carriers *Invincible*, which was worked-up, and *Hermes*, which was not, and included amphibious forces. The two carriers would have on board anti-submarine warfare helicopters, RAF and Sea Harriers. Task Force 324 comprised entirely submarines.

Argentina had long aspired to reclaim the Falklands, known to her as the Malvinas, which lay within what she regarded as her sphere of interest. The unpopular General Leopoldo Galtieri, de facto President for all of four months, had misread the signals emanating from London,[8] assuming he could move on the Falklands – and make the reclamation of the islands his legacy of office – and that the British, 8,000 miles (12,875 kilometres) away, would not intervene. He was content to have a presence on the islands, having made no preparations for their formal defence. What he had not considered was the effect the invasion would have upon an indignant British First Sea Lord and equally indignant Prime Minister: 'We were defending our honour as a nation, and principles of fundamental importance to the whole world – above all, that aggressors should never succeed and that international law should prevail over the use of force.'[9]

The man whose name has become synonymous with Goose Green never got there, he died before victory had been achieved. The first battle of the Falklands conflict, in which the 2nd Battalion The Parachute Regiment (2 Para) fought, was a twin engagement involving a battalion attack first upon the Darwin Line and then on the settlement of Goose Green.[10] It was on the Darwin Line that Lieutenant-Colonel H. Jones commanding 2 Para died.

Herbert Jones so disliked his Christian name that he adopted simply 'H', which was used as a form of address even by his own sons. 'H' went to Eton, Sandhurst and into his county regiment, the Devon and Dorsets. As a captain he was posted on attachment to The 3rd Battalion The Parachute Regiment where he won his red beret and was employed as battalion mortar officer. He returned to the Devon and Dorsets as adjutant, a position in which it became apparent he had little by way of diplomatic skill. 'He did not suffer fools gladly and he "wrote off" those he considered to be grey men.'[11] At Staff College his directing staff observed, 'tact and charm do not come easily to him' and 'I have talked about his arrogance and a tendency to ride roughshod over others'.[12]

Every officer aspires to command his regiment. Unfortunately for 'H', the Devon and Dorsets had three potential candidates, all with their eyes upon the ultimate appointment of Commanding Officer. That was still some way distant. After commanding a company, 'H' returned to the staff, this time as Brigade Major to 3 Infantry Brigade at Portadown, Northern Ireland. Here he met many battalion commanders passing through on roulement duty who would go on to greater and better things. One who was impressed by Jones was Lieutenant-Colonel Julian Thompson, commanding 40 Commando Royal Marines, and the future commander of 3 Commando Brigade, who would have 'H''s battalion under his command in the Falklands. Thompson wrote, 'I had considerable respect for Jones's quick wit, strong personality and soldierly qualities.'[13]

The ambitious Major 'H' would have been bitterly disappointed not to have been promoted at the first opportunity in the 1978 batch of promotions. Significantly, one of his battalion competitors had been. No less significant, as events would prove, was his spending the next year as an instructor at the School of Infantry. After 'H''s promotion had been announced in 1979, he went to Headquarters United Kingdom Land Forces near Salisbury. Halfway through that tour the command list was published. One of his competitors had been preferred to command the Devon and Dorsets. 'H' was given command of 2 Para, which required his re-badging. He assumed command on 3 April 1981.

The Paras regard those outside the maroon machine, the 'craphats', with a mixture of suspicion and disdain, as Chris Keeble, 'H''s second-in-command and immediate successor made clear:

> We are a body of people welded together by our traditions, by our regiment, by a feeling of togetherness. We're a family of people and you have to remember that. We all know each other, we know each other's families. This is a body of people who would die for each other . . . We have to win, the mission is paramount. It is more important than anything else.[14]

Fourteen pairs of brothers fought at Goose Green.[15]

What separates the Paras from others is not the jumping out of aircraft – something that occurs infrequently and besides is not really very difficult – but rather what happens on landing; their fitness, determination and the drawing on their family ethos to succeed. No battalion is forever in a state of excellence. What Jones did in his first year was to bring the battalion back to peak form as a parachute battalion after two years in Northern Ireland, focusing upon fitness and skill-at-arms, which proved to be a timely and valuable investment for what was to come. That was his real achievement. He trained his soldiers for conventional soldiering. In terms of all-arms engagements, only two members of the battalion had been previously under fire, B Company's Major Crosland and HQ Company's Major Ryan, both in Dhofar, Oman. The aim of any Commanding Officer is to plan and arrange training so that when the blanks give way to live rounds, his men take that less than subtle difference in their stride.

The regimental Signals Officer David Benest recounted how on exercise in Kenya, in October to December 1981, this laissez-faire attitude to live firing was encouraged when the Commanding Officer put his own tactical-HQ far forward, bending all the rules of live firing. The Kenya training came as a godsend for the battalion. There could not have been a better opportunity for them to bond, to train together as a prelude to war. The Commanding Officer proved to be a hard and impatient taskmaster. One of his least appropriate actions on blowing a fuse would be to tell the offending individual his fortune irrespective of rank and who was within listening range.

At the end of the Kenya exercise – Endex – Jones was left with only five months of his life remaining. There was no let-up in the tough training schedule. The training prior to deployment to Belize continued an arduous regime including 'hard fitness' battle marches of twelve to fifteen miles in full battle order. Basic battle skills underwent complete revision and were practised mainly at night. 'H', said John Crosland, 'came to us as a new broom, ambitious, relatively naïve and not experienced but he was prepared to listen and keen to learn. He was willing, wanting to get better, more professional.'[16] His achievement was to take to war a battalion that had perhaps not yet fully risen to the peak of its military effectiveness, but one that he endowed with an ambition to be unsurpassed by any other in that respect.

On return from a skiing holiday at Easter, Jones learned that the Falklands had been invaded and that a Task Force was being assembled to regain the islands. The plan was that the emergency standby Spearhead Battalion, 3 Para, the duty battalion on permanent reduced notice to move, would come under command of 3 Commando Brigade. That made sense. The second Army battalion nominated to join the Commandos was the Queen's Own Highlanders. To Jones, that did not make sense. He argued forcibly with his superior headquarters that 2 Para, being similarly equipped and used to operating with 3 Para, was a more sensible alternative to the Queen's Own Highlanders. 2 Para formed part of 5 Infantry Brigade, also nominated for the Falklands but requiring additional time to prepare for operations. 2 Para, insisted Jones, was ready now. The 1st Battalion The Parachute Regiment, 1 Para, was irretrievably ensconced on operations in Northern Ireland. All he was asking was to bring forward the battalion's date of departure.

The Ministry of Defence accepted Jones's logic although the Army as a whole believed a bad precedent had been created. He was to be granted his destiny, but what had he volunteered for? Obviously there was a probability that not everyone was going to come back, but that was equally true whether the battalion was in the first or second echelon. The truth is that the British military welcome having a part in active operations. Individuals wrote personally to Number 10 Downing Street asking that they be included. In the past, many a unit had been able to assume its Northern Ireland duty at full strength because those who would otherwise have been discharged extended their period of service to cover the tour.

Some might argue that Northern Ireland duty could not be as lethal as what would be experienced in the Falklands. On 2 Para's previous tour in Northern Ireland they had been caught by two separate IEDs planted by IRA terrorists at Warren Point. Eighteen men died, the same number as would die at Darwin and Goose Green. According to John Crosland, Officer Commanding B Company (OC B Coy), 2 Para, there was a difference. 'Northern Ireland had its very violent periods and some prolonged operations but none with the full orchestration of war . . . the Toms[17] in my company hadn't heard the noise of a sustained battle or felt the intense loneliness and fear that results from such an experience.'[18] Crosland, formerly SAS and veteran of Dhofar, had. He would go on to be the good shepherd of an inexperienced rifle company.

'H' Jones flew ahead of his battalion group to rendezvous with the advanced elements of the Task Force at Ascension Island. The battalion group under second-in-command Chris Keeble had exclusive use of the North Sea ferry *Norland*. There were three rifle companies: A Company, commanded by Major Dair Farrar-Hockley; B Company, commanded by Major John Crosland; and D Company commanded by Major Philip Neame. Of their voyage, Philip Neame said, 'It all looked likely that we would go for a nice South Atlantic cruise, a big show of arms and maybe even go ashore, but no one really thought that we were going to shed blood at that stage – they were all hoping we would, but didn't really believe it was going to happen.'[19]

On board *Norland*, 2 Para experienced three weeks of intensive graft, battle fitness drills, bayonet fighting, resistance to interrogation training, medical training, company sports activities and the consideration of battle awareness scenarios. Cementing all this together was the unlikely figure of the battalion chaplain, David Cooper. He trained the snipers 'so his street cred was respected'. As the *Norland* drew closer to the Falklands, attendance at his voluntary church services increased. He had told the Toms that on the way down they could acquire some credits by coming to church but there were no guarantees that would give them any luck. John Crosland recalls that at the padre's final service aboard *Norland*, attended by all, the chaplain's remarks offered them hope. 'Some of you will not be coming back. All I will guarantee is that you will be looked after whether you come back or whether you don't.'[20]

The Naval Task Force drew up into its pre-ordained positions to support landings at Port Carlos Bay. H-Hour, when 2 Para were to lead the infantry ashore, was at 2.30 a.m. on Friday 21 May. The plan was for *Intrepid*'s four landing-craft to come alongside *Norland*, taking approximately 650 of 2 Para's battalion group ashore for what could be an opposed landing. The craft did come alongside but not according to the battalion loading plan, resulting in 2 Para going ashore back to front. The landing-craft bearing Battalion Main HQ was first ashore. The principal concern of the Paras, with the then dreadfully cold and windy weather, was not to get their feet wet in the icy sea. That proved to be a fond but feeble hope as they all landed in two to three feet (0.6 to 0.9 of a metre) of water, with the consequence that a significant number would immediately suffer cold injuries to their feet.

The plan required the first troops ashore to rendezvous with the Special Boat Service (SBS), the Navy's equivalent of the SAS, who would make contact with torch signals and then move the arrivals quickly away from the beach. There were no signals. As B Company went ashore, there came a challenge in English from the beach. 'Who the hell are you?' '2 Para, who are you?' 'SBS. We were expecting you on the 24th.' 2 Para needed to know from the SBS before moving off to climb Sussex Mountains, their objective 5 miles (8 kilometres) away, whether they should expect to have to fight to secure it.

It took some time to sort themselves out before the sub-units moved off. Each man's pack averaged out at 100 lb (45 kg) for not only did he have to carry his personal kit but also an array of weapons. Rifle sections had been issued with an additional General Purpose Machine Gun (GPMG). Individuals carried the GPMG ammunition *au bandolier* with grenades either dangling off webbing or in pockets. Spare radio batteries were distributed among the riflemen together with 2-inch and 81-mm mortar bombs, 84-mm medium anti-tank weapons, 66-mm light anti-tank weapons and projectiles for the M79 grenade-launchers that were over and above the equipment to which the battalion was normally entitled.

Paras and Royal Marines are the best-qualified beasts of burden in the British armed forces, which was just as well because the number of helicopters available fell well short of what an operation such as this sensibly required. Support helicopters available numbered only eleven Sea King Mark IV and five Wessex. Two Royal Navy Squadrons, 820 and 826, were fitted for anti-submarine operations and of the others, only four Sea Kings were equipped for night-flying. General-purpose helicopters had been embarked aboard the *Atlantic Conveyor* which, on 25 May, was struck by one of two exocet missiles and sunk, taking with it six Wessex helicopters, three Chinook and one Lynx. The Harriers and one Chinook had successfully taken off prior to the attack[21] but the vehicles on board were also lost. Brigadier Thompson put the immediate helicopter problem into words. 'To lift one light gun battery and 500 rounds per gun, enough for one battle, takes eighty-five Sea King helicopters, or eight Sea King helicopters flying eleven times each, or any permutation thereof – and there were four light gun batteries.'[22]

As 2 Para dug in on top of cold and wet Sussex Mountain, the opening round of a five-day air–sea battle of attrition was about to begin and for their part they were to be virtual spectators. The first attack at 08.55 on D-Day was on the *Canberra* by a Pucara, followed at 09.38 when two Pucaras[23] interrupted 2 Para's defensive preparations. Out in the bay between 21 and 25 May, three more British warships followed HMS *Sheffield* to the bottom.[24] The Argentinians' mistake was to concentrate their attacks upon warships when the highest-priority targets were the logistic ships. The weight of fire from the Royal Navy's ships and Harriers served to cause the Argentinians to attack at low level, from which height the self-arming iron bombs they carried failed to arm and were in effect duds. In those five days, the Argentine Air Force almost ceased to be a potent fighting force, command of the air being wrested from them by the British.

Major-General Menendez commanded the Argentine land component from Stanley where he had the equivalent of six supported regiments[25] or over half the available manpower deployed. Two regiments occupied West Falkland and a further ad hoc regiment held the Darwin/Goose Green area. This deployment reflected that of an army of occupation rather than defence. The Argentinian rank and file were conscripts with very little training but, as was discovered on the Darwin feature, their line of defence had been well prepared. The non-commissioned officers came from Junior Leader Schools and assumed their rank without having first served as private soldiers. The officer corps was drawn from the social elite. It was not a successful symbiotic relationship.[26]

John Frost, a hero of Arnhem Bridge in the Second World War, described Goose Green as 'a rather lovely place and the greenness of the land and the abundance of geese confirmed the aptness of its name'.[27] His observation of the prowess of the SAS was less enthusiastic: 'some of the information given to the battalion was optimistic to a degree'.[28] The SAS assessed the enemy strength at Darwin not as the 100 men claimed by Frost, but as a light battalion group. CO 22 SAS told me: 'I passed this information on to 'H' Jones myself.' In reality, the actual enemy combatants (which excluded the Air Force) at Goose Green were reassessed to be one regiment[29] and, with one exception, their positions were also reasonably well known. But asking a battalion to attack a regiment was a tall order. 'H' Jones, however, was undeterred: 'if the enemy is hit hard, he will crumble'.[30]

In his 13 May orders to Brigadier Thompson, Major-General Jeremy Moore, the Land Commander, required him 'to push forward from the bridgehead area so far as the momentum of its security allows, to gain information to establish moral and physical domination over the enemy'. Brigadier Thompson, Commander 3 Commando Brigade, understood the requirement but saw 'absolutely no point in rushing out of the beachhead with a packet of sandwiches in one pocket and five rounds of ammunition in the other to engage the enemy who were some 50 miles [80 kilometres] away, until we had our logistics ashore'.[31] However, the Government required good news to counterbalance the bad. A strategic argument was mounted that an attack on Goose Green would not only isolate Argentine forces on West Falklands but also remove a threat to the beachhead.[32]

The solution to this lay with 2 Para, now bored silly sitting on a high, wet, cold, windswept hill. 'We are not winning. We are losing,'[33] declared an exasperated, impatient Colonel Jones. Then, on 23 May, seemingly as an answer to the prayers of a man anxious to go to war, came a serendipitous Warning Order from Brigade Headquarters. He was to leave one company to hold Sussex Mountain and take the remainder of the battalion forward to conduct 'a large-scale raid' on the Argentinian positions 19 miles (30 kilometres) distant at Darwin and Goose Green.

A 'raid' is something commandos do and something with which Paras are familiar: they launch a surprise attack on an enemy position, annoy them and then return from whence they came. In that manner, the Brigade Commander could be seen to be complying with his orders yet not get bogged down in a Goose Green sideshow which might so easily detract from the main effort to retake Stanley. 'The aim of the raid', reasoned Thompson, 'would be to cause as much damage as possible to the garrison and its equipment, including air defence guns and missiles.'[34] Brigadier Thompson reasoned that he had no need to take Darwin and Goose Green, out on a limb as they were. The position could be contained, bypassed and then dealt with after Stanley had been retaken. John Crosland expressed his concern with the detail. There was no deception plan, minimal fire support, exposed ground and a considerable number of enemy. 'But despite all this, 'H' accepted the task – there was no viable alternative.'

Keen as 2 Para was to be gone, there was not universal approval of the brigade's plan – but the brigade resisted every attempt to modify it. During the afternoon of 24 May, Major Philip Neame led his company down the mountain to secure the battalion assembly area some 8½ miles (14 kilometres) distant at Camilla Creek House, to be followed by the other two companies at last light. Then the fog of war intervened. Poor flying weather meant their direct support artillery could not be put in place. The raid was cancelled.

Jones would have recognized that without artillery support, the operation really was a non-starter, but that did not stop him venting his spleen: 'I've waited twenty years for this, and now some fucking marine's cancelled it.'[35] Thompson's Brigade Major, John Chester, whom Thompson described as having 'an acid, short fused temper under a quiet exterior'[36] apologized directly to Jones for having mucked him about. Jones proved to be sweetness itself. 'John, life's too short to worry about things like that.' It was 26 May. Suddenly the attack on Goose Green was back on schedule and Jones's lifetime ambition was about to come to fruition. The reason for the change of heart was all to do with high politics.

When Task Force headquarters occasionally wanted a one-on-one talk with Thompson to micro-manage operations, he was obliged to decamp to the brigade maintenance area where satellite radio reception back to Northwood was of exceptional quality. Thompson suffered a convoluted higher chain of command and the absence of a clear directive. One would think the availability of such high-quality communication systems would be welcome yet it had the potential to be the bane of the Commander's life. Margaret Thatcher had taken an enormous political risk but, having been given the task, the last thing the Commander wanted was real-time micro-management by the Prime Minister. Brigadier Thompson was already the recipient of orders from Northwood and from General Moore, Land Commander, emphasizing how vital it was that the responsible commander entrusted with the fighting of the conflict should have but one recognizable chain of command. Margaret Thatcher had let it be known that to snatch diplomatic defeat from the jaws of victory would be wrong, arguing forcibly that if the situation remained static, proposals for a ceasefire would gain momentum.[37] Thompson told his military superiors that he had cancelled Goose Green because he could not arrange artillery support. 'You do not need guns to assault Goose Green' came the reply from the London suburbs and he was thereupon ordered to put the attack on Goose Green back on schedule. He discussed 2 Para's mission with Admiral Fieldhouse; it was his intention that 2 Para 'raided' Goose Green. Fieldhouse demurred, telling Thompson to delete the word *raid* and insert *destroy* the enemy at Goose Green. Field Marshal the Lord Bramall, Chief of the General Staff, believed the wider intelligence picture to which they had access in Whitehall helped them to recognize the tactical dangers of 'getting stuck halfway across by weather'.[38] The 'going' was assumed to be boggy and bad, subject to further deterioration in the heavy rain and snow known to be falling at the time.

On the night of Wednesday 26th, 'H' sent Major Philip Neame's D Company back down the mountain to secure the battalion assembly area at Camilla Creek House. L Company 42 Commando flew on to Sussex Mountain, thereby releasing the balance of approximately 500 men of 2 Para who set off in fighting order to make rendezvous at Camilla Creek House. Here they spent a cramped, shortened night in the house and outbuildings. Robert Fox, one of 2 Para's embedded news-men, thought 'going into Goose Green was an act of almost foolish heroism because nobody knew quite what the strength of the opposition was'. 'H' Jones confided in him: 'Well, this is the only time I've ever done something like this.' He said he was worried because, 'I've got to get in there and lead these men and get them through it. I have every confidence in my men, but it's a difficult plan of battle.'[39]

'H''s six-phase plan of battle has been criticized for being too restrictive, *befehlstaktik*, the work of a control freak, but this was a night attack where 'H' Jones considered command and control to be of vital importance. Helmuth von Moltke insisted no plan survives contact with the enemy.[40] The plan has been described as a typical product of the School of Infantry, a training expedient so designed as to allow six different students the opportunity to express their own individuality in a convenient, continuous training package of different challenges. These multi-phase exercises are a training device to exercise students, in a format not meant to have any similarity with real life.

The plan might have been less susceptible to the claim of foolish heroism had the battalion been adequately resourced. A battalion in attack would have expected to have at least a battery of six guns in direct support with others in support. Jones was allocated three 105-mm Light Guns flown into Camilla Creek. As a make-weight for the shortage of artillery (45 Commando and 3 Para were also on the move), HMS *Arrow* took up position in Grantham Sound; but it would be of limited value because of a turret fault with her 4.5-inch gun and the need during daylight hours to be under collective protection arrangements in San Carlos Bay. Add to these difficulties the real problem of putting 81-mm mortars in position with ammunition and gaining sufficient purchase on the sodden peat, and it is unsurprising that there was only one section of two mortars to support the battalion. In order to boost the battalion's firepower, 'H' asked Thompson to detach a troop of the Blues and Royals' light-armoured vehicles. The Brigadier declined, believing wrongly that the tracked vehicles would sink into the peat surface.

In view of the paucity of 81-mm mortars to provide support, the option of taking 2-inch mortars forward was left to the discretion of company commanders. B and D

Companies did, A Company did not, reflecting different inter-
pretations of the Warning Order announcing a renewed raid.
Even worse was the performance of the three Light Guns.
'They were not at all effective,' said David Benest, author of
the battalion's Post Operation Report, 'mainly owing to the
close proximity of friendly forces and the effect of the wind.'[41]
The atrocious weather was also responsible for the frequent
unavailability of RAF ground attack fighters. When they did
fly, they had such a significant effect upon the Argentinians
as to be a major contributory factor in their capitulation. It
would be fair to say that this, the first battalion night attack
since the Korean War, was conducted virtually without the
benefit of fire support.

During the afternoon of the 27th, with the local time at
10.00 a.m., BBC World Service announced news of an
imminent attack on Goose Green by a parachute battalion.
The announcer said, 'They're saying, for example, that 2nd
Parachute Regiment has moved south towards Darwin area.'[42]
Jones went ballistic when he heard this. There was no one
in a position of authority at the top of the chain of command
he was not going to sue. The Argentinians at Goose Green
had heard the same report. Although a number in 2 Para
believed the Argentinians reinforced later that night, this appears
not to have been the case. The Argentinians attributed the
serious breach of security to a cynical attempt at disinformation
– they were not going to be taken in by such a clumsy ruse.
The media have the potential to have an adverse influence
in modern warfare. That was evident in the Falklands and
a lesson the Americans learned when they instituted their
media strategy for Grenada.

In all the accounts in this book there is a similar tension
between the media's belief in their right to know what's going
on and the military's insistence that their operations are not

prejudiced through breaches of security. The surprise is that in this case secret operational information could have been leaked from one of the most highly controlled media operations in modern history. Admiral Fieldhouse loathed the media. A coded signal, DIET, was allegedly sent from Northwood to the Task Force captains. Decoded, it meant 'starve the press'. 'Of all the wars I have covered,' wrote ITN's Michael Nicholson, 'the censorship then was the severest of any. I can recall only one instance when the reason behind a cut story was explained.'[43] When David Benest came to write the story of 2 Para's operations in the Falklands, he asked the BBC the source of their controversial news item. They said 'the MoD'. There is a belief within 2 Para that news of the attack on Goose Green had been deliberately leaked by Northwood's strategists in order to divert attention away from the main thrust on Stanley. That view is not supported by Brigadier Thompson, who has said the source of the leak was a member of the War Cabinet in the Garrick, the gentlemen's club in London.

> The fact that the indiscretion was allowed to leak further *may* have had something to do with Northwood believing that Goose Green had been taken by the night of 27/28 May whereas the battle did not *begin* until the night 27/28 May. If Northwood did think this, I can only guess that they assumed its capture on the afternoon of 27 May on the basis that I had told 'H' Jones to move down on the night 26/27 May. Northwood constantly underestimated the time it took to move on foot in the Falklands, and how the lack of helicopters slowed everything down.

'H' Jones returned to the crucial task of completing his orders. The mission paragraph read: '2 Para is to capture the Darwin and Goose Green area.'[44] The six-phase attack

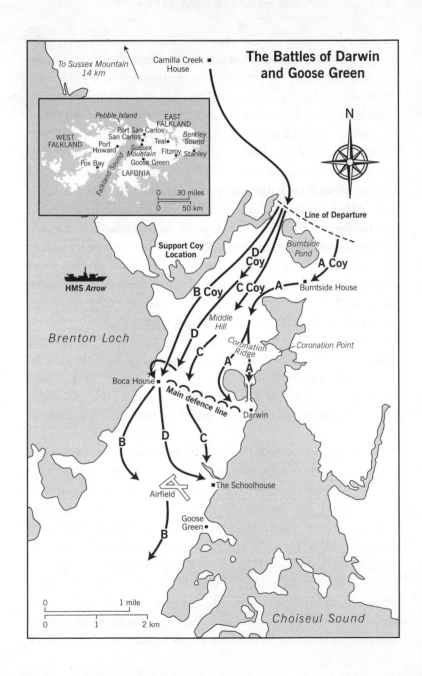

The Battles of Darwin and Goose Green

To Sussex Mountain 14 km

Camilla Creek House

N

Inset map:
WEST FALKLAND
Pebble Island
EAST FALKLAND
Port San Carlos
San Carlos
Port Howard
Sussex Mountain
Teal
Berkley Sound
Fitzroy
Stanley
Fox Bay
Goose Green
LAFONIA
Falkland Sound

0 — 30 miles
0 — 50 km

Line of Departure

Burntside Pond

Support Coy Location

D Coy
A Coy
B Coy
C Coy
A
Burntside House

HMS *Arrow*

Middle Hill

Brenton Loch

D
C
A
A
Coronation Ridge
Coronation Point

Boca House

Main defence line

Darwin

B
D
C

The Schoolhouse

Airfield

Goose Green

B

0 — 1 mile
0 — 1 — 2 km

Choiseul Sound

beginning at night on 27 May was to culminate in daylight assaults on Darwin Settlement and Goose Green. Not knowing precisely where the civilians were resulted in a deliberate intention to fight on in daylight when they could be easily identified. That intention did not come without problems of its own. Not without good reason was the surrounding, flat, featureless terrain named 'the billiard table' by 2 Para. The three rifle companies, A on the left flank, B on the right, D in reserve, and C (Patrol) Company were to advance on two axes based on known and possible enemy positions.

Preparing for a night attack such as that planned for that evening had to be slick. Everything flows from the Commanding Officer's orders. Company commanders then prepare and deliver their orders, after which platoon commanders do the same until every man in the section is informed of the overall intention. It is self-evident that the Commanding Officer's orders must be given at the earliest opportunity. 'H' had his orders written by mid-morning with a view to giving them to his 'O' Group at 11.00, allowing fourteen hours of darkness in which to travel the 8 miles (13 kilometres) from Camilla House to Goose Green down the 1½-mile- (2.4-kilometre-) wide isthmus.

When he arrived to kick-start the process, Jones discovered a number of key officers including a company commander absent. Apparently there had been a breakdown in communications. 'H' had no choice but to postpone giving his orders until the requisite individuals could be assembled. They were relatively close to each other, suggesting the delay should have been short. Unbelievably, 'H' delayed giving his orders for four hours, time irretrievably lost, reducing the number of hours of darkness available for the advance to contact and fight through opposition encountered along the way. There is no fathomable reason for this inordinate delay. There is a suggestion, only a suggestion, that 'H' Jones suffered a crisis of confidence compounded by the knowledge that the enemy now knew they were coming, forfeiting the element of surprise. 'H''s detailed orders took a laborious one and a half hours to deliver. Of the approaching fourteen hours of darkness, nine would be lost to battle preparations and moving down to the start line.[45]

'By the time I returned to brief my Company, the light was failing,' remembers John Crosland. 'I could barely see the platoon commanders and the rest of my Company Group. It was too late for models, so I kept my Orders brief, concentrating on how I saw the fight going and reinforcing our practised concept of operations – gain the momentum, keep moving under the cover of darkness to our advantage.'[46] Not everyone had maps at 'H''s orders group. There was therefore no requirement to repeat enemy locations or give meaningless grid references.

By the time 'H' gave his orders, the intelligence picture had improved. 2 Para's own reconnaissance revealed the enemy presence on Darwin ridge running NNE–SSW across the isthmus. The capture of an enemy Land Rover-mounted reconnaissance team had also generated further intelligence of the enemy. 'H' demonstrated his questionable grasp of tactics by instructing his officers to liaise with the battalion Intelligence Officer with regard to enemy positions *after* his orders. As a consequence, there was a serious disconnection between the intelligence and the plan and the responsibilities for attacking the enemy positions on Darwin ridge went unallocated.

What is strange is that, having listened at length to very detailed plans, no one present thought to ask the Commanding Officer what the company responsibilities were for capturing the enemy's vital ground along Darwin Hill.[47] 'The reasons are simple,' explained Dair Farrar-Hockley, 'first the vital ground was not expressed as such; second, the intelligence picture given – with 'H''s urging to hurry up – did not come across in a clear geographical sequence (the marking of maps followed rather than preceded the orders), thus the significance of what might have been there was lost.'[48]

In preparation for a deliberate battalion attack, it would be reasonable to have in place a belt-and-braces communication network so that if one system failed there was a back-up available. For the attack on Darwin–Goose Green, there was provision of neither battalion high-frequency nor administrative nets. Acknowledging this fact, the Signals Officer said, 'We were told "it's" on again, "it" had been the raid. We were not to discover the mission had changed to a full-blown attack until the Commanding Officer delivered his delayed orders. By then it was too late to put the additional two nets together.'[49] Unlike Arnhem where the signals problem derived from use of rudimentary equipment, the signals problems here lay in not making the best use of what was available. As a consequence there was a heavy flow of traffic coming through the one net, considerably annoying 'H' Jones.

At 18.00 on 27 May, C Company, led by engineers, set off in steady rain for the line of departure to clear the route for the rifle companies that would follow. The companies moved at 20.00, first A Company, then B and finally D. Jones was moving forward close to the front in his small tactical headquarters containing the command team. At 02.35, A Company crossed the line of departure, quickly pushing the enemy in platoon strength out of Burntside House. B Company faced lines of enemy in depth, section commanders responding to each situation accordingly. D Company, the reserve company, had what appeared to be the straightforward task of following on behind A and B, but in the rain and darkness they became disorientated in search of their guide. Philip Neame led his company back unguided on to the proper line and rested until the battle began. What Major Neame had not considered was 'H''s whereabouts. D Company had inadvertently gone ahead of the Commanding Officer. 'He came stomping down the track, found us there, and took this as a most immense personal affront that his reserve company was actually closer to the battle than he was.'[50]

The first lesson of night assaults is that they take longer than expected. B Company faced three engagements, the last involving artillery support which, despite the training, served to invert the company, putting platoons out of position relative to each other. 'H' had passed through D Company on the main track. Given that reorganization in B Company inevitably took longer than anticipated, 'H' had in all probability taken the lead of the battalion at the vanguard. When fired upon from an enemy position to his front, he returned to D Company, ordering Philip Neame to deal with the problem and maintain momentum. This he did, but an enemy position between B and D Companies was unwittingly bypassed. It then opened up on D Company, inflicting the first casualties of the battle, two dead and two wounded. D Company dealt with that problem but some of their fire fell around B Company, thereby emphasizing that in the deepness of a dark night, no element of the battalion had a clear idea where the others were. 'H' may have wanted close command and control at night but it was simply not possible. Progress was being subjected to further serious delays through the need to reorganize after every engagement in the pitch-black and featureless terrain. B Company suffered no casualties until just after dawn when they were caught on a forward slope by Argentinian machine gun fire coming from a westerly position on the Darwin feature.

Darwin Hill on the left flank rises 100 feet (30 metres) above Darwin Settlement. The ridge, which runs from the hill across the isthmus to Boca House, is also 100 feet at its highest point. The spur to the right of a gorse gully leading to the top of the feature was dominated by up to seven trenches which had to be cleared before A Company on the left flank could get into the gully. The top of Darwin Hill was unoccupied. It had no need to be occupied. Fixed-line machine guns from the Argentinian main defensive position precluded any movement along the top.

By 05.30 A Company had reached Coronation Point, its second objective, which Intelligence had said was a company position. Fortunately it was unoccupied. Dair Farrar-Hockley requested permission to continue the advance, making best use of the remaining darkness. 'H' could not believe Farrar-Hockley was where he claimed to be. He told him to stay where he was until 'H' had confirmed his position. He thereupon made the fateful journey over to the left flank to A Company's position. Satisfied that Dair Farrar-Hockley was where he said he was, the Commanding Officer authorized the advance to continue into the lightening dawn. 'We had been required to remain on Coronation Point for almost an hour, while the Commanding Officer made his way forward, thus losing the last important hour of darkness,'[51] said Farrar-Hockley.

The battalion had not progressed as well as the plan intended. Daybreak revealed in perfect clarity a battalion advancing towards the Argentinians' defended locations across open terrain unblessed by protective cover. Now, at first light, 2 Para was faced with attacking a prepared and alerted enemy able to engage them at long range. The battalion crossed a stretch of gorse bushes between Boca House and Darwin Settlement, just short of the Argentinian main positions on Darwin Heights. They were about to suffer for the delay in starting the advance. The first rays of daylight signified to the Paras the reality that the advantage had now swung to the defence.

Having stopped A Company, 'H' was now pressing the OC to get a move on with the advance southward. Farrar-Hockley had sent his 3 platoon around the Darwin inlet to cover the enemy located in the settlement while the remaining two platoons advanced in accordance with the plan. B and D Companies were to the right of the centre track. Unbeknown to 2 Para, there were not the sixteen trenches reported by their own reconnaissance upon Darwin ridge. In fact there were twenty-three, laid out in a horseshoe configuration, suggesting the expectation of an attack from the sea. This was occupied by ninety-two enemy. Yet despite the most comprehensive of plans, none of the companies was assigned to deal with what would appear to be a company position. A Company was focused upon Darwin Settlement and the gorse-covered gully which they would use to access Darwin Hill. The strength of the defensive line of Darwin rested upon the enemy company location to their right.

The Argentinians engaged A Company while it was still in the open. The troops in front were close enough to the gully to get there unscathed. For those bringing up the rear it was too far. One of them, Corporal Melia, a Royal Engineer, was shot dead. Battle drills learnt in training switched on automatically. Non-commissioned officers (NCOs) supported by a gunner captain did what they were trained to do, attacking the trenches on the enemy right with a mix of light anti-tank weapons, grenades and light machine guns. When soldiers were hit, their comrades braved Argentinian fire to recover them, a number of them becoming casualties as a consequence.

Strange things happen in lethal combat, such as that experienced by A Company. Second Lieutenant Coe lay on his back in a hole having arrived back from an expedition into the gully. He puffed on a cigarette, discussed cricket with Corporal Camp and listened sympathetically as his NCO described his concern that his wife had recently bought a car. This story should not detract from the fact that A Company was in dire straits. The artillery they called for was unavailable because the small amount of ammunition had been reserved for counter-battery tasks, and air strikes upon an ideal target could not be delivered because of fog at sea.

There seemed to be no option but to continue with time-consuming, sequential forays against the Argentinian line. They had to win the fire-fight and yet they had little support. There was no option but patiently to wage a battle of attrition, chipping away at the Argentinian defensive lines. 'H', who had been following behind A Company, became increasingly impatient. His battalion had been obliged to go to ground to the north of Darwin ridge and had been there for an hour, emphasizing that the initiative had indeed swung from the Paras to the Argentinians. Jones would have recognized his vulnerability to a counter-attack and the real possibility of defeat. To lose the first battle of the Falklands war would have had profound military and political consequences, and cast shame on 2 Para.

To the rear, and again in reserve, D Company was not as intimately engaged as A and B Companies, having freedom to move to avoid incoming artillery fire. Philip Neame, OC D Company, observed what he believed to be a door ajar to the right of Darwin ridge, along the western shoreline, inviting to be pushed to allow his company to outflank the defences on Darwin ridge. He could see Argentinians, bypassed earlier, taking that route. He asked the Commanding Officer for permission to exploit the opportunity. But 'H' had other things on his mind and said something like 'stop clogging the net; I'm trying to conduct a battle'.

Meanwhile C Company had come down the central track. Seeing the fire-fight ahead, the Company's twelve light machine guns were deployed in a line to engage the enemy positions on the ridge ahead. At that distance there was difficulty in differentiating between their own and enemy positions. C Company's second-in-command came up on the battalion radio net asking A Company to identify themselves so that he could provide fire support. 'I was ordered to stay off the radio by 'H'; he said he was trying to fight a battle. So was I, and found it frustrating to be ignored when we could so obviously help.'[52]

Annoyed by A Company's apparent lack of progress, 'H' moved up to join Farrar-Hockley, letting it be known that the present stalemate was unacceptable. The time was 08.30. He intended the mortar platoon commander to go forward to direct mortar fire on the Argentinian positions until Farrar-Hockley intervened to stop an action which he believed would result in a pointless death. Then, again, Philip Neame came up on the battalion net. Recognizing that the Argentinians did not have the strength to be everywhere, he earnestly attempted to persuade 'H' to allow D Company to go to the right flank to exploit through to the rear of the Argentinian position, thereby breaking the stalemate on the left. Angrily, 'H' said to him, 'don't tell me how to run my battle'. Both A and B Company commanders were well and truly stuck. It needed a battalion plan to unhinge the situation – which 'H' did not deliver.

Throughout this book we consistently discover that a battalion may have had no more than two or three soldiers with previous combat experience. 'H' Jones was not one of those. His reaction to being in combat for the first time was to permit no substantive action unless he himself had seen what was intended and given his personal approval. As a consequence, he stymied initiative among his company commanders, he slowed down the dynamic of the battle and, in so doing, unwittingly exposed the battalion to unnecessary additional risk. Such unexpected developments or behaviour arise in conflict. When we see examples, even the most implausible appear plausible; for example, the action of the Commanding Officer, played by Alec Guinness in the film, who attempted to stop the demolition of the bridge his battalion had built over the River Kwai.

Becoming impatient for a result, 'H' required Farrar-Hockley to proceed at a pace the latter did not consider sensible. An ad hoc section of all ranks assembled to go forward to take the crest above them but it made no tactical sense. 'H' saw three men die in the unnecessary attempt to force the pace. Even if smoke had been available to mask the Paras' movement, the strong wind would have dispersed it immediately.

Lance-Corporal Toole shouted out to Farrar-Hockley that if he did not go back now, he never would. Sniper fire had been responsible for the deaths of at least seven paratroopers, 'all head shots', said Corporal Abols. 'That is the main reason A Company was stuck.'[53] Heavy fire forced back small numbers attacking the Argentinian trenches: 'as we were going over, we were just losing blokes and coming back down, going up, losing them, coming back down . . . We had to get up there to find out what was actually going on so we could brief Major Farrar-Hockley . . . but each time we'd gain some more information about their strengths.'[54]

The three deaths had a devastating impact on 'H'. He

knew the clock was ticking, he knew they were vulnerable to a counter-attack which could roll them back from whence they had come, he knew he had little by way of external support with which to fight an equal battle. Enemy artillery continued its ceaseless pounding of 2 Para's exposed positions, scattering divots of peat. Casualties would have been far higher had not the peat cushioned the detonating artillery. Something had to be done and 'H' was not a person who would ask of his soldiers anything he was not prepared to do himself. He stood up, shouted out to those around him 'come on A Company, get your skirts off' and then, on a solo charge, was gone, followed by his bodyguard Sergeant Norman and Lance-Corporal Beresford. As he came round the spur he readied his SMG (sub machine gun) to attack an Argentinian trench, only to be cut down by a machine gun on the opposite side of the re-entrant, a mini valley, firing down on him. He was mortally wounded by a single round in the base of the neck which crashed through his body. Sergeant Blackburn, 'H''s radio operator, radioed those on the battalion net 'Sunray is down'.[55]

The great irony is that not long after 'H' had made his selfless sacrifice, A Company, after a sustained and aggressive fight by all ranks, finally broke the defended line. In total, this three-hour battle, phase five of the operation, involving 200 men of the two opposing companies, resulted in seventy-four casualties: twenty-four dead and fifty wounded. A Company inflicted over 60 per cent casualties on the enemy. Corporal David Abols's accurate firing of a 66-mm light anti-tank weapon into a command trench proved to be the tipping point against the Argentine force. The Argentinians had simply had enough and gradually, all along the line, the white cloths of surrender were raised. It had been a courageous defence and Lieutenant Estevez was to receive his country's highest gallantry award. A number of Argentinians had seen the writing on the wall from the beginning. 'My feeling', said one, 'was that if you tread on the lion's tail, it sometimes turns round and bites you.'[56]

Sergeant Norman was the first to reach the barely conscious 'H'; he removed his webbing and applied a saline drip. The Company Sergeant Major told Farrar-Hockley he thought Jones was dying. Farrar-Hockley saw 'H''s eyelids flicker but that was all. He held 'H''s hand until 10.00 when it was obvious that he had died.[57] Two Scout helicopters operating out of Camilla Creek House responded to the news that Jones was down. They offloaded ammunition and the two helicopters were flown forward for a straight casualty evacuation run to the RAP (Regimental Aid Post) to recover 'H' and other casualties. Unfortunately the two Scouts were intercepted by two Pucaras en route. One helicopter successfully avoided the Argentinian fighters but that flown by Lieutenant Richard Nunn was shot down and Nunn killed.[58] Some consolation was derived from the fact that one of the Pucaras returning to Stanley hit Blue Mountain, killing the pilot.

Sergeant Norman, 'H''s bodyguard and the man closest to him when he fell, was asked his opinion of his Commanding Officer's action. 'My own opinion was that he should not have been there, but being 'H' Jones, he was always going to be there because he was that type of Commanding Officer.'[59]

2 Para's second-in-command, Major Chris Keeble's heart leapt when he heard Sergeant Blackburn's voice frantically saying 'Sunray is down'. He radioed John Crosland, then heavily engaged on Darwin ridge, to assume command until he had moved forward. Theoretically, the Battery Commander should have assumed command after the loss of 'H' Jones. Keeble's mind was in a state of turmoil as he thought through

what had to be done. Then, composed and about to leave, the RSM (Regimental Sergeant-Major) called him back. 'What is it?' he asked sharply. 'You are going to do fucking well sir!' That really chuffed him. 'I felt a million dollars, a wonderful touch.'[60]

Over on the right flank, Philip Neame's D Company had taken time out for tea and porridge. His men may well have thought it odd to pause in mid-battle to take tea, but Neame was a successful Everest mountaineer and he knew well the importance of maintaining energy levels. There was no knowing when they would next have an opportunity for sustenance. Keeble told Neame over the radio to go forward and link up with Crosland's B Company. 'Well I was buggered if I was going to waste my porridge so this vagabond army got on the move with everyone trying to take the odd sip of their brew as they went and I was trying to get down the odd spoonful of hot porridge.'[61]

The next objective was Boca House, a ruin about a foot high, where the Argentinians had located a good proportion of their heavy machine guns. As he tried to link up with B Company, Neame and his Company HQ came under fire from these, so rather than risk being pinned down on the ridge as B Company was, he rapidly decided that supporting B Company was a more sensible option and pulled back to explore the right-flanking possibility along the shoreline that he had earlier identified. In the event, the ground did not allow this but it did allow Neame to get within 500 yards (457 metres) and effective machine gun range of Boca House.

Philip Neame of D Company had his twelve available machine guns lined up on the shore. Up on the hill, OC B Company set up the firing-post for the Milan anti-tank wire-guided missiles which he had called forward so that the Milan fire could shoot over the D Company machine gun fire. After four missiles had been launched and thousands of rounds of ammunition had been expended, the attackers saw a proliferation of white flags poking out around Boca House. Neame said to those around him that if the Argentinians wanted to surrender, it would be unwise to ignore their invitation. Standing next to him was Lieutenant Jim Barry. Neame readied to lead the heart-in-the-mouth move forward on to the exposed beach to take the surrender of the Argentinians, only to be checked by Corporal Harley who went ahead of him, saying 'This isn't your job sir, you're too valuable. This is Tom's work.' Neame did not argue. Despite poor communications on two occasions leading to unchecked firing from other 2 Para positions, the 500-yard (457-metre) walk of faith resulted in the Boca position being taken without further loss or expenditure of ammunition.

The Paras now advanced towards the settlement of Goose Green, which they could see a mile away. Their advance in the open, through tussocks of grass and minefields, reminded someone of the opening title sequence from *Dad's Army*. What was infinitely more significant than their being able to see the settlement was that the enemy in and around the settlement was able to see *them*. A seemingly endless barrage of artillery, mortars and anti-aircraft guns fired over open sights tracked every step taken forward.

The acting Commanding Officer told Neame to head for Goose Green. In fact, D Company was already heading directly for the settlement but was forced off the track and towards School House by anti-aircraft fire and the need to skirt around the minefield. A consequence of 'H''s death had been the liberation of the company commanders who, on the basis of mission-oriented orders, known also as *auftragstaktik*, now took the action which their experience told them to be the most sensible. C Company was also ordered to advance along the track from Darwin Hill towards Goose Green, without covering fire, but experienced difficulties when it became apparent the Argentinians were aiming for their radio aerials and, by virtue of relative positions, the individuals in Company HQ. One individual in C Company HQ said, 'Now I think I know what it must have been like to have been on the Somme.' B Company prepared to move off to encircle the enemy positions so that they hooked up from the south. There were two convenient watercourses which they were grateful to follow.

As he neared the school area, OC D Company ordered Lieutenant Barry to take a position near the track to provide covering fire for an attack on School House, which had been reported to be strongly held and which covered the final approach to the settlement. As the outlying buildings of the school were cleared, elements of C Company, approaching from Darwin Hill, joined D Company which was by then taking casualties from sustained enemy artillery fire. The two companies combined to launch an ad hoc attack.

Meanwhile, seeing white cloths flying from a position identified by a prominent flagpole on the high ground along-side the track leading to Goose Green, Barry (perhaps mindful of Neame's sentiments expressed prior to the surrender of Boca House), decided to approach and negotiate the surrender of the position. The Argentinian platoon commander, who spoke good English, believed it to be Barry and the two Paras with him who wanted to surrender. He was incredulous to discover the intention was the reverse. While they stood there, out in the open, a machine gun in the sustained fire role opened up on the group from the vicinity of Darwin Hill. Believing they had been hoodwinked, the Argentinians opened fire on Barry and his two escorts, killing all three. Sergeant Meredith assumed command of the platoon, successfully attacking the enemy positions, for which he would be awarded the Distinguished Conduct Medal.

The C and D Companies' attack on the school to the north of the airstrip had been successfully completed by mid-afternoon. Fire had taken hold of the school. B Company's enveloping manoeuvre made good progress, the OC taking his men forward below the angles of depression of the anti-aircraft guns. The Paras had been told to expect an RAF air strike. The reassuring sound of jet engines could be heard in the distance, closing on Goose Green. Philip Neame remembers looking up: 'Hang on a minute,' he thought to himself, 'those are enemy Skyhawks.' As they came in, he and other members of D Company found themselves trapped between a raging inferno on one side and a minefield on the other. Corporal J. Montgomery continued, 'We were glad to see a Skyhawk shot down by our troops to the west. No sooner had we finished congratulating each other than suddenly a Pucara flew in from behind us. The reaction from everyone was to put immediate fire into the Pucara. To our sheer joy it was hit. Our joy turned to sheer terror as the plane banked towards us and crashed about 30 metres [32 yards] from us, the wing taking an ammo belt off a man's back without injuring him and sprayed us with fuel from its burst tanks.'[62]

Air activity was intense that day. In a tactical surge, six helicopters delivered Argentine reinforcements to the south of B Company – merely adding to the number of prisoners of war to be repatriated aboard the *Norland*. Next, it would be the RAF's turn, in a surgical strike which contributed to the eventual outcome of the battle.

'I could see the settlement of Goose Green and the target peninsula laid out directly in front, just like a model,' wrote Squadron Leader Jerry Pook, one of three RAF Harrier GR3 pilots arriving over 2 Para towards the end of daylight. Their targets were the 35-mm guns (Oerlikon) on the periphery of the airstrip. The lead Harrier pilot saw the gun positions just to the right of his aiming point; 'Come right, 50 yards [46 metres] from that!' said the Leader. 'His cluster bombs exploded in a spectacular array of sparks from right to left across my front; then I fired all 72 of my rockets in a half-second burst,' said Pook. The RAF Harriers had not been shy of Goose Green's 'flak trap'.[63] Within ten days of war operations they had had half their Harriers shot down.[64] Some of B Company thought the Harriers had come too close for their liking. This indication of the Harrier's capabilities made a lasting impression on the Argentinians.

For the Argentinians, the RAF attack had an acute psychological effect, the last straw after having been consistently and persistently hammered by the Toms. They did not share the junta's affection for these desolate islands and certainly had no intention of dying for them. 2 Para's Second-in-command Chris Keeble halted the advance. It was dark. He ordered a break to eat and sleep with a view to resuming hostilities in the morning. He entertained the notion that the Harrier attack had demoralized the enemy, that their will had been broken and that in the morning they could go for a surrender.

That night, Chris Keeble sat among the gorse bushes with a weary Dair Farrar-Hockley and ran his Plan A and Plan B for the morning past him. 'We will walk down the hill, tell the Argies the game is up and defeat was unavoidable.' Apparently Farrar-Hockley's reaction was to look at him as though he had lost his marbles. But that was Plan A. Plan B, to attack the encircled Argentinians in the settlement with overwhelming violence, was complicated to the extent it was barely credible because they knew that 112 inhabitants were under lock and key in the community centre. 'We had not journeyed 8,000 miles [12,875 kilometres] merely to destroy the very people we had come to save.' It was also doubtful whether they had sufficient ammunition to do the job.

Plan A had to work. The great unknown is what would have happened had this bluff been called. While the rest tried to sleep in the snow and bitter cold, Keeble wrote out the surrender document with the assistance of Robert Fox,[65] and sought approval for his plan from the Brigade Commander. J Company 42 Commando was positioned as a reserve to reinforce an attack on Goose Green but would not be needed.

In the early morning light of 30 May, two Argentinian Warrant Officers could be seen leaving the British lines walking towards the settlement. In their hands they held white flags and one carried a letter written in Spanish. In that letter Keeble told the Argentinian commander his situation was hopeless; he was surrounded. To avoid further casualties, Keeble proposed he release the civilians and surrender. The two Warrant Officers returned almost immediately. Air Vice-Commodore Wilson Pedroza agreed to a meeting to discuss the situation.

At 08.30 Keeble led a small group of unarmed officers and the two embedded correspondents down to the agreed rendezvous point on the airstrip. Pedroza arrived accompanied by a naval officer. The release of the civilians was immediately agreed. The surrender arrangements were more difficult because this was something only Brigadier Menendez in Stanley could approve. Pedroza said that if approval was forthcoming its implementation would be conditional upon the Argentinians not being humiliated. Pedroza was made particularly ill at ease by the presence of the two correspondents. 'They can do whatever they like if they surrender,' Keeble told the interpreter.[66] They waited for the reply from Stanley. Pedroza was authorized to do as he saw fit under the circumstances.

The first to arrive to lay down their arms were 150 of Pedroza's airmen. Keeble relieved Pedroza of his pistol. Then the army contingent led by Lieutenant-Colonel Italo Pioggi marched on to the airfield where they threw down their arms. Later, a number of Paras exchanged their own weapons for the better ones discarded by the enemy. After singing the Argentine national anthem, soldiers and airmen passed into captivity. At 09.05 Brigade Headquarters received a message from 2 Para. 'Argies in area Goose Green and Darwin not to be fired upon without permission. Body of men manoeuvring looking as though they're going to surrender.'[67] D Company began a head count of the captured enemy. There were in excess of 900 army personnel, more than twice the number of 2 Para attackers.

This had been an amazing feat, put into perspective by Philip Neame who joked that he had been more afraid of 'H' Jones than the Argentinians. Regarding the Argentinians, Keeble believed 'one of the principal causes of the collapse of will was the breakdown in relationship between officer and conscripted soldier, which in itself reinforces the strength of a volunteer, albeit smaller force'.[68] Max Hastings recorded the startling fact that throughout the length of the battle only one officer had been captured and only one had been killed. 'Most of them, it seemed, had stayed as far to the rear as possible throughout the struggle.'[69] Seventy-five per cent of 2 Para's casualties had been officers and NCOs. At 12.42 a message to Brigade HQ came through the artillery net. 'The Union Jack has been raised over Goose Green Settlement.'[70]

As recently as 25 May, a pessimistic ITN correspondent, Michael Nicholson, had written in his war diary: 'This is our lowest ebb. We have lost five ships, 54 seamen have been killed, over 100 wounded, many critically.' Two days later, 2 Paras' advance on Darwin and Goose Green commenced.

'It was the battle for Goose Green that turned things around,' wrote Nicholson, 'a tiny settlement of no strategic value but Mrs Thatcher needed good news and the Paras' overnight victory provided it.[71] Come daylight we filmed the aftermath. [Nicholson did not arrive until after the battle ended.] The Argentine dead were still out there, half submerged in the mud and water of their trenches. I saw too that the Paras had used bayonets as well as bullets.'[72] Chris Keeble denied Nicholson permission to film the surrender ceremony after Benest had refused to allow him to go forward, 'but he managed to hitch a ride and get in on the act'.[73]

The battle of Darwin and Goose Green had cost eighteen British dead and thirty-five wounded in action. Fifty Argentinians were buried at Goose Green and 1,100 captured. Thompson remained convinced that Goose Green had been an unnecessary diversion from getting on to Stanley. 2 Para had been profoundly under-resourced to do what was asked of them. Who did the asking? With the benefit of hindsight, the Brigade Commander considered that he should have commanded the battle for Goose Green and used an additional battalion and also allocated armour. 'He reflected that he asked more of 2 Para than he should have done.'[74]

There is a strong possibility that the Falklands war could have ended at Goose Green but again, media reporting had done what the Argentinians had specifically asked should not happen, that is, from their viewpoint, to humiliate them. The only course left open to them was to fight on, to show that Goose Green had been an aberration.

The Argentinian conscripts fought bravely but were psychologically defeated. They were beaten by better soldiers, soldiers determined not to give up, soldiers who did make mistakes but who recovered faster than their adversaries. The Paras were not older than their enemy. Their strength and fitness allowed them to fight a continuous battle which required them to be on their feet for seventy-two hours. It was their willpower and determination to move forward which proved to be the battle winner. It comes down to training. All the soldiers had had to pass selection tests, corporals are required to pass the Section Commanders' Battle Course in the Brecon mountains;[75] sergeants have to qualify at the Sergeants' Battle Course; and, in addition, Paras are recruited from among those with the highest intelligence grades.

2 Para won the first battle of the Falklands Campaign and they did this by fighting a numerically superior defending force to a standstill.[76] That achievement would have been noted by the Soviets and also by a Guatemalan government with designs on Belize. Their next engagement, under the command of 5 Infantry Brigade, involved a heliborne operation – 28 miles (45 kilometres) inside no man's land – to secure two settlements within 12 miles (19 kilometres) of Port Stanley, thus creating a southern flank.

On rejoining 3 Commando Brigade, 2 Para marched north around Mount Longdon in preparation for an assault upon Wireless Ridge. After that success, 2 Para led the follow-on assault into Stanley, maintaining the momentum and forcing surrender. After the surrender, 2 Para, along with the rest of 3 Commando Brigade, were put on standby to clear through West Falkland. Brigadier Thompson sent 40 Commando, who cleared Port Howard and Fox Bay. They were, however, required to take their turn as duty battalion to deal with law and order problems in Stanley, thereby concluding an outstanding operation for a group of men described by Margaret Thatcher as 'the bravest of the brave'.[77]

There is no doubt in OC B Coy John Crosland's mind to whom that success was principally due: 'H's leadership and inspiration had produced a battalion that was "second to none" in terms of dogged determination, courage, physically and mentally very tough, yet totally focused on achieving its task.'[78]

Endless discussions have ensued as to whether 'H' Jones as Commanding Officer had been right to charge headlong into a defended enemy position. Dair Farrar-Hockley reiterated what he said in Mark Adkin's book:

> It cannot be said that 'H''s courageous sortie – or whatever he had in mind – inspired the soldiers at that moment, because few, if any, were aware of what he was doing. But his enterprise on our right did distract the enemy there to one degree or another. I do not agree that a particular piece of ground was taken on this account. Most important was 'H''s standing and drive in the battalion. He put us to a difficult task; he inspired us in the undertaking; he was up front from the beginning and hence provided the dynamic needed for the impetus of attacking and continuing to attack until we had succeeded. His inspiration and example were to remain with us for the rest of the campaign.[79]

'In the final analysis,' reflected John Crosland, 'no matter what happened between the start and the finish, it was a glorious victory vindicating 'H' and the award of his VC.'[80]

However there is one issue which an independent observer who has examined this battle can reasonably raise. Honours and awards are a source of controversy and this was the case at Goose Green. The Victoria Cross, which since 1856 has been the highest award for gallantry in Britain's armed forces, was posthumously awarded to Lieutenant-Colonel 'H' Jones OBE. Of the survivors, the Distinguished Service Order was awarded to Major C.P.B. Keeble and Military Crosses to Major J.H. Crosland, Major C.D. Farrar-Hockley and

Lieutenant C.S. Connor. Had he lived and been awarded the Victoria Cross, Colonel 'H' Jones would no doubt have insisted that the award was not his alone but also that of his battalion. Major P. Neame, the only rifle company commander not to receive the Military Cross, was among twenty to be mentioned in dispatches. Chris Keeble attributed the outcome of the battle to having been 'really achieved by the skill of Phil Neame's and Johnny Crosland's D and B Companies'.

The inclination here is to avoid issues of political and personal ambition. Nevertheless, two omissions are evident in this the concluding phase of Goose Green, which is why Chris Keeble's views have been included here. The first, Keeble's failure to mention Dair Farrar-Hockley and A Company, appears a strange oversight given Philip Neame's comment, 'No one can fail to be stirred by the harrowing three hours of A Company's battle for Darwin Hill – ending with unequivocal success – and surely by a margin the hardest fought and most demanding single engagement of the battle.'[81] The point is that it was Neame and Crosland who were in the then Commanding Officer's mind, remembering that 2 Para had three Commanding Officers within a fortnight.[82]

This brings us to the second omission. Neame's name for suitable recognition never crossed the relatively short distance between battalion and Brigade Headquarters. Dair Farrar-Hockley's, John Crosland's and a subaltern's did and, as a consequence, these were the three 2 Para officers awarded Military Crosses.[83] The skill and determination of Neame and his company would be repeated during 2 Para's later battle for Wireless Ridge.

The Brigade Commander, to whom all citations within his brigade went, admits that the matter of Falklands citations 'irks me to this day'. 3 Commando Brigade were given forty-eight hours to get their citations to divisional head-quarters, under pressure from Northwood to expedite submissions. The effect of this was to give Commanding Officers twenty-four hours to comply:

> This meant that in a number of cases, people were not put up because there was not time for proper reflection and investigation. I sent a number of citations back for rewriting, to reinforce the case for a decoration. I did not turn down, or 'write down' any. If Neame had been put up for a decoration I would have supported it. In essence, I knew of no cases where people were decorated undeservedly, and several where people were not decorated or received something less than they deserved.[84]

The subject of medals might seem a strange issue, whether that be campaign medals, medals for successful leaders or medals for the brave and courageous, but it is an important one. Campaign medals or bars are awarded for the first but not subsequent tours of duty, which means there is invariably a greater commitment to and interest by the soldiery in their first rather than subsequent tours of duty. This book is replete with stories of courage, of bravery beyond the call of duty; yet while fairness and the implementation of common standards is of course desirable, the conclusion is that it is not always achievable. The issue is examined further in the penultimate chapter.

The battle for Goose Green could not be described as a grand battle yet its analysis reveals an important modern battle replete with lessons for the future. A dismounted night–day and attack–defence between two conventional forces of approximately equal strength on the battlefield was unusual in that it simply had not happened for a long time, perhaps not since the Second World War.

The Goose Green battle is generally regarded as a triumph of the human spirit and leadership over impossible odds. The evidence reveals such an assertion to be too strong, but that is the common view. The battle demonstrated the limits of the then current tactical doctrine, above all the need for Mission Command – something which runs through this collection of battle accounts – a matter which only really came to the attention of the military after the death of 'H' Jones. Mission Command is also known as *auftragstaktik* and mission-oriented orders. The commander still gives his subordinates their orders but only within a framework of his intentions. His subordinates are then free to fight the battle as they see fit, conscious of their commander's concept of operations.

We saw useful improvisation in the battle. The wire-guided MILAN missile, for example, is an anti-tank weapon. At Goose Green it was used for the first time against bunkers, to great effect – to the extent that arguably it overturned the then commonly held understanding regarding force ratios for attack and defence, offering the attacker a distinct advantage over the positional defender. Convention had it that the ratio of attack to defence was three to one. This revolution in thinking would have been further strengthened had light tanks been deployed forward.

Command and leadership at battle group level was poor. The battle group headquarters did not operate as a team. HQ 2 Para had been identified as weak by GOC (General Officer Commanding) South East District, General Sir Paul Travers, prior to deployment to the Falklands. It is curious how 'H' Jones had been so focused upon standards within his rifle companies that he had not brought his own head-quarters up to standard. Leadership cannot be conducted by fear alone. This is borne out by an examination of the leadership at company level, which was found to be consistently outstanding. What had become self-evident was the value of experience from previous campaigns, especially Dhofar. (This is important since almost without exception all the later accounts in this book are of the activities of virtual combat virgins.)

The single greatest weakness of Goose Green was 'H' Jones's plan, especially the failure to identify Darwin Hill as the vital ground and to exert sufficient control to ensure that it was taken before daylight. Given a long approach to contact in deep darkness, the rationale behind his decision to maintain absolute command in a multi-phase operation is understandable, yet matters such as this are rarely black and white. Another could equally well have taken the opposite view: that by virtue of the darkness and the presence of a number of intervening defended localities lying between the point of departure and the vital ground, a planned multi-phase operation made little sense. A commander may be an inspirational leader but such an attribute can be negated by a poor plan. The unanswered mystery is why a raid transformed into a deliberate battle group attack without subordinates having been informed.

The Task Force's mission was to seize Stanley, the core of the Argentinian defence. While in pursuit of that mission there were other, subsidiary, related battles. Goose Green was a separate, one-off battle since it was not directly related to military operations against Stanley. It has to be remembered that at the outset the Royal Navy was being hammered by the Argentinian Air Force. Bad news came on a daily basis. 2 Para were in a position to attack Goose Green, a defended location that might otherwise have been bypassed, before the main body had closed on Stanley. Mrs Thatcher wanted good news and it is for that reason that 2 Para was ordered to make the risky attack upon the Argentinian positions in and around Goose Green. It was a close-run thing but Mrs Thatcher had her victorious battle, followed by other victorious battles in the lead-up to the fall of Stanley. It is for this reason that Goose Green has been selected over other engagements as the representative battle of the Falklands conflict.

As has been seen, military–media relations and command and control were problem areas in connection with the Goose Green battle. Almost without exception, these continued to create difficulties almost to the end of the series of battles under examination. Command and control issues manifest themselves in many different ways, whether in the micro-management of a battle by a superior headquarters or the obsessive insistence of the heroic 'H' Jones to maintain absolute command and control at Goose Green.

In 1982, the production and giving of formal orders to subordinates as adopted by 'H' Jones were taught at the staff colleges and School of Infantry in preference to the consideration of more flexible mission-oriented orders. Although mission-oriented orders instruction was not held in favour in the British Army's teaching schools, it does not mean that as a concept it was not practised. The intuitive nature of British officers is evident in their not being dedicated adherents to military doctrine, being inclined more towards the use of their own initiative. As was seen at Goose Green, the death of 'H' Jones liberated his company commanders to do what they thought best to achieve the given mission. For the British, Goose Green marked the beginning, if not entirely the end, of lengthy formal orders in favour of mission-oriented orders.

Relations with the media are another continuing issue. Apart from Helmand, where they were good – although this was mainly attributable to the special circumstances related to operations in Helmand Province – management of the media was often challenging. In Grenada, the subject of the next chapter, and the Falklands, while not having a great deal operationally in common, the management of the media was broadly similar. That is understandable given that the campaigns were fought on distant islands, not easily accessible by the uninvited press. Immediately the conflict of interest is identifiable, there is tension: the military are intent upon maintaining operational security, the press on exercising their rationale of the right to know. The lessons learned at the end of both campaigns introduced measures to meliorate what are inevitably going to be to a large extent irreconcilable aims between the military on the one hand and the media on the other.

3

Grenada
1983

'When the Army sees we're American, they will give up'

On 24 October 1983, Major-General H. Norman Schwarzkopf commanding 24th Armoured Infantry Division, Fort Stewart, Georgia, stood at his kitchen table preparing some recently caught bass for the family dinner. The phone rang. It was Major-General Dick Graves, Director of Operations at Forces Command. He asked Schwarzkopf what his plans were for the next few weeks. Graves dodged the 'what's this all about' questions, noted that Schwarzkopf could be available and promised to ring back once he had spoken to General Cavazos. A curious General Schwarzkopf put two and two together and got five. The day before, the Marine barracks in Beirut had been bombed, killing 241 US Marines. He suspected he might be required in connection with a retaliatory strike. Graves rang back, telling Schwarzkopf – just Schwarzkopf, none of his command – to get to Atlanta as quickly as possible. The General packed desert and temperate uniforms. He would need neither; he was going to Grenada.[1]

The United States' interest fell upon Grenada after 13 March 1979 when the Marxist Maurice Bishop overthrew the Prime Minister Eric Gairy, whom he described as corrupt and brutal, installing himself in Gairy's place as head of the People's Revolutionary Government (PRG). The coup – it was not a revolution – had the popular support of a large percentage of the 110,000 population and Bishop retained much of the support of the masses until his end. Washington's unease with Bishop stemmed not so much from his Marxist leanings but from his close friendship with arch-villain Fidel Castro.

The possibility of the orchestration of a counter-coup by his deputy Bernard Coard would have appeared nugatory for the ambitious Coard was also a Marxist, allegedly drawing his support from Moscow. Both men owed their positions to Communist sponsorship. 'The greater Communist of the two was Bishop, not Coard,' insisted publisher Leslie Pierre.[2] Bishop had a way with words, was charismatic and had a good rapport with the people, who lionized him.[3] 'We have this anomaly', declared Grenadian Member of Parliament Winston Whyte,[4] 'of the good Bishop and Coard, the evil genius. Nothing could be further from the truth. It is a myth being perpetuated by Bishop's supporters who envisage him as Grenada's Che Guevara.' Coard owed his position to his being an excellent organizer. The former Finance Minister, Coard insisted there was no ideological difference between himself and Prime Minister Bishop. 'I was a Marxist economist – I used Marxist analytical models but we ran a market economy.'[5]

Strangely, given its interest in Grenada for over four years, the United States had no CIA representation on the island and precious little Intelligence. In March 1983, seven months before the invasion, President Reagan gave a television address expressing his concerns with regard to developments on the island. As the United States invariably wished to be seen observing international law, however, its options were severely constrained. From a public relations point of view, the picture of a superpower acting to remove the de facto government of a small state without just cause was one that required careful management. The opportunity would be fleeting and the justification would presumably need to be based upon Article 51 of the UN Charter, collective self-defence.

Christopher Columbus discovered Grenada in 1498. The island then passed from Spanish to French and finally British ownership, from whom independence was achieved in 1974. Grenada is a constitutional monarchy represented at this time by a Governor General, Sir Paul Scoon. As head of state, the Queen has to act on the advice of the Grenadian Prime Minister, not the British Government. Margaret Thatcher's government had no authority in Grenada, nor any right to interfere or give advice. The Queen acts through the Governor General who acts on the advice of the Prime Minister. As for Sir Paul Scoon, he had been the ousted Prime Minister Gairy's Governor General. 'We retained Sir Paul,' explained Coard,[6] 'because we valued his concepts of patriotism and duty.'[7]

Grenada, known as the Spice Island, is a tri-island state with a reputation of outstanding natural beauty. Grenada itself is corseted inside a mere 133-square-mile (344-square-kilometre) island – at its maximum 25 miles long by 10 miles wide (40 by 16 kilometres) – whose exotic cash crops did little to balance the books between income and expenditure. The islands lie between the Caribbean Sea and the Atlantic Ocean, north of Trinidad and south of St Vincent. Grenada is a volcanic island with steep slopes and heavy vegetation. The flatter terrain, which might otherwise have been used to land helicopters, is dedicated to the cultivation of bananas and cocoa. From here either secondary jungle or rainforest rise up mountainous slopes.

In 1983, the captain of the tanker which delivered fuel to the islands had instructions from the owners not to call at Grenada. The bursar of the American medical school situated at appropriately named True Blue received a request to advance payment of fees to the Government so that a British contractor working on the building of the Point Salines International Airport on the island's southern tip could be paid. The school enjoyed a strange relationship with the Marxist Government. To Bishop, the facility acted as a sacred *milchkuh* in whose welfare and survival he took a particular interest. No government has ever done anything to upset the smooth running of the medical school which became St George's University.

The aims of Bishop and Coard did little to achieve fiscal stability. Bishop bought massive stocks of arms and ammunition with the view, eventually, that every Grenadian would have his or her personal weapon. By 1983–5 Bishop intended to take receipt of a final tranche of military equipment (including Soviet instructors) numbering 50 APCs, 30 76-mm guns, 30 57-mm anti-tank guns, 50 portable launchers, 60 82-mm mortars and 2,000 AK-47 rifles.[8] The Americans should have made the investment to fathom out the reasons why this minute island state would require such large quantities of arms and ammunition. Arguably of more concern was Bishop's New Joint Endeavour for Welfare, Education and Liberation (New Jewel) Party's initiative to develop Point Salines airport with a 9,000-foot (2,743-metre) runway. The Grenadian Government said the new airfield would feed an expanded tourist industry, yet there had been no corresponding development of island tourism. Cuba supplied the workforce, which also included an element from the Cuban Armed Forces. Grenada is a significant distance from both Cuba and the United States and it was the intention of Cuba to use the new airport as a staging base for aircraft servicing Cuban interests in Africa and Nicaragua after its completion date in 1984.

Bishop's visit to the United States in May 1983, where he met middle-rank government officials, caused consternation in Moscow, Havana and among the New Jewel political wing led by Coard. Grenada had become an important thorn in the side of the United States whose Monroe Doctrine[9] had been formulated around a determination to allow no European presence within her Central and South American spheres of influence. Questions began to be raised in Grenada by Bishop and his followers as to the benefits of private enterprise, of the wisdom of further Communist investment in Grenada's People's Revolutionary Armed Forces (PRAF), a people under arms, and the Point Salines airport. Newspaperman Leslie Pierre was left unconvinced by Bishop's apparent movement towards the right. 'He was pulling wool over people's eyes, another chimera', but a dangerous one.[10]

Coard allegedly decided that none of these achievements should be put at risk and accordingly decided to take action to remove Bishop from office. He persuaded former gaol warder General Hudson Austin to swing the regular military component behind him. The People's Revolutionary Militia (PRM) remained loyal to Bishop. On 13 October 1983, the faction allied to Coard ordered Bishop to stand down and placed him under house arrest. The same day, US contingency planners began to take a more active interest in events developing on the island. The heirs of the concept of the domino theory (which speculated that states would fall successively to Communism) would not only know what had to be done but also why it had to be done. Grenada was of immense strategic importance to the United States. As the southernmost of the Windward Islands separating the Caribbean Sea from the Atlantic Ocean, the nearby sea lanes supply America with 56 per cent of her imported oil.

Six days later events came to a head: 'It was to be a momentous day in the history of the Caribbean. The climax of the struggle between the two Marxist leaders would push the United States into mounting its largest military operation since Vietnam'.[11] Bishop, followed by his supporters, moved into Fort George, the Army and Police headquarters. He was head of the armed forces and in need of a communications centre.

Hearing of these developments, the military commanders in Fort Frederick despatched three armoured personnel carriers (APCs) to drive the 2 miles (3.2 kilometres) to Fort George to bring the fort back under military control. The soldiers drove up to the fort, the men sitting on top of the vehicles, some waving unthreateningly. Shots rang out from the fort, killing Warrant Officer Raphael Mason and the popular officer in charge, Officer Cadet 'Connie' Mayers. Two other soldiers were reported killed. An Army officer admitted to the subsequent inquiry that they 'lost it', firing back at those firing on them. 'Oh God,' said Bishop, 'they have turned their guns on the masses,' something no one thought the Army would do. The number of civilians killed in the fifteen- to twenty-minute shootout ranged from the fifteen alleged by Coard – four soldiers and fifteen civilians, eight unlawfully – to fifty, reported by other sources. Certainly, a number did throw themselves off the fortress wall to escape the firing. The eight unlawfully killed included Bishop and seven followers at 14.05 in front of a hastily convened firing squad and apparently in the heat of the moment. 'The history of soldiers retaliating for the loss of friends is a distinct feature of combat, where discipline breaks down and revenge follows,' said Coard.[12] 'Morally objectionable as it was, it was a change of degree rather than in kind,'[13] commented Margaret Thatcher.

'There had been no problem on the campus until Bishop's assassination, then no one, Americans or Grenadians, was sure what was going to happen,'[14] said a university representative.

Of the 600 staff and students of the American medical school only 10 per cent asked to be repatriated. They were never in danger but neither they nor their Government could have been certain. The number desiring repatriation increased dramatically after the first American attacks. Coard's administration treated the school with kid gloves. They knew that if America intervened they would be catapulted into an unwinnable conflict. The safety of American nationals would have been uppermost in President Reagan's mind in determining whether or not to invade. That truth was also conveyed to Grenada by Havana recommending a total hands-off policy towards the medical school, allowing those who wished to leave to do so.

Castro also announced Cuba's policy of non-intervention in Grenada's domestic affairs. This happened to be a qualified declaration of non-intervention. Castro was only too well aware that presentationally the total abandonment of his followers in Grenada would not send a reassuring message to his supporters around the world. He made available to the Grenadians those Cubans already on the island. Advisers would fight alongside the advised. The Cuban airport workers received orders to defend the facility under local Cuban command. The effect of these decisions, therefore, was to place the defence of Grenada almost entirely in Cuban hands. The situation would have looked different from the White House, where the word 'hostages' is emblematic of political risks and potential disaster.

American initial plans revolved around the evacuation of American and other foreign nationals. Urgent Fury, the name of the Grenada operation, took as its model Ocean Venture 81, which had taken place partially in the Caribbean. During Ocean Venture 81, a force of Rangers, Marines, Paratroopers and Special Forces rehearsed the rescue of American hostages

held in a hostile Third World state.[15] In these circumstances
the plan envisaged the establishment of a security cordon,
the assembly of American nationals at Pearls Airport, their
evacuation to offshore naval ships and onward movement to
Bridgetown, Barbados.

In Washington, the Chairman of the Joint Chiefs of Staff
instructed Atlantic Command, Norfolk, Virginia to draw up
plans to neutralize Grenada's People's Revolutionary Army
(PRA). Tom Adams, Prime Minister of Barbados, discussed
a proposed intervention in Grenada with the willing agent
of the US Government in Barbados, Ambassador Milan
Bish. Bish emphasized to Adams the vital importance of a
written invitation from Grenada inviting intervention. The
Governor General Sir Paul Scoon obliged, eventually (the
circumstances in which this was achieved will be examined
at the chapter end).

There were two overlapping regional organizations with
different views as to whether or not to intervene militarily
in Grenada. The Organization of East Caribbean States
(OECS), the lesser of the two organizations and certainly the
most benign, comprised a grouping of seven small islands:
Antigua and Barbuda, Dominica, St Kitts-Nevis, St Lucia,
St Vincent, the British Dependency of Montserrat and
Grenada. The Caribbean Community (CARICOM) was
larger, comprising thirteen members: the OECS states, the
Bahamas, Barbados, Guyana, Jamaica, Trinidad and Tobago
and the British Dependency of Belize. A principal requirement
before regional action could be taken was the reaching of
consensus; a simple majority would be insufficient.

For years Guyana of CARICOM had encouraged
revolution in Grenada. Tom Adams could not be certain
that other states within CARICOM would not be steered
towards non-intervention by Guyana's leftist President,

Forbes Burnham. He arranged to circumvent any potential problem arising within CARICOM by excluding the organization from the discussions. He formed an ad hoc group of interested, positive parties which included OECS, Barbados and Jamaica. Representatives of these states assembled in Barbados on 21 October, the day before a scheduled CARICOM meeting, also held in Barbados. The OECS group decided to initiate collective defence in support of future military intervention in Grenada. The reinforced OECS had stolen CARICOM's thunder. By the time President Burnham arrived in Barbados to attend the CARICOM meeting, the way forward had already been determined.

Tom Adams's perception vis-à-vis other CARICOM states' reluctance to support a military option proved prescient. Bahamas, Belize and Trinidad joined Guyana in opposing intervention. Allegedly, President Burnham gave an account of the events within OECS and CARICOM to Fidel Castro, who then informed Coard.[16]

The United States' intervention record was not good. What impressed Washington's decision-makers with the Grenada situation was the certainty of success, the predictable generation of self-respect and the generation of a mood of national self-confidence similar to that which the British had enjoyed after the Falklands Campaign. America could not afford to be 'seen as a paper tiger in the eyes of both friendly and hostile Latin American countries'.[17]

The Vietnam experience had been forgotten neither by the public nor the military now in senior posts. Marines had failed in a 1975 rescue attempt in Cambodia that proved not to have been necessary. Five years later came another disaster in a hostage rescue attempt in Tehran, which certainly did not presage well for Grenada. In Washington, the hawkish

Deputy Secretary of State for Political Affairs, Lawrence Eagleburger, referred to the Tehran disaster, insisting that if the Administration failed to rescue American hostages in Grenada, Washington would lose face in the Caribbean and Central America at a time when America had to stand up to left-wing challenges.[18] Then, just as planners and decision-makers contemplated intervention in Grenada, came the dreadful news of the deaths of 241 Marines in Beirut. It was this last factor which determined President Reagan, with an eye on re-election, to intervene in Grenada.

Operational security would be vital. The need to know had to be rationed appropriately. Admiral Wesley L. McDonald, Commander-in-Chief of Atlantic Command, with his headquarters in Norfolk, Virginia, had enormous experience in maritime–air missions. The appointment of Atlantic Command rather than US Forces Caribbean Command to lead the Grenada operation surprised many. The Pentagon's contingency plan for intervention in Grenada, number 2360, designated US Forces Caribbean Command to lead the operation.[19] McDonald's staff was predominantly naval- and NATO-oriented. The Grenada operation would be predominantly land warfare.

At 16.45 on Monday 22 October, the Joint Chiefs of Staff gave McDonald his mission for an operation they wanted concluded in days. Four days would be sufficient, but the Americans had enormously good fortune in their favour. Had the opposition been in any way a coherent force, they could have experienced serious difficulties. McDonald was to 'conduct military operations to protect and evacuate US and designated foreign nationals from Grenada, neutralize Grenadian forces, stabilize the internal situation, and maintain the peace. In conjunction with OECS/friendly government participants assist in the restoration of a democratic government on Grenada.'[20] There was neither a strategic aim nor a joint force theatre commander controlling and tasking military assets.

Major-General Dick Graves met General Schwarzkopf off his aircraft at Atlanta's Charlie Brown Airport. There, in the Army terminal, Graves told Schwarzkopf of the Grenada problem and of hundreds of American medical students allegedly detained in dormitories. The Navy was to launch a major operation to go ashore, liberate the students and restore the legitimate government. The Army would be a major player in the operation, alongside Special Forces, 82nd Airborne and the 1st Ranger Battalion. 'Washington wants to make sure that the Navy uses them correctly. That's where you come in . . . as adviser to the Navy.' Inter-service rivalry being as it was, the Navy was not known for being receptive to Army advice, particularly the Marines. Graves reassured Schwarzkopf that if he did encounter difficulty, 'just let us know and we'll get it straightened out'.[21]

On Tuesday 18 October, two Navy Task Forces had sailed for the Mediterranean on pre-planned operations. On 21 October, the two Task Forces received orders to change course for Grenada. The helicopter carrier *Guam* led Task Force 124, supported by four landing ships carrying 1,900 Marines of 22 Marine Amphibious Unit (MAU). Embarked on *Guam* were the helicopters of a reinforced Marine Medium Helicopter Squadron 261 which would add to the available airlift of 107 helicopters, a number which would have made Brigadier Thompson of Falkland Islands fame mighty envious.[22] The availability of these helicopters contributed to the speed and success of the operation. 22 MAU had the task of the nominal replacement of 24 MAU at Beirut International Airport, Lebanon. Assessments of the Grenada campaign should take into account that when 22 MAU sailed they were going to Lebanon, not Grenada – not that they were sorry. Warriors always prefer proper operations to 'peacekeeping'. The carrier USS *Independence* led the second Task Force, or carrier battle group, supported by cruisers, destroyers and the aircraft of Carrier Air Wing 6. During the evening of 20 October Atlantic Command ordered naval forces to divert closer to Grenada, the MAU to take up station 500 miles (805 kilometres) to the north-east of Grenada. No reason for the detour was given.

The abiding criticism of modern conflicts is of their under-resourcing in terms of manpower and equipment. Such a claim could not be made in respect of the Grenada operation, Urgent Fury. On a relatively small operation such as Urgent Fury, however, everyone wants a share of the action. This is as much a reflection of the tyranny of the military budget as anything else. When government is consistently accused of under-resourcing military operations, it appears to be in a no-win situation when an operation such as Urgent Fury is generously resourced. An adequate provision of manpower is the best guarantee of preventing the enemy withdrawing into the jungle and urban environment to establish a guerrilla campaign.

In Grenada, a substantial, powerful American force of 20,000 men, or 6,000 active combatants,[23] with the most modern equipment would confront directly a maximum of 1,200 to 1,500 Grenadian regular soldiers, 2–5,000 territorial reservists and the Cubans. There were 636 Cuban construction workers. The Cuban Government produced the job specifications for each one of them. Those who were not capable of bearing arms were told to go away and lie low. Dependants went aboard *Viet Nam Heroica* anchored in St George's Harbour. The core of the Cuban military expertise lay in the fifty-three members of the Cuban Military Mission.

On 22 October, two American diplomats and one Briton departed Barbados for Grenada for discussions with the Revolutionary Military Council. Neither they nor John Kelly, the only British diplomat on Grenada, believed their nationals to be in immediate danger.[24] On Monday 24 October, following their final meeting with the Revolutionary Military Council, the American diplomats departed from Pearls Airport. Later, a Cubana An-24 airliner landed. On board was a Cuban Colonel, Pedro Tortolo Comas, a former commander of the Cuban Military Mission on Grenada. Comas graduated from the Soviet Frunze and Voroshilov military academies and presently served as Chief of Staff to an Army-sized formation in Cuba. His mission was to take charge of the Cubans on Grenada and organize the defence.[25]

Intelligence did not rate the Grenadian military and Cubans as a significant challenge. 'Don't worry. When the Army sees we're Americans, they'll give up . . . Don't worry. The gunners are poorly trained and don't represent a real threat.' As for the Cubans, 'Don't worry. They're not going to fight.' The plan which became the lot of the Rangers reflected this sense of an easy ride. Rangers were to drive to the Cuban compound and announce: 'We are here to reinstal the legitimate government of Grenada. You will not be hurt. Please stay here while we get this thing over with.' As optimistic a plan as there could be, yet a worrying thought continued to run through General Schwarzkopf's mind: 'How do we know the Cubans aren't going to fight?'[26]

The last two American diplomats to leave Grenada before the invasion had spent the two previous days visiting students at the campuses of the medical school – one-third at True Blue and the remaining two-thirds at Grand Anse, some 1½ miles (2½ kilometres) distant. It appears to have been common knowledge that the facility was divided between the two sites, but the incoming military was informed by the National Intelligence Center on 22 October that all the students were domiciled on the True Blue campus. When the advance rescue forces arrived at True Blue, they heard for the first time of the second campus's existence. 'None of us knew a thing about Grand Anse Campus,' said the then Ranger Captain John Abizaid. 'We did not understand its significance until we had a chance to talk to some of the American students from True Blue immediately after the parachute assault.'[27] An intelligence breakdown such as this could have had unfortunate ramifications. Surprise is a principle of war. It is, however, supposed to work[28] in your favour. Having said that, the insistence upon speed and surprise was the driving force of the whole operation. In Norfolk, the plan was rejigged. General Schwarzkopf attended the planning conference with two other Army Major-Generals, Major-General Ed Trobaugh – who allegedly had a disconcerting habit of prefacing his remarks by shouting 'Airborne' – and Major-General Dick Scholtes, Special Forces Commander commanding the Ranger battalions, Delta Force, SEAL (Sea, Air, Land) Team 6 and Special Forces helicopters. The conference room had a familiar feel to General Schwarzkopf; he had served under the Navy for two years at Pacific Command and knew their ways. Admiral McDonald, Commander-in-Chief Atlantic Command, came up to Schwarzkopf and asked him to try to be helpful. Schwarzkopf would report to Vice-Admiral Joseph Metcalf, 'We've got a tough job to do and we don't need the Army giving us a hard time.' McDonald prefaced the discussion of the operational plan with a caveat similar to one which had been relevant to the Falklands Task Force, '. . . everyone should bear in mind the strong possibility that we won't have to carry it out'.[29] If diplomacy worked, there would be no conflict.

For any hot plan to succeed, ideally it has to be kept simple. At Grenada, the cast of players were all found jobs, although finding appropriate roles for the Special Forces stretched planners' imaginations. The joint plan shook out initially into Navy, Army and Special Forces' independent operations, requiring no abnormal cross-fusion of services and thus reducing the risk of complications. Planners allocated the northern part of the island to the Navy and Marines and the southern part to the Army and Air Force. This arrangement offset the problems which might otherwise have arisen through the absence of a joint doctrine or the ability of the Army to communicate with the Marines. The absence of a common map with common co-ordinates was one problem which proved almost insurmountable. Urgent Fury was a combined operation yet local Caribbean forces were not called upon for substantive assistance until the post-conflict phase.

The Navy had the task of putting a *cordon sanitaire* around the island. Their Marines were then to land on the east coast, their objectives being the small Pearls Airport in the northeast (being replaced by the Cuban-built Point Salines Airport) and the garrison town of Grenville. Simultaneously, Rangers were to seize Point Salines Airport in a *coup de main* attack and secure the True Blue campus where it was believed the American medical student potential hostages lived. Once the Rangers had notified the securing of Salines Airport, two 82nd Airborne Parachute battalions were to relieve the Rangers. The Special Forces under their own commander had been allocated three separate tasks, the Navy's SEAL teams the first two, the Army's Delta Force the third:

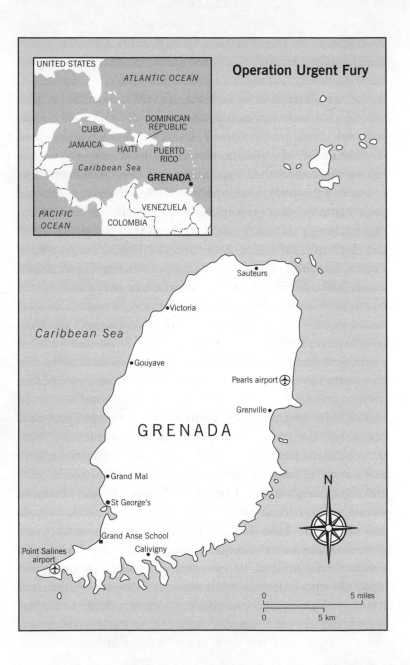

- to rescue Sir Paul Scoon at his residence in the capital St George's (they had need of him)
- to capture Radio Free Grenada with Fort George
- to capture Fort Frederick and Richmond Hill Prison, where Coard's opponents were believed to be incarcerated[30]

The Rangers had therefore been allocated the task of rescuing the medical students, a task for which Special Forces were better trained and equipped. Instead, two of their three assigned tasks were non-tasks. The radio station was a regional facility. Taking it out would have no effect upon broadcasts within Grenada, which had its own domestic studio to the rear of Grand Anse beach. Precisely who was in the prison was not known, 'but to employ the army's top anti-terrorist unit to secure their early release, in preference to American nationals, must remain one of the most extraordinary decisions of Urgent Fury'.[31] The Governor General could have been the subject of other arrangements. Special Forces had no significant impact upon the military operation.

Commanders were not being helped by the poverty of intelligence, consequently risks were being taken. The Grenada intervention has been described as 'policy making without intelligence'.[32] Each service was responsible for its own reconnaissance. The condition of the Point Salines runway was of inestimable importance in deciding whether the Rangers could adopt the preferred air-landed option or would have to parachute in. A Navy SEAL team was parachuted in in advance to answer that precise question but failed: four of their number died in the rough sea. The planners were none the wiser. Major-General Scholtes's recommendation that the operation be postponed for twenty-four hours until this vital information became available met the flattest of negatives from Admiral McDonald. 'I can't believe what I am hearing around this table. All you're going to face is a bunch of Grenadians. They're going to fall apart the minute they see our combat power. Why are we making such a big deal of this?' Put in his place and outranked, Scholtes insisted H-Hour be delayed for at least two hours in order that time be made available for reconnaissance. He wanted to know what he was sending the troops into.[33] Admiral Metcalf delayed H-Hour a further hour until 5 a.m., fifteen minutes before first light, meaning a night operation would now take place in daylight. A second SEAL reconnaissance fared no better. The men had not trained for such a contingency in rough seas.

Between 19 and 24 October there had been a flurry of diplomatic activity. The British Foreign and Commonwealth Office had as High Commissioner in what was usually the diplomatic backwater of Bridgetown, Barbados, a bright, imaginative man, Giles Bullard. He had his finger well on the pulse, keeping London informed of developments. Twice, Barbados Prime Minister Tom Adams gave a verbal invitation to Bullard for Britain to join the OECS-sponsored intervention into Grenada. The promised, essential, formal letter requesting British participation never arrived. It is understood that Adams was dissuaded from sending it.[34]

News of what was happening was also flowing from the British Military Attaché in Jamaica to the Ministry of Defence, which had alerted members of the House of Commons. On the basis of assurances given to London by the US State Department, Sir Geoffrey Howe, Secretary of State for Foreign and Commonwealth Affairs, made a statement in the House at 4 p.m. on Monday, 24 October, which 'saw his reputation as Foreign and Commonwealth Secretary buried, perhaps for good'.[35] Howe fed to the Commons the great American deception: that the island was calm but tense and the Governor General and British citizens appeared to be in no danger. Pressed by the Opposition, he confirmed: 'I have no reason to believe that American intervention is likely.'[36] HMS *Antrim* was on hand to effect the evacuation of British citizens.

At 7.15 p.m. that same day, a staff member interrupted Margaret Thatcher's hosting of a cocktail party in Downing Street with an urgent message from President Reagan. Reagan explained that the OECS request for military support left him inclined to oblige. Did his good friend Margaret have a view? She certainly did. She replied that she strongly opposed intervention. At her second engagement that night, a dinner party, she met the American Ambassador. What was going on in Grenada, she asked. He knew nothing. Then she was notified that a second message had arrived from the President, requiring her to leave the dinner and return to Downing Street. Reagan had decided 'to respond positively to the request for military action'. Consulting her advisers, they drafted a reply: 'This action will be seen as intervention by a western country in the internal affairs of a small independent nation however unattractive its regime.'

Twenty minutes later Mrs Thatcher rang President Reagan on the hot line. She asked that he carefully consider the full reply which she had sent him. This he agreed to do, but then said, 'we are already at zero'. The next morning, at 07.45, another message from the President advised that he had carefully weighed Mrs Thatcher's objections but 'believed them to be outweighed by other factors'. Then he revealed information he would have found painful: American forces had invaded Grenada that morning. The Prime Minister now faced up to the unpleasant reality of having 'to explain how it had happened that a member of the Commonwealth had been invaded by our closest ally, and more than that, whatever our private feelings, we would have to defend the United States' reputation in the face of widespread condemnation'.[37]

At 18.30 on Monday 24 October *Guam*'s senior officers sat down in the Admiral's mess to a turkey dinner. Only then, when Admiral Metcalf's Chief of Staff entered the wardroom, did they hear, 'It's a go. It's a go.' 'We're going. H-Hour has been bumped back one hour. It's a go at 05.00.' The mess hall thinned until only Schwarzkopf remained, the only senior officer present with nothing to do. The General climbed up towards the bridge and stood there in the dark, aware that this time tomorrow the United States would once again be at war. Understandably, the significance of that truth affected the Vietnam veterans more than either the younger junior officers or their subordinates.[38]

The Revolutionary Military Council's worst dreams were about to be realized. Their entreaties for assistance from Castro had led merely to his sending Colonel Tortolo as co-ordinator of Cuban nationals, seventeen hours ahead of the Americans. Castro had been explicit: 'That they have to find a way to reach reconciliation with the people, perhaps one way would be to clarify the death of Bishop – and seek out those responsible.' He refused reinforcements, refused to put the Cubans on Grenada under Grenadian command and placed conditions on the employment of the Cuban nationals on the island. 'If Grenada is invaded by the US, the Cuban personnel will defend their positions in their camps and working areas with all their energy and courage.'[39] The murder of Bishop had removed at one stroke almost the entire militia force which would otherwise have been available to defend Grenada. Gaps in the regular order of battle went unfilled. 'When the execution squad opened fire that afternoon, they killed the people's will to resist, just as surely as they killed their prime minister.'[40]

There was precious little available to the PRA with which to face the looming onslaught. A mobile force had been cobbled together from the eight armoured personnel carriers, BTR-60 PBs, gifts from the Soviet Union. There were a number of antiquated anti-aircraft guns with low ceilings, yet likely to be effective against helicopters. The high command correctly recognized their anti-aircraft guns as being of significant importance. They also recognized that with, at best, four infantry companies, they could not be strong everywhere and decided instead to concentrate on the south-west. The sole infantry battle group, drawing upon the mobility of the armoured personnel carriers, was the 110-man-strong company commanded by Second Lieutenant Nelson. General Hudson deployed a small number of anti-aircraft and medium machine guns in the capital, St George's, protecting Fort George and Fort Frederick. As the minutes ticked away, a pervading sense of doom fell upon a regular component with low morale and low pay – $100 a month.[41] Those about to die deserved more.

The Grenadian Army never played or ever considered playing their trump card, taking American hostages. Had they done so, a deal in the short term might have been possible. To Washington's intense relief, their worst possible fear never came to fruition.

When the American people were alerted to the news of the invasion, they doubted its wisdom and necessity although it did not take long for them to swing behind and support a president with an eye on re-election. The Caribbean gave broad support but elsewhere criticism proved well nigh universal. Understandably the Soviets were incandescent with rage, not only at the American invasion but also at Havana's refusal to play an active role in halting this imperialist advance. Soviet television news told their horrified public that 'US troops had invaded Spain, dropped on Andalusia and captured the city of Granada'.[42] At 15.30 on 26 October Sir Geoffrey Howe stood up to address the House, at the conclusion of which he reminded an observer of something 'more like a strangled chicken than a minister of the Crown'.[43]

During the night 24/25 October, a SEAL team had made the first reconnaissance of the beaches adjacent to Pearls Airport and Grenville. They found the surf heavy and plunging, unsuitable for amphibious landings. Fortunately Admiral Metcalf had the assets available to switch the attacking force on to helicopters. SEAL teams also made a further attempt to gain intelligence on the state of the Point Salines Airport. Again, the sea proved too rough for their inflatable boats and the mission had to be aborted. As a consequence, when the Rangers went into the assault they did not have an adequate reconnaissance report. The Ranger battalions were already on their way from Savannah, albeit thirty minutes behind schedule, uncertain whether they were to be air-landed or parachuted in.[44] 'The radio nets on board the aircraft were very confused,' admitted Captain Abizaid, 'with contrary reports and orders. Rig for drop, derig, rig again were orders on the net. On board my aircraft we knew the recon had failed, knew the runway was blocked from an aerial recon made by AC-130s and thus we stayed rigged.'[45] The AC-130 Spectre is a sophisticated, hi-tech C-130 Hercules gunship with an alternative reconnaissance role. The fire control system is computer-based, day and night. Weapons on board include a 105-mm cannon firing eight rounds a minute, a 40-mm gun, two 20-mm Vulcan cannons firing 2,500 rounds per minute and two six-barrelled 7.62-mm machine guns firing 6,000 rounds a minute.

The Marines knew precisely what they were doing, they were in the air ready to hit H-Hour at 05.00 on 25 October.

There would be a lack of co-ordination, however, between what were intended to be concurrent attacks. Metcalf sought Schwarzkopf's advice. The General told the Admiral to let the Marines go, their helicopters could be heard ashore and if they were not given the go-ahead, surprise would be completely lost. The Marines landed at Pearls which they took almost uncontested. At 06.30 another group of Marines helicopters took the town of Grenville without contest.

The SEAL teams' attack from two Blackhawks on the Beauséjour transmitting station went well. Locating the facility had been simple. A massive radio mast indicated its position. Overpowering the guard also proved simple. By 06.30 the radio station was in American hands. The SEAL team was not to destroy the station, merely to sit where they were and await relief. Their leader established defended positions around the station. A number of Grenadians fell into the trap, including a group of lorry-borne territorials, five of whom were killed. The arrival of an APC at 09.30, together with other vehicles carrying regular force Grenadians, posed an immediate threat to the lightly armed SEAL team. Mortars and the APC's gun raked the transmitting station building, inflicting casualties upon the Special Forces. Unable to respond effectively, unable to raise close air support, the SEAL team reluctantly withdrew to the beach, from where they swam out to the USS *Caron*.

While attempting to find a landing site, the two Blackhawks with a SEAL team of twenty-two assigned to rescue Governor General Sir Paul Scoon from Government House had such a hot reception that they began to take casualties, who then had to be flown back to the *Guam*. The second approach proved successful, only for the attackers to find themselves attacked by APCs. Admiral Metcalf tasked a Spectre gunship, which succeeded in holding the Grenadian forces at bay, but then the anti-aircraft positions at Forts Frederick and George interposed so that there could be no guarantee that Sir Paul Scoon could be brought safely over to the American side. The Grenadians shot down two Cobra helicopters.

With one SEAL attack unsuccessful and another with the outcome in the balance, American Special Forces operations appeared to be following an established pattern of failure. The Army's Delta Force regard themselves superior to the Navy's SEAL teams in the same way as the SAS regard themselves superior to the SBS. Delta Force's mission had more to do with them being there, needing a job, rather than the attack on the prison being an appropriate task for Special Forces and the associated speed of response. Such debate is largely academic to Delta Force personnel. For them there is no substitute for complete success. The five unescorted Blackhawks headed off for the attack on Richmond Hill Prison although no one on board had the benefit of any useful intelligence of their mission. There was no difficulty in identifying the high-walled prison but the sight of it sitting on the raised spine of a steep ridge surrounded by watchtowers and with no suitable landing sites nearby proved to be one of those breathtaking moments. That was not all. Three hundred yards (274 metres) to the east, on ground 150 feet (46 metres) higher than the prison, sat Fort Frederick with its two anti-aircraft guns. Close air support had largely been dissipated upon other tasks. Spectre operations concentrated upon the opposition at Point Salines.

The lot of the five Blackhawks and their crews represents an interesting study of consequences, the consequences of an executive decision and the reason for particular individuals to be in a particular place at a particular time. The decision had been the President's, a reaction to events in Grenada. The Blackhawks were a component of Task Force 160, an elite, secretive unit whose function was to insert and extract Special Forces into or out of secret missions. The mystery of Operation Urgent Fury is not so much the numbers of Special Forces members to be given appropriate work but the consideration of what work was deemed to be appropriate. The five Blackhawks' complement of Special Forces had the mission to raid the prison to release incarcerated Grenadians. There had been no reconnaissance. The helicopters arrived over the target seventy-five minutes after the operation had commenced, thus forfeiting the element of surprise, and the field they were to use to put down their military passengers, adjoining the prison, was either not identified or its use was deemed to be suicidal. As mentioned, the mystery was not so much the zero intelligence but the reason why the release of Grenadian prisoners took precedence over the release of American hostages, supposedly one part of America's *casus belli.*

The ground was a crucial consideration if the operation was to be successful. The volcanic nature of the hills surrounding the port of St George's provided innumerable pinnacles and ridges upon which to build a circle of forts. Fort Rupert, named after Bishop's father who was killed by Gairy's men, now known as Fort George, guarded the entrance to the port. To the south-east, on a sharp ridge with perpendicular sides, stood the seemingly impenetrable Richmond Hill Prison, but more important was the 'jewel in the crown' in this defensive circle, Fort Frederick. Fort Frederick lies 500 yards (457 metres) to the north-east of Richmond Hill Prison. The PRA had placed two anti-aircraft guns in Fort Frederick and four in Fort George, thereby establishing a veritable flak-trap for any air-mounted operations in the area to the immediate south of St George's.

Into that flak-trap flew the five Blackhawks, one of which

was flown by Captain Keith Lucas and co-piloted by Warrant Officer Class II Paul Price. On board were two loadmasters manning M-60 machine guns and a relief co-pilot-navigator. Precisely how many Special Forces were on board Lucas's aircraft with its capacity of eleven fully equipped troops is unknown. Looking down upon their objective for the first time, described as 'impregnable as Alcatraz',[46] the five pilots considered their options while at the same time coming under small arms and anti-aircraft fire from Fort Frederick. With that weight of heavy, accurate fire, hovering over the target for the Special Forces to fast-rope down was good for neither crew nor passengers. They had an urgent need either for Spectre gunship support or maritime air support from USS *Independence*. Since no support aircraft were bid for at the air-tasking meeting, none had been allocated.

The rugged Blackhawk had an armoured cocoon to protect the crew although such protection could be no more than partial. In the passenger section there was little protection at all. As pilots zig-zagged between the forts, searching out a solution to their predicament, their passengers were suffering grievous injuries from incoming fire. 'Legs and arms were smashed, blood spattered everywhere, men screamed. The panic inside the aircraft was real.'[47] A bullet hit Lucas in the right arm. Another hit a loadmaster, smashing his right leg. The order came to withdraw, to regroup over the sea.

There were no more constructive ideas than to return to the task in the hope of making a breakthrough. Bullets entered the windscreen of Captain Lucas's aircraft above the armour plating, hitting him in the head and chest, killing him instantly. The co-pilot, with a graze to his head, assumed command of an aircraft now belching smoke and with panic rife among the passengers. He turned the damaged craft southward in the hope of reaching American-held territory. Another

Blackhawk shadowed the badly damaged helicopter. The co-pilot had come inland to avoid the air defences but unfortunately flew into an anti-aircraft site at Frequente where Lucas's Blackhawk suffered irredeemable damage, crashing on a ridge above the sea at Amber Belaire Hill. The soundly built aircraft broke apart, its rotor blades hitting the sea. After a momentary period of grace, the fuel tanks ignited, detonating the Blackhawk on the ground. In that short period of time the surviving crew escaped and a number of Special Forces men were either thrown clear or escaped, all of them injured or wounded.

As a general rule, the wounded should receive treatment within two hours. Another Blackhawk arrived to provide force protection but no Blackhawks were employed to take the wounded back to USS *Guam* for life-saving medical attention. Their pilots were not trained to land on helicopter carriers. Eventually a naval helicopter arrived to take the wounded and injured to the *Guam*, three and a half hours after the Blackhawk had crashed.[48]

Watching from *Guam*, General Schwarzkopf saw two Army helicopters fall into the sea. A number did manage to land on *Guam*'s flight deck, 'shot full of holes and leaking hydraulic fluid all over'. Admiral Metcalf received an urgent warning from the Comptroller of the Navy. He was not to refuel the Army aircraft because the accounting procedure was yet to be established. The General saw Metcalf read the instructions. 'Bullshit!' said the Admiral. 'Give them fuel.' Of the Special Forces operation General Schwarzkopf wrote: 'It was total chaos and confusion.'[49]

A Spectre AC-130H gunship flew ninety minutes ahead of the main body of Rangers from the USA to Grenada. On board were men of Captain John Abizaid's A Company 1st/75th Rangers, the Pathfinders, commanded by Lieutenant-Colonel

Wes Taylor. Their task was to reconnoitre and clear the runway at Point Salines. The remainder of A Company and the balance of the depleted battalion[50] followed in two MC-130s and five C-130s. The 2nd/75th Rangers formed a second echelon. Lieutenant-Colonel Taylor took the news of the failure of the second SEAL reconnaissance mission philosophically. 'We always planned to drop at 500 feet,' explained John Abizaid. 'The Pathfinders did not adjust to go in below the angle of depression of the guns . . . in fact I believe that my aircraft was hit as we dropped.'[51]

The other Rangers in the first four C-130s looked for their main 'chutes, discarding that kit which they could no longer take. Time was not on their side. There would barely be time to check each other out. There were seven C-130s in this sortie. The order to prepare to parachute in had not reached the rear three aircraft. The senior officer in the fifth aircraft anticipated the order to prepare to jump and instructed the Rangers accordingly. An airloadmaster, however, told the soldiers they would definitely be air-landed; they were to take off their parachutes.

Shortly afterwards, when the Rangers had de-rigged, the loadmaster re-emerged and told the Rangers the aircraft had sufficient fuel for only thirty minutes. They would definitely be jumping in twenty minutes. The pilot of the MC-130 responsible for navigating the Rangers to their drop zone radioed that his navigational equipment was not functioning and he was unable to guarantee an accurate drop. A seasonal rainstorm then hit the immediate area of the airport, meaning that the MC-130 Talon could not be satisfactorily replaced by another. General Scholtes slipped H-Hour to 05.30. The aircraft of 1st/75th Rangers were in different stages of preparedness to drop over the airport, meaning the drop would not be instantaneous as it should have been but drawn out over ninety minutes, giving rise to the possibility of having insufficient men on the ground to dominate the area. Surprise had been lost. Cubans trained their anti-aircraft guns on the approaching aircraft. Nearby, armed with his camera, stood Joseph Gaylord.

Flying in from the south at low altitude, the coast of Grenada came into view. Colonel Hugh Hunter in the lead Spectre in this mix of thirteen aircraft ordered 2nd/75th to replace 1st/75th as first to drop on the runway. The weight of heavy anti-aircraft fire aimed at the incoming aircraft surprised Hunter. There was then another change of plan. Hunter aborted the drop, calling forward the other two Spectres in the armada to take out the guns below. The first two transport aircraft overflew the airport as directed but in the third, unaccountably, the green light came on. The load-master, having stood the Rangers in the door, shouted 'Go! Go! Go!' The first of the main body to land in a 20-knot ground wind were the Commanding Officer of 1st/75th and his headquarters.

While the command group prepared to receive their battalion, the Spectres attacked the guns being bravely fired at them by the enemy below, causing retaliatory strikes on them and the transports. Lieutenant-Colonel Taylor's 1st/75th's 'assembly area turned out to be a Cuban machine gun position', said Captain Abizaid.

> It was necessary to assault that position. We took it with a commandeered bulldozer and an infantry assault. We continued on, took the highest ground on the ridge overlooking the airfield, captured an anti-aircraft gun and turned it on the Cuban camp below us. We did not have the capability to co-ordinate naval gunfire despite the fact that destroyers were clearly visible off to the south of the airfield. Thus when we assaulted the Cubans

on the high ground we could not use the 5-inch guns that we could see on the ships. Similar problems with naval and Marine air took place because of different 'grid systems' on their maps vs the Rangers' maps.[52]

Once the weight of fire had been suppressed, Hunter ordered the transports to drop their incoming Rangers over the airport at 500 feet (152 metres), which was believed to be below the angle of depression of the anti-aircraft guns sited on the ridge along the runway. Amazingly, only one man was injured in the jump; two died in an earlier accident. Good fortune favoured the Rangers for, in the same way as at Goose Green, the PRA and Cubans assumed the Americans would make an amphibious landing and, as a consequence, two-thirds of the defenders had been deployed along the beach. The Goose Green similarity did not end there, for the Rangers, after attacking the Cuban camp at the airport and inflicting casualties, sent a prisoner in with an ultimatum – surrender, or face the consequences. One hundred and seventy-five chose to surrender. Colonel Tortolo escaped, eventually making his way to the Russian embassy, where he sought asylum.

The Americans turned their attention on the Cubans in defended locations along the beach, not that they were a fighting force as we know it. Among the construction workers were forty-three Cuban all ranks, four of whom were colonels, nine lieutenant-colonels and twenty-one other officers. Only six of the total were assigned to the infantry training teams; the others were technicians, including one woman; almost all would have been conscripts. This would be the Americans' penultimate encounter with Cubans in strength, ordered to fight only if attacked and to remain on or around the airport. The remainder of Grenada became solely the area of operation of the PRA. It was no contest, the Rangers and Spectres swatting away an over-ambitious assault by three Cuban-manned APCs.

Meanwhile, Captain Abizaid's three platoons advanced towards the medical school at True Blue, lying to the immediate east of the runway, where they were met by the relieved Americans who then, at 10.28, came under their protection – not that that had been necessary. Only then did the Americans discover that the majority of the students were at the second, larger campus on Grand Anse. Moreover, there were numerous students who were not on either of the campuses but scattered around in houses. Work on clearing the runway had progressed well, so much so that by mid-morning the transports had landed and the Rangers' jeeps off-loaded. At Point Salines Airport, Major-General Edward Trobaugh, Commander 82nd Airborne Division, who arrived at Salines aboard the first C-141 Starlifter at 14.05, radioed Pope Air Force Base: 'Keep sending battalions until I tell you to stop.'[53]

Signals Intelligence (SIGINT) identified Fort Frederick as the hub of the PRA defensive position. Admiral Metcalf turned to General Schwarzkopf: 'I want to bomb it, what do you advise?' Metcalf's orders required of him not only minimal US casualties but the need also to avoid casualties among non-combatants. Fort Frederick is relatively close to the town. 'Bomb it,' said Schwarzkopf. 'If we let them keep up an organized resistance, we'll take a lot more casualties and eventually have to bomb it anyhow.'[54] Had the Admiral and the General had the benefit of adequate intelligence, they would have known that Fort Matthew adjoining Fort Frederick had been converted into a mental hospital. Orders went to the *Independence* to launch a full-scale attack on the forts, including Fort George. The A-7s proved very effective, severely damaging Fort Frederick, Fort George and Fort Matthew. Thirty mental patients were killed. Those who survived and were able fled into the surrounding area.[55] As was the case with all collateral damage, at war's end the Americans built a new facility nearby.

At close of play on the first day, the command team aboard *Guam* assessed their achievements and failures. The two airports were in American hands and the naval blockade in position. Otherwise, there was very little about which to rejoice. Anti-aircraft defences had prevented Special Forces from taking St George's. Plan B – the move of amphibious forces from Grenville to the north of St George's and disembarkation of a company of Marines supported by another brought in by helicopters – set in place, saw the Marines in position at Grand Mal ready to go into St George's the morning of Day 2. The unfinished business included Governor General Sir Paul Scoon and his SEAL rescue team, still surrounded, the Government still in power and, the result of another intelligence failure, the majority of the medical students still not rescued.

Admiral Metcalf asked General Schwarzkopf to write the orders for the next day's ground operations to take Army and Marines into St George's and Grand Anse to rescue the students. Had the Americans had to face a remotely competent, well-equipped opposition on the first day they would have been in serious trouble. The availability of surface-to-air missiles would have changed the nature of the conflict, prohibiting the use of unprotected helicopters. Metcalf, who had been up for thirty-six hours, prepared to turn in. Schwarzkopf gathered his people to plan the next day. A call came from Atlantic Command, Norfolk, Virginia requiring the body count.

'We need to stay away from this body-count business,' the General said to Metcalf. 'It caused terrible trouble in Vietnam and it'll cause terrible trouble here. Let's just concentrate on accomplishing the mission.'

'You're right,' said Metcalf and, instructing his staff accordingly, he left for his cabin.

Atlantic Command would have none of this, telephoning back thirty minutes later ordering a body count. Metcalf's staff showed Schwarzkopf the summary of returns: Army 13; Marines 133.

'This is the biggest bunch of bullshit I've ever seen,' said Schwarzkopf angrily. 'The Marines weren't even in battle today. Where did they get this 133?' The General sensed a shocked atmosphere among the naval staff. 'Guys,' he said in a conciliatory tone, 'don't you realize how much grief there was over body counts in Vietnam? We can't send numbers that make no sense.' The staff went back to the Marines, who explained the enemy fatalities had been caused by helicopters. Unconvinced, Schwarzkopf, with other matters to attend to, told the naval staff to send that particular body count if they must. 'But please, aggregate the reports into one number, so we don't start a body count competition between the Army and the Marines.' General Schwarzkopf sensed from the naval staff's demeanour that they believed his concern was the Marines showing up the Army.[56]

The majority of Americans who had fought or stood and waited on that first day had had no combat experience.[57] That is a pattern which is apparent in almost all modern conflicts. The older or more senior, however, had had the experience of Vietnam. They would have noticed that that which had been conspicuously absent in the first twenty-four hours was the media. Three hundred of them could be found on Barbados chafing at the bit because the military who controlled both airports and dominated the sea around the island would not allow them access. Six reporters and a photographer did reach the island but found no means with which to report back. Four of the reporters had invitations to be taken on board *Guam* to file their dispatches, but once there no facilities were offered.[58] Eight hours after the invasion began, Secretary of Defense Caspar Weinberger and Chairman of the Joint Chiefs of Staff General Vessey held a press conference in Washington regretting the exclusion of the press. This had allegedly been done to preserve secrecy and protect the correspondents. The ban lasted for two days, after which a restricted pool system was introduced.

One lesson the military would be wise to learn is to resist confiding in a reporter hungry for a story, for not to do so is as dangerous as whispering in an alligator's ear. A lieutenant-colonel told a correspondent that 'we learned a lesson in the Falklands'. This comment was widely circulated among the media, incensed at not having their way and exercising their right to know. Two months after the conflict ended, Secretary of State Schulz admitted the real reason for the Government barring journalists: it doesn't like them. In past wars, said Shultz, 'reporters were involved all along. And on the whole they were on our side. These days, in the advocacy journalism that's been developed, it seems as though reporters are always seeking to screw things up. And when you're trying to conduct a military operation, you don't need that.'[59] Of two conflicting philosophies, Otis Pike wrote after the Grenada conflict: 'Our military is trained to win. Winning requires secrecy and an image of skill, courage, stamina, strength and sacrifice. Our media are trained to report. Reporting must avoid secrecy and must also report blunders, cowardice, exhaustion, weakness and agony, all of which demoralize us.'[60]

As a result of this closed-door policy, correspondents drew their news from Havana or invented stories or reported inventions, a situation which was clearly undesirable – as undesirable as allowing the military a free hand. The foundation for the way forward in military–media relations came for the British after the Falklands in a report prepared by the House of Commons Defence Committee, and for the Americans in the Sidle Report commissioned by General Vessey as a result of lessons learned in Grenada. Both established the idea of creating a press pool, fed as though fish with information. It would not be long before correspondents discovered the best stories were to be found away from the pool.

In the early hours of Day 2 – 26 October – the Marines at Grand Mal close to St George's set out for Government House. Their attack met little resistance. At 07.00 they had married up with the SEAL team and Governor General Sir Paul Scoon. He, his wife and staff set off to make rendezvous with a helicopter bound for *Guam*. Having received permission to press forward, by last light the Marines had secured the Queen's Park Race Course and Forts Frederick and George. Fort Adolphus, over which there flew an unidentified flag presumed to be Cuban, was selected for preparatory bombardment. An element of uncertainty persisted and the flag's identity was sought. It proved to be the flag of Venezuela flying over its embassy. Elsewhere, specialists in search of intelligence found documents suggesting there might be 1,700 Cubans on the island.[61]

Out at Point Salines, the airport had become severely congested. Two under-strength Rangers battalions had been replaced by four battalions of paratroopers and their artillery, obeying Trobaugh's orders to keep coming. There were a further two to arrive, totalling six battalions. Metcalf told him to stop once two battalions were on the ground but a larger-sized force was already in the pipeline. Consolidation took time. Intelligence reported a strong enemy force blocking the route towards Grand Anse and as a consequence nothing was happening at that end to rescue the remaining medical students. A signal arrived from Atlantic Command: why had they not rescued the students? General Schwarzkopf recalls the atmosphere in the command centre having become increasingly tense. He went outside for some fresh air.

During the night, *Guam* had steamed south down the Grenada coast. Now, in daylight, General Schwarzkopf looked across to the island and found himself looking into the students' dormitory buildings above an idyllic white, sandy beach. His mind began to race as his gaze shifted on to the reinforced squadron of unemployed Sea Knights and Sea Stallion Marine helicopters sitting out on the deck. He went back inside and said to Metcalf, 'Come with me, I want to show you something.' Coming out on to the bridge, he pointed landward. 'That's where the enemy is, right over there. Look at that beach. It's a perfect landing zone. We've got all these helicopters here and all these Rangers and Airborne troops down at Point Salines. Why not pick up the troops, fly in from the sea and rescue the students?' Suitably impressed, Metcalf told Schwarzkopf to make it happen.

Schwarzkopf called Trobaugh at Point Salines telling him to bring his men to readiness and to await the arrival of the Marines' helicopters. Pleased that a plan was coming together to avoid the present impasse, he called the Colonel command-ing the helicopters to come to the bridge, where he explained the plan.

'I'm not going to do that,' said the Marine Colonel.

'What do you mean?'

'We don't fly Army soldiers in Marine helicopters.'

'Colonel, you don't understand. We've got a mission, and that mission is to rescue these students *now*. Your Marines are way up in Grenville securing that area, and your helicopters are right here. The way to get the job done is to put Army troops in those helicopters.'

'If we have to do it, I want to use my Marines. They'll rescue the hostages,' said the Colonel.

'How long would that take?'

Looking General Schwarzkopf straight in the eye he said, 'At least twenty-four hours.'

'Listen to me very carefully, Colonel. This is a direct order from me, a Major-General, to you, a Colonel, to do something that Admiral Metcalf wants done. If you disobey that order, I'll see to it that you're court-martialled.'

A number of the Colonel's subordinate officers had arrived with him on the bridge. 'Sir,' said one to the Colonel, 'can we talk to you outside?'

When he returned he said, 'Well all right. I guess we'll do it.'[62]

This angry exchange between General Schwarzkopf and the Marine Colonel was symptomatic of a lengthy animosity which had existed between the two services. The Army's resentment was attributable in part to the Marines' greater success at publicizing their cause or mobilizing their lobbies. President Harry S Truman, a former captain of artillery, was but one of many serving or retired Army men who resented the Marines and their successful publicity machinery. 'They have', he said, 'a propaganda machine that is almost equal to Stalin's.' The harmful divisiveness ran from the First World War to operations in the Pacific in the Second World War, through Korea and Vietnam. Grenada, 1983, revealed minimal change for the better. In the interest of operational effectiveness, the introduction of a joint operation command and control regime was clearly overdue. The grasping of that particular nettle was finally consolidated in 1986 in the form of the Goldwater–Nichols Department of Defense Reorganization Act.

The joint Rangers–Marines rescue of the students proved

to be the undoubted success of the operation. There had been careful liaison and surprisingly good communications between the parties involved and, for a change, good intelligence. The medical students received their briefing in great detail in terms of what was expected of them and what would happen. They had telephone contact with the airborne forces at the airport. There would be a softening up of the known PRA positions around the periphery of the campus, then the Marine helicopters would bring in the Rangers to hold and consolidate the position while the students were flown out on the empty seats. At 16.15, curious students found the temptation irresistible to look out to sea in response to the increasing sound of throbbing, urgent engines coming in their direction. One described what he saw as 'something right out of *Apocalypse Now*'[63] as a line of helicopters, skipping the waves, closed in upon the campus. America had arrived to rescue her own. Two hundred and twenty-four American nationals were lifted out under fire.[64] Three helicopters were hit, one destroyed.[65] The extent to which the rescue of the students had been a *bona fide casus belli* has been the subject of long debate. It was the invasion that put the students in potential danger. Mark Adkin makes the sound point that the second campus lay only 1½ miles (2½ kilometres) from Point Salines Airport yet it took the military thirty-three hours to get there, which appears an inadequate response. The fact is, however, that the Army's manoeuvre in the south had been ponderous as unacclimatized soldiers struggled in the 82°F constant temperature with their 120 lb (54 kg) packs apparently welded to their backs. 'We attacked to secure the airhead. We were like slow-moving turtles. My ruck weighed 120 pounds. . . There were all these guys sitting on the side of the road with IV tubes in them. There's no way the guys could [have gone on].'[66]

Mark Adkin is right to suggest the rescue of the students was a beneficial smokescreen to conceal the real reasons for intervention: 'The seizing of an unprecedented opportunity to rid the Caribbean of an expanding Communist threat and at the same time permit the military to regain credibility in a situation in which they could not lose.'[67] Documents seized in those first few days revealed the extent of Soviet intentions for the development of Grenada as a strategic Soviet outpost. The victory which had been achieved by the end of Day 2, but not recognized as such, represented 'for the first time, a strategic reverse for Soviet expansionism, thus demonstrating that the spread of Soviet-style Communism envisaged by Lenin . . . is not, after all, fatally inevitable'.[68]

On 26 October, the PRA leadership decided that further contest would be pointless. Taking off their uniforms and changing into civilian clothes, they disappeared into the surrounding jungle and towns. On that day, at the Cuban compound at Little Havana, B Company of 82nd Airborne's 2nd/325th attacked the Cubans, bringing to an end their formal military resistance on the island. Eighty-six surrendered and sixteen had died at the cost of two American lives. The Americans had no idea that success, less mopping up, had been achieved. Having had access to so little useful intelligence throughout this operation, it is unfortunate that unnecessary risks would now be taken to locate what bad intelligence had identified as a core of 1,500 Cubans loose somewhere on the island. Nevertheless, Metcalf and Schwarzkopf, now officially designated Metcalf's deputy to avoid further misunderstanding, were reasonably content with the day's work. Day 3 – 27 October – would not be such a happy day, a day when General Schwarzkopf lived up to his nickname 'Stormin' Norman'.

The morning of the 27th began with the Marines'

containment of St George's, belated relief brought by 82nd Airborne – in place of the Rangers – who slowly but surely began to clear northward. Metcalf and Schwarzkopf prepared themselves for a visit to Point Salines for a briefing by the Army. No sooner had the Admiral and General taken their seats for the briefing than they were handed a message which had come from the Joint Chiefs: they were required to have taken the barracks at Calivigny by the end of the day. Calivigny was a collection of huts and a rifle range lying 5 miles (8 kilometres) east of Point Salines and believed to be a Cuban-run training camp. The camp had been included in 82nd Airborne's 'to do' list as they advanced from the south. The mission would have been accomplished by the 28th. That information went back to Atlantic Command, from where the reply came: 'Absolutely not. JCS orders you to take Calivigny barracks by tonight.'[69]

An operation was accordingly assembled without the benefit of having had time to reconnoitre. A massive weight of preliminary fire from the air levelled the camp, allowing heliborne Rangers to follow up at 16.45.[70] Three Blackhawks in the first wave of four crashed into one another on the narrow landing site. Spinning, breaking rotor blades cut into and through dismounting Rangers. Three died and four were badly injured. The Rangers sent back a situation report (SITREP) to *Guam*: 'The camp is clear, there's no one here.' A flight of four A-7s over Calivigny responded to an air support squadron request to neutralize snipers in a nearby house. They got the wrong house, hitting instead a Brigade Headquarters, causing seventeen casualties, one of whom died.

General Schwarzkopf saw the badly injured brought aboard *Guam*. He hurried down to the sick bay. He met a Rangers lieutenant who tried to stand, forgetting that a few hours earlier he had lost a leg. 'I was angry as I climbed back up [to] the bridge,' wrote Schwarzkopf, furious at the micro-management of operations by someone in a distant headquarters. 'Soldiers had died, this kid was lying there mutilated, and there had been no military reason that we had to take the Calivigny barracks that day. I wondered which son of a bitch had ordered the attack.'[71]

Clearing through the island, taking the Grenadian hierarchy into custody and securing numerous weapons caches lasted until Tuesday 1 November. On Wednesday, 2 November Admiral Metcalf declared the campaign over. Featuring on the butcher's bill were 24 Cubans killed, 59 wounded and 602 prisoners of war. An estimated 67 Grenadians died. The number of inmates who died in the mental hospital was declared as 17 when the true figure is believed to have been 30. As many as 358 non-combatants may have been wounded. Of the American casualties, there is some suspicion of creative accounting, particularly in the under-declaring of Special Forces losses. The overall, official figure was nevertheless remarkably low: 18 dead (another died later) and 115 wounded, in an operation in which 152 Purple Hearts were awarded.[72] A local person, Paul Slinger, suggested that the reason why American casualties were low was because their military comprised a high percentage of soldiers the same colour as the Grenadians. He suggested there had been a reluctance to fire upon brothers.

Admiral Metcalf gave General Schwarzkopf a lift home in his jet as far as Norfolk, Virginia. Both men were surprised and overwhelmed by the enthusiasm and razzmatazz of their welcome. They shook hands, General Schwarzkopf making his way to the small jet which would take him to Fort Stewart airstrip. Twice before he had come home from war but on neither occasion had he been welcomed. As his plane taxied at Fort Stewart, a crowd of upward of sixty people and his divisional band were there to greet the conquering hero.

Reflection upon the importance of the Grenada operations fits the aphorism 'where you stand is where you sit'. From a global perspective, Governor General Sir Paul Scoon believes that 'it was in Grenada that the fall of Communism began'. The Caribbean Islands were for the most part very satisfied, not least Grenada, which saw democracy restored and elections held in 1984. Something like 85 per cent of the population had greeted the Americans with the kind of enthusiasm that Mr Chalabi promised Defense Secretary Donald Rumsfeld would be the case after America's invasion of Iraq. The Grenadians afforded the Americans every possible assistance, pointing out former military personnel and indicating the location of weapons and arms caches. For them, this operation had been not so much an invasion as a liberation. 'It freed me from prison,' said newspaperman Leslie Pierre, editor of the *Grenadian Voice*, 'as well as the whole country from under the iron fist of nascent Communism.'[73]

America had the satisfaction of restoring democracy to Grenada, frustrating the wider ambitions of the Soviet Union and resolving a perceived threat to her national security. As an operation, it had not quite lived up to the expectation of a *coup de main* but the overall aims were achieved in what was, after all, an operation put together in a matter of days. America had her victory; the sign that her Vietnam tragedy had now been expunged, that the image of burnt-out aircraft in the Iranian desert was something in the past. The tragedy of Lebanon and the loss of so many Marines had been counterbalanced to a large degree by the efforts of their own brothers in arms. A new, confident America buoyed by self-esteem looked forward to the future.

The question of the legality of the invasion remained. The

international community heard Washington's justification but was not so naïve as to be taken in. America gave three reasons to justify the invasion. She took part in an OECS regional operation; she intervened at the request of the Governor General to restore law and order; and it had been necessary to intervene to protect the lives of US nationals.

The cornerstone of America's case was founded upon the idea of regional action. It seems that the OECS had no authority to invite intervention. Its Charter makes no provision for the right to intervene, although Article 8 does permit the protection of a member state from threats originating from outside the OECS. The decision to take such action must be unanimous. Grenada did not take part in the process and Montserrat, represented by Britain, did not vote. As for external influence, Cuba had no involvement in Bishop's murder and had nothing to gain from his death.

The case that intervention had been formulated around an idea of regional peacekeeping does not stand up to close examination. Peacekeeping is about consent. The Government of Grenada did not give its consent to the American-led intervention. Besides, under Article 53 of the UN Charter, a regional organization may engage in enforcement action only with the permission of the Security Council. Moreover, who, in all seriousness, would insist that Grenada was facing an imminent armed attack?

There is then the matter of the invitation given by the Governor General to the OECS and US to intervene. There is no doubt that the letter exists, but equally, there is no doubt that the letter was signed by Sir Paul Scoon after the intervention had begun. Then there is the question whether a former figurehead in the Grenadian constitution had the authority to invite intervention. At the beginning of hostilities Grenada still had a de facto Government. Arguably, only if it had not could the Governor General, as the last remnant of legal authority on the island, have invited the intervention. In reality, this is legal semantics. The Prime Minister had been murdered, his deputy was in custody. Grenada required, above all, leadership – something willingly and professionally provided by Sir Paul Scoon until an interim administration could be established. 'Life in Grenada had to go on and, as Governor General, I could not allow any hiatus in the governance of the country.'[74]

Sir Paul explained how the application for military intervention dated 24 October was not signed until the 26th:

> I am the last person to ask anyone to come to invade my country but things had deteriorated so badly after the murder of Bishop, I called the Roman Catholic Bishop and the Anglican Archdeacon. The RMC [Revolutionary Military Council] sought out Maurice Bishop's supporters over a period of six dreadful days. We decided something had to be done to restore order. I had a visit from David Montgomery, British Deputy High Commissioner in Barbados. He told me OECS had decided they should intervene in Grenada to restore law and order but in view of the large number of sophisticated weapons in the hands of Coard's men, they felt they needed American help. I said to David, 'then do it, ask the Americans to come in to restore order. OECS could not do it by themselves. If Tom Adams drafts the letter asking the Americans to intervene militarily, I will sign it.'[75]

Sir Paul therefore made no request for Britain to intervene in Grenada.

> I was whisked off to USS *Guam* where I had a welcome meal and tidy up. When I returned to Grenada proper on the 26th, I was presented with the application letter by Brigadier Rudyard

Lewis commanding Barbadian forces. I had expected the letter, dated 24 October, two days previously but for obvious reasons we were unable to marry up. I read the letter, made two changes, my wife typed it and I signed it before handing four copies[76] back to Lewis. While this important business took its course, we were intensely irritated by a foppish American presuming to give orders to all and sundry around him. So you see, the intervention action did begin prior to the document being signed but Eugenia Charles and President Reagan were both aware of my position.[77]

Cases of intervention to protect nationals are generally recognized as legitimate. Britain's Lord Palmerston was never loath to intervene to protect Britons, justifying the action where a breakdown in law and order had occurred in the term *civis Romanus sum*. The American students were not at risk, but the American Government was not to know that. Time is relevant because, come the day, the rescue of the 'hostages' had not been blessed with an overwhelming sense of urgency. Nor, in terms of proportionality, can it be said that an island-wide operation could be justifiably related to the protection of nationals for whom an Entebbe-style rescue would appear to have been adequate. In the final analysis, while the foregoing legal reservations are legitimate, in Grenada's case it would be fair to say that we saw the right outcome for the wrong reasons. Within a year of their evacuation, the medical students returned to Grenada to resume their studies.

When the matter of the Grenada intervention came before the Security Council, the United States vetoed criticism while the United Kingdom, another permanent member, meekly abstained. In the General Assembly, the United States' action was almost unanimously condemned by states making the point that the domestic jurisdiction of those states was non-negotiable, an attitude which changed profoundly eight years later when a coalition of states attacked Iraq.

'One of the key lessons taken from Grenada was the need to fight jointly and we began to correct the deficiencies almost immediately,' said John Abizaid. 'The jointness issue is one frequently missed by most commentators on Grenada. Joint failures there led to much greater rigor in joint operations thereafter. The difference between joint operations today and in 1983 is astounding.'[78]

General Norman Schwarzkopf has been used deliberately as the catalyst in this account. He served his apprenticeship in Grenada for an event of huge international significance, the first Gulf conflict, 1991. He wrote in his memoirs of the shortcomings identified in Grenada, 'an abysmal lack of accurate intelligence, major deficiencies in communications, flare-up of inter-service rivalry, interference by higher head-quarters in battlefield decisions, our alienation of the press and more'.[79] Many but not all of these shortcomings would be rectified in time. He ensured that when the day came, he would be the sole responsible ground commander, responsible for a plan in which he had set forces for courses according to their skills and capabilities, namely, the Iraq Conflict 1990–1.

4

The Iraq Conflict
1990–1991

What if?

In 1980, Saddam Hussein attacked Iran in an offensive he believed would last no more than two weeks. In this ill-conceived conflict, Saddam Hussein received generous support from an Arabia concerned at the prospect of Iran's regional expansionism and the development of worrying Islamic fundamentalism. Iraq's ruler grew to see himself and Baghdad at the centre of an imaginary pan-Arab state. To Saddam Hussein, his war against Iran was not just Iraq's but also the entire Arab world's war. No sooner had the war started than Iraq's financial haemorrhage began. Eight years later, with Iraq's economy in ruins and hundreds of thousands of lives lost, Hussein and Ayatollah Khomeini agreed to abide by UN Security Council Resolution 598, drawing their bloody Gulf War to a conclusion.

Kuwait first came under threat of invasion by Iraq in 1961, the year she gained independence from Britain. Baghdad had claimed Kuwait as a province of hers throughout the duration of the Ottoman Empire. The boundaries were claimed to have been artificial, the work of imperialists. Foremost in the claim for Kuwaiti territory were the strategically placed Warba and Bubiyan Islands dominating access and egress into the Gulf. That is not to suggest that the land boundaries were not also extremely important to Iraq. The Iraq–Kuwait border runs through the rich al-Rumeilah oilfield believed to hold oil reserves valued at $750 billion. Attacking Kuwait as opposed to attacking Iran was always going to be viewed differently in the Middle East. Unpopular as Kuwait's ruling al-Sabah family may have been, the Emir's people were Arabs, far removed from the traditional enemy, Iran.

Saddam Hussein had been Washington's man in the same way that Osama bin Laden and the Panamanian dictator General Manuel Noriega had been. He was no less the man of other states with arms to sell and oil to buy. Moscow's reaction to Iraq's invasion of Kuwait, however, was not what might have been expected. Tass News Agency reported Iraq's aggression as having been intended 'to resolve at one go all its acute political and economic problems: to boost the price of crude oil, to get from Kuwait $2.4 billion in compensation and to write off its $15 billion war debt'. Moscow suspended Soviet arms supplies to Iraq. While that move may have been pragmatic, it was not replicated elsewhere.

The British Government as good as ignored Iraq's judicial murder on 15 March 1990 of the *Observer*'s Iranian-born, British investigative journalist charged with espionage, Farzad Bazoft. Frenetic were the efforts to ensure trade links were not damaged by the resultant public outcry. In 1982 Iraq became Britain's largest Middle East customer after Saudi Arabia. Immediately following the 1988 chemical attack on the Kurds at Halabja, Britain doubled Iraq's export credits guarantee; *The Times* later commented: 'Observers believe that the episode convinced President Saddam Hussein that, as long as Iraq had money to spend abroad, all avowed concern for human rights in the world would remain hypocrisy.'[1] As pathetic as the British action may have been, it paled into insignificance compared with that of the United States, providing Saddam Hussein with what he believed to be an open invitation to have his way with Kuwait.

Congress's reaction to Iraq's initial sabre-rattling on the Iraq–Kuwait border was to enact a series of economic measures against Iraq. The State Department and White House intervened because they saw in Congress's sanctions a weakening of their leverage over Saddam Hussein. The Under-Secretary of Commerce, Dennis Kloske, who had previously approved millions of dollars' worth of sensitive US technologies to Baghdad, testified before the House that he had recommended the implementation of stringent control measures on the export of US high technology to Iraq. The next day he left office. There were parties within government concerned at the direction the Administration was taking in the Middle East. On 15 June 1990, the State Department's Assistant Secretary of State for Near Eastern Affairs appeared before the Senate Foreign Relations Committee to explain why America appeared to be appeasing Saddam Hussein. Why, for example, were trade sanctions not being applied against Iraq? 'Because our competitors in Canada, Australia, Europe and Japan would step in quickly to fill the breach.' In August, Democrats blamed the State Department for a 'policy premised in fiction and fantasy' which they believed had encouraged Iraq to invade Kuwait.

The misreading of political intentions had contributed to the Korean War and the Falklands conflict. In the case of the Gulf conflict there is an arguable case that the messages had not been misinterpreted in Baghdad. According to BBC World Service, Assistant Secretary of State for the Near East and South Asia, John Kelly told Congress that there was no treaty obligation with Kuwait which would require US forces to come to the defence of the country. In discussions held on 25 July 1990 between Saddam Hussein and America's Ambassador to Iraq, April Glaspie, the dictator warned Glaspie that he would take whatever steps might be necessary to bring Kuwait's economic war against Iraq to an end. According to the Iraqi transcript of their meeting,[2] Glaspie, allegedly speaking on the instructions of Secretary of State Baker, said the USA had 'no opinion on the Arab–Arab conflicts, like your border disagreement with Kuwait'. The *Washington Post* provided corroboration. 'The substance of Miss Glaspie's recorded remarks closely parallels official US positions stated in Washington at the time, in which other state officials publicly disavowed any American security commitments.'

In an interview with the *New York Times*, Miss Glaspie said, 'Obviously I didn't think and nobody else did, that the Iraqis were going to take *all* of *Kuwait*.'[3] It may well have been that the intended message was to signal to Iraq Washington's contentment for Iraq to make the limited acquisition of Warba and Bubiyan Islands. In April 1991 when Miss Glaspie appeared before the Senate Foreign Relations Committee, she insisted the Iraqi transcript had been so extensively edited as to be 'disinformation'. She left her interrogators with the choice 'Saddam's words or mine'.

Saddam Hussein would have been encouraged by the messages emanating from Washington. While it is true that there had been criticism of Iraq's human rights record and the use of chemical weapons, economic considerations took precedence. Saddam Hussein was convinced America would not be prepared to take the number of casualties required to remove Iraq from Kuwait. He told Glaspie, 'Yours is a society which cannot accept 10,000 dead in one battle.' His calculations proved well off the mark, for the coalition forces that is. The 'mother of all battles' led to the comprehensive defeat of Iraqi forces.

On 2 August 1990, having promised President Mubarak of Egypt that he had no designs on Kuwait, Saddam's forces crossed the border into Kuwait allegedly in support of a popular uprising against the Emir and his family. In New York, the UN adopted Resolution 660, a Chapter VII enforcement measure condemning the Iraqi invasion[4] and demanding immediate and unconditional withdrawal. That resolution having had no effect, the Security Council reconvened on 6 August to adopt Resolution 661 imposing mandatory sanctions upon Iraq and Kuwait.

On the day of the invasion, President George Bush's schedule had him opening the Aspen Institute conference in Colorado. Margaret Thatcher had arranged to be present. A review of what was going on elsewhere revealed that the Arab League foreign ministers, meeting in Cairo, had failed to issue a joint declaration opposing Iraq's invasion of Kuwait. None had believed an Arab state would invade another. King Hussein of Jordan suggested Kuwait had got what was coming to her. In reality, he believed that to denounce Iraq would put his crown at risk. Saddam Hussein had become a hero of Palestinians in the occupied territories and Jordan for his defiance of Israel. President Hosni Mubarak of Egypt publicly denounced Saddam Hussein and called for unconditional withdrawal.

What the two Gulf conflicts of 1990–1 and that commencing in 2003 had in common was that the stimulus to engage came from the British Prime Ministers.[5] When the two leaders met in Aspen, Bush asked Thatcher what she thought of the situation. She made two points. First, that aggressors should never be appeased. 'We learned that to our cost in the 1930s.'[6] This would be a theme repeated by Bush a week later. 'If history teaches us anything, it is that we must resist aggression or it will destroy our freedoms. Appeasement does not work. As was the case in the 1930s, we see in Saddam Hussein an aggressive dictator threatening his neighbours.' Second,

Margaret Thatcher said that if Saddam Hussein were to cross the border into Saudi Arabia he would then control 65 per cent of the world's oil reserves, a prospect which would have set alarm bells ringing in Bush's mind. 'This was no time to go wobbly,' she told him. At Aspen, Margaret Thatcher added a few additional lines to her prepared speech. 'Iraq's invasion of Kuwait defies every principle for which the United Nations stands. If we let it succeed, no small country can ever feel safe again. The law of the jungle would take over from the rule of law.'[7] The Thatcher view should be compared with the Bush–Blair illegal invasion of Iraq in 2003. Recognition should also be given to the Islamic view that a double standard was at work here. George Bush asked Margaret Thatcher to return with him to Washington where she was taken into the confidence of the nation's decision-makers to a degree she had never previously experienced.

The Arabs wanted to find an Arab solution, but in the meantime American and Royal Navy ships were ordered to the Gulf as the first components of a multi-national fleet. On 7 August, US Secretary of Defense Dick Cheney travelled to Riyadh to ask King Fahd of Saudi Arabia for permission to station American land and air forces on Saudi soil against the possibility of an Iraqi invasion. King Fahd agreed to a brigade of 82nd Airborne Division – 4,000 men and 48 F-15 fighters – being deployed to Saudi Arabia conditional upon no announcement being made until the forces were in place. This happened while Resolution 661 was being discussed by the Security Council.

In coming to this agreement, the modest forerunner of a far larger commitment, King Fahd set himself a narrow, dangerous path to tread. As Custodian of the Two Holy Mosques, he put himself in a potential position to agitate internal and external Islamic sensitivities – something seized upon after the battle by Osama bin Laden to justify his terror campaign against the West.[8] For their part, senior coalition commanders had the additional duty to ensure culture clashes did not arise. That meant, among other things, no alcohol, no overt signs of competing religions and no female exhibitionism – no girlie magazines and no dancing of the type which in the West might be offered as 'entertainment'.

Thatcher found herself at odds with the Administration regarding the matter of the UN and international law. Her position in 1990 was opposite to the line the British Government would have ideally wanted to take in 2003. Thatcher desired to proceed solely on the basis of Resolution 660 bolstered by Article 51, the inherent right of self-defence. What she said sounded emblematic of what might have been expected to be said by Bush and Baker. 'I did not like unnecessary resort to the UN, because it suggested that sovereign states lacked the moral authority to act on their own behalf. If it became accepted that force could only be used – even in self-defence – when the United Nations approved, neither Britain's interests nor those of international justice and order would be served.'[9] Baker disagreed. He said UN authority was crucial to sustain the support of American public opinion for military action.[10]

Orders went out from the Pentagon to build up the defence force being sent to Saudi Arabia. Within two weeks the ground forces would be tripled by increasing the number of airborne forces, adding a brigade of Marines and a Special Forces group. After a month, the second or heavy echelon would begin to arrive: an air assault brigade and a mechanized infantry brigade bringing with them heavier firepower than that possessed by light airborne forces, including Apache attack helicopters and Abrams tanks. According to the Commander of Central Command, General H. Norman

Schwarzkopf, based in Tampa, Florida, three months would be needed to build up sufficient combat power 'to be absolutely assured of fending off a full-scale Iraqi attack'.[11] The planning and execution of Operation Desert Storm was organized jointly by the United States, represented in the field by General Schwarzkopf, and Saudi Arabia, represented by Sandhurst-educated Lieutenant-General Prince Khalid bin Sultan bin Abdul Aziz Al-Saud. Agreement had been reached that the Americans were to be *primus inter pares* in so far as final decisions rested with them.

The first states to pledge support for the allied coalition were two states owed considerable amounts of money by Saddam Hussein. France made the 6th Light Division available, appointing Lieutenant-General Michel Roquejeoffre their coalition commander based at the Coalition Head-quarters in Riyadh. The United Kingdom sent a squadron of Tornado F-3 air defence fighters and a squadron of Jaguar ground attack aircraft, followed by Nimrod maritime recon-naissance and VC-10 tanker aircraft. Later, in August, a squadron of Tornado GR-1 ground attack aircraft arrived in Bahrain. The American request for a British armoured brigade however reflected their sensitivity vis-à-vis the unknown quality of the Republican Guard's armour, particularly their Soviet-built T-72s.

It was Margaret Thatcher rather than the Ministry of Defence who decided to commit 7th Armoured Brigade. Their forebears, 7th Armoured Division, had fought and beaten Rommel in the Western Desert in the Second World War. Thatcher told Bush the self-contained brigade comprised two armoured regiments with 120 tanks, Mk 3 Challengers – the latest,[12] a regiment of field artillery, a battalion of Warrior-borne armoured infantry and anti-tank helicopters.[13] The ministry made good shortages in peace establishments, then brought the brigade up to its war establishment, an increment of approximately 20 per cent, adding extra arms and supporting services and bringing its strength to 7,500. The reinforcements came from other regular units in Germany, thereby undermining operational effectiveness.

Margaret Thatcher described how she wanted as the commander in the Gulf someone in whom she and the servicemen had complete confidence. She chose Lieutenant-General Sir Peter de la Billière, a distinguished officer who spoke colloquial Arabic and was within one week of retirement. For no known reason, Secretary of State for Defence Tom King did not support the de la Billière appointment as Commander British Forces Middle East. Thatcher told him that de la Billière either did that or would be appointed personal adviser to Downing Street on the conduct of the war. 'He went to the Gulf,' she wrote.[14]

On 5 October the General, taking leave of Headquarters South East District where he had served for two and a half years, gathered his staff together to bid farewell. He told them of developments in the Gulf, recommending that they keep their eyes on their newspapers over the period leading up to Christmas. A reporter's account of what the General said was interpreted by Reuters as the General forecasting there would be war by Christmas. The General found reassurance in adversity: '. . . even if I had damaged my standing in the United Kingdom, I had positively enhanced it in the Gulf, where rulers such as Sheikh Isa of Bahrain were to congratulate me heartily on taking such a vigorous approach'.[15]

On 20 September, Brigadier Cordingley, Commander 7th Armoured Brigade, and his recce party flew the 373 miles (600 kilometres) from Riyadh to the port of Al Jubayl, 'a scruffy place . . . four times the size of Dover . . . The characteristic smell of a Middle Eastern town hung in the air, a mixture of spice and incense with a strong hint of animal dung.'[16] He found the port congested with the equipment and weapons of war. Al Jubayl was to be 7th Armoured Brigade's assembly area where they would marry up with the American 1st Marine Expeditionary Force, under whose tactical control they were to come. The Marines were short of armour and in view of their part in the Schwarzkopf deception plan, approaching Kuwait City from the south, it was important that the Americans and the small British armoured component trained to work as one.

The British brigade was neither designed nor equipped to fight as an independent command and was therefore provisionally allocated to the Marines' First Division, subject to always being under the national command of General de la Billière. General Schwarzkopf's deception plan was to persuade the Iraqis that there would be an amphibious landing from which the Marines would advance from the south. The Iraqi deployments indicated that they had swallowed the bait and had established their defences to confront the Marines, when the reality was that they would be hammered by the left hook of an armoured fist coming through Iraq. The plan therefore left the Marines having to face the prepared defensive lines and obstacle belts of Iraqi forces in Kuwait. At his debrief at the Joint Force Headquarters, High Wycombe, Brigadier Cordingley sensed 'an unease with the idea of large numbers of British casualties'.[17] Little wonder that Marine Lieutenant-General Walt Boomer gave Brigadier Cordingley the warmest of welcomes. When would he be up and running in Saudi Arabia? 'We'll be operational by 16 November,' said Cordingley.[18] Unknown to both men, there was a parallel development which would impact upon all their plans and training.

The problem was that shortly after being appointed General de la Billière was 'already looking round for ways of increasing the number of troops at my disposal'. He saw the disadvantage of deploying one armoured brigade to the desert as being the obligation of attaching it to an American division 'which would severely limit its freedom of action'. How that would be, he does not say. 'If on the other hand, we had a British division, it would have far more scope to do itself justice.' His French opposite number commanded a light division, albeit not an ideal contribution. 'And yet, to raise a complete division from BAOR [British Army of the Rhine] would leave defences in the British zone of Germany substantially depleted.'[19] The British armoured division comprises three, sometimes four brigades. In view of the easing of tension in the Central Region, the release of an armoured division to the Gulf would be a calculated risk, but in view of the parlous situation under which the under-resourced 1st British Corps in Germany worked, the extraction of one fully supported division was bound to hobble and bring the other two armoured divisions to a virtual standstill.

I once commanded a squadron and a regiment in the 1st Armoured Division. We exercised regularly. We thought we were well trained. Even then, in 1982–4, there were increasing pressures upon training areas and what the German authorities would or would not permit. The 7th Armoured Brigade in Soltau and Fallingbostel was undoubtedly in the best position of any of the British brigades to train by virtue of their proximity to nearby training areas, including Fallingbostel and Munsterlager. Two of the three regiments had recently completed battle group training at Suffield, Canada, where there was space to manoeuvre and train with live ammunition. When the brigade arrived in the desert, they carved out their own ranges and training area where, with time on their hands for training, they saw a quantum leap in standards. Their training priorities were expressed as 'firing, fitness, first aid and f—ing NBC warfare'. There was an implicit assumption that Saddam Hussein might use nuclear, biological and chemical (NBC) weapons. The wearing of protective NBC suits and respirators in the desert brought normal activity to a state of slow motion. On 20 October, the first of 7th Armoured Brigade's tanks arrived at Al Jubayl port. The media had arrived before them.

The Times of 19 October carried a photograph on its front page, taken in the residential area of the port, of two soldiers in T-shirts and shorts carrying rifles. There was no armoury for weapons. The men were therefore obliged to carry their personal weapons wherever they went. It was the caption which was the cause of a multitude of politicians, civil servants and armchair-warriors choking on their morning cornflakes. 'Dressed to kill; Corporal Myles Sharman and John Shonfield on patrol in Saudi Arabia.' The act, fraudulent and unworthy, served as an early warning to the military to be constantly vigilant when dealing with the press. The media have a right to report the good, the bad and the trivial but, at a time of national crisis, what it reports must above all be true, or not knowingly inaccurate. 'I was always disappointed', wrote General de la Billière, 'when I read inaccurate reports written simply to attract attention and create a story where none existed.'[20]

By the end of October, a sufficiency of forces had arrived with which to defend Saudi Arabia. Desert Shield by itself had therefore become a satisfactorily redundant aspiration as General Schwarzkopf and his planners looked towards raising the force level to take the offensive on Desert Storm to remove Saddam Hussein and his 545,000-strong army from Kuwait. The Muslim holy month of Ramadan, beginning on 15 March, stood as a significant limiting factor on military operations. As a result, ground attack would need to be launched around mid-February and be concluded before the start of Ramadan. In April, the hot weather really settles in and would reduce soldiers obliged to wear full NBC protection to a blob.

General Schwarzkopf turned his attention to force generation. Serendipitously, he had in the new Chairman of the Joint Chiefs of Staff, General Colin Powell, a resourceful ally. Powell had a personal doctrine of not skimping when allocating troops to task. After Schwarzkopf had submitted his wish list to the Pentagon, Powell virtually doubled the numbers requested. Two armoured divisions were requested; three were made available with an additional brigade, all equipped with the Abrams M1A1. Another Marine division was found, together with an extra brigade. Other additional Navy resources included two aircraft-carrier battle groups and a second battleship. The number of Air Force planes increased by 300.[21] Two-thirds of the coalition was American yet the other third, an odd mixture of forces, all had a role to play. Setting aside the UK, USA and France, other troop contributors included Afghanistan, Bangladesh, Bahrain, Egypt, Kuwait, Morocco, Nigeria, Oman, Pakistan, Qatar, Saudi Arabia, Senegal, Syria and the UAE. None of the military representatives of the Arab states would enter Iraq. States which for one reason or another did not volunteer for a military role, supplemented the funding provided by the Arab states to ensure that all intervention costs were met.

Numerous were the visitors to 7th Armoured Brigade. On his fact-finding tour of Al Jubayl, the Chief of the Defence Staff, Marshal of the Royal Air Force, Sir David Craig, heard Brigadier Cordingley admit his concerns with the media. 'I am not at all convinced we are getting the right message put over or even if the press is behind us.' Craig reassured him he would deal with media problems. Cordingley should 'worry about the Iraqis'.[22] The brigade attracted a disproportionate amount of interest, possibly because of the 'Desert Rats'[23] connection. The press had a preference to hear the latest news from the horse's mouth rather than from a staff officer. Answers to their questions were going to be that much more authoritative. The pool system was intended to exercise control over the press. There had been seventeen correspondents in the first pool to deploy in August 1990. Everything seemed to work well for a fortnight. As troop numbers increased, so too did the media presence – 800 by December and 1,600 at war's end[24] – and so, correspondingly, did the potential hazards facing the unwary military.

On 28 November 1990, Brigadier Cordingley was tasked to address a group of visiting British correspondents. The brief lasted thirty minutes, after which came the tricky part, the questions. Some could be simply side-stepped – future intentions, for example. Then, up stood the *Guardian*'s man. What sort of casualties did he expect? This was one Cordingley was content to answer but, upon reflection, perhaps wished he had not. 'It is inconceivable that if two armies of the size that are facing each other here went to war there would not be considerable casualties.' He qualified this statement by saying the majority would be suffered by Iraq.[25] Frenetic scribbling continued. They wanted percentages. 'Two? Ten? Twenty?' 'It's not really possible to put a figure on it,' said the Brigadier. There then occurred what can be described as the tipping-point when a staff officer said: 'We are planning on 15 per cent.' One of the numerate among the press exclaimed: 'That's over 1,500 from your brigade alone.'[26] Brigadier Cordingley engaged in damage limitation, repeating the facts: that the majority of casualties would be Iraqis, how reinforcements would reduce the British total even further, how excellent was the medical support. 'Before I go,' said the Brigade Commander, 'I hope none of you are going to go away saying that Brigadier Cordingley says there are going to be lots of casualties in the Gulf.' Hope springs eternal. The next day, the London papers carried the story and, since it contradicted the official Government line of low casualties, this caused a rumpus in the Ministry of Defence. The *Mail*'s John Junor concluded, 'If I had my way, Brigadier Patrick Cordingley would be on the next plane home.'[27] Secretary of State for Defence Tom King quickly intervened in support of Brigadier Cordingley.[28]

General de la Billière had been one of those who reassured the press that this would be a war of short duration, with low casualties. His staff left a message for the Brigadier to ring the Commander at 10.00. Brigadier Cordingley knew instinctively that this would not be a social call. 'It's a bloody stupid business and quite frankly, Patrick, it shows poor judgement on your part.' The General had overlooked his own 'war by Christmas' scare. 'You laid yourself open.' To his credit, the General recognized Cordingley had been misquoted and said he would have his backing. 'I think you were perhaps naïve. But mind you, Patrick, you have a reputation for speaking out of turn. Make sure it's the last time here.'[29]

The reference to speaking out of turn may have had its origins in a meeting the two had had with General Walt Boomer on 15 November when the brigade was put under tactical control of the US Marine Expeditionary Force. In view of the General's hidden agenda to create a British division, it seemed incongruous to be going through the motions of handing over a brigade vital to the Marines' success but hinting that this might not be the final solution.

It was a riddle beyond Boomer's comprehension. 'I felt desperately uncomfortable', wrote Cordingley, 'and wished I was
elsewhere.'[30] On 22 November, Tom King stood up in the
House and announced that 7th Armoured Brigade was to be
joined by 4th Armoured Brigade, four additional artillery
regiments, additional support units and the 1st Armoured
Division Headquarters to command and control these units.
Meanwhile, in the Gulf, President Bush pumped Brigadier
Cordingley's hand. 'General Cordingley,[31] I would like to thank
you, your men and your government, for your contribution.
It means a lot to us to have the Desert Rats fighting alongside
us.'[32] The President said how saddened he had been by the
sacking of Margaret Thatcher. She had been removed by
the grandees of her party who, in so doing, removed one
of the most powerful influences upon the course of the war.

On 27 November, Lieutenant-General Wilkes, Commander
UK Land Forces, accompanied Lieutenant-General de la
Billière on a visit to 7th Armoured Brigade. General de la Billière
announced his intention that the brigade would remain with
the Marines until 1st Armoured Division was complete,
thought to be in the New Year, when they would transfer
to being under tactical control of VII US Corps. The outline
plan was for VII and XVIII Corps to execute the main
thrust through Iraq into Kuwait. De la Billière espoused his
preference for the British to form part of this main attack
rather than be a component in the Marines' diversionary
role. Cordingley disagreed, describing this as a nightmare
scenario. He over-egged the logistical difficulties. His
perception of the operational difficulties found him on firmer
ground. 'We were asking the 1st Armoured Division, which
had never trained as a division, to operate with a strange
Corps whose concepts of manoeuvre warfare were bound to
be different. If the division stayed with the Marines, they

would find their tactical battle easier to comprehend.'
Brigadier Cordingley concluded his summary of reservations
on the question of loyalty. 'We have trained with the Marines
now for some time. We know how they work, how they
think, we understand each other. They need us and I don't
like the idea of walking out on them now.'[33] The intervention
had no effect; the die had been cast.

4th Armoured Brigade had a different organization to that
of 7th Armoured Brigade in that it comprised one armoured
regiment and two Warrior armoured fighting vehicle-borne
infantry battalions. 7th Armoured Brigade had the opposite
components and was now trained to a high standard. 4th
Armoured Brigade was a composite brigade, had not
previously trained together and had three weeks to ready
itself for armed conflict. In that respect, this was a lopsided
division. 7th Armoured Brigade had established a level of
training which allowed for mission-oriented operations. The
4th Armoured had had neither the time nor opportunity to
reach this standard and was obliged to adapt to less flexible
brigade drills.

Cordingley sensed de la Billière's disappointment in his
contradicting him in front of General Wilkes. The problem
was that Cordingley suspected de la Billière had two reasons
for taking 7th Armoured Brigade away from the Marines.
First, that he thought there was a risk of sustaining high
casualties on the obstacle belt south of Kuwait City, and
second, because he saw the attack from the south as a
sideshow. The proof of the pudding was that by altering the
angle of his approach, Lieutenant-General Walt Boomer
succeeded in his mission with negligible casualties. It would
be difficult to argue that the task given to the 1st Armoured
Division as flank guard to VII Corps could be described as
a high-profile mission.

General Schwarzkopf wanted the 1st Armoured Division to support Boomer's attack into Kuwait. De la Billière asked Schwarzkopf to reassign the division to VII Corps' main attack. The change was made, 'over the strenuous objection of Boomer, who was impressed with the Desert Rats and wanted the combat power of their tanks'. Schwarzkopf rearranged the order of battle, assigning the Marines the Tiger Brigade from the 2nd (US) Armoured Division in Germany with additional air support. He switched the 1st Armoured Division to the tactical control of VII Corps, who allocated them a supporting attack role on their right flank. The French, under Khalid's command not Schwarzkopf's, took their position on the coalition's left flank. Major-General Bernard Janvier's light armoured vehicles were no match against Iraqi armour.

On 30 November, the Security Council adopted Resolution 678 issuing Iraq with an ultimatum to comply with previous resolutions by 15 January or the UN would use 'all necessary means' to restore international peace and security to the region. China abstained but, surprisingly, Russia voted in favour of the resolution. The two votes against had been reasonably consistently cast by two temporary members, Yemen and Cuba. The President of the Yemen exasperated President Bush when he likened Saddam Hussein's seizure of Kuwait to America's operation in Grenada. Notwithstanding the action of the 'awkward squad',[34] the international community welcomed Resolution 678 as a sign that the UN was now behaving in the collegial manner intended by the drafters of the Atlantic Charter. So great was the enthusiasm among the peace professionals that they took Resolution 678 as the foundation upon which to build new doctrine. This is the origin of the concept of wider peacekeeping, the product of authors unable to comprehend that what was happening in the Gulf did not set a precedent for the future. Sir Anthony Parsons was among those realists who believed a recurrence improbable. He could not believe there could be another leader as inept as Saddam Hussein whose aggression was so undeniable as to unite international opinion against him. Saddam Hussein then compounded his ineptitude by threatening friends of the sole remaining superpower and other important states who had an interest in maintaining the flow of oil. Saudi Arabia ensured states would not suffer shortages by increasing production. The terrain upon which the counter-offensive was to be launched suited manoeuvre warfare. Other than Kuwait City, there were massive sweeps of barely inhabited desert, ideal for the competent operation of armour and air power. Then, of course, money was no object. 'Such a conjuncture', concluded Parsons of the wider peacekeeping role for the UN, 'is the stuff of war games in think tanks, not of real life.'[35]

There were the usual, tentative, 'not going anywhere' interim political meetings between both sides aimed at preventing the war, but they came to nothing. On the night of 16/17 January 1991, the war began with comprehensive air attacks from allied aircraft and Tomahawk cruise missiles against Kuwait, the Baghdad infrastructure, forward command and control centres and air defence capabilities. The coalition established command of the air except for the Scud missile threat. The neutralizing of the Scuds required the importation of US Patriot anti-aircraft missile systems from Germany, the Netherlands and the United States, the allocation of a disproportionate percentage of one-third of offensive air assets which would otherwise have been utilized elsewhere, and the deployment of Special Forces to laser-guide cab-ranked aircraft on to mobile Scud launchers. The Iraqi Air Force avoided air combat by flying to Iran, where they were impounded for the duration of the war. The naval ships were being used essentially as platforms from which to launch gunfire, missiles and aircraft. The Royal Navy alone sank approximately half the Iraq Navy as they led the combined fleet up the Gulf, clearing mines and defeating at least one missile attack on a US capital ship as they did so. The naval presence contributed towards engraving the deception plan in the mind of Saddam Hussein, the conviction that the main attack would flow from an amphibious landing. The conflict was essentially a combined operation dominated by land warfare, heavily supported by maritime and air.

At the commencement of the air war, land forces had been drawn up parallel to the Saudi–Kuwait border, but none had encroached upon it. All that was about to change as General Schwarzkopf now began the enormous move of two corps, their equipment and logistics, westward to assembly areas facing Iraq. This was the preparation of the left hook upon Saddam Hussein's open flank. Coalition planners with time to think contemplated the reason for this flank being unprotected. Was it a 'come on', would it be a nuclear killing zone? One of the initial tasks in the air war therefore, unsurprisingly, was upon Saddam Hussein's reconnaissance assets. The Russians moved two satellites and placed them over the future battlefield. Surprisingly, it appears that Saddam had no forewarning.

Saddam Hussein had not thought through his exit strategy, there being but two possible routes running north–south from Kuwait to Baghdad. The marshy valleys of the Euphrates and Tigris and their collapsed bridges would serve to guide any forces seeking to withdraw hurriedly towards the choke point at Mitla Pass. The coalition, with laser sights, GPS and night vision supported by AWACS and JSTARS[36] were capable of fighting day and night, thereby deriving the greatest advantage from manoeuvre warfare. The ultimate purpose of Lieutenant-General Chuck Horner's Air Force was to so massage by extreme violence the Iraqi forces below that they were prepared, set up, softened, to be hit so hard by ground forces as to squeeze them out of Kuwait as toothpaste from a tube. While the support of ground forces was clearly the priority, there were other tasks making demands upon each day's 2,500 sorties – air defence, strategic bombing and battle-field interdiction.

On 29 January, the Iraqis launched armoured and infantry raids into Al Wafra and Khafji in Saudi Arabia, possibly in search of intelligence, having been blinded by the coalition air campaign. These moves took the coalition by surprise, leading to defensive positions being dug deeper and one of the fiercest engagements of the war. The US Marines confronted the Iraqis at Al Wafra, destroying twenty-two tanks with on-call aircraft. The casualties they suffered were from one of their own aircraft whose pilot's competence in recognition left much to be desired. On 30 January, Saudi and Qatari forces attacked the Iraqis in Khafji but were initially unsuccessful. They regrouped and attacked the next day, forcing the surviving Iraqis back over the border.

The Iraqis launched their first Scud missiles on 17 January against Tel Aviv and Haifa. These obsolete Soviet missiles had formerly been intended as tactical nuclear weapons. Those fired into Israel were fitted with conventional warheads, yet Israel and the coalition were aware of the possibility that the missiles could deliver biological or chemical material. The original missiles had a range of 190 miles (306 kilometres) with the prospect of landing within half a mile (0.8 kilometres) of their intended target. The Scud has been compared to the German V2 rocket, yet despite its accuracy being played down, the weapon was substantially more accurate than a V2. Accuracy to within 900 yards (823 metres) is tolerable when delivering a tactical nuclear warhead. The Iraqis learnt to extend the Scud's range by joining two bodies end to end. In increasing the range to 300 miles (483 kilometres), there was a corresponding decline in accuracy to within 2 miles (3.2 kilometres) and a reduction in warhead size to 160 lb (75 kg).[37] The Scud threat was therefore more political and psychological than military.

The Israelis wanted to retaliate, requesting permission to over-fly Saudi Arabia. The Saudis refused. If Israel had joined the war against Iraq, the Saudis would probably have remained alongside America. How many other Arab states would have done likewise was never put to the test. If it had been, the Arab contribution to the coalition would certainly have been substantially reduced. Keeping Israel out of the war became one of the coalition's principal aims, its achievement conditional upon its success in neutralizing the Scud sites. Israel's compliance did not come without strings. They wanted their own people working in Coalition Headquarters Riyadh and required the coalition air forces to strike targets on a list supplied by them. General Schwarzkopf asked the Joint Chiefs, 'How can anyone think the Israelis have better target information than our Air Force?' Dutifully, targets were attacked but nothing was found. What rankled with General Schwarzkopf was the threat posed to his successful cultural sensitivity programme. 'I couldn't believe I had to explain that the presence of Israeli officers could wreck Central Command's credibility with the Arabs – assuming the Saudis would even let them in.'[38]

The Allied air forces located and destroyed thirty-six fixed Scud sites and ten mobile ones. The latter were the source of the problem, having the freedom to hide and roam at will. The opportunity suddenly presented itself 'to devise a

worthwhile role for our Special Forces'.[39] De la Billière
enjoyed a good rapport with General Schwarzkopf; both
brought considerable experience to the higher echelon of
the campaign's command. General Schwarzkopf however
had good reason to reflect upon the Special Forces' performance in Grenada. The Scud threat related to an uneasy
Israel meant that nothing should be ruled out. Delta Force
also wanted a share in the action. On 29 January, General
Wayne Downing, appointed to command US Special
Operations Forces in Iraq, arrived in Riyadh to establish
a role for his men. The parties agreed that the SAS would
remain in the south and the Americans would take the
northern box.

There appear to be no figures to quantify what either party
managed to achieve, whether as 'assists' – the *coup de grâce*
taken by an aircraft – or, failing the availability of an aircraft,
the destruction of mobile launchers by Special Forces using
anti-tank missiles. The desert had wide-open spaces yet there
was so often someone around when operators did not wish
to be seen – goatherds or patrols looking for downed pilots.
Someone also failed to appreciate the weather conditions in
Iraq's north-western uplands – hot in the day, and so cold
at night that men could, and did, die of exposure. The fact
is that after 26 January, no further Scud attacks were made
on Israel. That is not to say the threat had gone away, for
a month later on 26 February a Scud hit a warehouse being
used as a barracks in Khobar, Dhahran in eastern Saudi
Arabia. Twenty-eight troops were killed and many injured
in what had been a random strike. The Khobar Scud had
been one of 81 missiles launched by Iraq: 38 against Israel,
41 against Saudi Arabia and 2 long-shots against Bahrain
and Qatar.

Press relations continued to be difficult. At Christmas, a

time when the General was engaged with Secretary Cheney and General Powell, Schwarzkopf had told his deputy, General Cal Waller, to brief the press. General Waller had been in theatre for only a month and was unused to dealing with the press's thrusting questions. When would Central Command be ready, they asked? He told them the ground forces would not be fully prepared until mid-February, which lifted any sense of urgency for Saddam Hussein to reach an accommodation in December. Cheney had recently fired Air Force General Dugan for a breach of operational security. Schwarzkopf sportingly accepted the blame for putting his deputy up front. Neither Cheney nor Powell was concerned. 'It's not always bad to send the enemy mixed signals,' said Cheney.

On 4 February, General Schwarzkopf told General Powell that the press was unhappy and growing increasingly so. Of the thousand out there at that time, only seventy-five could be accommodated in pools. The other 925 sat around and complained. Two weeks later, General Schwarzkopf noted there to be 180 correspondents out on front line pools from 1,300 in the war zone. He had sat down to watch a CNN White House press conference preceded by live coverage from a pool correspondent. 'There has just been a major artillery duel in my location between 82nd Airborne and the Iraqis.' The Iraqis watched the same programme. They could put two and two together, find out where there had at that moment been artillery firing, and no doubt be horrified to discover that they had an American division sitting, waiting to attack through an exposed front, thereby ruining three weeks of deception planning. 'Son of a bitch!' shouted Schwarzkopf.[40]

A solitary security breach by a reporter could have a catastrophic effect upon military operations. But then, the press has an essential role in reporting the progress of the conflict to the international community. The embedding process which developed out of the Gulf experience went some way towards reconciling the irreconcilable through shared risks. The effect of the press on the conflict overall was positive.

While ground forces positioned themselves in their assembly areas, air forces continued the process of wreaking attrition upon Iraqi forces with no hiding place out there in the desert. Their front line divisions had been reduced to half their fighting strength. The Republican Guard divisions on the Iraq side of the Iraq–Kuwait border were singled out for special treatment including the carpet-bombing by B52 bombers. Tomahawk cruise missiles reached out to attack operational targets in and around Baghdad. A strike of two laser-guided bombs upon what was believed to have been a communications bunker fell through the ventilation shaft of an air raid shelter, leading to heavy loss of life among the 400 non-combatants who had sought refuge there. The resultant horrific images led to further attacks upon urban areas being minimized.

The Land Commanders each presented their operational possibilities to General Schwarzkopf. His undoubted favourite was from a successor of his, commanding his former 24th Armoured Infantry Division. After the battle, he rated Major-General Barry McCaffrey the most aggressive and successful ground commander of the war. The Commander-in-Chief admitted to being less convinced by the VII Corps plan which he described as 'plodding and overly cautious'.[41] General Schwarzkopf left his Central Command commanders in no doubt as to how he viewed the subject of command. 'I cannot afford to have commanders who do not understand that it is attack, attack, attack, attack, and destroy every step of

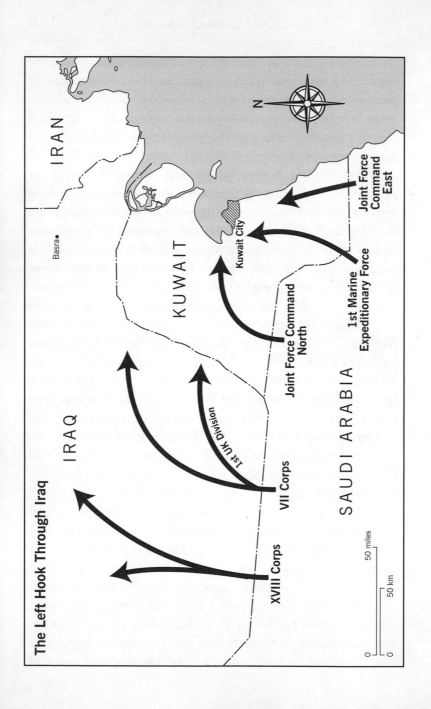

The Left Hook Through Iraq

the way. If you have somebody who doesn't understand it, I would strongly recommend that you consider removing him from command and putting in somebody that can do the job.'[42]

Commanders are free to fight their formation battles as they wish, within boundaries, subject to satisfying the mission. One of the problems with short wars, but not long wars, is that there is little opportunity to identify weakness in a commander and little time in which to remove him from command. The selection of the right people to command is never more important. Major-General Rupert Smith, formerly of The Parachute Regiment and commanding 1st Armoured Division, discussed the subject of command in his first Directive and its applicability at all levels: 'Those leaders who failed in my own Regiment in the Falklands were those who required all their moral and physical resources to maintain themselves in the line and had no capacity to discipline and lead their commands which, in turn, were mediocre.'[43]

General Smith's plan took as an absolute given the complete absence of any ground of tactical advantage, from which he deduced he would not fight for ground but would bypass occupied pockets and attack instead lines of communication and supply between commander and commanded. 'This reduced my needs for infantry and for close-quarter battle, all of which reduced my anticipated needs for men and supplies. These in turn added to the speed at which I could move, and therefore interdict the command arrangements in the depth of the Iraqi positions.'[44] Arguably, this was the course of action of a commander of a two-brigade division. The subordination of a US brigade was discussed but did not happen. 'With hindsight of the battle,' said General Smith, 'if a third brigade had been available, it would have been tasked and might have contributed to further increase our speed and sustainability.'[45] The decision how the division is to be fought is not a matter to be decided upon at the last moment since it touches upon training, organization and equipment. General Smith explained his reason for choosing to fight the division in depth rather than width: 'I had to fight the division in such a way that if I got stuck in a hole I could pull myself out of it, equally if we had success I had to be able to capitalize on it rapidly.'[46]

VII Corps, on the left of 1st Armoured Division, believed the enemy would assess the 1st Division's position as the coalition's point of main effort, for which reason the division disguised its presence. During 14–23 February, the divisional artillery took part in VII Corps' programme of preparatory fire plans known as 'artillery raids'. These 'raids' served a number of purposes: they contributed to the deception plan, obscuring the points at which breaches in the defence line would occur; they afforded gunners unprecedented, hands-on familiarity with their equipment; and they maintained the process of attrition upon Iraqi ground forces and high-value targets.

On Friday 22 February, President Bush, on television, issued Saddam Hussein with a final ultimatum. He gave the Iraqis less than twenty-four hours in which to begin their withdrawal, forty-eight hours in which to have left Kuwait City and one week in which to be out of Kuwait. There having been no response to the ultimatum, the two-phase land campaign began in the early hours of Sunday 24 February 2001.

At 04.00 on the wet morning of 24 February, D-Day, the Marines began their first-phase advance towards Kuwait City. In the north, the French 6th Division and 82nd Airborne Division crossed into Iraq to provide flank protection for the force. The rain was not what the Marines wanted because the associated low cloud restricted vital air support for a force light on artillery. General Boomer made spectacular progress.[47] The Iraqis were on the run. Oilfields had been torched and the desalination plant wrecked, meaning the Iraqis were not going to linger in Kuwait. Given these indicators, General Schwarzkopf brought forward the main, second-phase attack to 15.00. The British, held back in their concentration area as greyhounds in the slips, carried out last-minute checks on their armour. Meanwhile, concurrently, VII Corps' 1st Infantry Division had opened up gaps in the main obstacles, the berms and the minefields, so that when ordered to go, 7th Armoured Brigade followed by 4th Armoured Brigade could begin a journey that would end in the suburbs of Kuwait City. The coalition mission: 'to inflict maximum destruction, *maximum* destruction, on the Iraqi military machine. You are to destroy all war-fighting equipment.'[48]

The two British brigades entered Iraq sequentially, beginning at 12.07, advancing towards the contact battle with a view to destroying the enemy at ranges in excess of 1,094 yards (1,000 metres). The divisional commander 'thought it best to fight lots of little fights quickly, over a period, rather than a few big ones over the same period'. What then developed is what can best be described as a pinball battle of bagatelle. Every area in which there were Iraqi armed forces had a code word named after a metal. As subordinate formations hit occupied positions they bounced away and around Bronze, Copper, Zinc, Brass, Steel, Platinum (thought, for example, to be the main element of the Iraqi 12th Armoured Division), Tungsten and Lead. The score after sixty-six hours' constant engagement over 180 miles (290 kilometres) added up to 3 Iraqi divisions destroyed, 7,024 prisoners including two division commanders, 400 pieces of equipment captured and 2,000 small arms. A separate, specially assembled Prisoner of War Guard Force (PWGF) handled all PoWs. Most Iraqis had fought only tentatively after days of being subjected to bombing and artillery fire. Commander 4th Armoured Brigade, Brigadier Christopher Hammerbeck, called up the Division Commander. 'Will you give me loudspeakers to persuade them to surrender?', to which the response was, 'I might give you some MLRS [Multiple Launched Rocket System]'.

It is no easy matter to estimate the number of Iraqi casualties within the divisional boundary or indeed elsewhere. There was constant attrition. Arabs bury their dead soon after death. Many of the wounded had terrible injuries. British casualties were light, notwithstanding earlier fears of substantial casualties. Twenty-four British servicemen were killed in action, including SAS and Tornado crew.[49] One of 1st Battalion The Staffordshire Regiment's soldiers took a rocket-propelled grenade on his chest, dying instantly, but the highest casualties in any one single action occurred in 4th Armoured Brigade when two Warrior APCs were struck by American A-10s flown by incompletely trained pilots. Nine infanteers died; others were wounded. The brigades fought through each metal-coded reference point, passing countless Iraqis trying to surrender until at 09.15 on 27 February the first squadron entered Kuwait. The Brigade Commander followed fifteen minutes later, called a halt and asked the crew for a cup of tea. 'It seemed a quintessentially British thing to do.'[50]

Men were becoming tired. Up until that point, orders had been given over the radio, now they were to be written. Flags of all descriptions were found and flown from the vehicles, if only to cast doubt in the minds of trigger-happy flanking formations or cowboy pilots.

At 05.30 on the morning of Thursday 28 February,

Brigadier Cordingley, having reached his objective, received orders to go one stage further: 'to attack east to cut routes from Kuwait City so as to prevent the Iraqi army from retreating north to Basra'. Apparently the ceasefire was due at eight o'clock that morning. 'I want you on that road by then,'[51] said General Smith. There were no formal orders, just an instruction to be ready at 06.00 for a 40-mile (64-kilometre) cavalry charge across the desert. In a strengthening dawn, the crews encountered 'the detritus of an army not just defeated but utterly routed'.[52] VII Corps never quite made up the time lost in a ponderous start. At 08.00 the left hook stopped short of having engaged all the Republican Guard divisions. Kuwait City was back in coalition hands. The equivalent of three battalions of correspondents released from their minders headed straight for the capital to report what they found there and along the highway of death on the road to Basra.

To say that the men of 1st Armoured Division had fought to a state of exhaustion would be to understate the case. Theirs had been a remarkable achievement. Of their Challenger tanks, whose reliability had been in question, 95 per cent had been running at any one time. To assist in the achievement of that commendable situation, the manufacturers sent their own team of engineers out, supported up front by a sufficiency of spare parts and power-packs. There is no doubt what the 1st Armoured Division's battle winner was, it was its officers and men, heirs of the men who had also gone into the desert as virgin warriors, blooded in 'no holds barred' battles against the Afrika Korps. As elsewhere in this collection of battle accounts, this is a story of skilful, courageous and committed men, having never previously been to war, accepting the challenge, applying their willpower and rising to the occasion.

Elsewhere, the 24th Infantry Division fought on after the ceasefire. The terms of that ceasefire provided for retaliation by coalition forces:

> General Barry McCaffrey's 24th US Division staged a four-hour assault against retreating Iraqis near the Euphrates river, destroying more than 750 vehicles including a busload of women and children, and killing thousands of soldiers. An Apache helicopter crewman was heard yelling 'say hello to Allah' as he launched a Hellfire missile at the Iraqis. Not a single American was killed.[53]

President Bush had reassured these non-combatants and conscripts that his fight was not with them but with their leader, Saddam Hussein. The purpose of destroying war-fighting equipment had been to ensure its non-appearance in any future revisitation of the region. It is difficult to talk of proportionality in life and death moments but the images taken along the 62-mile (100-kilometre) road from Kuwait City to the border town of Safwan haunted many of those who would soon be confronted with the results of their hand-iwork. If there were any laurels to be awarded, it was to a formation described by General Schwarzkopf as the one responsible for an 'absolutely superb operation' which 'will be studied for many years to come as the way to do it',[54] The United States Marine Corps. Among the principal players, that which impressed the General the least was VII Corps.

This was one of those rare conflicts where people had had no idea what was going to happen or how the battle was going to end. The worst case had to be provided for, as was evidenced in the battle casualty provisions and the provision of medical facilities for massive casualties that never materialized.

The black smoke from the oil wells masking the light of day, the wrecked vehicles, disassembled bodies or bodies turned to carbon, left as good an impression of Dante's Inferno as imaginable. The worst of the killing ground, on the road at Mitla Pass, lay a short distance from where 1st Armoured Division had halted. A route had to be cleared through the tangle of vehicles, bodies and plunder in order that the road could be used. Engineers came forward with their equipment: units detailed off burial parties to attend to those bodies on the road. A far bigger engineer effort would follow when bulldozers excavated trenches for a more substantial burial of remains in mass graves. The British had heard how the Iraqis had been caught in a traffic-jam caused by the road being sealed ahead. The killing had been done by the American Air Force and the Second Marine Division. 'There were not thousands of bodies, as the media had claimed,' wrote Brigadier Cordingley, 'but certainly hundreds; it was a reminder to us all of the horror of war.'[55] Two subalterns, Andrew Nye and Roy Monk, were on burial detail, disposing of the dead, including women and children, Iraqi, Kuwaiti or Egyptian refugees. Nye said: 'You have to feel this to believe it. There are booby-traps here and the Iraqis who died on this road were stripping Kuwait City. But I shudder to think what it would have been like in their position.'[56]

The images transmitted back to people's comfortable living-rooms so revolted the public that they and their leaders said 'enough'. But what if the coalition had gone on to Baghdad and removed Saddam Hussein from power? Would it have rendered the invasion in 2003 nugatory?

Margaret Thatcher wrote in her memoirs that it had been one of her abiding regrets that she had not been in a position to see the issue through:

The failure to disarm Saddam Hussein and to follow through
the victory so that he was publicly humiliated in the eyes of his
subjects and Islamic neighbours was a mistake which stemmed
from the excessive emphasis placed right from the start on
international consensus . . . In war there is much to be said for
magnanimity in victory. But not before victory.[57]

The well nigh universal argument within the coalition against
heading north to Baghdad to overthrow Saddam Hussein
was the expression of the absence of a mandate. What is
curious with regard to the interpretation of international law
is that it is one of the stronger justifications for extending
the conflict in so far as an arguable case did exist. Margaret
Thatcher had been on the wrong track in her insistence on
using Article 51, collective self-defence, as the case with which
to prise the Iraqis out of Kuwait. The Article 51 route would
have been difficult to extrapolate into a justification to have
gone beyond the liberation of Kuwait. What the Americans
had done in insisting on the backing of a specific UN Security
Council resolution was to keep the option of driving to
Baghdad open.

The fact that Resolution 678 authorized the coalition to ensure
that Iraq complied with all relevant Security Council resolutions and to 'restore international peace and security in the
area', strongly suggests that the Kuwait action was seen by
the Council as enforcement action, rather than as an exercise
of the right of collective self-defence and it was this mandate
to restore peace and security which justified the coalition in
going beyond the immediate aim of liberating Kuwait and
taking action to reduce the capability of Iraq to pose a military
threat in the future.[58]

To believe, however, that Resolution 678 could be dusted off and made to fit the 2003 situation appears a step too far.

For the armed forces to move from their locations in or near Kuwait to continue the offensive to Baghdad would have brought them into conflict with a defeated, demoralized army unable to defend itself. Sixty thousand had been taken as prisoners of war. A coalition tank commander is in no position to second-guess the intentions of an Iraqi T-55 tank crew. He has to play safe. There's no doubt that the coalition could have been in Baghdad forty-eight hours after departure, but the slaughter en route would have been so horrific that there is reasonable doubt the military and air force could have continued the attrition of Saddam Hussein's armed forces. There was talk of 'low pilot morale', as amplified by Douglas Hurd: 'In fact, once the Iraqi forces had effectively lost their capacity to defend themselves, many pilots were reluctant to continue the fight.'[59]

The situation among the Army was no different. General de la Billière flew over Mitla Ridge en route to visiting the division and '. . . saw for myself the legacy of the Iraqis' doomed attempts to escape. More than five hundred burnt-out vehicles lay scattered about where they had tried to circumvent the road block ahead by taking to the desert.' The General observed the exhausted state of the men he had come to visit. 'It was a measure of how exhausted they were that Arthur Denaro, a close friend, who had performed admirably during the battle, almost lost his temper with me in public when I said that I could not yet tell him anything definite about when his regiment would be repatriated.'[60] These were men who had been in the desert for five months. The stress of being subjected to NBC attack at any moment and suffer its grim effects is progressively debilitating. But, seemingly against all odds, they had survived, they wanted to go home to see their wives and families, certainly before any politician could convince others that it would be a good idea to go on to Baghdad.

The mechanics of extending the conflict do not bear thinking about. The whole logistic supply chain would have had to be repositioned if the risk of outrunning the force's sustainment were to be avoided. The coalition garrison for Iraq could only be found from the Americans, the British and possibly the French. Having achieved their mission, the Arab leaders would not only refuse to go into Iraq but might also face local difficulties with their continuing support of the coalition. The manning of the Iraq garrison would have to be found from the warfighters. Time would be required to arrange their relief. Originally, 7th Armoured Brigade was to be replaced by 4th Armoured Brigade. In Britain's case, the placing of two brigades in the desert had brought the British Army of the Rhine to a virtual standstill. The truth is that the British would have had difficulty in achieving the timely replacement of the men of the 4th and 7th Brigades with appropriately trained reliefs. How fortunate the Warsaw Pact never crossed the inner German border.

The principal reason for the failure of the 2003 invasion of Iraq was the inadequate provision for post-conflict resolution. The 1991 coalition forces would have been less prepared than their successors to replace a government which they had removed and would have been obliged to sustain a role as belligerent occupants, including the cost of government, education and utilities. Moreover, the back door out of Baghdad would have been open, allowing Saddam Hussein to slip away to be a thorn in the side of the new army of occupation.

What if the coalition had gone on to Baghdad? The

effects of the 2003 invasion would have been replicated in 1991. To quote General Schwarzkopf, the architect of victory: '. . . the armed forces of western and Arab nations fought side by side against Iraq's aggression and when Kuwait was liberated the western nations withdrew their military forces and went home. For once we were strategically smart enough to win the war and the peace.'[61] Peace is the military's profession. As General Douglas MacArthur once said, 'The soldier above all others prays for peace, for it is the soldier who must suffer and bear the deepest wounds and scars of war.'

The 1990–1 Gulf intervention proved to be an outstanding success on a large scale and had a significant influence upon future events. Undoubtedly a great battle, it was nevertheless different from other battles under consideration. It was legal, it was a UN-sanctioned operation and it had universal support. The 2003 Iraq invasion, by contrast, could not be described as an outstanding success. It was illegal, was declared as such by the UN Secretary-General and suffered almost universal public opprobrium. The unhelpful legacy of the 1990–1 conflict was the impression left in the minds of peace professionals that it had established a new, repeatable norm in the field of international relations. One unhelpful lesson which did arise in the minds of those opposed to the US was that asymmetric means represented the only reasonable prospect of defeating the US and NATO. The ease with which victory had been achieved left the unfortunate, though valid, conviction in Washington's mind that an invasion of Iraq was 'do-able'. To a large part such a justification was based on the massive technological divide between the US and her allies and Iraq. Valuable new and widely distributed technology included night vision and global positioning systems. One technology identified as essential, Identification Friend or Foe (IFF), had still not been issued to British forces in Helmand, partly due to technological difficulties and partly due to cost.

After having made essential cultural adjustments, Saudi Arabia proved to be an excellent host state. Should it be necessary to face up to other real or imaginary regional rogue states, she will doubtless be called upon again to play the same role. The concept of combined American–Saudi command worked well in both a diplomatic and military sense. The crucial role played by General Schwarzkopf as the enabler should not be underestimated. He had excellent relations with the senior military representatives of the force providers and particularly with the allied air commander, General Chuck Horner. Air Force and Naval Air Power made the success of the stunning ground war possible. Coalition air forces had flown 30,000 missions in under two weeks, systematically destroying Iraq's air defences. By the end of January, the coalition controlled the air space over Iraq. 'We were accomplishing exactly what we had set out to do,' explained General Schwarzkopf, 'cripple Iraq's military system while leaving its agriculture and commerce intact and its civilian population largely unharmed.'[62] Coalition air power then focused upon Iraqi ground forces, striking with devastating effectiveness at deployed formations with smart weapons.

The United States' change of fortune in military operations as seen in Grenada was consolidated in the Gulf conflict. In the next chapter we move out of the desert to the complex, urban environment of southern Mogadishu.

5

Mogadishu
1992–1993

'If you liked Beirut, you will love Somalia'

'How could this happen?' demanded President Clinton of his advisers. He had been in his room in California's Fairmont Hotel watching the television news. The date was Monday 4 October 1993. He watched incredulously as he saw Somalians dragging the corpse of a dead American soldier through the dusty streets of southern Mogadishu. The newscasters spoke of two helicopters lost and significant American casualties. Clinton reached for his telephone and rang the White House.

There were two sides to his question. How could it happen that the Administration had been caught unprepared, and what were the antecedents to an operation he described as 'dumb at a minimum to put US troops in helicopters in urban areas where they were subject to ground fire'.[1]

The answer to the first part of the question is shorter and less convoluted than the answer to the second. Those responsible for foreign policy were transfixed by events in Moscow, where Boris Yeltsin was engaged in a see-saw, bloody struggle with political opponents attempting a *coup d'état*. Another significant factor was the new President's apparent lack of interest in foreign policy, his time dedicated almost entirely to domestic policy. The President let it be known that he did not want to be troubled with foreign policy unless there was a crisis. The situation in Somalia had drifted out of Washington's control, becoming the subject of local initiatives. When the Principals of the Administration did involve themselves in Somalia, it was as an exercise in damage limitation rather than within the context of coherent, joined-up foreign policy.

On Tuesday 5 October, forty-eight hours after the attack, the President returned to the White House intent upon regaining control. Already the public was demanding withdrawal from Somalia. Clinton asked David Gergen, formerly President Reagan's Director of Communications – meaning spin – how Reagan was able to overcome the fall-out when in 1983 219 Marines died in a truck-bomb attack on their Beirut barracks – the single most severe loss of life suffered by the Marines since Iwo Jima? The answer was, 'Because two days later we were in Grenada, and everyone knew that Ronald Reagan would bomb the hell out of somewhere.'[2]

The lesson future enemies drew from America's ignominious retreat from Beirut, in a war of choice, linked forcible American disengagement to the inflicting of casualties upon them. Casualty-aversion arose out of the rubble of the Beirut accommodation block in 1983. Ten years later, inflicting casualties in Somalia similarly led to precipitate retreat, the memory of which had a deadening influence upon American military operations from Rwanda to Bosnia.

The answer to the second strand of the Clinton question requires a return to 1960. In that year, Somalia entered the world stage as an independent, post-colonial state arising from the union of British and Italian Somaliland. The outlook appeared promising for the debutant, 'ethnically and linguistically as homogeneous as any country in the world',[3] 99 per cent of its people adhering to the Sunni Islam faith. The weakness lay in the structure of a population, now 7 million strong and divided into six main tribes overseen by fifteen warlords seemingly most content when fighting one another. The principal instruments of war were pick-up trucks, 'technicals', with medium machine guns or light artillery mounted in the back.

Superpower competition in the strategically important Horn of Africa served to fuel domestic confrontation. In 1969, the military dictator Siad Barre seized power, pandering first to the Soviets and then to the Americans in order to maintain pre-eminence, something he managed until overthrown in 1991. The ramifications arising from the demise of dictators have been seen in Yugoslavia and Iraq. Somalia was no different, degenerating into an orgy of killing which in turn exacerbated famine.

The town of Baidoa became a central feature in Somalia's crisis. Siad Barre, the deposed dictator, occupied Baidoa in September 1991 with a view to advancing on Mogadishu. He remained there until April 1992 with 8,000 troops and during that time they ravaged the grain stores. The population of Baidoa is not nomadic and thus starvation came about as a direct consequence of Barre's occupation of the town. Accounts attributing Somalia's problem to anarchy and famine are inaccurate. This had not been a natural but a man-made disaster. General Aideed confronted Barre and in a six-day war forced Barre out of Somalia into Kenya. If the Baidoa incident had not taken place, there would have been no requirement for Operation Restore Hope.

Aideed's power increased to the extent that he became recognized as the leading warlord, a man who over a few short months exposed the paucity not only of the UN's power but also of the superpowers. When the *Washington Post*'s Keith Richburg met Aideed for the first time, 'I thought he was crazy. He seemed neurotic, edgy, his wild eyes constantly shifting, unable to focus . . . he was a ruthless man who cared little about human life and suffering. He was a first-class liar, a cynical role-player, and a wily guerrilla fighter who understood, among other things, the importance of an inflated body count in what was essentially a television war.'4 What was out of the ordinary was the fact that one of Aideed's sons served as a US Marine; not only that, he did a tour of duty in Somalia.

Boutros Boutros-Ghali served as Egyptian Ambassador to Somalia during part of the time Barre was in office. They were friends. Boutros-Ghali also knew the principal challengers for power, the so-called interim 'President' Ali Mohammed and the warlord whose muscle had been responsible for shifting Barre, General Farah Aideed. Neither had the strength to consolidate his power base and, as a consequence, thousands became victims of their power struggle. In Mogadishu alone, 20,000 died during November 1991. Refugees streamed south into Kenya. The Organization of African Unity (OAU) appealed to the UN Security Council to intervene. On 3 December 1991, the Cairo-born Boutros Boutros-Ghali was appointed to the position of UN Secretary-General, replacing the South American Pérez de Cuéllar. On 31 January 1992, the Security Council imposed an arms embargo upon Somalia, called for a ceasefire and requested the Secretary-General to negotiate a political settlement.

UN Security Council Resolution 751 of 24 April 1992, with a non-enforcement mandate, established UNOSOM I (United Nations Operation in Somalia I) which originally comprised fifty unarmed observers. They were ineffective. Warlords ran business in Mogadishu, protecting non-governmental organizations (NGOs) and the aid they wished to distribute for the price of half of that aid. That was a good deal because up to 80 per cent of unprotected food supplies were being lost to armed gangs. More troops were required to escort the humanitarian supplies. Five hundred arrived in September 1992, followed by incremental reinforcements until UNOSOM's strength reached 4,000. UNOSOM found itself unable to control the situation. Moreover, it was held in contempt by the Somalis. Logistics was not appropriate work for warriors. 'It was clear that there would have to be a far larger, far more muscular military action to take Somalia back into the orbit of civilized nations.'[5] Rumours suggested the UN was spending up to $3 million a day on extortion, bribes and payment to gangsters.[6] The warriors recognized that power rested with whoever controlled the food supply. Thousands had been left to starve in order to achieve political advantage or profit. Food was being used politically and economically as both stick and carrot. Drought now intervened to make a desperate situation even worse.

Somalia's tragedy had not struck a chord in the West. Boutros Boutros-Ghali chastized Western leaders for the resources being ploughed into Yugoslavia's 'rich man's war' when no fingers were being lifted to help Somalia. Reporters in Somalia became increasingly active with words and pictures aimed at shaking decision-makers out of their self-enforced lethargy. One such was Keith Richburg, the *Washington Post*'s man in Mogadishu. 'I could force them to care by rubbing their faces in it every day, by showing the pictures of starving kids in front of people's noses as often as I could, in the newspaper seen daily by the White House and members of Congress.'[7] Three thousand people a day were dying of starvation.

Gradually the voice of public opinion, stirred by public conscience, cried out for something to be done. President Bush, defeated in the 1992 presidential election by Bill

Clinton, but prior to Clinton's inauguration on 20 January 1993, responded to an appeal from a coalition of US-based NGOs that something could and should be done. The White House tasked the Pentagon to conduct a feasibility study of launching a humanitarian intervention into Somalia. The planners consulted Lieutenant-Colonel John Abizaid among others who had been involved in Operation Provide Comfort, the provision of humanitarian assistance in northern Iraq. That operation and the proposed operation were seen in the Pentagon as being similar, risk-free tasks. The White House received the Pentagon's 'can-do' appraisal with some surprise. George Bush had been a good president to the military. They believed they 'owed' him. They were much less relaxed at the prospect of Bill Clinton becoming their Commander-in-Chief. A commonly held view considered that Operation Restore Hope would be successfully concluded before the incoming president's inauguration.

On 25 November, Washington advised the UN that if it were the will of the Security Council, America would be prepared to lead a humanitarian intervention into Somalia. On 3 December 1992, by a unanimous vote, the Security Council adopted Resolution 794 couched in the language of the enforcement chapter, Chapter VII, 'to use all necessary means', in much the same way as Resolution 678 had authorized UN action to liberate Kuwait. The Somalia operation became only the fourth occasion the UN had sanctioned a Chapter VII enforcement operation, the previous occasions being Korea, the Congo and the Gulf crisis. A high proportion of the troops in Somalia went there on the understanding that this was a peacekeeping mission, namely the delivery of humanitarian aid. The major flaw in this resolution was to link the objective of the delivery of humanitarian aid with the restoration of peace, stability, law and order, national reconciliation and a political settlement. The certitude of mission creep had therefore been factored in. A secondary though important flaw was to permit the Secretary-General input into the conduct of the operation, notably his insistence upon 'a show of force' and the disarmament of irregular groups as a preliminary to 'post-conflict peace-building'.[8]

Providing the Secretary-General and the Security Council with some visibility in the conduct of the operation arose through concern expressed by some states that during the Gulf conflict, the United States had ridden roughshod over lesser states. America was not going to concede command and control. An editorial in the *Washington Post* explained: 'In circumstances where Americans are supplying the leadership as well as the preponderance of forces, an American President has reason to keep the principal reins.'[9] The end result 'amounted to a slight restriction on the absolute carte blanche enjoyed by the United States in Korea and the Gulf'.[10] To some, this little spat was a matter of insignificance compared with other weightier issues. Smith Hempstone, America's Ambassador to Kenya, questioned the wisdom of tackling head on a xenophobic, heavily armed, anti-colonial, anti-Christian collection of clans susceptible to fundamentalist influences from the north. In a confidential letter to the State Department, he wrote, 'If you liked Beirut, you will love Somalia.'[11]

General Farah Aideed welcomed the news of the American-led intervention. 'We believe the American move will solve our political, economic and social problems. The United Nations has failed to save the unity of Somalia, the reconciliation process and the recovery programme.'[12] It is curious that the Somalis, noted for their xenophobia and virulent racism, were prepared to give the Americans the benefit of a honeymoon period; something they denied their fellow Muslims the Pakistanis, so tainted by association with the UN.

The United States Marines assigned to Operation Restore Hope or United Task Force, Somalia (UNITAF) effected their traditional beach landing, forcing their way through a multitude of TV cameramen forewarned by a White House with an eye on prime-time television viewing. They established their headquarters in the compound of the former US embassy. Not seen on camera were the Marines' coalition partners soon to be at sixes and sevens over their precise role. It is never axiomatic that all parties in a coalition will be bound by common rules of engagement (ROE). The representative armed forces of twenty-eight other states – a total of 37,000 men – which Marine General Robert Johnston was obliged to take under his wing were of the peacekeeping tradition, trained to resort to lethal armed force only in self-defence. The American ROE were no less stringent, only permitting their forces to open fire on someone pointing a weapon at them. There was a host of reasons why this limitation was impracticable and ignored.

General Johnston received no strategic plan from New York. The state of training of his attachments was unknown and many arrived without essential equipment in the belief that a munificent Uncle Sam would provide. The Americans chose not to wear blue helmets and did not bring UNITAF to an end until 4 May 1993 when the operation became redesignated UNOSOM II. The American component of UNITAF had refused to become involved in the disarming of the militias, thereby avoiding friction. The militias had no need to confront UNITAF because the operation was working under a sunset clause, albeit one that had slipped from 20 January to 4 May 1993. They laid low. 'The delivery of food and medicine was protected, and NGOs expanded their relief operations. The result was a dramatic drop in malnutrition and the number of deaths from starvation.'[13] In one of those 'Mission Accomplished' moments, the President welcomed representative soldiers on the White House lawn, congratulating them on a job well done. The truth is that the worst was still to come; so reminiscent of Iraq.

On 26 March, the Security Council acceded to Boutros Boutros-Ghali's recommendation that the transition from UNITAF to UNOSOM II should take place on 2 May, with a view to establishing a peace enforcement operation under UN command.[14] Somalia expert John Drysdale wrote that the Secretary-General's 'ambition was to use chaotic Somalia as an experiment to prove the viability of his new doctrine: that the absolute sovereignty of nations in the post-Cold War era was over and that universal sovereignty had taken its place'.[15] 'This would involve preventing, by force if necessary, the resumption of violence, maintaining control of heavy weapons, seizing small arms from irregular groups, and security communications, including forceful action to neutralize armed attacks.'[16] There were three aspects to this plan (which also involved the continuation of humanitarian support) that patently included its own self-destruct mechanism. The first was Aideed's contempt for the UN; second, the certainty that the warlords would not allow themselves to be disarmed; and third, the failure to grasp that the multi-missions they had set themselves were beyond the capability of the force they had assembled. General Sir Michael Rose, formerly Commander of the UN Protection Force in Bosnia, coined the phrase 'crossing the Mogadishu Line' to represent the move from peacekeeping to enforcement operation.

Conceptually, the change from one state to another, Chapter VI peacekeeping to Chapter VII enforcement, is rarely that stark. There is a wide grey area lying between

Chapter VI and Chapter VII, what former UN Secretary-General Dag Hammarskjöld described as Chapter VI½, in which low-intensity conflict takes place.

Force protection concerns led to an American Quick Reaction Force (QRF) being added to the forces available. The QRF comprised a brigade-level headquarters and a light infantry battalion task force from the 10th Mountain Division with its own combat service support,[17] which brought the total US representation in Somalia to 4,000 men.

The command and control arrangements for UNOSOM II appeared complex. They were, and they would become even more complicated. This issue is a significant theme throughout this account, notably in Delta Force's insistence upon a separate chain of command in order to preserve operational security. The question of unity of command, when Delta Force and the Rangers get into severe difficulty and call for help, only to discover that there is general ignorance of their whereabouts and what they are doing, is also discussed. Observe, for example, how UN-assigned troops were kept out of the loop and then slandered for the delay in executing the rescue of those who had not confided in them.

Command within international coalitions is never absolute. Governments will rarely, if ever, place their armed forces entirely under the command of a non-national. It lies invariably within the gift of national commanders to produce a red card if they believe they are being asked to take action that is, to them, militarily or politically unwise. The British Major-General James Cassells did so in Korea and Lieutenant-General Mike Jackson did so in Kosovo. Governments of a number of European forces deployed to NATO in Afghanistan in 2007 explicitly refused to allow their military to be deployed into dangerous areas or work after dark.

From March 1993 it became evident that opinion with regard to the way forward in Somalia had polarized into a US view and a UNOSOM view. The passive element believed that the UN had no option but to work with the *in situ* leaders and institutions, while the vigorously less passive took the view that Somalia's problems could be addressed only through a fundamental restructuring of the country. Those associated with the latter position included the American envoy Robert Gosende, April Glaspie and Major-General Montgomery. There was a distinct impression that this group was subconsciously pursuing American interests on the assumption that these were also UN interests. Observers in the country at the time reported how some Americans became increasingly irritated by the apparent impertinence of Aideed in 'taking us on', and how the intention emerged to teach him a lesson. If there was a whiff of vindictiveness in the American camp, that was also true of the pinnacle of UN headquarters, New York. Aideed was not insensitive to the American plan to marginalize him, strengthening his resolve not to be factored out. Professor Tom Farer,[18] called in by Boutros Boutros-Ghali to investigate the murder of UN soldiers in June 1993, also commented upon the US/UN attitude to Aideed. He observed the undisguised preference April Glaspie had shown towards Aideed's principal political opponent, Mohammed Abshir, 'and was less than discreet about her hostility to Aideed'.[19] Abshir derived no benefit from the favour bestowed upon him. It was, said one political observer, 'a kiss of death for Abshir'.

The State Department proposed that a retired American admiral, submariner Jonathan Howe, be appointed the Secretary-General's Special Representative as Head of UNOSOM II. 'Our understanding', wrote Boutros Boutros-Ghali, 'was that Howe would serve for a short period and then be replaced by a non-American, but this did not turn out to be the case.'[20] The Secretary-General's choice as his Special Representative had been Ambassador Lansana Kouyate, the Guinean Permanent Representative at the UN. He became Howe's deputy but, having been heavily marginalized, resigned. The State Department responded by appointing a former ambassador to Iraq to act as Howe's political assistant, to manage the interface between the UN and USA. Her name: April Glaspie. John Drysdale described how she was 'undoubtedly a diplomat of extraordinary vivacity and of an inexhaustibly enquiring mind', yet exercised 'policies which ran counter to UN principles of neutrality'.[21]

Washington approved as *de jure* Commander UNOSOM Force a Turkish Lieutenant-General Cevik Bir, identified as someone with whom they could work. The *de facto* UNOSOM Force Commander through whom Washington worked was Bir's deputy, the Commander US Forces in Somalia, Major-General Thomas Montgomery. Montgomery, who commanded the Quick Reaction Force, reported to General Joseph Hoar, Commander US Central Command (USCENTCOM). 'Under such heavy military influence, politics was never in command in Mogadishu while Howe was in charge.'[22]

Admiral Howe was by no means in the same camp as his fellow Americans. He did take important initiatives without consulting New York, although he was essentially the Secretary-General's man. When he took over in Mogadishu from Robert Oakley, President Bush's Special Envoy to Somalia, Marine General Johnston advised him: 'Look, do not take on Aideed. You have to understand who the guy is in this country. You do not need to make him an enemy.'[23] Both Oakley and Johnston, who admittedly had different mandates, were determined not to suffer unnecessary casualties among their force and recognized that they had no choice but to deal with Aideed. Not only was he the most powerful of the Somali warlords but his own power base lay among his Habr Gidr clan in southern Mogadishu, which became the centre of US/UN operations. Much the same words of caution were given to the Admiral by John Drysdale, political adviser to Special Representative Howe: 'we are not just dealing with Aideed; we are dealing with the whole clan'. Drysdale, a Briton, had served with the Somali battalion in Burma during the Second World War and was a Somalia expert and linguist. He found the Americans prepared to heed his advice in the early stages of UNOSOM's life but before long they preferred their own judgements.

A growing problem in Mogadishu was the sparring conducted along the airwaves between the UN's radio and Aideed's radio. The diplomatic Admiral Howe's solution was to recommend to Aideed the establishment of a joint committee to exert control over the radio. Although expressing himself supportive, Aideed did nothing to establish his side of the committee. American hawks intent upon the political reduction of Aideed saw the gaining of control of his radio station as an essential step towards stopping the undermining of UNOSOM. The last thing they wanted was to see the Admiral introduce yet another ad hoc committee. They discussed how best to take Aideed off the air. Their parallel concern was to confront the leakage from the dumps of confiscated arms and ammunition collected by General Johnston during the life of UNITAF. The NGOs appeared the best, or rather easiest, source of weapons. Of the eighty-four weapons seized in one particular month, fifty-four belonged to the NGOs.[24]

On 3 June 1993, General Montgomery sent the Admiral

a copy of a letter that outlined the surveillance plan for the arms dumps, and controls to be placed on Aideed's radio station. Addressed to one of Aideed's minor functionaries, the intention was that it should be delivered on the afternoon of Friday 4 June, which happened to be a local holiday. Howe called Glaspie into his office, five minutes before she was due to depart for Nairobi on holiday. He asked her to give political clearance to the Montgomery plan. It seems that the significance of the plan was misjudged for there was no attempt to call a meeting of political advisers. 'Ms Glaspie was leaving the country so she glanced rapidly at this piece of paper setting out UN intentions and said, "I approve this".'[25] 'If I had seen the proposal,' said John Drysdale, 'I would have acted against it.'[26]

UN planners were well aware of the effect their plans would have on Aideed's camp. In order to minimize the impact of their action, Aideed was given fourteen to fifteen hours' notice or, 'enough time to make the UN appear less aggressive in his eyes but not enough to allow him to move his heavy weapons'.[27] The Pakistani brigadier whose troops were assigned to the mission had discussed the operation a week earlier, when he expressed his reservations as to the political sensitivity of the operation as well as the obvious danger. When the UN's intentions were revealed by two officials to Aideed's head of security, Colonel Qaaybdid, he was astonished: 'This is unacceptable. This is war.'[28]

In pre-emptive strikes, 'on the morning of 5 June, UN Pakistani forces were attacked almost simultaneously in places scattered all across southern Mogadishu: at Brigade head-quarters in the National Soccer Stadium, at two feeding stations and at several strong points as well as at key points along streets connecting these places. But the principal attack fell on Pakistani troops at Checkpoint 89 on 21 October

Road.'[29] Twenty-four Pakistani soldiers were killed and fifty-six wounded, of whom eleven were crippled for life. 'The massacre was ugly, too; dead Pakistani soldiers were disembowelled and some had their eyes gouged out. It was a type of attack particularly vicious for Muslims: mutilate the body, leave it unburied, violate one of the basic tenets of Islam.'[30]

When the news reached their homes in a tightly knit recruiting area in central Punjab, their relatives and friends were dumbfounded. How, they asked, could such a thing happen on a peacekeeping mission? It was not peacekeeping: there was no peace to be kept. Reported Médécins Sans Frontières:

> Blue helmets go on the military offensive without formal recognition as fully fledged combatants subject to the laws of war – laws that impose strict limits on the use of force, irrespective of the cause at stake and the conduct of the enemy . . . The consequences on the ground are disastrous. In Somalia, the UN attacks civilian districts and relief compounds without early warnings or prior evacuation. UN troops prevent civilians from reaching hospital during fighting and prevent aid workers from bringing relief to the wounded.[31]

As indicated earlier, the UN Secretary-General appointed Professor Tom Farer of the American University Washington to investigate the circumstances of the murder of the Pakistani soldiers. His report concluded that the attacks could have been carried out only on Aideed's orders.[32] Boutros Boutros-Ghali determined something had to be done lest it be assumed that representatives of the UN could be attacked with impunity. UN Security Council Resolution 837, passed unanimously, authorized the Secretary-General 'to take all necessary measures against all those responsible for the armed

attacks . . . including to secure the investigation of their actions
and their arrest and detention for prosecution, trial and punishment'. President Clinton declared that a warrant had been
issued for Aideed's arrest. Admiral Howe called for a Delta
Detachment, equivalent in concept to the SAS, to arrest Aideed
so that he might be brought to trial. Washington refused his
request but did despatch four AD-130H Spectre gunships
capable of firing 105-mm–20-mm ammunition round the clock.
Not on the face of it weaponry suitable for a densely packed
city.[33] Nevertheless, they were engaged to destroy Aideed's radio
station while the QRF's Cobras attacked four other targets.
The UN had taken sides and was prepared to use all necessary
means to neutralize Aideed and his followers.

Co-ordinated air and ground attacks in the name of the
UN followed. Aideed's headquarters, his home and that of
his deputy felt the full force of Spectre and Cobra gunfire and
missiles. UN infantry and armour used the massive weight of
covering fire to advance through southern Mogadishu engaging
Aideed's men until the latter chose to break contact. The UN
and US assumed Aideed would be reeling from this attack on
his heartland, but the reverse was true. Some Somalis who
previously might not have given Aideed the time of day flocked
to his support. Howe's idea of offering $25,000 for Aideed's
capture and dropping the reward posters by helicopter was
treated with contempt. 'Aideed had made the city streets so
unsafe that the only place they could tack up their "WANTED"
posters was inside the walls of the fortified embassy compound
itself.'[34] The collateral damage had been severe.

On 2 July, Aideed's men attacked an Italian checkpoint on
another warlord's territory. Three Italians died and twenty-
four were wounded. Half a dozen Somalis working for the UN
propaganda newspaper *Maanta* were kidnapped and killed.
Howe recognized he had to respond to these attacks. The UN

had an unfulfilled aspiration to attack the home of Aideed's security minister, Abdi Qaaybdid. Howe reluctantly decided that the time had come for the UN to approve an assassination, the first-known occasion on which this had occurred. Cobra helicopters put sixteen TOW anti-tank missiles into the building, supplemented by 2,000 rounds of cannon fire. 'No call for those inside to come out and surrender. No warning to vacate the premises. Just a straight-out, bloody massacre.'[35] This had been a clan meeting involving others than militiamen. The Red Cross estimated seventy people had died. Four pressmen rushed from the Al-Sahafi Hotel to cover the attack, only to be attacked themselves by the mob, killed by flailing fists, stones and knives. The attack on Qaaybdid's house is a recognizable tipping point when the Habr Gidr clan became so riled that, forthwith, Westerners entered their territory at their peril.

The tit for tat killing continued. Four military policemen died in an IED attack on their Humvee. Aideed continued to take his attack to the Americans, this time in a mortar attack on Mogadishu airfield which damaged aircraft and injured six. Again the obsessive Howe requested Special Forces to track down and account for Aideed. The 'WANTED' notices did not specify 'dead' or 'alive'. This time his wish was granted. As Les Aspin, Secretary of Defense, recalled, the simple question was, 'If Aideed is killing Americans, even if there's only a one in four chance of catching him, shouldn't you do everything you can?' The question was not intended to be rhetorical but when the military asked Aspin to release armour for use in Somalia, he declined. He would be heavily criticized for that decision but it was entirely logical. To send armour into Somalia at a time when the military were supposed to be lowering their profile in Somalia did not make sense. The Senate Review decided differently. 'US Bradley fighting vehicles and tanks definitely would have been used in the rescue effort, would have allowed a faster rescue and possibly resulted in fewer casualties in the rescue force.'[36]

It is said 'they also serve who only stand and wait'. Delta Force had stood and waited to be called for a long time. The problem with Delta Force was their high profile and low success rate. Their *modus operandi*, going in hard with massive use of firepower, was not thought necessarily the best solution for Mogadishu. Generals Hoar and Powell strongly advised against using the Task Force Ranger in Somalia but had to give way to 'civilian control'. The Iran hostage mission in 1980 had gone wrong. In Grenada, Delta Force had pressed to intervene alone. Considered for employment in Panama to intercept and pick up General Noriega, they gave way to the preferred choice of conventional forces. Delta Force developed a contingency plan to pluck Saddam Hussein out of Baghdad but General Norman Schwarzkopf refused to allow them into his command. The Special Forces were regarded as too gung-ho and difficult to control. 'Special Ops people are hard to deal with. They are arrogant, they overestimate their own capability, and they're very secretive. This all came back to bite them in Somalia. When they needed help, no one knew what they were doing.'[37]

At the time the decision was made to send a significant, high-profile reinforcement to Somalia, the Administration had a policy of reducing the emphasis placed on a military solution in favour of a political one. In his commentary to the Senate Committee on Armed Services on the 3–4 October raid, Senator John Warner said Task Force Ranger should not have been sent to Somalia to capture Aideed:

The overwhelming majority of the military leaders who were consulted regarding this mission advised against it, pointing out this was a very high risk mission with low probability of success. Unfortunately, the significant professional advice of our most senior US military leaders was overruled. The arguments of senior US civilian policy makers, in co-ordination with UN officials, prevailed. The upshot of all this was as described in a 15 July 1993 statement by Senator Byrd: 'Mr President, this Senator and this Senate did not vote to send American forces to Somalia to go from house to house to disarm the participants in internecine battles between Somalian warlords . . . to chase down competing warlords . . . to confiscate weapons. I thought I voted to allow United States forces to go to Somalia and feed hungry people.'[38]

'Unity of command means that all the forces are under one responsible commander. It requires having a single commander with the requisite authority to direct all forces employed in pursuit of a unified purpose.'[39] It was this concept, seen as too restrictive, which had so upset Delta Force in Grenada. Joint Special Operations Command (JSOC) was convinced that they could and would snatch Aideed in the same way that they had intended to snatch Saddam Hussein. They had assembled and trained a force to do just that. The Delta element comprised 130 men of C Squadron, 1st Special Forces Operational Detachment, supported by a reinforced Rangers rifle company. They had a mix of helicopters available from 160th Special Operations Aviation Regiment which included gunships and MH-60 Blackhawk support helicopters. Intelligence, without which there would be no success, was provided by Intelligence Support Activity (ISA). They would dock in with the in-country CIA assets with a view to locating Aideed and his lieutenants.

Commander Joint Special Operations Command, Major-General William F. Garrison, slipped into Somalia a few days before the main body arrived in six giant C5 Galaxy transports. Wearing Lieutenant-Colonel rank, his arrival went unnoticed. Among his many initial tasks was to resolve the difficult question of command and control. Having Garrison reporting through the UN's General Cevik Bir did not attract one moment's consideration. The prospect of Garrison reporting to Montgomery who commanded the QRF was considered but rejected because Montgomery's headquarters was not considered leak-proof. Garrison proposed that he should have a direct link, reporting to the President. General Hoar would have none of that. If Garrison was within his tactical area of responsibility then he was to be answerable to Hoar.

If they came under pressure, the command and control arrangements agreed carried the seeds that could render a difficult operation impossible. All might have been well had not unforeseen problems arisen during the course of the operation. What was agreed was:

> Garrison reported through General Hoar, CinC US Central Command (Tampa, Florida) and General Powell of the Joint Chiefs of Staff (Washington) to Clinton and Secretary of Defense Aspin (Washington) with a co-ordination line to the CinC US Special Operations Command (Tampa, Florida) and Montgomery in US Force Somalia (Mogadishu). It was understood that Hoar would not interfere except in extraordinary circumstances and that Montgomery would be permitted to stop Task Force Ranger missions only if that endangered US or UN troops. In essence, Garrison still worked in the usual special operations 'stovepipe' right into the White House, as the Delta folks preferred. This satisfied JSOC. Unfortunately, it also created one UN and two US chains of command in Mogadishu, about two too many for an operation as fraught with perils as chasing Aideed.[40]

One American officer in the chain of command circus said: 'Unity of command is one of the [American] principles of war. We complained when other units in the UN force referred orders back to their own headquarters, but when it comes to unity of command, we are the worst.'[41]

As soon as kit had been sorted, Task Force Ranger looked for a mission. Unfortunately, Aideed had gone to ground. Nothing had been heard of him since July. What happened next was not in the best tradition of Special Forces but an operation lampooned in the press as having some empathy with the Keystone Kops. At 03.00 on 30 August, a dozen helicopters lifted off from Mogadishu airfield in an operation intended to prove the utility of Special Forces. Before long, helicopters came over a villa in the city, ropes snaked down, first the Rangers to secure the perimeter and then Delta Force in black to enter the building and arrest those inside. Intelligence said Aideed's men were there, yet outside the entrance to the building stood a sign identifying it as the HQ of the UN Development Programme (UNDP). The UN flag flew from the roof of the building. The Delta men apprehended eight UN officials, tied them up and bundled them away. An Irishman and a Canadian showed the soldiers their passports but to no avail. Many of General Garrison's men had not previously been in combat. He did not want them to develop a 'bunker mentality', recognizing the importance 'to get my guys up and operating'. Nevertheless this, the first raid, was confirmed by General Powell as 'an embarrassment and I had to unscrew myself from the ceiling'.

The UN press conference which followed the débâcle proved revealing because it managed to turn the negative into the positive by blurring the issue. The comprehensive intelligence failure was not discussed. Instead, the UN public relations officer described the raid in glowing terms as having been a textbook example of how these operations should proceed, using lightning speed and overpowering force. The fact the operation had been an embarrassing cock-up received no mention. Fortunately no one had been killed, not this time.

The raid had also revealed the presence of Special Forces in Mogadishu. Their effectiveness depended upon high-quality human intelligence (humint) as well as the element of surprise. General Garrison had adequate technical intelligence at his disposal. The surveillance means available allowed him 24-hour visibility of any area of southern Mogadishu he wished, brought to a screen in his HQ. Human intelligence was far less reliable and led to embarrassing situations. In response to Special Forces' humiliation, suppressed mumblings of *schadenfreude* reverberated around the camps of the conventional military. General Garrison recognized that there was just so much embarrassment his unit could take; so much so that the viability of putative operations became subjected to intensive scrutiny, but not quite enough to avoid the episode of Somalia's chief of police, General Jilao.

The next snatch caught General Jilao, head of the Somali police agency and most decidedly a man on the UN's side. They said he was Aideed: he said he was not, so they hit him with their rifle butts. Envoy Gosende gave Washington an account of the Jilao mission:

> We understand that some damage to the premises took place . . . General Jilao has received apologies from all concerned. We don't know if the person mistaken for General Aideed was General Jilao. It would be hard to confuse him with Aideed. Jilao is approximately ten inches taller than Aideed. Aideed is very dark. Jilao has a much lighter complexion. Aideed is slim

and has sharp, semitic-like features. Jilao is overweight and round faced . . . We are very concerned that this episode might find its way into the press.[42]

They persevered and the next time apprehended Aideed's head of finance, Osman Ato, their first success. The conflict grew in intensity, the militia choosing not to draw the Special Forces but to attack UN soldiers and meet each reaction by attacking again. Some Nigerian soldiers were killed. Cobras intervening to relieve Pakistani soldiers killed Somali women and children. Four CNN men died in retaliation, then two Italian soldiers died. All the while, Aideed's men harried the UN and Americans. On 16 September, the airfield came under mortar fire. A Blackhawk took off to act as a spotter, intending to bring down counter-fire. Instead, it attracted fire, an RPG (rocket-propelled grenade) round hitting the aircraft between where the two pilots were seated and the three crew in the back. The Blackhawk fell to the ground. The pilots escaped. The rest of the crew died when the ruptured fuel tanks exploded. This was the first time in Somalia that an RPG had been used against a helicopter. Until then, conventional wisdom assumed that the back-blast effect from an RPG militated against its use in confined areas as a ground-to-air weapon. The helicopter had been travelling – that is, not hovering – making it a far less easy target to hit. Aideed's men had watched Task Force Ranger operations, observing their *modus operandi*; the hover, snaking ropes, fast-roping troops, all of which lasted seconds but long enough for someone nearby with an RPG to get a shot off. 'If you use a tactic twice,' said one of Aideed's colonels, 'you should not use it a third time.'[43]

While the violence escalated, seemingly out of control, questions began to be asked. Should the pursuit of Aideed be continued or should a political settlement be sought?

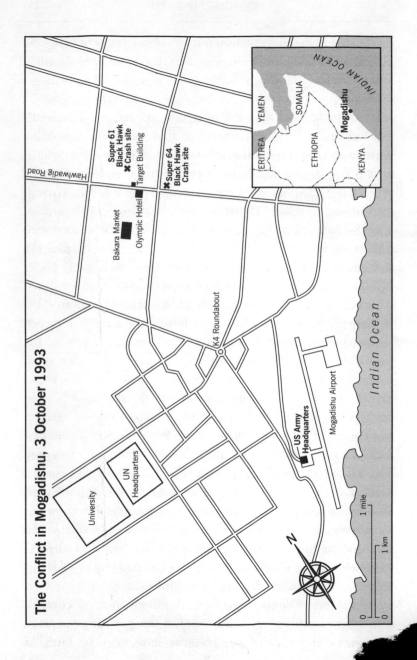

The Conflict in Mogadishu, 3 October 1993

Hawlwadig Road

Super 61
Black Hawk
✗ Crash site
■ Target Building

Super 64
✗ Black Hawk
Crash site

Bakara Market
■ Olympic Hotel

K4 Roundabout

University

UN
Headquarters

US Army
Headquarters

Mogadishu Airport

Indian Ocean

N

1 mile

1 km

ERITREA
YEMEN
SOMALIA
INDIAN OCEAN
ETHIOPIA
Mogadishu
KENYA

Boutros Boutros-Ghali, arguably too literally minded, said he had no option but to persevere because the Security Council resolution had mandated that Aideed be captured and brought to justice.[44] A US official said they thought Boutros-Ghali's problem was inertia, but it was not: 'It was opposition.'[45] He had become part of the problem, as had America's Permanent Representative to the UN, Madeleine Albright, whose language could have applied equally to Iraq a dozen years later: 'The decision we must make is whether to pull up stakes and allow Somalia to fall back into the abyss or stay the course and help lift the country and its people from the category of a failed State into that of an emerging democracy.'[46] Others sought an alternative to what was being conducted as an entirely military solution. Congress was becoming anxious but Bosnia and the role America was to play there became the more important foreign policy question.

While the tooth-sucking went on Stateside, something happened in Somalia to hasten an end to political procrastination. At 13.00 on 3 October, a rare Somali spy reported that Aideed's clan intended to hold a meeting deep in clan territory near to the Olympic Hotel, close to the Bakara Market. Among the two dozen likely to be there would be two of Aideed's principal lieutenants. In order to confirm precisely which building in the warren was to be used, the informer had instructions to drive to the spot, stop and lift his car bonnet, all of which would be seen and identified by a circling helicopter. So nervous was the informer and so indistinct his actions, he was told by his handlers to repeat the process more slowly. Meanwhile the Delta/Rangers members of Task Force Ranger had been warned to stand by for an immediate operation.

Task Force Ranger comprised Delta and Ranger components. Not only did they look different, they also operated differently, the former flexible, the latter having faith in doctrine and recognized drills, so in principle the plans established a clear demarcation between the two representative groups. On the British Operation Barras, 2000, for example, a river separated the assigned Parachute Regiment company from the SAS. The Delta group also comprised Navy and Air Force Special Forces: opportunities for glory tend to be shared. They wore large, black flak jackets, plastic hockey helmets and communicated with one another via wrap-around microphones and earpieces. Older and more mature than Rangers, they wore their hair long. Delta men had a far higher threshold of military skills than the Rangers, most had combat experience and were used to operating independently.

The majority of Rangers would still have been in their teens. Unusually, there were only two Afro-Americans in the reinforced company. They dressed conventionally, desert camouflage, rudimentary flak jackets and helmets. They were not combat experienced. They were however very fit, disciplined and brimming with confidence, their motto being 'Rangers Lead the Way', and they had a virtually Masonic style, greeting one another with 'Hoo-ah'. They were convinced they were the Army's best, many having as their ultimate aim acceptance into Delta Force.

Nineteen aircraft were allocated to the mission, four on surveillance including the Orion C-130. Spectre gunships had not been included. 'This weapon system was never designed to fire into civilian populated areas.'[47] Four of the ruggedized Blackhawks, each with fifteen Rangers aboard, had the task of securing the perimeter around the target building. A fifth Blackhawk carried a team of fifteen Rangers to act as reserve or back-up. A sixth became an airborne command post. The seventh and eighth Blackhawks would take in the twelve Delta men they each carried, whose task it would be to effect the snatch and return with Aideed's lieutenants. The method of entry from the hovering helicopters was by way of the dependable fast-rope. No one minimized the dangers or risks involved in conducting such an operation in broad daylight into an enemy stronghold sufficiently well armed and equipped to defeat it. A mix of eight additional small helicopters, four AH-6 and four MH-6, had the task of bringing fire to bear in the target area and delivering the advance guard. The Americans had the habit of sitting along the side of the helicopters, their feet dangling out, the soles of their boots passing above the inhabitants – for Muslims, an insult.

At 14.14 the QRF's Tactical Operations Centre heard that certain sectors of central Mogadishu would be 'off limits to UNOSOM air and ground force'. The fifty-strong truck-borne Rangers, led by Lieutenant-Colonel Danny McKnight, specified the sectors in which they would be operating. Their mission in their nine Humvees and three 5-ton (5-tonne) trucks was to bring out those taken in by helicopter together with their detainees.

At the same time as Task Force Ranger was preparing to go, activity was also taking place within the American chain of command. Lieutenant-Colonel William David and the first echelon of the QRF mounted in sandbagged Humvees and 5-ton trucks had been placed on stand-by, although the purpose was by no means clear. Montgomery's deputy, Brigadier Greg Gile, reported to Task Force Ranger command post to respond to whatever eventuality presented itself. His own boss had not been taken into the confidence of Task Force Ranger planners. Informing the UN and national components was out of the question, certainly until the operation had been launched. 'The possibility that the Americans could need help from the UN troops had not been considered at all.'[48] At 15.37 QRF, located at the university compound adjacent to the former US embassy compound, heard Task Force Rangers' notification that they were about to launch their 'capture mission'. Eight minutes later, the QRF heard from Task Force Ranger that the cordon and search elements were in place in the area of the Bakara Market, close to the Olympic Hotel.

The five-storey Olympic Hotel could be found on Hawlwadig Road standing proud of surrounding buildings, mostly single-storey dwellings with tin roofs. Another relatively tall building of three storeys stood diagonally across the crossroads from it. This was the target building close to the Bakara Market, a three-minute flight away. The market, in the heart of Aideed's territory, was a UN no-go area. Weeks before the raid was planned, General Garrison penned a memo: 'If we go into the vicinity of the Bakara Market, there's no question we will win the gunfight, but we might lose the war.'[49]

At 15.40 the Delta men and Rangers disgorged from their helicopters, the former into the target building, the latter around it. In twenty minutes, the Deltas emerged with twenty-four prisoners, clinically cuffed in plastic handcuffs. Their transportation to take them out of what they called 'Dodge City' under McKnight pulled in. While in the process of putting the prisoners aboard, Rangers on the outer perimeter radioed that they were coming under pressure. The heavy weight of fire, though badly aimed, would by virtue of its sheer volume lead to casualties. Soon, at 16.10, RPGs were introduced into the fire-fight, not just to seek out ground targets but also helicopters. At 16.15 a Blackhawk – call sign Super 61 – was hit, falling to the ground immediately below, 546 yards (500 metres) north-east of the Olympic Hotel. The loss of Super 61 dramatically changed the nature of the operation, for it was Special Forces lore that friends could not be left on the battlefield or in this case to the mercy of enraged Somalis high on the narcotic weed *khat*, an emboldener of warriors.[50]

The decision to rescue the crew, though understandable and noble, was not on balance wise. They might have perished in the crash. At sea, sailors in a damaged part of a ship are sacrificed by the closing of watertight doors so that the ship survives and others might live.

Garrison called forward the air-mounted reaction team, the diversionary part of the assault force, and sent a warning order to the QRF to be prepared to make rendezvous with Task Force Ranger in the vicinity of the Bakara Markets. One of the small helicopters, an AH-6, was the first to squeeze between the buildings to the crashed helicopter. While the pilot fired into the masses, his co-pilot eased two of the Blackhawk crew out of their damaged machine and into his own craft, now under heavy fire. Bravely, the pilot lifted off safely and returned to the airport. No sooner was he away than the quick reaction Blackhawk hovered over the crash site. Rescuers tumbled down the 3-inch- (7.6-cm-) thick ropes on to the ground while at the same time the Blackhawk was enduring almost unsustainable damage. The pilot struggled to hold the helicopter steady as he hurriedly re-embarked the rescuers whom he carried off back to the airport in the barely airworthy craft.

Rangers who had been part of the perimeter security guard converged on the downed helicopter, arriving moments before Aideed's people. Men firing AK-47s or RPG-7s used women as shields to close on the Rangers. If the women thought they were inviolate they were wrong. As one Ranger said, 'I hosed the guy and the ladies.'[51] McKnight, who had the prisoners and Task Force Ranger wounded aboard his vehicles, received orders to move to the site of the crashed helicopter. To access the Blackhawk, McKnight had to run an unending gauntlet of fire – machine guns and RPGs – to make rendezvous at a location of whose whereabouts he had only the vaguest of ideas, in a tightly packed warren of buildings from which an unending barrage of lead poured into his vehicles. Unsurprisingly, he lost his way. An Orion's crew passed down directions but by the time those directions were relayed by Garrison's HQ the convoy had already passed the point at which they should have turned. Only after passing the Olympic Hotel for the second time was McKnight told to abort and return to base with the prisoners and American wounded. In taking Aideed's lieutenants and their associates into custody, the mission could be claimed to have been achieved.

At 16.49 news came through that a second Blackhawk had been brought down. While seeking to assist Call Sign 61, Call Sign 64's tail took an RPG. Severely damaged, the pilot turned the helicopter homeward towards the airfield in what proved to be an unequal task. The tail gave way, leaving the aircraft to come down, its forward momentum taking it skidding over low roofs until it came to a tangled halt half a mile (0.8 kilometres) south-east of the Olympic Hotel. Three of the four crew escaped the aircraft, only to find themselves facing a baying, heavily armed mob intent upon killing them. Covering and rescuing Americans from two contested crash sites was beyond the resources available to Garrison, who had no option but to call out the QRF – quickly.

By 17.00 all the QRF's company commanders had gathered in the Tactical Operations Centre at the university but remained in the dark as to what was happening. Intelligence and information had not been disseminated to them although they had been listening to Task Force Ranger radio. They were unable to put aircraft above the area of operations because Task Force Rangers retained operational control of the air space. At 17.11 Lieutenant-Colonel Bill David came under Task Force Ranger 'control' and at 17.25 was briefed on the tactical situation. His mission was to deploy with his leading company to the southern crash site to protect the crew and Rangers in that vicinity. The clock was ticking. Away from the airfield, men were being killed. Time was nevertheless required to allow David to brief his own men, men who learned for the first time what had been going on during that afternoon, no more than 3 miles (4.8 kilometres) to their north-west. David, believing the task required more than a company, asked Garrison for permission to take his battalion. Garrison considered it more important to move, to take what he had. There was no time to delay; his own men were in danger.

With the minimum of briefing, at 17.47 David led his small convoy of sixteen heavily armed vehicles out of the airfield behind a packet of six Rangers' vehicles which had rushed on ahead. The QRF had adapted their 5-ton trucks for purpose. They were heavily sandbagged and mounted medium machine guns, resembling enlarged 'technicals'. They did not have the agility of the technicals nor, as soft-skinned vehicles, did they have anywhere near sufficient protection against RPGs. There were armoured vehicles available in Mogadishu but the Americans had none and the UN was blissfully unaware of what was happening because the Americans had no intention of including them in the information loop.

The QRF reaction had been anticipated by the Somalis for no sooner had they left the confines of the airport than they came under heavy fire, but not too heavy to hold up the rescue mission. The convoy crossed the K4 roundabout and it was here, at 17.54, they were checked. Two of the lead Rangers' Humvees were hit and as a consequence the convoy concertinaed. Heavy fire fell upon them from all directions including from an estimated two to three hundred RPGs. Dismounting, the Americans engaged their attackers. David's radio went dead. Those at the command post feared the worst. They could see black smoke rising into the air in the vicinity of K4 and heard the sound of an intense fire-fight. Surprisingly, only two Americans were wounded by the heavy though inaccurate Somali fire. At 18.15 David's radio came back to life to tell those at the airport headquarters that there was no way through. There would have been a number on the radio net that night mortified by the news. At 18.21, Task Force Ranger HQ ordered David to return to base.

The commander of the helicopters heard the news that the QRF had aborted its advance. Below him, he could still see heavy fighting around the crashed Super 64. He found himself in a difficult position. Should he leave the crew of Super 64 to their fate, or make a final attempt – which would probably fail – to lift out the handful of Americans surrounded by hundreds of Somalis? He called forward Super 62 which had on board two Delta snipers. Landing 100 yards (91 metres) from Super 64, the two snipers – Gordon and Shughart – ran forward, their weapons firing as they closed on the mob in a charge reminiscent of the last moments of *Butch Cassidy and the Sundance Kid*. Super 62, now airborne, attempted to cover the Delta men with a curtain of fire, until an RPG went through the cockpit. The explosion knocked out the co-pilot and, on its way through the cabin, the RPG took off one of the air gunner's legs. The pilot turned the badly damaged helicopter for home but it did not make it, crashing in the docks area.

Remarkably, the two Delta snipers reached Super 64 and found the pilot, Warrant Officer Durant, still in his seat. He had a broken leg and a damaged spine and therefore virtually no mobility. They released him, lying him down so that the hull of the aircraft lay between him and the mob. They turned their attention to the surging mob, picking off the assailants. It was an unequal struggle. Both Delta men fell, killed in the massive weight of fire directed at them. The Somalis who found Durant, the sole survivor, did not kill him but took him prisoner, selling him to Aideed. He would appear live as an unwilling agent in Aideed's propaganda releases. The bravery of the two Delta snipers epitomized the high levels of courage on display during this remarkable engagement. They were both posthumously awarded the Congressional Medal of Honor for their bravery, the first such awards since the Vietnam War. For the dead, there had been little by way of dignity, their bodies desecrated by jubilant Somalis.

Malaysia had a mechanized battalion in Mogadishu and the Pakistanis had a number of M48 tanks. Major-General Montgomery made a bid for this armour to attempt to crash through the obstructions to rescue the Americans still engaged in fire-fights close to where they had been dropped off. Brigadier Gile assumed command of the rescue operation, working out the rescue plan with Colonel Casper between 19.00 and 21.00. They ordered Lieutenant-Colonel David to link up with the Rangers at the Super 61 crash site and then return via Super 64 to rescue survivors and pick up bodies. Out in the city, near the Olympic Hotel, the beleaguered Special Forces vented their spleens on 'those bastards', meaning the UN who had thus far failed to rescue them. The changed circumstances threw Delta and Rangers together, one consequence of which was further to complicate command and control by virtue of having two commanders of the same operation.

At 21.30 the vehicle-mounted rescue force was ready and

assembled – over five hours after the first helicopter had gone down. The difficulties inherent in controlling a battalion of Malaysian Russian-built BRDM APCs, a Pakistani tank company, three companies of the QRF and the residue of forty Special Forces was well recognized. The Americans persuaded the Malaysians to allow Americans to take their places in the APCs although the Malaysians insisted their own soldiers drove and operated the vehicles' machine guns. At least their commanders all spoke the same language. Graphics outlining the plan had been distributed throughout the column. At H-Hour – 23.00 – the plan had the tanks leading, followed by the APCs. The intervening period had been set aside for liaison. Prior to H-Hour, problems arose with the Pakistanis and the order of march. At 22.56 the order of march was changed so that two Malaysian APCs would lead, followed by the Pakistani tanks. After reconsideration, the Pakistanis agreed to lead the column and at 23.24 – over seven hours after the first aircraft had gone down – the seventy-strong convoy left New Port for the objectives, covered by attack helicopters.

The Pakistanis showed they were nervous at taking tanks into such confined spaces. Shortly after the convoy began to roll, the driver of the lead tank refused to proceed beyond a Pakistani-controlled checkpoint. An American urged him forward. Soon after, the Pakistani company commander intervened, refusing to allow his tanks to lead any further. The Malaysians were still confident to lead but in so doing took the wrong turning, thus again exposing the Pakistani M48s as the lead vehicles. The tanks reluctantly edged forward towards the sound of battle but then, a quarter of a mile (0.4 of a kilometre) short of the Rangers' outer perimeter, they declined to advance further. The Delta and Ranger defenders of the Super 61 area could hear their long-awaited rescuers' progress according to the increasing noise of the approaching gunfire. With the onset of darkness, the by now tentative Somalis were unable to consolidate their success. For their part, the Americans were unable to dominate the area. Their desire to travel light on what was assumed to be a short in-and-out mission meant their night observation devices had been left behind in their hangars. Their water bottles were also empty.

For a so-called Operations Other Than War (OOTW), the situation on the ground seemed exceedingly warlike. But why was this happening to them, pinned down by Sammies? They were, after all, the cream of America's fighting machine. They should not be in this intolerable position. Their rules of engagement had not survived the first engagement. Weapon and ammunition-carriers were targeted, as was any figure who appeared to be an opponent. The actions of their light heli-copters, gunning and rocketing assemblies of Somalis, served to emphasize the incongruity of rules of engagement confined to those who pointed weapons at them. These helicopters, which introduced *Armageddon Now* to downtown Mogadishu, were key force multipliers enabling the Americans to stay in the fight. The QRF edged forward and at 01.55 made contact with the Rangers surrounding Super 61. Another company peeled off for Durant's Super 64 crash site but found neither the living nor the dead. Once the rescuers regained the seats on which they had travelled out in order to return back to base and room had been found for the dead and wounded, there was no room for anywhere near the number that had survived the fourteen hours of battle. To them fell the indignity of having to run after the vehicles of their rescuers.

When the news came through, President Clinton, for the first time, understood that being Commander-in-Chief attracted responsibilities. He had difficulty, anxiety even, in accepting that the responsibility for the loss of those eighteen American lives was his. Recognition of this fact depressed him: 'He really needed some hand holding.'[52] What would have hit hardest, if true, is the report that at the Medal of Honor ceremony, the father of the deceased Sergeant Randy Shughart told President Clinton he was not fit to be Commander-in-Chief.[53]

Casualty-aversion can flow downward from the top and the consequences of what happened in the streets of southern Mogadishu impacted upon the 1994 belated deployment into Rwanda when, long after the conflict had ended, a visitor to the US headquarters in Goma saw the declared number one goal to be 'no casualties'. 'Many recall the curious juxtaposition between unarmed NGOs going anywhere they wanted and the armed-to-the-teeth [American] military having to be in before dark while not being allowed in the refugee camps at all.'[54] Similarly, ground troops would not be permitted a role in the Bosnia intervention. The President told the UN that in the future, if they expected the USA to say 'yes', they should learn to say 'no'. Washington issued a new set of rules for intervention entitled 'The Clinton Administration's Policy on Reforming Multilateral Peace Operations', alias Presidential Decision Document 25 (PDD 25). Boutros Boutros-Ghali declared the new rules to be 'so tightly drawn as to scope, mission, duration, resources and risk that only the easiest, cheapest and safest peacekeeping operations could be approved under them and many current UN operations could not'.[55]

In American politics, someone has to be identified as being blameworthy for an action that has been politically or militarily embarrassing. Uppermost in the blame game were Clinton's foreign policy advisers. He felt he should have been consulted about the Special Forces mission but the disastrous mission had been their seventh. Clifton Wharton, the Secretary of State's deputy, was sacked, as was the US envoy in Somalia, Robert Gosende. Secretary of Defense Les Aspin had been pencilled in for a 20 January 1994 retirement but served on longer because of administrative problems. The UN envoy Admiral Jonathan Howe could not be sacked by the American authorities despite his being blamed for much of what had gone wrong in Mogadishu. However, the Admiral had been appointed by Washington. When he visited the capital on UN business, he attended official briefings while his UN colleagues waited in the outer office. The solution to the problem of how to demonstrate the loss of confidence in Howe was to call upon the Special Envoy Robert Oakley in a unilateral move bypassing Howe. The UN's authority had been undermined. An angry Boutros Boutros-Ghali said to Albright: 'You have already confused the military situation: now you want to confuse the diplomatic situation too.'[56]

In October 1993, Oakley returned to Somalia to resume the appointment of political controller which he had held in December 1992. His mission was to 'engage Aideed in an effort to make peace'. America's armed forces became non-operational. Although they were reinforced to provide force protection, their new mission was to sit on their hands 'under American command' in their compounds until March 1994 so as not to appear to have been drummed out of Somalia by Aideed. The emphasis placed on 'under American command' was disingenuous, as if to suggest that American forces had not previously been entirely under American command. When America abandoned UNOSOM II, others in the coalition were quick to follow suit.

On 9 October, Aideed agreed to a ceasefire, releasing his Delta captive, Warrant Officer Durant, in exchange for his lieutenants and their associates. It had therefore been a pointless operation. In November, thirty 71-ton M-1A1 Abram tanks and forty-two Bradley Fighting Vehicles arrived in Mogadishu. As a matter of prestige, the new Task Force commander, Major-General Carl Ernst, wanted to take the militia on. He was strongly discouraged from doing this by General Bir. Neither Oakley nor Howe would have been impressed by the idea.[57] In December, the Americans provided Aideed with transport to Ethiopia to participate in a peace conference. Conscious that forty-two Americans had died through the actions of this man, the apparent pandering to him caused a storm of outrage in America.

The truth was, the military had not been provided with the force structure required to operate in UNOSOM II against a well-organized urban enemy. The American fatalities numbered much the same as in another under-resourced venture – Goose Green. A military victory in Mogadishu, however, was never going to be possible. Those who do not learn from history have little prospect of success. Far too often, military commanders underestimate their enemy and, in their planning, work against themselves by eschewing the simple in favour of the difficult and unmanageable. Aideed died in 1996. On a number of occasions, the President asked: 'Why the hell were we chasing after him?'[58]

In testimony before the Senate Committee on Armed Services, the father of a serviceman killed in Somalia said:

I shared with President Clinton my dismay at the October 3 raid after he had already obviously embarked on a course of diplomacy. I asked him to confirm what I had heard and was pretty sure it was true that President Carter had met with Aideed and had in fact reported back to the President that truly a diplomatic solution was the only solution, and he confirmed that. So I said, well, Mr President, if that is the case, why the October 3 raid?

And the President shared my dismay. He said when he got the reports of the casualties, that was his first question: what in the world are they doing conducting a raid? That is not the environment in which we should be operating today. We should in fact be seeking a diplomatic solution. So that was enlightening for me, that the President shared my dismay and basically said he thought that was the key question that had to be addressed.[59]

In the blame game that followed Somalia, it was the more sinned against than sinning UN that the Americans chose to blame for the fiasco in Mogadishu. Les Aspin told the President that most of the blame fell on 'a UN command and control structure that had been unable to rush well-equipped troops to the Rangers' rescue'.[60] Why did the Secretary-General not react to such a blatant untruth? 'The UN exists to help member countries to solve their problems,' he said. If attacking the UN helps President Clinton with Congress, 'I am not going to answer back.'[61] Perhaps the Secretary-General had his eye on a second term. In that respect he would be disappointed. America had the measure of him. As Albright is reputed to have said, 'I will make Boutros think I am his friend; then I will break his legs.'[62] James Rubin, described as Albright's 'tart tongued janissary', explained how 'it was unfortunate that Boutros-Ghali did not have the skills to successfully manage the most important relationship for any Secretary-General which is smooth cooperation with the United States'.[63] 'The UN', continued Rubin, 'can only do what the US lets it do.'[64]

Among the most reprehensible features of the Somalia experience had been the absence of honesty among the ranking American political players. They used the UN as a convenient scapegoat to shield their own inadequacies and keep their ambitions and reputations intact. They found no difficulty in justifying their actions to the domestic body politic, inclined to see in the Somalia experience the confirmation of all their prejudices. A senior adviser later admitted: 'They decided to blame the UN for Somalia policy without realizing this would make the President look inattentive and wouldn't wash.'[65] It was as a direct result of this failure of moral courage that in future global crises, when leadership was anticipated and looked for, it was not there.

The opportunity to rehabilitate the failed state that is Somalia was squandered. Instead, Somalia is destined to stagger from crisis to crisis. The tragedy is that there is no prospect of there being a substantive effort to resolve its agony.

The Mogadishu experience cast its long, dark shadow into Bosnia, where NATO had gone outside its Cold War borders of the Central Region. America exerted her influence over NATO to ensure NATO did not adopt a ground role except, as a last resort, on a rescue mission. America's interest was political, to ensure that no American ground forces deployed into Bosnia. This did not mean that there were no NATO states with a troop presence in Bosnia; it was just that their presence came under UN not NATO auspices. Thereby ran a schism between the United States on one side and the Europeans including the UK, France and the Netherlands, on the other. The Europeans endeavoured to abide by the rules of peacekeeping; to use lethal force only in self-defence, to act impartially and with the consent of the warring parties. America's positive support for the Bosniacs and her overwhelming desire to bomb the Serbs created division between her and the Europeans. Britain was engaged in the largely unreported conflict in the safe haven of Gorazde, an operation which confirmed the concept of peacekeeping in such circumstances to be irredeemably flawed.

The concept of unity of command had been at its self-defeating worst in Mogadishu. To simplify what we saw, there was the Special Forces chain of command, the American non-Special Forces chain of command and the UN, all endeavouring to work in the same small area of southern Mogadishu, with disastrous results. The battle taught us that the Americans had little experience of fighting in an urban environment and had made the fatal mistake of grossly under-estimating the determination of their opponents. We must remember that the arrival of foreign troops intent upon lethal conflict on the home territory of opponents determined to defend that territory will, as often as not, presage a potent reaction. We saw that in Iraq and to a lesser extent in Afghanistan.

American tactics in Fighting in Built-up Areas (FIBUA) – the US call it Military Operations in Urban Terrain (MOUT) – were tentative. To take one example, there was the extended debate as to whether armour was appropriate to fight in an urban environment. When the decision was taken to send armour to Mogadishu, the political process was so far advanced as to preclude its use. The British had for a long time believed tracked vehicles were inappropriate in urban areas. In 1972 Londonderry, where the IRA set up barriers to denote no-go areas, the engineer-armoured vehicles employed on Operation Motorman to remove the barriers had 'Royal Engineers' painted along each side and their stubby 165-mm demolition guns had been swung through 180 degrees to point rearward. The British did employ Chieftain main battle tanks in Basra, as the Americans used Abrams in Fallujah, albeit in a city from which the non-combatants had fled. Since much of future war is increasingly to be fought in an urban world, it behoves all future combatants to establish an appropriate, timely doctrine for Operations in Urban Terrain. New anti-armour weapons, a number developed in Iran, mean that tracked vehicles cannot be employed with impunity in these areas.

General Rose wrote: '. . . the fact of war-fighting objectives by UNPROFOR [in Bosnia] would take the mission across the Mogadishu Line, with potentially the same catastrophic results as had occurred in Somalia in 1993'.[66] The UNOSOM II mission in Mogadishu was a Chapter VII enforcement operation, the UN having taken sides against General Aideed's tribe, against whom they were authorized to use force. UNPROFOR on the other hand was a Chapter VI peacekeeping mission in which the use of force was confined to self-defence. An attempt to interpret Mogadishu from Bosnia does not involve a like-for-like comparison. The theory is somewhat removed from the actuality. The significance of Mogadishu for the Americans is that it represented a return to the bad times prior to Grenada.

It will be seen, in the next chapter, how in Bosnia the USA adopted their nugatory, pro-Islam policy in accordance with the prevailing foreign policy. As would be seen, no benefit would accrue from their support of the Bosniacs and Iranians. The American anti-Serb line should not have involved the active use of force, for which there was no mandate. Similarly the British and French were anti-Serb by virtue of their sustainment of the Bosniacs. Despite Mogadishu being an enforcement operation, it did not experience bombing and shelling such as that of the Serbs by NATO supporting a peacekeeping mission. In Gorazde, as will become clear, there was no peace to be kept.

6

Gorazde
1995

'The Serbs will not dare to harm any
of my Royal Welch Fusiliers.'

The distinguished diplomat Sir Anthony Parsons wrote, prior
to the Iraq War: 'I cannot recall any operation which has
generated such an intensive, continuing and wide-ranging
public debate and so strong a day-to-day interest as the civil
war which erupted in Yugoslavia in June 1991, first in
Slovenia and Croatia and thereafter in Bosnia-Hercegovina.'[1]
The public became conscious of the reality that they were
witnessing a new type of post-Cold War conflict – one that
was extremely complex. Much has been written on the strategic infantry and artillery battles around Sarajevo, a city
enduring the first post-Cold War siege, principally because
of its importance and because the press were there. Similarly,
much has been written of Srebrenica, not because the press
were there but because of the grotesque slaughter of more
than 7,000 unarmed Muslims by Serbs in July 1995.
Comparatively little has been said about the stand-off between
the UN, NATO, Serbs and Muslims in Gorazde.

Sarajevo, Gorazde and Srebrenica, and others declared
as 'safe areas', were components in a complex political,
diplomatic and military experience that signified a collapse
in the nature of conflict. In reality, the 'safe areas' were among
the most unsafe places in the northern hemisphere. The Bosnia

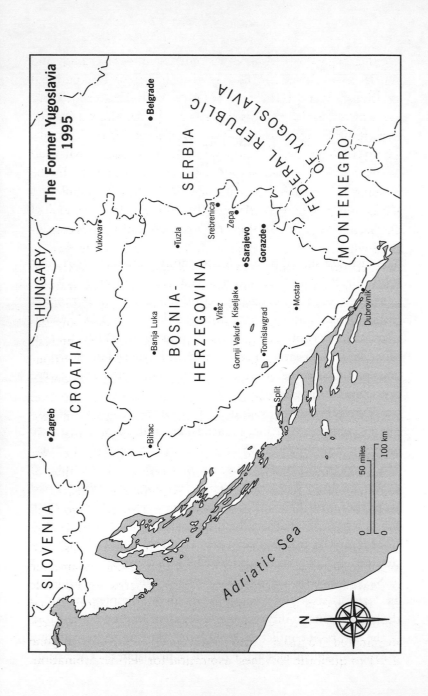

The Former Yugoslavia
1995

HUNGARY

SLOVENIA

CROATIA

•Zagreb

•Bihac

•Banja Luka

BOSNIA-
HERZEGOVINA

Vukovar•

•Belgrade

SERBIA

•Tuzla

Srebrenica•

Zepa•

•Sarajevo

Gorazde•

Vitez•
Gornji Vakuf• Kiseljak•
△Tomislavgrad

•Mostar

FEDERAL REPUBLIC
OF YUGOSLAVIA

MONTENEGRO

Split•

•Dubrovnik

Adriatic Sea

50 miles

100 km

0

0

N

conflict begged questions of the current understandings and ideals respective states had of the theory of international relations. At the heart of the military and political endeavour were the multiple attempts made at nation-building in Bosnia, something which was made doubly difficult due to the multiplicity of interested nations involved, Bosniacs, Croats and Serbs, and the United States' patronage of one side. In the ensuing mêlée there occurred one of the largest population shifts and bloodiest battles seen in Europe since the end of the Second World War. Potential interventionist states considered whether it was in their national interest to intervene in a failed state and responded accordingly, unfortunately not all pulling in the same direction. International organizations similarly considered their positions. A seemingly redundant NATO tested the question of its future by examining engagement out of area, beyond its traditional area of interest. Europe persisted in the search for a meaningful role. Tensions soon arose between Europe and the USA, principally due to the USA's refusal to put men on the ground, a situation reversed in 2008 Afghanistan. Ethnic cleansing re-emerged as a cultural, political and military tool. Here were the early indications of Muslim radicalism on the march with the most improbable of sponsors – the United States – at the time of the appearance of new, post-Cold War military threats.[2]

Before his death in 1980, President Tito of Yugoslavia created for his multi-ethnic country a plan to establish six administrative areas which cut across ethnic boundaries, each republic providing a president in turn. Belgrade became the capital of Serbian territory, yet a third of Serbs lived outside the designated Serb republic. Assuming the international community had enough concerns elsewhere, the Serb-dominated Yugoslav Army intervened in Slovenia in June 1991 to quell the Slovenes' aspiration for self-determination.

By September, the reality dawned upon the Yugoslav Army that their task was hopeless.[3]

Ethnic groups accordingly made immediate claims to the international community to be recognized as independent states and for admission into the UN. Slovenia easily passed the requisite tests, Croatia less so, and the more difficult matter of Bosnia-Hercegovina went to a referendum. The Serbs, 32 per cent of the population, boycotted the election, giving a free run to the majority (44 per cent) Muslim Bosniacs. Anthony Parsons wrote scathingly of the EC for its failure to point out to the Bosnian Muslim leader, Alia Izetbegovic, the political facts of life, that 'it was madness to proceed to independence on the basis of a constitution rejected by a powerful minority which controlled virtually all the heavy weaponry in the country and had the military backing of the JNA [Yugoslav Federal Army] itself'.[4] Some believe that Izetbegovic deliberately opted for a referendum, fully aware of the consequences and hoping for international intervention even at the risk of losing a large number of his people. To add insult to injury, the UN withdrew Serbia's right to represent the Federal Republic of Yugoslavia in New York (having welcomed Slovenia and Croatia), insisting that Belgrade reapply for membership.

Serbia would not be entirely disadvantaged. UN Security Council Resolution 713, adopted on 25 September 1991, endorsed an earlier imposed EC arms embargo on the Balkans, thereby favouring the Serbs and the Yugoslav Army enormously. 'The Muslims did have very few weapons,' commented the UN Secretary-General, 'while the Bosnian Serbs had access to the vast resources of the Yugoslav People's Army and the Bosnian Croats were being armed by Croatia.'[5] Continual images and reports of ethnic cleansing finally provoked an international response and February 1992 saw the formation of a 13,000-strong Chapter VI UN Protection Force (UNPROFOR). UNPROFOR's original mission was in Croatia to protect the Croatian Serbs in the Krajinas and two other areas. These were called UN Protected Areas (UNPAs).[6] Nora Beloff famously described the architects of such a plan as 'the do-something-know-nothing brigade'. Sarajevo, home of the Bosniac Government, hosted the UN Forward Headquarters in Bosnia-Hercegovina, the original mission of which had been the escort of humanitarian convoys.

In May 1992, UN Resolution 752 set in train self-defeating and disastrous mission creep. Humanitarian relief convoys were now to be protected by UN armed escorts and peace-keepers were expected to disband and disarm irregular forces, in effect going beyond action permitted for Chapter VI peacekeeping operations, crossing what would become known as the Mogadishu Line. The first London Conference of 26 August 1992 set out to divide responsibilities between the UN and EC. Cyrus Vance and David Owen, co-chairs of the Steering Committee, were set the task of formulating a UN/EC peace plan.

Deterioration of the security situation around Sarajevo airport led to the UN reinforcing Resolution 752 with a no-nonsense Resolution 770 phrased in the language of Chapter VII of the Charter, authorizing states to take 'all measures necessary' to deliver humanitarian relief. However, this was soon replaced by Resolution 776 which confined UNPROFOR to the use of positive Chapter VI measures. The message to the Bosnian Serb military commander, Ratko Mladic, was that the UN had no intention of being sucked into Bosnia's civil war. States did however reinforce UNPROFOR's strength of blue beret, white vehicle-borne peacekeepers. Lieutenant-General Sir Michael Rose, commander of 22 SAS in the Falklands and now UNPROFOR's regional commander in Sarajevo,[7] reported the remark of one of his soldiers: 'If you want to go to war, you do not do so in white painted vehicles.'[8] In September 1992, Britain increased her presence to an under-strength brigade, 11th Armoured Brigade. The UN Secretary-General, Boutros Boutros-Ghali, commented, 'I believed that the UN Protection Force was being used by Europe and the United States to show that "something" was being done about the hell that Bosnia had become, as well as a scapegoat for the failure to stop the horror altogether.'[9] By November 1992, half of Bosnia-Herce-govina's people, 2 million, had become refugees and 17,000 had been killed.

There was little discernible commonality in the aims and approaches of the leading Western allies. Russia, a shell of her former self, remained an unknown quantity but supported her fellow Slavs, the Serbs. The British and French did their utmost to remain in impartial support of the UN, but since that meant protecting aid essentially destined for the benefit of the Bosniacs it represented a strange form of impartiality. The United States did not pretend to be impartial. Such a policy, at variance with that adopted by allies, left a serious gap, allowing the Bosniacs to play America off against the UN. America's regional foreign policy goals were to contain Iraq and Iran and to be seen to be supportive of Islam. Following President Clinton's inauguration on 20 January 1993, his Principals Group advising him on the Balkans was unashamedly pro-Bosniac, anti-Serb. Indeed, a central plank of Clinton's election campaign had been the lifting of the arms embargo against the Bosniacs. The subject was so polit-ically uncontentious that it was shared by the Republicans and the press. America's support for General Rose began to wane towards the end of his tour as Washington regarded him as pro-Serb.

Among those in the Principals Group most vehemently opposed to the Serbs was the former Marie Korbelova, born in Prague in 1937 of Czech parents of Jewish extraction, now America's Permanent Representative at the UN, Madeleine Albright. In view of her early experiences in modern history, her prejudice against dictatorial figures is understandable, but in that prejudice lay inconsistency. Washington supported Croatia's dictator Franjo Tudjman, a man as evil as Serbia's Slobodan Milošević. Al Gore had as his principal political advisor, Leon Furth, a Croat. Therein lies a lesson of Balkan Wars painted in black and white yet far removed from the truth. Misha Glenny wrote: 'Tudjman almost certainly did not care that he was a monster because, unlike Milošević, he was our monster.'[10] America had as her local aim the uniting of Croats and Bosniacs into a new federation to counter-balance and confront Bosnia's Serbs.

The Albright solution to the Bosnian Serb problem became known as 'lift and strike', meaning lift the arms embargo and strike from the air at the Serbs laying siege to Sarajevo. America's Secretary of State, the dapper Warren Christopher, attempted to persuade London, Paris and The Hague to support a bombing campaign against Bosnia's Serbs. They refused. To them, to have acquiesced would have escalated the conflict, leaving their lightly armed peacekeepers on the ground at the mercy of well-armed Serbs and leading to the collapse of humanitarian support to the Bosniacs.

Clinton blew hot every time he saw on his TV images of excesses in the Balkans, only to cool with the realization that there were no sensible options available to him. He resisted his advisers' attempts to persuade him to ignore British and French concerns by bombing the Serbs unilaterally. He had no wish to risk embarrassment. He knew only too well that the long, dark shadow of Mogadishu meant he could not, and did not wish to, put American forces into Bosnia. At a time when UNPROFOR's strength had risen to 27,000, Lieutenant-General Barry McCaffrey testified to the Senate that it would take 120,000 troops to make humanitarian assistance in Bosnia work.[11] As a contribution, Washington agreed to an action of last resort, guaranteeing the availability of American forces to assist with the extraction of UNPRO-FOR should that prove necessary.

NATO had a presence, feeling its way in a new environment of out-of-area operations. Unsurprisingly, NATO followed America's lead in refusing to put ground forces into Bosnia. Washington used her pre-eminent position in NATO to pressurize the membership into first agreeing to the no-fly zone and then the exclusion zones around safe areas. Instead, there were blockading Naval ships on Sharp Guard, unseen, out to sea in the Adriatic, and 200 aircraft enforcing Oper-ation Deny Flight, the no-fly zone, but available on call for close air support or for the bombing of Serb targets. 'Dual Key' described the system of aircraft-tasking, requiring the agreement of the designated representative in both NATO and the UN before air–ground attacks could be confirmed. Those allies who had troops on the ground insisted that UN commanders must have control over the use of NATO; hence NATO decided on the Dual Key.

Intelligence is worthy of examination here. As late as 1995 the UN regarded the spying or investigation of member states as contrary to the spirit of the Charter. States which had their own intelligence services deployed, or who accessed NATO intelligence, almost universally refused to pass on intelligence to the DPKO, insisting this was a national prerog-ative. Speaking of UN headquarters, one intelligence officer said: 'You know how it is in this place. If you even think about something in this building, it is known in 189 capitals the next day.'[12] At the tactical level, where The Royal Welch Fusiliers would work, the British were assessed as receiving 98 per cent of their intelligence 'primarily from their own soldiers on patrol'.[13] At the strategic level, the most profound intelligence failure was said to have been the absence of a mole within General Ratko Mladic's headquarters. Some have their doubts that there was no mole there. The allies are said to have had no idea of his future intentions. Within the broader working environment of the coalition of the selectively willing, national prerogatives were exercised and frequently details of important measures were not passed to the closest of allies. Such coyness is understandable in a situation where states were deliberately ignoring UN resolutions as a matter of policy.

Professor Cees Wiebes, engaged by the Dutch government to investigate the causes of the fall of Srebrenica and the subsequent massacre, became conscious of skulduggery in the surreptitious arming of the Bosniacs contrary to the prevailing arms embargo. As a consequence, he investigated the situation and published his findings in a sensational book, *Intelligence and the War in Bosnia, 1992–1995*, part of a larger study (7,500 pages) commissioned by the Dutch Government. Given the United States' policy to monitor and contain Iran, it came as a surprise to discover that during 1992 to 1996 in Bosnia, the United States approved Iran's arming of the Bosniacs and their provision of 'advisers'. Moreover, Mujahidin fighters were brought into Bosnia from a number of Osama bin Laden's training camps in Afghanistan.[14] The CIA was aware of the blatant supply of weapons to the Bosniacs by Iran Air Boeing 747s operating through Zagreb, which 'creamed off' a part of the cargo. In a three- to five-month period in 1993, approximately 35,000 Muslim soldiers had been armed and equipped by Iran and

Turkey.[15] From this point, the trade temporarily dried up when Bosniac forces unwisely turned their attention on the Croats.

On 27 April 1994, Croatian officials approached America's Ambassador in Zagreb, Peter Galbraith, to enquire what the Administration's attitude would be to reopening the Iranian arms supply channel. Galbraith replied that he had no instructions, meaning 'go-ahead'.[16] Clinton attributed the Mogadishu fiasco to his having been kept out of the information loop. He could not argue the same case here. The United States was actively supplying the Bosniacs with weapons by 'Black Flights' – C-130s with no identifying markings. British Intelligence sources observed new equipment arriving in the Muslim 2 Corps area, 'shoulder launched SAMS (possibly SA-16) . . . may be significant when linked to sightings of SA-7 Grail in Maglaj area and a possible Stinger in the Gorazde area. Reportings of these lightweight high value weapons may support conjecture about recent unexplained flying activity at Tuzla.'[17] There was no apparent need to allow Iran greater influence in the Balkans. Deputy Secretary of State Strobe Talbott and National Security Advisor Anthony Lake discussed the matter with President Clinton on board Air Force One on 27 April 1994. The Administration had expressed its concerns regarding Iran's sponsorship of radical groups and terrorists and for arming Hezbollah in Lebanon and Hamas on the West Bank.[18] Nevertheless, the decision was made aboard Air Force One, 'to give a green light to the arms supplies from Iran to Croatia'.[19] Between 1992 and 1996 the United States is said to have approved the arming of the Bosniacs by Iran as well as the provision of advisors. By the time in March 1995 when The 1st Battalion The Royal Welch Fusiliers (1RWF) arrived in Gorazde, Iranian arms cargoes were landing in Zagreb three times a week.[20]

There may have been over 2,000 Mujahidin who came to Bosnia from Yemen, Algeria, Chechnya and Afghanistan. In April 1993, as a declaration to prevent the Bosnian Serbs seizing Srebrenica, the Security Council declared Srebrenica a 'safe area' to be spared armed or hostile acts. It was the refugees who had crowded into Sarajevo who needed to be made safe, not the place itself, something which was also true of Gorazde and Zepa. Some weeks later, Sarajevo, Tuzla, Zepa, Bihac and Gorazde were added to the list of safe areas. Security Council Resolutions 824 and 836 were not what they appeared to be. They offered no guarantees, being explicit in the words used, not to *defend* or *protect* but to '*deter* attacks against the safe areas'.[21] The idea of 'safe areas' represented a case of collective flight of fancy for 'it can only work if all the parties to a conflict respect the agreement'.[22] There were no maps or geographical boundaries delineating the areas, no disarmament, no authorization to search houses and barns for weapons (the USA resisted this in the Security Council). Efforts were now made to find UN forces to occupy the 'safe areas' as deterrent forces. The 'safe areas' all had one thing in common: they were Bosniac havens. No effort was made, for example, to make the Serb Krajina a 'safe area' – essentially, American policy depended upon its removal in order to form a viable Croat-Bosniac state in Bosnia.

The search for peace and agreement in Bosnia continued, hopes raised and hopes dashed, one step forward, two steps back, a process complicated by the presence of two major international organizations, the UN and NATO/USA, which rarely saw eye to eye with each other. That is not to say there were no positive achievements. Within two weeks of taking up his post as Commander UNPROFOR in Bosnia, General Rose was obliged to use strong-arm tactics in the crisis of a 5 February 1994 mortar attack on a Sarajevo market, forcing the withdrawal of heavy weapons from a 12-mile (20-kilometre) radius around Sarajevo airport. The big guns within the total exclusion zone (TEZ) fell silent for the first time in almost two years. The images and effects of precision smart-bombing during the recent Gulf conflict would have still been indelibly printed on military minds. It should be remembered, however, that these weapons had, for the most part, been delivered from a great height, in the clearest of skies, upon relatively easily identifiable targets, at little risk to the aircraft or pilot. It could be argued that insufficient recognition had been given to the Serbs' sensitivity to being bombed. The concern for the effect reprisals would have upon UNPROFOR ground operations was probably overstated. The indigenous forces were more often than not in a strong position to take lightly armed peacekeepers hostage whenever the mood took them. Now held in check in Sarajevo, the Serbs turned their attention elsewhere, to Gorazde.

The message the 9 February airport agreement conveyed to the Serbs was that in a controlled environment they could not achieve total military victory over the Bosniacs. They had no option but eventually to agree to a political settlement. In March 1994, however, the Serbs still occupied 70 per cent of Bosnia-Hercegovina. The time had come to consolidate. In 1992, in a rare reversal, the Serbs in Gorazde had been driven out, not least by the increasing number of Bosniac refugees from other towns. Honour and face required the restoration of Gorazde to Serb possession before the final political solution and before the military forces of the Croat-Bosniac Federation gained any more ground. The Serbs were enraged that the 'safe areas', notably Gorazde and Srebrenica, were being used openly as launch pads for

The collection of Argentinean Prisoners, including wounded, at Goose Green.

Lieutenant-Colonel H. Jones, VC.

Sir Paul Scoon, Maurice Bishop and Bernard Coard in more convivial times.

Richmond Hill Prison, the objective of Delta Force, as seen from Fort Frederick.

St George's with Fort George, centre.

The Mitla Pass – a scene of total destruction.

Brigadier Cordingley's fateful press briefing on 28 November 1990 when the question of casualty levels in the forthcoming battle in Iraq arose.

The British Army Challenger Main Battle Tank.

The Army MH-60K Special Operations Blackhawk.

Mike Durant's Super 64 helicopter over Mogadishu, 3 October 1993.

Lieutenant-Colonel Jonathon Riley with Lieutenant-General Rupert Smith.

Alpha and Bravo bridges, in the town centre of Gorazde, as seen from Observation Post 2.

Observation Post 2 from the rear. The Saxon is fitted with snow chains because of the condition of the tracks.

The British Army's 'technical' Land Rover carrying a 12.7-mm (0.5-inch) Browning in a Weapons Mounted Installation Kit (WMIK) known as the 'Wimik'.

'If you can't beat them, join them.' Many West Side Boys reported to Benguema Camp to join the Sierra Leone Army.

A confirmed insurgent stronghold goes up in smoke after a strategic aerial strike, 10 November 2004.

Howitzer gun crew of 4th Battalion, 14th Marine Corps shelling enemy positions inside Fallujah.

American soldiers entering a building in Fallujah, 12 November 2004.

Two members of a rescue team who volunteered to locate Lance-Corporal Mathew Ford, on board an Apache WAH-64 attack helicopter returning to Jugroom Fort, Helmand.

Captain Mackenzie-Green, M Company, 42 Commando RM, sends a situation report during the initial breech into enemy compounds, in an operation to clear buildings used by the Taliban in the area of Barijko in Kajaki.

Lieutenant-Colonel M.J. Holmes RM giving orders to 42 Commando RM Group for Operation Silver, 6 April 2007, prior to the assault into Sangin.

offensive hit-and-run operations into Serb territory despite protests from the UN.

On 10 April 1994, General Rose heard from his Chief of Staff that Serb armour had opened an offensive against Gorazde; parts of the town were aflame and the Bosniacs were observed to be in general retreat. The UN had a number of military observers and joint commission officers in Gorazde. General Rose immediately set in motion the request procedure for close air support. When aircraft arrived over the target, however, the results did not live up to expectations. The atrociously wet, cloudy weather forced pilots to hug the ground, permitting only fleeting glimpses of the targets below. In accordance with theatre operational procedures, a small number of aircraft had been scrambled as a proportional response to the Serb attack. As General Rose said, '. . . as long as the level of force used by NATO remained within the limits set by the UN mandate, there remained a chance that we could revert to the peace process'.[23]

On 14 April, UN Forward HQ in Sarajevo heard the news that another 'safe area', Tuzla, had come under artillery fire and 150 UN soldiers and aid workers had been taken hostage. The UN's senior representative Yasushi Akashi protested to General Mladic, and Mr Akashi and General Rose also met with the Bosnian leaders President Izetbegovic and Prime Minister Haris Silajdzic. General Rose explained that the UN could not fight other people's civil wars, nor could their actions exceed what their mandate prescribed. On 17 April, NATO air attacks on the Serbs outside Gorazde continued but on this day a Royal Navy Sea Harrier was shot down near Gorazde. The pilot survived. The loss of a NATO aircraft caused a perceptible wobble within NATO headquarters, Naples, to the extent that the commanders refused to authorize the further use of aircraft for tactical strikes and pilots were ordered to stay above 10,000 feet (3,048 metres).

UN leaders in Sarajevo assembled to discuss this serious development. General Rose recorded: 'We agreed that the shooting down of the NATO aircraft had probably altered the political and military situation in Bosnia',[24] but this was not perhaps in the way he imagined. Russia's Special Envoy to former Yugoslavia, Vitaly Churkin, telephoned from Pale to say that the Serbs had agreed to stop fighting, to withdraw 3 kilometres (1.8 miles) from the town centre and to adopt a 20-kilometre (12-mile) TEZ around Gorazde. This was stunning news, particularly since the Serbs had been within a whisker of overrunning the Bosniacs in Gorazde. Radovan Karadzic, the Bosnian Serb leader, agreed to disengage by 26 April. Now UNPROFOR would need a military presence in Gorazde to oversee the separation of Serbs from Bosniacs. The problem was that Gorazde was within the French area of responsibility and President François Mitterrand refused to allow a French battalion to deploy there. Perhaps he shared the same view as Richard Holbrooke, the last in a long line of negotiators, who spoke of 'Dien Bien Gorazde'.

Faced with a French 'non', General Rose turned to the British for a 'yes', which was immediately forthcoming. A British battalion, The Duke of Wellington's Regiment, recruited in West Yorkshire and commanded by Lieutenant-Colonel David Santa Ollala, was promised to be in Gorazde twenty-four hours later, thus setting in train a series of consequences with far-reaching implications. Meanwhile, the first convoy left for Gorazde carrying a Ukrainian company and a Norwegian medical team.

On 18 December 1994, the former US President Jimmy Carter and his wife arrived in Sarajevo. By the end of the month he had secured a four-month Cessation of Hostilities

Agreement from Karadzic and Izetbegovic. It had been a diplomatic coup. The Bosniacs could not afford to risk losing support in the USA and Karadzic believed Carter to be the only American of influence who would listen to Serbs.[25] The Duke of Wellington's Regiment had come and gone, to be relieved by Lieutenant-Colonel Patrick Davidson-Houston's Royal Gloucestershire, Berkshire and Wiltshire Regiment. Not for them so much the conflict between Serbs and Muslims but, on their winter watch, the real dangers of negotiating winter mountain tracks in their far from ideal Saxon APCs.[26]

During the interregnum, on 23 January 1995, General Rose bade farewell to his Sarajevo staff, leaving a bottle of champagne on his empty desk for his successor, Lieutenant-General Rupert Smith. A note tied to the bottle with a pink ribbon read: 'Good luck. Your life will never be the same again.' Thoughts had already turned to what might happen if the Cessation of Hostilities Agreement was not extended. If that were the case, the Serbs intended to remove the Bosniacs from the three enclaves in the Drina valley in eastern Bosnia – Gorazde, Zepa and Srebrenica – forcing them to accept a Serb-dictated peace.[27] The Bosniacs and Croats used the pause to rearm from the various channels available to them. Meanwhile, the changing of the guard continued with the completion of The Royal Gloucestershire, Berkshire and Wiltshire Regiment's tour of duty and their replacement by The Royal Welch Fusiliers.

As is so often the case with modern intervention operations, other than the Commanding Officer, Lieutenant-Colonel Jonathon Riley, one of his company commanders and one or two others, no other soldier of the The Royal Welch Fusiliers had any experience of the earlier years of Bosnia's tragedy. Infantry battalions tend to deploy as complete entities rather than be subject to the trickle-feeding principle applicable to support units. That is not to suggest that 1RWF was under-trained. The contrary is true since their training included mechanized operations, battle group live-firing exercises in Canada and frequent Northern Ireland operational roulements.

The first sight the young soldiers had of Gorazde in late February 1995 made an overwhelming impact. The town had quite clearly suffered enormous destruction. This is where they were going to live for the next six months. Precisely how many would not be coming home again to Wales was one of life's unknowns. 'I was determined,' said Colonel Riley, 'if humanly possible, to see that every one of my Fusiliers who had come in with me would go back.'[28]

They drove through bleak, limestone mountains as high as anything seen in Wales. The river Drina, upon which Gorazde sat, had for many millennia sliced through the limestone now towering above battered homes below. This east Bosnia enclave spread over 124 miles (200 kilometres) of outstanding natural beautiful, rugged country populated by approximately 45,000 Bosniacs, of whom 17,000 lived in the town, 11,000 of them having come there from the surrounding area in search of sanctuary. The pre-war Serb population now comprised a mere 150. The enclave lay 87 miles (140 kilometres) from the nearest UN troops, in Serbian territory, 11 miles (18 kilometres) from the Serb border. Other than food grown in the hinterland, the Muslims depended entirely upon United Nations High Commissioner for Refugees (UNHCR) humanitarian relief for their survival. The population and UN military were therefore dependent upon UN convoys obliged to transit through Serb territory. Seeing no reason why they should support their enemies, the Serbs consistently and deliberately obstructed the flow of humanitarian relief; after all, it would not be unusual for the Serbs to have neither food nor fuel nor other basic commodities.

The water of the Drina was mud-coloured rather than the blood colour immortalized in folklore. The 3-kilometre (1.8-mile) TEZ put in place on 23 April 1994 had its centre point midway along Gorazde's main river bridge. What the local TEZ agreement had achieved in reality was to create an exclusion zone applicable to the Serbs but not the Bosniacs. Gorazde had been an important medieval trading route owing its status to the strategically important river and road networks under the town's control. Compared with the other two eastern enclaves, its contemporary strategic importance during this bloody civil war derived from its position astride the Serb lines of communication.

Nothing else in the Gorazde situation enjoyed the exactitude of the measurement of the TEZ. As the situation changed so too would 1RWF's response, but they never had a precise mission. On arrival, the battalion inherited a number of mission statements to: maintain the Gorazde 'safe area'; maintain the Gorazde TEZ for as long as consent lasted; maintain the safety of UN personnel and accredited agencies and the security of installations; observe and report warring faction activity; and assist all humanitarian agencies and projects.[29] These multi-missions had been fashioned around the concept of traditional peacekeeping and would have a short life. From May 1995 onward, the situation had deteriorated into all-out civil war. There was no longer any peace to be kept.

The 'safe area' had never been geographically defined and resisted bureaucratic definition. The fundamental requirement that both parties should be demilitarized was never addressed. Lieutenant-General Rupert Smith intervened to assist the

Commanding Officer with his own definition: 'The Safe Area exists to safeguard the civil population as far as it is practicable to do so in war.'[30]

An imposed manpower ceiling of 500 deprived Commanding Officer 1RWF of the satisfaction of having his whole battalion under command. The 120-strong Ukrainian company commanded by a lieutenant-colonel and the 20-strong Norwegian Field Ambulance were still *in situ*. Headroom also had to be found for a troop of engineers and two patrols of SAS, thereby limiting the number of 1RWF able to be accommodated in the Gorazde enclave to approximately 350.[31] The sub-units allocated to Gorazde were: Battalion HQ, A (rifle) Company, B (rifle) Company, C (Pioneer, reconnaissance and signals platoons) Company. The 200-strong D (rifle) Company Group had to be placed under command of The Royal Highland Fusiliers at Bugojno. Each rifle company took under the command mortar and anti-tank sections and medium machine gun sections manned by the Drums.[32]

RWF had as their principal occupation the manning of observation posts (OPs) interspersed between the warring factions, some no more than 22 yards (20 metres) apart. Each OP had a complement of six to twelve men. Here were shades of the First World War, sturdy shelters manned by vigilant soldiers observing the territory not only in front but also behind their lines. Gorazde camp was muddy in winter, dusty in summer, overlooked from every side, indefensible. A Company deployed to the west bank, B Company to the east bank, while C Company patrolled the rear of the TEZ entirely in Muslim territory. The Ukrainians had their camp outside Gorazde in the nearby village of Vitkovici. Some regarded the separation as fortuitous. The obligation to police both the TEZ and the 'safe area' meant the RoE were more robust than that applicable to traditional peacekeeping, the Commanding Officer being permitted to use lethal force to defend his troops and the civilian population. 1RWF's operational chain of command went directly to General Smith in Sarajevo.[33]

One of Colonel Riley's first tasks was to acquaint himself with the local warring parties. Liaison was a vital part of the monitoring process. Brigadier Hamid Bahto commanded the local Bosniac troops of the 81st Division. When his assets are examined, it might be concluded that this division was pathetically weak, yet it was far stronger than its sister formations in Zepa and Srebrenica; not an easy nut to crack. Bahto had 8,000 men under command but the largesse arising from illicit arms deliveries had not reached this far east. It seems that the best they received from the CIA Black Flights cargoes were new uniforms. A number in the Bosniac community were convinced that they were being deliberately neglected by the Sarajevo Government, which they believed was prepared to forfeit Gorazde in exchange for Serb areas of Sarajevo. That might be a reason why Bahto had sufficient personal weapons for only 6,500 men, enough for a partially mobilized division. The support weapons in his armoury included one tank, three field guns, approximately twenty mortars and some heavy machine guns. The amount of ammunition at intense rates of fire would last a month of engagements.[34] Were it not for the presence of an ammunition factory in the Bosniac territory, the situation would have been far worse. Bahto divided his resources into six brigades: five holding brigades and one Special Forces brigade.

The Serbs surrounded Gorazde with representative elements of three corps, which is one reason why offensive action was poorly co-ordinated. An inter-corps boundary ran along the Drina. Brigade organization reflected the nature of

the terrain over which they fought. These were mountain
brigades without integral armour. There were 1,000 men in
each brigade but only 300 in the line at any one time. Among
the Serbs besieging Gorazde were many embittered warriors,
able to see their own former homes from the wrong side of
the confrontation line. To some degree, the poor quality of
soldier was compensated for by the availability of large
quantities of good weapons including anti-aircraft guns,
mortars and artillery.[35]

1RWF assumed duties and responsibility for Gorazde on
St David's Day. In accordance with tradition, leeks were
added to the ration-runs out to the OPs, one for the youngest
fusilier in each location. Inside Gorazde camp and in the
same way as a military Christmas is celebrated, the members
of the officers' and sergeants' messes served the men their St
David's Day lunch. More leeks were consumed while fifes
and drums sounded as the musicians marched around the
tables. A goat had been acquired, a stand-in for the regimental
goat safely ensconced in his quarters in Wales. 'The goat, an
ill-tempered beast, caused quite a stir, since nothing could
convince the owner that we did not intend to eat the
creature.'[36] Early the next morning, a burst of firing awoke
the Commanding Officer from his slumbers. The firing
continued throughout the day but in comparison to what
was to come, it was of little consequence. After all, the date
was 8 March; the Cessation of Hostilities Agreement still
had until 30 April 1995 to run.

1RWF were soon to learn how much the quality of their
military life was related to the nature of the commander of
the opposing forces. The Serb Rogatica Brigade commanded
by a Major Kusic, the Butcher of the Rogatica, for example,
had been cited as 'difficult'. Colour Sergeant Garbutt and
Sergeants Cassemis and Howell described a convoy run from

Kiseljak to Gorazde and their grave sense of unease when, at the halfway point, they came to the Rogatica checkpoint. Kusic's men came forward to inspect documents and vehicles. During the fighting and ethnic cleansing a year previously, he had offered free passage out of Serb territory to any Muslim who wanted to leave. Those who refused were put through the local sawmill. Those who left were given one hour's start and were then hunted. If caught they were nailed to trees.[37]

On 11 March, the Royal Welch had the first of two fire-fights with the Rogatica Brigade at Podkevacev Dol, 5½ miles (9 kilometres) north of Gorazde. A platoon had been out on reconnaissance and was preparing to leave the house they had used for two days when their sentry came under fire from Serb lines. The sentry returned fire and in retaliation all hell was let loose from the Serb side of the confrontation line. So heavy was the fire from 40-mm anti-aircraft guns and heavy machine guns that the platoon house began to disintegrate. 1RWF returned the fire and once a form of equilibrium had been reached they used smoke to withdraw from their position. For two days the OP overlooking the Rogatica Brigade became the subject of nuisance firing and the occasional mortar round. On 15 March another 1RWF patrol came under fire from the Rogatica Brigade. Told that he was firing on the UN, Kusic said he did not care. A-10 and F-16 aircraft were called up and a Milan anti-tank section brought forward to ensure he did care. Lives were at risk. The Commanding Officer was prepared, if necessary, to fully engage but preferred to be patient and eventually, after five hours under fire, the patrol was able to withdraw.[38]

These examples of conflict were far from common, partic-ularly in this consensual period of peace when relations were generally good. A game of football could not fail to be an ice-breaker. Food was exchanged although it was never certain who benefited most from the deal. As the piggy in the middle, the impartial wearers of the blue beret, The Royal Welch, were never shy of telling their war stories to any Bosniac or Serb prepared to listen. That they could not understand a word seemed not to matter. On occasions, for political reasons, the Bosnian Serbs in Pale passed instructions to their outposts to shell their Bosniac opposition. The rationale for this would relate to some distant Bosniac-on-Serb attack or vice versa. On 26 March 1995, the Serbs bombarded the headquarters of the 81st Division but it was the civilians who bore the collateral damage. 'Why', they asked Jonathon Riley, in Gorazde's streets, 'had there been no air strikes against this violation of the Agreement?' He explained the need to avoid escalation, something he found himself having difficulty believing as he visited the hospital,

> short of everything from safety pins to surgical equipment. There is one operating theatre and the doctors are mostly GPs who have had to learn other skills: they are, after three years, exhausted. The Regimental doctor, surgeon and medics together with the Médecins sans Frontières doctors do their best to supplement or relieve Gorazde's own doctors.[39]

As the snow disappeared, the thoughts of the Serbs and Bosniacs turned more intensely towards the spring warring season. From 11 April to 30 April, when the Cessation of Hostilities Agreement would end, both sides manoeuvred to be in the most advantageous position once the restrictive conditions to which they only paid lip service fell away. On 11 April the Serbs again bombarded Gorazde but there were no casualties. 1RWF conducted a vigorous patrol programme within the safe area, occasionally going outside the area to deal with events which fell within the moral responsibility of the UN. One such example was to find a Serb sniper firing into the school and at civilians in the small village of Vitkovici, 3.7 miles (6 kilometres) south of Gorazde. The British action deterred any recurrence. Patrolling did not come without risk, particularly from mines strewn haphazardly within the 'safe area'. On 18 April, three fusiliers were injured in an unmarked anti-personnel minefield. Muslims went in to bring the British casualties out and the Serbs were quick to authorize a helicopter to land at Gorazde – one of only two flights in six months – to evacuate the casualties.[40] They all recovered and returned to duty.

Between 17 and 26 April an increasing number of heavy-weapon impacts were logged – 348 from direct-fire weapons and 38 reports of mortar and artillery strikes. The effect of the Serbs' stringent interference with the flow of supplies into the enclave also affected 1RWF who, by the end of April, found themselves virtually under siege. 'The entire force had to run on only 200 litres of fuel per day – this meant no electricity for lights, hot water, or laundry; walking every-where; and cooking on wood. The loss of the deep fat fryer, and with it, chips, was deeply felt by the Fusiliers.'[41]

At the strategic level, every time a 'safe area' was attacked by the Serbs, no matter how minor or whether the Bosniacs had provoked it, Mrs Albright and General George Joulwan (Supreme Allied Commander Europe (SACEUR)) would press for air strikes.[42] Mr Akashi, who took his neutrality very seriously, struggled to keep this aspiration in check yet was vilified by the media for 'being soft on Serbs'.[43] On 26 April, the British Government announced that after 1RWF had completed its tour of duty there would no longer be a British presence in Gorazde. Downing Street imagined the risks, visualizing hostages or British peacekeepers hanged from lamp posts. John Major appeared totally mesmerized by this prospect and his attitude was that as 1RWF had been the third consecutive British battalion to undertake an enormously difficult task in what was, after all, a French zone, it should be someone else's turn.

Colonel Riley's diary entry for 8 May notes that because of Serb obstruction no fuel convoy had entered Gorazde since 22 February, no supply convoy since 21 April and no mail since 28 April. The fuel shortage was particularly taxing because supplies had to be carried on foot to the OPs. Invariably these ration-runs came under fire from the Serb lines. The Commanding Officer's difficulty lay in deciding whether to return the fire or depend on liaison to resolve the problem. Thus far, liaison had worked, but at the risk of encouraging further incidents in the future. The resupply problem led to at least one inspired improvisation. Someone found an old cart to which two mules were attached. As soon as the cart had been loaded with precious supplies, the latter-day waggoners set off for A Company OP.

> This spectacle, as it hove into view of the Serb lines, was clearly too much for the watching Serb soldiers to resist – if, that is, they could believe their eyes. A few rounds cracked overhead, the mules shed their load and bolted with the Company Sergeant-Major being dragged after, hanging on like fury, with Company Quartermaster Sergeant Poole and Fusilier Jones 94 in hot pursuit.[44]

The reduction of the RWF ration was inevitable. No one could say when the next supply convoy would get through the Serb checkpoints and as a consequence the ration was reduced by a third, not a choice the Commanding Officer took lightly in view of the arduous work undertaken by his men. The cherished chips had given way to powdered potato mixed with murky river water and known as 'Drina mash'. The Commanding Officer recalled how he had been 'reliably informed that it can be used either for eating or building bomb-proof shelters'.[45] Then a convoy arrived, the first in a month, but with less than two days' rations on board.

Operations continued. Some episodes left the RWF wondering why they bothered. During one of two attacks on them at Osanica bridge, a hotspot 6 miles (10 kilometres) away, a number of B Company's Saxons escorting a UN civilian police vehicle came under fire from both Serbs and Bosniacs. 'The action by the Muslims,' said the OC, 'whom we are to assist and at whose request this action was carried out, was nothing short of disgraceful.'[46] Here was a parallel with Srebrenica.

Mladic's unwillingness to respond to General Smith's ultimatum that all heavy weapons circling Sarajevo were to cease fire by midday 25 May and be withdrawn to beyond the 12-mile (20-kilometre) boundary, resulted in Pale being bombed. Mladic ordered the launch of artillery attacks upon each of the six 'safe areas', with a threat particularly aimed at Jonathon Riley that his battalion would be shelled if more air strikes took place. As a precaution, the Commanding Officer reduced manning in the camp to twenty-five, sending all non-essentials to a secure hide area where they could not be reached by Serb artillery. Bomb shelters were strengthened. Radio security became the subject of a cunning idea. Both the Serbs and Bosniacs had excellent signals intelligence capabilities:

Military information transmitted in the mountains of eastern Bosnia now leaves the Balkan warlords as mystified as most of the Welsh when they hear Serbo-Croat. Three Companies of Welch Fusiliers stationed in the besieged enclave of Gorazde turned to their native language when they found the Balkan combatants mimicking the British on the radio network and threatening the regiment's effectiveness.[47]

The Commanding Officer recalled this idea having worked against the Japanese in Burma in 1944.

On 28 May, the Commanding Officer returned from a visit to 81st Division to be told that three of his A Company OP positions on the west bank had been overrun by heavily armed Serbs. He immediately ordered his men from the two remaining OPs to withdraw. Meanwhile, reports from the east bank told of the assembly of large numbers of Serb soldiers in the vicinity of B Company's OPs. OC B Company's orders were: be prepared to withdraw, open fire if attacked. The Serbs overran one OP but the remainder withdrew under fire. The lucky Royal Welch's luck held out. There had been no casualties but thirty-three fusiliers had been taken prisoner, a small proportion of the 500 UN troops seized throughout Bosnia. The Serbs had not been so fortunate, the fusiliers having aimed to kill. The area in front of the B Company position could be seen to be littered with Serb corpses. The effect of these attacks would have been far worse had they been co-ordinated. The attacks on the OPs were the prequel to intensified attacks upon Gorazde which became the Commanding Officer's principal concern. 'I was not worried about the fate of the hostages,' said Colonel Riley, 'I knew nothing would happen.'[48] He knew that much from his daily dealings with the principal officers of the parties involved. In a short period, eighteen hostages were released, including a number injured in a road traffic accident. The Commanding Officer knew the remaining five fusiliers would be released shortly and he was proved correct.

The Serbs, capitalizing on the OPs being unmanned,

launched a surprise 1,000-man attack on Gorazde. The RWF intervened, fighting the Serbs for a good two hours, keeping them off the ridge overlooking the town, Gorazde's vital ground. Saxon APCs deployed on the eastern side of Gorazde provided fire support to keep the Serbs away from the area. The defence of Gorazde brought a whole new interpretation of the term 'peacekeeping'. The aim of the Royal Welch had been to hold the high ground until the Bosniac 81st Division could mobilize, allowing the Welch to step away from the ongoing civil war. 'The delay battle on the west bank gave Bahto time to move up and secure the high ground occupied by us, from which the Serbs could have destroyed the town,' said Jonathon Riley. 'This was not exactly impartial conduct, but we had no moral choice. It was this battle which saved Gorazde from the fate of Srebrenica.' Serb fought Bosniac. By the end of June they had reached stalemate, but, said Riley, 'my mandate had gone'.[49] That did not mean the Royal Welch could withdraw. London believed that if they did, it would set in train a general UN withdrawal from Bosnia; besides, the ever active Madeleine Albright convinced the Security Council of the pressing need to keep UN troops in the 'safe areas'.[50]

The history of The Royal Welch Fusiliers reveals them as having been in similar predicaments before, at Minorca in the Seven Years War and at Yorktown in the American Revolutionary War. In London, the Government responded by ordering 24 Airmobile Brigade to Bosnia as an element of a Rapid Reaction Force that included British and French armoured infantry battle groups and an artillery group that also included a Dutch unit. It is not clear whether such a deployment made sense or whether it was a symbolic gesture, but such speculation is academic – the brigade arrived too late to make a practical contribution. What arguably did make a contribution was the declaration of intent explicit in an apparent willingness to take the battle to the Serbs. Generals such as Mladic respect such displays of determination and strength. As a consequence, it seems probable that General Mladic focused his attention on those 'safe areas' where he might meet with less resistance.

In Paris, President Chirac received his defence staff's response to his question, what should be done about Gorazde? The military advised airlifting 1,000 French troops in American helicopters into Gorazde. Washington took the French plan seriously, not that they liked it or would go along with it, not least because it risked sucking American forces into the Balkan quagmire. Washington's solution was to put a plan of their own on the table to achieve a consensus in favour of calling in strategic air power in the event of Gorazde being attacked.[51]

On 7 June 1995, in Haverfordwest, south Wales, a gathering of ladies in colourful summer dresses, some wearing hats, some practising their curtseys, waited nervously for their distinguished guest. These were the wives of the men of The Royal Welch Fusiliers. Shortly, a large, highly polished Rolls Royce pulled up outside the Trafalgar Road estate Community Centre. Out stepped the Colonel-in-Chief of the regiment, Her Majesty Queen Elizabeth II. The Queen then spoke privately to the wives of the five soldiers still held hostage. She reassured them, 'the Serbs will not dare to harm any of my Royal Welch Fusiliers'.[52]

That evening, in Gorazde, Colonel Riley received a signal. It came from the Queen. 'I visited the Regiment's families today in Haverfordwest. Despite the grave situation you are facing, I found them in good heart and supporting each other in the finest traditions of the Regiment. You can be proud of them, as I am proud of you. I send my warm good wishes to you all.'[53] An elated Commanding Officer wrote in his diary: 'The press would have us believe that royalty has lost its magic, but the effect of that message on all of us here was pretty magical.' The Colonel had a powerful ally. It seems strange that he should have been in need of one.

Prime Minister John Major had telephoned Jonathon Riley on 2 June prior to his own visit to Wales. The call came as no surprise. He had been warned to expect it by the Chief of the General Staff who told him to be completely honest – 'so I was'. Riley told the Prime Minister that his men were serving no useful purpose in Gorazde, that peacekeeping was an impossibility where there was no peace to be kept. When John Major relayed the contents of his twenty-five-minute discussion to the Ministry of Defence, it was not generally well received. The staff were quite content to persevere with peacekeeping while being resolutely opposed to progressing to enforcement. One very senior officer at Joint Headquarters Wilton, angry at Riley speaking out, is alleged to have said that Riley 'should get back in his trench and die' and 'stop thinking too much'.[54] Others were hugely surprised that the Prime Minister should cut through all the chains of command to speak directly to Commanding Officer 1RWF deep in his bunker, sheltering from up to 500 rounds a day of incoming artillery fire passing over his head. The Chief of the Defence Staff and General Smith came forward to support what Riley had said. As a consequence, the *bêtes noires* lowered their profiles.

Cook Sergeant Wayne Taylor found his imagination stretched trying to produce the same old tinned food in different and satisfying ways. Rationing was still in force and there had been no resupply convoy for over a month. Supply officers in the British Army have a happy knack of producing fresh rations in the most unlikely of places.

Evidence of that kind of magic would have been welcomed by those presently under siege in Gorazde. Then, out of the blue, there came a radio transmission: 'Allo Wellington . . . ici Napoleon . . . do you copy . . . over?'[55] It was the first logistic convoy in over a month, commanded by a determined Colonel Phillippe Coiffet, four days on the road dropping off supplies en route until reaching Gorazde, the last stop on the line. The French convoy stood out on the road between the two warring factions and in front of a Serb minefield. Fortunately, preoccupation with events in Sarajevo had brought a lull in fighting around Gorazde. Sappers were sent forthwith to let the convoy into the camp. Imaginations ran riot. The French have an excellent reputation for their food, but not this time. They had come so far, taking enormous risks, to bring pasta to the chip-loving soldiers of Wales. 'I am already sick of it,' Colonel Riley confided to his diary. More positive was the fuel brought to Gorazde, sufficient to keep communications open for a month. Colonel Coiffet's was the last logistic convoy to have to endure hassle from Serb checkpoints. Convoys forthwith drove the longer, quicker, 620-mile (1,000-kilometre) route authorized for UNHCR, avoiding for good the psychopaths of Rogatica.

The Serb attack on Srebrenica was a major Intelligence failure. Intelligence, for what it was worth, insisted no enclaves would fall, but it was in both Serb and Bosniac interests that the 'safe areas' should come under local domination. Milosevic wanted Mladic to attack Srebrenica in order to generate long-awaited diplomatic action from Washington.[56] The Sarajevo Government was of a similar mind. They were content for Srebrenica to fall in order to increase pressure on the international community. Oafish Serbs without a scintilla of diplomacy played into their hands. A man of Bosniac and Serb parentage told me that if the reverse situation had applied to Srebrenica – i.e. Bosniacs attacking Serbs – the result would have been the same.[57] 'Most of the extremists on all three sides think alike. Circumstances placed the Serbs in the best position to do what was done.' The Croats, Serbs and Muslims were fighting total war or, as Ripley says, a war of survival. It is a terrible indictment that a nation appears to have been content to have so many of its own people killed in the interest of a higher cause.

The pressure shifted off Lieutenant-Colonel Riley's 1RWF and on to Dutch Lieutenant-Colonel Thom Karremans's Dutchbat, whose life forthwith would be tragically blighted. A Serb General agreed, 'Srebrenica did happen but Serb territory was being attacked from these safe areas on a daily basis. Even before we liberated Srebrenica, terror groups entered our villages to burn them down. We asked UNPRO-FOR to control the situation but they did not.'[58] Following the Serb attack of 11 July 1995, the enclave of Srebrenica fell into Serb hands. 'The defenders and almost all the able-bodied men and some women tried to break out of the pocket,' wrote General Smith:

> The majority were taken prisoner and subsequently murdered, others were killed on the march and a few made it to safety. The Dutch stayed in their compound; they did not intervene as the remaining men were separated from the women and taken away to be murdered. The women, children and old men were bussed by the Bosnian Serbs to the front line where they were directed towards the Bosnia positions and subsequently moved to Tuzla and some other places – a grim journey.[59]

Over 7,000 Bosniac men and boys were killed between 14 and 17 July 1995 and buried in mass graves throughout north-east Bosnia.

There was a belief among some that air strikes would never be authorized to stop attacks on civilians alone.[60] Others dispute civilians having a lower priority for air support when attacked than soldiers. Indeed, a mutual defence plan had been worked out between the Dutch and the Bosniacs but, come the day, it never came to fruition. Without military engagement, there was no prospect of the UN mandate being interpreted so as to allow air power to be used to defend Srebrenica.[61] It was not for the want of the many itching to deploy it. Sixty aircraft were on standby to intervene. Lieutenant-General Janvier, French UNPROFOR Commander, warned the Security Council, in the same way that Colonel Riley had warned John Major, that the UN's task in the enclaves was an impossible mission. At the prompting of Madeleine Albright in the UN Security Council, his warnings were ignored.[62]

In Gorazde, the Commanding Officer's stress management regime had been tailored to each separate circumstance. After the hostages had been debriefed by Intelligence, he sent them off to D Company in Bugojno to wind down for a week under the supervision of one of the regiment's medical officers who, by chance, was a psychiatrist. Only then were they granted two weeks' home leave. The error of sending them directly on leave had been avoided. The one person in 1RWF most susceptible to stress was the Commanding Officer. He would constantly attempt to think his way into the Serb thought cycle but found second-guessing them virtually impossible. He kept alert, inventing wargame scenarios based on the Srebrenica experience so that he remained aware of all the options. The most difficult problem in search of a solution was how to protect the refugees. His best course of action towards de-stressing would be to take a short break from Gorazde, to undertake something – anything –

constructive within Bosnia. The fact remains however that the best antidote for stress is the creation of a sense of family, of belonging, within a professional battalion. 1RWF took to Bosnia 54 Joneses, 29 Williamses, 11 each of Thomases, Hugheses and Evanses, and of course many others.

In Zepa on 16 July, while under Serb attack, the Bosniacs turned on eighty UN Ukrainians, robbing them of their personal items, weapons, equipment and armoured vehicles. For a year, the Ukrainians had been there to protect the Bosniacs. The Ukrainians were detested by the Bosniacs and their Serb brothers. It was perhaps one of the few issues upon which the warring factions were in agreement. The Ukrainians, sturdy peasants capable of being reasonable soldiers, had a reputation as gangsters, pro-Serb, but while some undoubtedly indulged in wheeling and dealing collectively they did not deserve this reputation. 'They suffered from exposure to the immediate post-Communist period, corruption, black markets and prostitution.'[63] By 20 July, the Bosniacs had shelled the Ukrainian camp.[64]

That the Zepa betrayal had been the Bosniac Government's policy soon became clear when the process was repeated against the Ukrainian camp at Vitkovici in the Gorazde enclave. Bahto told the RWF's second-in-command not to interfere, it would all be over and done with very quickly. 'If you intervene, a lot of people will be killed.'[65] A fire-fight began but the Ukrainians, finding themselves in a hopeless position, began to neutralize weapons and immobilize vehicles. They stopped their equipment denial only when their lives were threatened by their erstwhile charges who dishonoured them by surrounding them and stripping them of their clothes. Six Bosniacs took hold of the OC and threatened to kill him if their demands were not met. Suddenly finding his Ukrainian neighbours defenceless and entirely

dependent upon 1RWF for protection seriously affected
Colonel Riley's ongoing plan to move all his own non-
essentials out of the area. Colonel Riley wrote scathingly:

> . . . nothing can justify attacks, and seizure of Ukrainian vehicles,
> weapons and equipment, not to mention the theft of money and
> personal belongings . . . Here in Gorazde we have experienced
> all sorts of harassment – not from the Serbs, but from the people
> who depend upon us to risk our lives breaching the Serbs' mine-
> field every time a UNHCR convoy comes in.[66]

Colonel Riley had the first of two excursions in mid-July.
The Americans wanted him to brief their Ambassador in
Sarajevo, John Menzies, as to how he saw the overall situation
in Republika Srpska. 'Jonathon Riley', explained a senior
British UNPROFOR officer, 'is ambitious, not only for
himself but also for his regiment. They have performed
outstandingly well out here but have suffered from not having
a journalist with them to tell the world what they have been
through. He is bright and intelligent which some of his less
astute superiors confuse with being opinionated.' The problem
with the international bureaucracy was that they were only
receptive to information which reflected what they wanted
to believe. The Americans did not agree with Riley's view
that the Serbs would continue to resist being forced into a
one-size-fits-all state. Menzies had considerable sympathy for
UNPROFOR's position but when Holbrooke heard the tape
of the Menzies–Riley discussion, he expressed his concern to
General Smith. Smith and Menzies had lengthy talks about
their different objectives. Menzies explained all this to Riley:
'You are an impartial peacekeeper, I am not impartial – it
is US policy to support the Bosnians.'[67] Menzies was said to
belong to a group known as the 'Dirty Dozen', a group of

diplomats and members of Congress committed to do more for Bosnia's Muslims.

At the London Conference held at Lancaster House on 21 July those present included the Ministers of Foreign Affairs and Defence of the countries of the Contact Group and of the most important troop-contributing nations, the UN and NATO Secretaries-General and senior members of the European Commission. Also invited were Generals Janvier and Smith. When it came to General Rupert Smith's turn to address the conference, he stood up, listed his objectives and then told those present he did not see any prospect of achieving any of them. 'There was a cowed silence in the room.'[68] Srebrenica had fallen, Zepa was close to capitulation, which meant Gorazde would be the next to tumble. The Americans wanted to hit the Serbs with heavy air bombardments, the French pretended they wanted to reinforce Gorazde (there was now a Rapid Reaction Force but it took an inordinate amount of time to deploy).[69] The British wanted out. What emerged from these apparently irreconcilable differences was a decision to tell Mladic that if he attacked Gorazde, the full weight of NATO and the UN would fall upon him. The United States abandoned Mrs Albright's unrealistic insistence of UN troops remaining in the enclaves. The UN believed an attack on Gorazde unlikely due to the Serbs' commitments in western Bosnia. General Smith reminded the conference that he filled an international appointment. He was responsible not only for deterring an attack upon Gorazde but also upon the other remaining safe areas – Sarajevo, Tuzla and Bihac. The decision to threaten to attack the Serbs if Gorazde came under pressure was duly extended by the North Atlantic Council on 2 August to include Sarajevo and Tuzla. NATO decided to leave Bihac out in the cold due to its imprecise demarcation and the complex numbers of warring factions involved.

A delegation of British, French and American officers took the NATO ultimatum to Mladic. The wording left little room for doubt: '. . . if you undertake military action against Gorazde, or if you put the lives of UNPROFOR peacekeepers there at risk, we will use substantial air power against you'.[70] Even the British and French, who had striven to remain impartial, recognized that now the time had probably come to hit the Serbs if they did not terminate their unending quest to extend their territory.

Krajina fell at the end of July. On 10 August, General Smith made his first visit to Gorazde. That it took so long to gain permission to visit the enclave is another indicator of the Bosnian Serb hold on it and its control of UNPROFOR. General Smith decided to take Commanding Officer 1RWF with him to negotiate 1RWF's withdrawal with Mladic:

> I wanted Mladic to give the order to his subordinates to give clearance for the RWF to withdraw through the Bosnian Serb territory into Serbia at a time to be decided by the Commanding Officer in front of the Commanding Officer; so that in the event there would be the least room for questioning and doubt. The Commanding Officer would be having enough trouble with the Bosniacs.[71]

On 20 August, Riley received instructions to make rendezvous with General Smith at 11.00 a.m. at Rogatica before going off to see Mladic at Boreke. What followed was, for Colonel Riley,

> one of the most significant experiences of my life . . . General Mladic is an imposing, indeed dominating figure both physically and in terms of his personality; it was easy to see why his own men adore him and his enemies fear him. I viewed him then, and still do, in the same way as Hyde viewed Cromwell: 'A great, bad man'.[72]

In 1994, Sergio di Mello, the UN Head of Civil Affairs in Bosnia (he was killed in Iraq) had an interesting insight into Mladic, the butcher of Srebrenica. Di Mello arrived at Kopaci, near to Gorazde, to supervise the onward movement of a convoy which had been held up. Kopaci has one of the oldest Orthodox Serb churches in the former Yugoslavia. On reaching the head of the convoy, di Mello saw in the truck's headlights the unmistakable figure of Mladic. The church had been desecrated. Mladic took di Mello to show him. They entered the graveyard where, by the light of a torch, Mladic illuminated smashed headstones and the graves of his men killed in the recent fighting. Di Mello noticed that hard man Mladic was weeping, 'reduced to tears by the sight of the graves of his young soldiers'.[73]

It is hatred which mobilized the parties to the extent that something so extreme as Srebrenica could and did happen. This comment is not intended to excuse but to help to understand. 'Being under Serb shellfire did not necessarily make us pro-Muslim,' admitted Colonel Riley. Serbs had been Britain's traditional Balkan allies. They had good cause to feel aggrieved at the manner in which the referendum on the country's independence had been staged; their cause was sound but it was played so badly it defied support. There's no doubt they felt very threatened by the Bosniac entity to the extent that their desperation was readily identifiable. They had this perpetual idea that their fears were never considered. Where the fighting was, were the worst villains who had been nobodies in peacetime. 'It was to the Serbs that the warning to the West of the green Islamic spear poised at the soft underbelly of Europe was attributed.'[74]

The recovery of The RWF was seen by many observers as a clearing of the decks as a preliminary to a NATO bombing campaign. Quite what would act as a trigger to start that campaign remained to be seen. The British presence had not been in Mladic's interest. Mladic appointed a Colonel Popovic as liaison officer for the extraction of 1RWF via Belgrade, but taking with it all its vehicles and weapons. Mladic feared more weapons and equipment falling into Bosniac hands, as had occurred with UNPROFOR's Ukrainian representatives. The difficulty would arise once the decommissioning team arrived to take away the camp's accountable stores including heavy plant and equipment. Unconsumed fuel and food would be given to UNHCR for distribution to the needy on both sides. The Bosniacs could not fail to notice the signs of a British withdrawal. When the low loaders rolled in, so the obstruction began. The Sarajevo Government announced that the British battalion, 'on which the enclave had depended for every mouthful of food for the past year and a half'[75] would only be 'allowed' to leave if all its weapons and equipment were put in a weapons control point. Colonel Riley had an uncompromising meeting with the Commander of the Bosniac 81st Division, telling him that any attempted repetition of the Ukrainian attack would be met with lethal force. In reality, the British appeared too tempting a source of almost everything the Bosniacs needed to allow the opportunity to pass by.

The probing of the perimeter fence by Bosniac military police and men of the Special Forces brigade began during the afternoon and evening of 24 August. Firing broke out at 20.00 as a preliminary to a concerted attack on Gorazde camp at 23.00. The RWF strength had been reduced to one company and it became a matter of all hands to the pump. Covering fire came from Bosniac positions on the high ground overlooking the camp on the east side of the Drina.[76] Flares went up. In the floating light, the Welshmen took careful aim and fired at the advancing Bosniacs, a number of whom fell. Some found their way in. Lance-Corporal Ganeshbahadur Gurung of the Gurkha Transport Regiment, one of a number of drivers of the decommissioning vehicles, had been detailed as sentry. In the darkness, he saw Muslims attempting to wrestle a man's personal weapon away from him. He intervened, 'kicking and punching the intruders until the soldier was released'.[77] While the fighting was at its height, a Serb liaison officer called in on the radio asking whether the Serbs could assist the British.

The attack had been an opportune attempt to steal food, fuel and weapons. General Smith used the event to embarrass the Sarajevo Government, undoubtedly successfully because within the space of twelve hours, three convoys (including the Ukrainians) set off for safe territory without interference. There are always consequences to unauthorized action such as the Bosniac attack on the British in the Gorazde enclave. That event proved far less serious than the occasion on 28 August when a Serb unit outside Sarajevo put five mortar rounds into the city's Markale Market. Twenty-three non-combatants were killed in what was a repeat of an earlier attack. The ramifications for Colonel Riley and his small band of eighty 1RWF were profound. Those looking for such an event, a trigger to launch reprisals against Serbia, were not slow in coming forward. A NATO response might be unavoidable but not until the UN keyholder – General Smith had taken control of the UN key from Mr Akashi – agreed, and General Smith said there would be no aerial retaliation until 1RWF were safely on the right side of the Bosnian-Serb border.

The Commander of the 81st Division told Colonel Riley that to stay another night would be unwise. Renegade elements within his division were likely to launch a better-prepared attack, not only in revenge for the death of Bosniac soldiers but also because the British had so much of what they did not and were determined to get. The gate sentry, Fusilier Jones 35, had been shot by a sniper but fortunately suffered only a slight wound to the hand.

Riley maintained regular contact with General Smith. He knew he had to go and he knew he had to go now, if only to keep ahead of Mladic's information flow. He had a valid one-way ticket for the remnants of his battalion group all the way through to Belgrade, the shortest route through Bosnian-Serb territory. General Smith asked whether the convoy could reach the Yugoslav border, 18½ miles (30 kilometres) distant, that night. Riley said they could. 'OK,' said the General, 'get going and tell me when you are across the frontier with all your Fusiliers.'[78]

Engineers opened a gap in the Serb minefield, allowing the last convoy out of Gorazde to begin what could have been a perilous journey. It was 16.45. The vehicles – twelve Saxon APCs and a dozen of assorted makes – were closed down ready for action, supported by on-call, cab-ranked fighter-bombers.[79] They crossed the confrontation line forty-five minutes later, leaving the possibility of an attack by Bosniacs behind them and at the same time taking on the risk of attack by the Serbs. 'Meanwhile,' wrote General Smith, 'it was important to conceal my intentions from Mladic, so telephone calls continued to be made as we investigated the mortaring of the Markale Market. Mladic wanted a joint commission, I said we would have to consult my higher HQ. I was stalling.'[80] The air forces began to confirm future targets for Operation Deliberate Force.

Serbs waved 1RWF through, their convoy having the benefit of clearance from no less a person than General Ratko Mladic. Rumbling through the early dusk, the convoy passed through Visegrad, receiving friendly waves from customers in colourful cafés, and on to the border. Special arrangements had been made to keep the border open and, sure enough, the plan worked. There too, inside Serbia, they made rendezvous with their logistic support, which had come down from Belgrade to effect replenishment, thus allowing 1RWF to drive on through to Croatia and Zagreb. Colonel Riley used his satellite phone to General Smith, confirming 1RWF's great escape:

> The relief as I sent the message over the satellite to General Smith was indescribable – followed by the realization that we had done what everyone had thought to be impossible: to extract from Gorazde and cross the Serbs' territory in good order, with all our equipment and without the loss of a single life. It was that realization and the lingering adrenaline which kept us all awake during the long eight hours that followed as we drove northward to Belgrade in the darkness and pouring rain.[81]

Lieutenant-Colonel Riley was awarded the Distinguished Service Order for his outstanding command and leadership of The Royal Welch Fusiliers during their tour of duty in Gorazde.

On 29 August, General Smith told General Mladic that there was no doubt the mortar fire had come from the Serb lines. Mladic made it perfectly clear what would happen to the battalion in the Gorazde enclave if the Bosnian Serbs were to be bombed. Presumably he was referring to 1RWF who had been given the open-ended guarantee of a safe passage to Zagreb under General Mladic's personal orders. 'The thought gave me pleasure at the time,' wrote General Smith. 'I then turned the UN key, and Admiral "Snuffie" Smith, the NATO Southern Region commander turned the NATO key.'[82]

NATO started the bombing campaign to an UNPROFOR plan. General Smith selected the targets and agreed the air defence targets that NATO wanted to hit throughout the operation. The Rapid Reaction Force was fully engaged, the artillery group firing over 250 fire missions.

Under the terms of the Dayton agreement, the parties agreed to Bosnia-Hercegovina being divided 51 per cent in favour of the Croat-Muslim Federation and 49 per cent to the Serbs. That formula had been on the table one and a half years earlier, since when over 10,000 of Bosnia-Hercegovina's people had been killed and many more joined the growing lines of refugees.

If anything is to be learned from the Bosnia experience, perhaps the most important lesson is that states should be absolutely certain what they are doing before volunteering to interpose themselves between the warring factions in other states' civil wars. These were not just common or garden belligerents but a deadly cocktail of Catholic Croats, Orthodox Serbs and Islamists.

Bosnia did not pass any of the tests by which traditional peacekeeping is recognized as being conducted, namely: with the consent of the states involved; that the peacekeepers act impartially; and lethal force is used only in self-defence.[83] The Americans never attempted to be impartial. They were pro-Bosniac as a matter of policy. UNPROFOR was unintentionally pro-Bosniac in so far as without UNPROFOR's support the Bosniacs would have succumbed. The 'safe areas' became springboards from which the Bosniacs attacked Serbs with the connivance and outright military and logistical support of the US and various Muslim countries of the international community. The enclaves served the purpose of blackmailing the West. They were virtually open prison camps whose inmates were sustained by the UN.

The Rules of Engagement applicable to the use of lethal force varied throughout UNPROFOR. The rules for Gorazde were less restrictive than for the remainder of UNPROFOR in that the Commanding Officer was permitted to defend his mission and the civilian population. 1RWF withdrew having had no set piece engagement, no fatalities, few wounded. The Serbs and Bosniacs fought each other, suffering relatively high losses, but in their engagements with the British their losses were few. Gorazde had been no Fallujah where the opposing sides came face to face, employing extreme violence one against the other. Nevertheless, Gorazde deserves to be regarded as a great battle because of its subtleties – it had been a battle of wills. A small, heavily under-strength, British, family regiment was interposed between the forces of two extreme, frequently barbaric, national armies and made its will prevail. After stepping aside, the way became clear for robust action which led to the Dayton Peace Agreement.

The Gorazde experience also casts light on modern battle strategy and the complexities of peacekeeping issues including consent and impartiality, as Colonel Riley told me:[84]

> Our understanding of doctrine at that time was based on the Cold War model of peacekeeping. If consent was given, it remained fixed, there was no way back. That was not our experience in Gorazde. Consent could exist at the political level but not tactical, and vice versa. We crossed and re-crossed the consent divide every time we fought a combat engagement and we were generally able to pursue a full range of activities; monitoring, humanitarian assistance, mediation – so consent is a relative, not an absolute, and the concept of no way back is flawed. We would have wished to have been scrupulously impartial but the manner in which we were tasked rendered that ideal impossible. We have also identified that a division exists between

peace enforcement and war with a divide of impartiality between them. We have also identified – and I hope learned – a number of important lessons.

First, when peacekeeping troops are committed, the military – if not political – end state should be clear, and their extraction should be planned at the same time as their insertion.

This point is one of the Cambridge Principles,[85] particularly applicable to Iraq and Afghanistan. Likewise, where situations are unstable, a peacekeeping force must be capable, if necessary, of the transition to enforcement, or fighting in self-defence. And, as John Major said, 'we should only try to peace keep where there is peace to be kept'.

Secondly, our Army philosophy of training, equipping and preparing for war – and then the stepping down to Operations Other Than War – is right, up to a point. When time is tight, commitment levels high and reserves scarce, we need to train for the worst thing that can happen to the man on the ground. 1RWF went to Bosnia trained and prepared for war – it was just as well. If our army ever loses sight of that philosophy, we are finished, as Srebrenica proved.

The Dutch experience of military operations had been far less extensive than that of the British Army, which has been on continuous operations since 1945. Moreover, caution has been consistently impressed upon the Dutch by their Government and Ministry of Defence. 'The failure of Srebrenica in July 1995, a dark page in Dutch military history, is still alive,' wrote Lieutenant-Colonel Dr Marcel de Haas. 'For months the Dutchbattalion (Dutchbat) had been deprived of rations and ammunition and was stuck in an isolated location with decreasing manpower. In preparation for the mission the Commander-in-Chief of the Army demanded that in order to emphasize the peaceful nature of the operation, the heavy guns on the armoured vehicles were to be replaced by machine guns.'[86] Given the paucity of resources and manpower available to the Dutch and their relatively poor standard of training, they were unable to fight in the same way as 1RWF.

'Thirdly,' continued General Riley, 'there is the philosophy of manoeuvre' – the antithesis of trench warfare.

> If we have such a philosophy, then it must underpin everything we do: it is not something we pick up for warfighting and then put down for Operations Other Than War. I tried to approach our operations from a manoeuvrist point of view – I hope successfully. I also feel that Mission Command [also known as mission-oriented orders and *auftragstaktik*], the tool of manoeuvre, is vindicated in Operations Other Than War. I received few direct orders and very limited guidance – this was due to political turmoil and the lack of any defined end state – but I always knew what General Smith's intentions were (and he was, I am sure, in the same position as me) and I was thus able to frame orders for my subordinates.

These orders would have given a bare outline of the Commander's intentions, leaving his subordinate commanders free to extemporize within the boundaries established by the Commanding Officer's mission. Mission Command is therefore quite unlike the detailed orders given by Lieutenant-Colonel 'H' Jones to 2 Para at Goose Green. 'One note of caution,' warned Colonel Riley, 'a principle of Mission Command is obedience to orders – which indicates that orders should, indeed must, be given. Mission Command is not an excuse for woolly thought, nor is it a let-out for commanders not to give their subordinates adequate orders.' The battalion has the capacity to generate sufficient intelligence for most contingencies. The Intelligence must however be properly assessed and sensible conclusions drawn – not as happened with 2 Para at Goose Green.

It does seem however that 1RWF were prisoners of a doctrinal trap: UN operations meant no intelligence should be gathered, therefore they would not be given any. The credibility of the UN is entirely dependent upon the capabilities of the contributors. It follows therefore that deploying forces on multi-national operations does not absolve higher command of the responsibility to provide the greatest capability possible to national troops deployed in harm's way. 1RWF received almost no additional intelligence, even nationally. Colonel Riley elaborated:

If we had stayed at Gorazde, we would certainly have been the target for Serb malevolence and wholly dependent upon air power to hold our position: not a happy thought given the Balkan weather even in September. We would also have been exploited by the Bosniacs for their own political end. Extraction was the right thing to do – it reduced exposure and increased our freedom of action. I hope no one is ever again put in the position I was in.

In Sierra Leone 2000, there was none of the chicanery or hubris associated with allies, NATO or the UN because the British chose to act unilaterally – not a frequent occurrence but something to be encouraged whenever the opportunity arises. Here, Operation Barras, undertaken by a small, select, joint UK force, proved one of the most highly successful hostage rescue operations in military history. In examining Barras and its predecessor, Palliser, we identify one of only two occasions in these battle accounts where no major difficulties were experienced with command and control (the other was the second phase of the Battle for Fallujah).

7

Operation Barras – Sierra Leone 2000

'A brilliant surgical strike which saved a nation'

In the research I have carried out for the writing of this book [Damien Lewis, *Operation Certain Death*, 2004], I have come across just one, authoritative account of the assault, written a year after the event. Richard Connaughton, formerly the British Army's Head of Defence Studies and now a security consultant, wrote a short article entitled 'Operation Barras' in the academic journal *Small Wars and Insurgencies*. . . . Other than that far from widely read publication, the story of the hostage crisis and Operation Barras seemed to have disappeared without trace.

Operation Barras, the codename given to a Special Forces mission to extract twelve hostages in Sierra Leone 2000, became known as one of the most highly successful rescue missions in recent military history. It is the story of the bold rescue of seven hostages from rebel camps in the Occra Hills, Sierra Leone, by a small, dedicated team of Special Forces. One can imagine how, within the Special Forces community, as information built up regarding the hostage situation, there would have been immediate recognition among that community that if there was to be a Special Forces rescue operation, nothing in recent times came as big or as complex. Any warrior worth his salt would have been clamouring to be included.

Knowing that I had been in Sierra Leone, in 2001 the editor of *Small Wars and Insurgencies* asked me to write a short article on the mission. I had no access to Special Forces sources. I knew the odd piece of information to be true but my final article was put together on the balance of probability. The point is that then, as now, the Ministry of Defence will neither acknowledge nor discuss Special Forces operations – those of the Special Air Service Regiment (SAS) and the Royal Navy equivalent, the Special Boat Service (SBS).

It transpired that some of my guesswork had been off target but, on the other hand, self-regulation excluded some information which would have been on target. Since 2001 however there has been systematic leakage – not all of it accurate – and a number of books written on the subject. The time has come to provide a revised account and I shall do so by drawing upon that which I believe to be true and which has already appeared in the public domain.

I do, however, have serious reservations regarding the restrictions imposed by the Minstry of Defence: I do not believe it is fair and reasonable to members of the Special Forces to impose a blanket ban on discussion of their operations. The Paras are not Special Forces and their participation in Operation Barras is not subject to censorship. A Company, 1st Battalion The Parachute Regiment played a vital supporting role and from the news which was released after the event, it might be possible to conclude that Operation Barras had been a Parachute Regiment operation. There is a need for control, but a discriminate form of control which recognizes the difference between releasing an outline of the Special Forces operation after the event and the preservation of anonymity.

One example of the Ministry of Defence's arbitrary censorship affected the Army's in-house magazine *Soldier*, the editor of which is permitted under Queen's Regulations to act as a self-regulator without reference to the Minstry of Defence. In an innocuous article, the editor wrote in general terms of the highly successful SAS[1] operation to release the British Army hostages from the clutches of the so-called West Side Boys bandits. The pulping of the entire print run of *Soldier* was ordered, not because there had been a breach of security but rather because the Ministry insisted on making the point that it was unequivocal when it came to matters of either discussing or acknowledging Special Forces participation in specific operations. In today's terrorist-suffused climate, the matter of anonymity is obviously not negotiable except, arguably, where a member of the Special Forces has lost his life on operations. The Ministry of Defence refused to admit that one Operation Barras fatality had been a member of the Special Forces, thereby denying him and his family recognition for having reached the zenith of military excellence.

Sierra Leone's natural harbour, by far the best on the west coast of Africa and where the capital Freetown is situated, is what most impressed its Portuguese discoverers in 1460. The country's name is derived from the Portuguese name Serra Lyoa, meaning Lion Mountains. Freetown was so named to acknowledge that it was to this place freed slaves had come for repatriation. This fertile land, the size of Scotland, has a population of 5.7 million. Cash crops include cacao, coffee, ginger, kola nuts and palm derivatives such as palm oil. The country is rich in minerals – aluminium, titanium and diamonds, the quest for the latter having been largely responsible for the state's instability. Controls were established shortly after diamonds were discovered in quantity in the early 1930s. In 1935 the colonial authorities appointed De Beers as the sole agent authorized to manage the exploitation of swathes of diamonds found close to the surface in the north and east of the country. So accessible were the diamonds that within two years 1 million carats of them had made a substantial contribution to the colony's GDP. It was this very accessibility that proved to be the source of the new country's problems after independence from Britain in 1961 following 174 years of colonial rule.

In 2001, 75,000 Klondikers in the diamond fields had been siphoning the state's lifeblood away. The country's GDP was estimated at £440 million – a per capita annual income of £91.3 – in large part because only £16.5 million of diamond sales were passing through official channels. Ninety per cent of the country's diamonds, so-called 'blood diamonds', were being traded by insurgents for Liberian weapons and ammunition, through a strange mixture of Israeli and Lebanese intermediaries. The life expectancy of the people had fallen to forty-nine years. The country was among the poorest of the world's states and held the unenviable record of having the world's worst healthcare. 'Sierra Leone', said the *Economist*, 'manifests the continent's worst characteristics. It is an extreme, but not untypical example of a state with all the epiphenomena and none of the institutions of government . . . it is unusual only in its brutality: rape, cannibalism and amputation have been common, with children often among its victims.'[2]

What the correspondent did not reveal was the fact that it was often drugged children of the Small Boys Units who were responsible for the crimes. These young thugs operated within criminal groups using amputation as a means of achieving leverage. The amputation of arms fell into two categories – 'long sleeve' or 'short sleeve', the former where amputations, single or double, were made at the wrist and the latter above the elbow. There is an amputee centre close to the Army barracks in Freetown which offers artificial limbs and comfort to countless amputees. I had gone there when I was in Sierra Leone on a familiarization visit in 2000. I felt a tap on my leg and the oft-heard plea of a child, 'sweets, sweets'. I had no sweets but I did have a pocketful of pencils for such an occasion. I turned to see a smiling little girl with amazingly white teeth. She wore a faded print frock upon which were large sunflowers. I bent down, offering her a pencil. She raised her arms. She had no hands. What has to be borne in mind regarding Operation Barras is that although its mission was the rescue of twelve hostages, its consequences went much further, changing the whole psychology of rebellion.

In January 1991, Foday Sankoh became leader of the Revolutionary United Front (RUF). He had come to prominence earlier when as a corporal photographer he accused the Government of neglecting the Army. An unreformable barrack-room lawyer, he spoke up in the name of the other ranks and received a gaol sentence of seven years for his trouble. After completing five, he went to Libya, returning to Sierra Leone in 1991 when he became leader of the RUF, originally part of Liberian President Charles Taylor's National Patriotic Front. For eight years, Sankoh led a war against all comers in Sierra Leone. It was not an ideologically driven crusade but one based on settling scores by seizing control of the country's diamond resources. Sankoh argued that the gap between rich and poor had grown too large, having in mind the 'fat cats' who lived on the Peninsula.

The conflict in Sierra Leone began in March 1991 when the RUF launched an attack into Sierra Leone from the east, close to the Liberian border, with the intention of overthrowing the Government of Major-General Joseph Saidu Momoh. Momoh clung to power for a year before being overthrown by a group of young officers concerned that their men had not been paid. The coup leader, 25-year-old Captain Valentine Strasser, negotiated a defence agreement with a Pretoria-based private military company, Executive Outcomes (EO). Strasser intended to pay EO's monthly fee of £840,000 from diamond production. The fee was not excessive and the danger self-evident, with the RUF 25 miles (40 kilometres) from Freetown.

EO formed an Air Wing with former Soviet helicopters which they used to search out and destroy the RUF. With a force of approximately 150 men, EO began rolling back the RUF and training the Kamajor people of Sierra Leone to bolster the strength of the Army. In March 1996, Ahmed Tejan Kabbah, leader of Sierra Leone's People's Party, became the democratically elected president of Sierra Leone. The reality of a serious dichotomy soon became apparent. The responsibility for paying EO's men fell to the Sierra Leone Government but it could not afford the freedom they brought. Kabbah unilaterally reduced EO's fee from £840,000 to £391,000 – insufficient to finance its operations. The drying up of funding and growing international pressure from countries ill at ease with the notion of employing mercenaries forced EO to leave Sierra Leone in January 1997, owed almost £11 million by the Government.

Sierra Leone's volatile military did not care much for the responsibilities being given to the Kamajors and the plan to reduce the strength of the military as a cost-saving measure. Sandhurst-trained officer, Johnny Paul Koroma, came forward to lead a coup which overthrew Kabbah. He led the Army into the formation of a junta with the RUF and the Armed Forces Revolutionary Council (AFRC), which jointly took control of all but a small part of the country – the Aberdeen Peninsula, from where foreign nationals were

evacuated. Sierra Leone was suspended from the Commonwealth and the UN applied sanctions, including a weapons
embargo.

Lieutenant-Colonel Tim Spicer, formerly Scots Guards
and a Falklands veteran, headed a company – Sandline
International – to supply arms to the democratically elected
government of Sierra Leone. Beneficiaries were friendly forces
supporting the Government. One group, formed in 1997,
called itself the West Side Boys. Sandline's business was of
course contrary to the arms embargo, an embargo aimed at
circumventing the excesses of the bad, not the best intentions
of the good. UN Security Council Resolution 1132, drafted
by the UK, did not make that distinction. Resolution 1132
prohibited the export of both weapons and oil to Sierra
Leone, to insurgents and Government. Spicer was not
conducting his business covertly; he did so with the full
knowledge of the Foreign and Commonwealth Office. One
consequence of the Sandline initiative was President Kabbah's
return to power on 10 March 1998.

When the nature of Sandline's work became public knowledge, it caused considerable embarrassment to the architect
of Britain's ethically flavoured foreign policy; the Foreign
Secretary, Robin Cook, entered a plea of plausible denial –
apparently he had not been told what his subordinates were
doing. Twice, private military companies had successfully
intervened to save democracy in Sierra Leone only to see
these successes frittered away by a misplaced sense of idealism
within the international community. 'Where 13,000 UN
peacekeepers with an annual budget of over half a billion
dollars failed dismally in 2000, a force of just 150 mercenaries
deployed by Executive Outcomes succeeded four years earlier
with an annual budget of $20 million.' If the UK alone could
or would have found a process whereby London financed

Executive Outcomes, the cost benefit to the UK would have been enormous.[3] UN Secretary-General Kofi Annan believed the world was not yet ready to privatize peace.[4]

The appearance of contractors, a term which also embraces mercenaries, in modern conflict reflects the well nigh predictable inability of intervening governments to resource their interventions adequately with military personnel. No one could describe the motives of EO or Sandline as altruistic but that does not mean they were not a force for good. Use of contractors is a feature in a number of the studies in this book, and they could be categorized as the good, the bad and the ugly. The former applies to Sierra Leone, the bad to American mercenary support of the Croatian attack on the Serbs in Krajina and the ugly to Fallujah, with particular reference to the Blackwater security company.

Sankoh enjoyed a charmed life while consistently orchestrating thousands of deaths and mutilations. Nigeria, which was the major regional power which led the military operation in Sierra Leone for the Economic Community of West African States Ceasefire Monitoring Group (ECOMOG), captured Sankoh in 1998 and sent him into exile in neighbouring Togo. A Freedom Court sentenced Sankoh to death in absentia for his crimes against humanity. In June 1998, the UN Security Council established the totally inadequate United Nations Observer Mission in Sierra Leone (UNOMSIL). The observers were unarmed and entirely dependent upon ECOMOG for their protection. On 6 January 1999, the RUF again invaded Freetown, to be confronted by the armed forces of ECOMOG, who cleared the city and reinstated President Kabbah, a friend of UN Secretary-General Kofi Annan.

For some reason the death sentence against Sankoh was not put into effect. To the contrary, America's Secretary of State Madeleine Albright and British Foreign Secretary Robin

Cook managed to persuade Kabbah not only to rehabilitate Sankoh but also to appoint him vice-president and give him a Cabinet position – unbelievably, Minister for Natural Resources, a position whose responsibilities included the nation's diamond resources. It is said that the mines provided Sankoh with $90 million with which to pay his adherents. Kabbah had been persuaded to give the fox the key to the hen house. This extraordinary arrangement became formalized in the Lomé Peace Agreement of 7 July 1999. Moreover, UN Security Council Resolution 1270 of 22 October 1999 provided for the creation of the United Nations Mission in Sierra Leone (UNAMSIL) to monitor the process of the agreement and disarmament. UNOMSIL was terminated. Sankoh flattered the optimists in London, Washington and New York with a token, partial disarmament but retained sufficient weapons with which to continue terrorizing and intimidating those outside his group. Sankoh supported President Charles Taylor's seizure of power in Liberia and it was Sierra Leone's diamonds that helped Taylor maintain his position.

UN Security Council Resolution 1270 was framed under Chapter VII (enforcement) of the UN Charter and attracted for its policing African and Asian troops of a basic standard required to monitor a traditional peacekeeping agreement where the consent of both parties – i.e. Kabbah and Sankoh – was in place. Indian and Nigerian troops were of a good standard and were exceptions to that rule. In a very short time, the parties to the Lomé agreement began to dispute the terms and conditions of Resolution 1270. The withdrawal of Sankoh's consent and the support the UN gave to Kabbah made nonsense of two of the essential peacekeeping criteria, namely consent and impartiality. The problem revolved around Resolution 1270 and the absence of precision.

Although mandated by reference to Chapter VII, the conditions of Resolution 1270 were pacific and what might be thought to be applicable to a peacekeeping force. The all-important authority 'to use all necessary means' was not there.

The head of the Economic Community of West African States (ECOWAS), Lansana Kouyate, insisted that, 'If the UN Security Council hesitates in changing the mandate, ECOWAS countries may be forced to go on their own in Sierra Leone with a peace enforcement mandate', but it was an empty threat. UNAMSIL's mandate was restricted to using force in self-defence, to defending the capital, to protecting civilians and to aiding operations. Only the final proviso could be interpreted as permitting offensive operations against the RUF. UNAMSIL chose not to interpret Resolution 1270 as was intended: they would resort to lethal force only if attacked. One wise head commented: 'The RUF understood fully what they were doing when they signed up to Lomé but they do not have the people to guide them with the due process. Too much emphasis is being placed upon the military aspects of the agreement and insufficient upon the political.'

Sankoh's backtracking on aspects of the Lomé agreement and the murder of a number of peacekeepers confirmed that UNAMSIL had become a peacekeeping operation in name only. Sankoh all along had pursued a separate agenda to keep the diamond wealth to himself and take over the country. It was an impossibility to emphasize political considerations to the RUF, which had no political organization. It was a collection of bush chiefs. The weak, 8,300-strong UN force had neither the presence nor the capability to intimidate the RUF, who systematically seized a large number of UN men and disarmed them. The UK had a sprinkling of officers working for the UN in the demobilization camps and they were among the hostages taken. These acts caught the attention of the Permanent Joint Headquarters (PJHQ) in Northwood, which had been newly set up to mobilize Rapid Reaction Forces to participate in operations deemed to be in the national interest. It in turn liaised with the UK Special Forces. In the event, the Special Forces would not be needed because the British officers had the guile and initiative, with or without assistance, to effect their escape.

More seriously, the RUF captured 500 UN peacekeepers, thereby hugely embarrassing the UN and once again raising the question of the viability of peacekeeping in Africa and elsewhere. Sankoh's 'seizure of the UN battalions that were operating the demobilization camps follows directly from their success in providing a way out for boy soldiers and other villagers conscripted by the RUF', reported an editorial in *The Times*. 'His commanders saw their private armies melt away; his fellow smugglers suspected that the UN operation would eventually cut off their supply of diamonds.'[5]

UN Secretary-General Kofi Annan realized that if Sankoh was permitted to force upon the UN the kind of humiliating withdrawal seen in Mogadishu 1993, the UN's credibility would count for nothing. Annan appealed to the United States, the United Kingdom and France to send Rapid Reaction Forces into Sierra Leone. All three nations declined Annan's initial invitation to put combat troops into Sierra Leone. On Friday 5 May, British Foreign Secretary Cook said that the UK would only be providing technical and logistical support to the UN. Despite that statement, the planning of offensive action was already in the process of consideration at PJHQ.

News of the RUF's advance on Freetown in May 2000 posed a moral quandary for the British Government. This was a crisis partly of its own making. It had made an initial investment of £60 million ($120m) to bolster the Kabbah Government. Arguably, as the former colonial power the UK had a residual obligation to act. The British Government had been the subject of valid criticism for having been too slow to respond to the humanitarian flood crisis in Mozambique earlier in 2000. PJHQ had not thus far been fully tested. Soon it would be.

In 1994, the UK had an inefficient system of responding to crises and there was a constant, though apparently contradictory, political intention to improve military efficiency and yet at the same time achieve savings against the defence budget. Prior to the creation of PJHQ it was usual for the arrangement of command and control of joint forces deployed on overseas operations for the Chief of the Defence Staff to appoint one of the three single service commanders – Navy, Army or Air Force – to be the Joint Commander, employing his own headquarters as the Joint Headquarters.

This selection process did not normally begin until after the Cabinet has decided to commit British forces. The three-star Chief of Joint Operations commands PJHQ. One of his subordinates, a brigadier from the Army or Royal Marines, the Chief of Joint Force Operations, commands the Joint Force Headquarters. The resources he is supplied with for each specific operation are drawn from the Joint Rapid Reaction Force, comprising a pool of combat and support forces from which the UK meets all short-notice, crisis action, planned military contingencies. The units in the pool are those that are the best trained across the whole range of military capabilities and include Special Forces. The pool is configured into two echelons according to readiness requirements. First echelon forces' readiness varies from forty-eight hours for Spearhead Forces and Joint Force Headquarters to completion within ten days; the second echelon's more substantial capabilities have a phased entry of eleven to thirty days.

At 10 a.m. on 5 May 2000, Britain's Joint Force Head-quarters' commander, Brigadier David Richards, was ordered to deploy to Freetown prepared to oversee the evacuation of British, Commonwealth and EU nationals from the country, in military parlance known as Non-Combat Evacuation Operation (NEO). An NEO had been practised in Sierra Leone over Christmas 1998 and two operations were conducted there in 1999. The Brigadier and his small advance party arrived at Lungi International Airport at midday on Saturday 6 May.

Lungi Airport is separated from the capital Freetown by a 5-mile- (8-kilometre-) wide strip of water. The two are connected by a strategic, 75-mile- (121-kilometre-) long, horseshoe-shaped road, two-thirds of which, in May, was susceptible to RUF interference. On reviewing the situation where the Nigerians had stopped the RUF advance at Waterloo, Brigadier Richards requested PJHQ to release immediately the lead company of the Spearhead land element followed by the remainder of the group. Operation Palliser had been set in train.

The Falkland intervention had been assumed to be the last British unilateral intervention, but it was not. British forces in Sierra Leone operated independently of UNAMSIL. At last, recognition was being given to the essential requirement of unity of command. NEO could not be conducted without helicopter support. Four CH-47 Chinooks were ordered to Sierra Leone via Gibraltar, Tenerife, Mauritania and Dakar. The first pair arrived during the evening of Sunday 7 May to support NEO, only thirty hours after being tasked. The Commanding Officer 22 SAS, two SAS squadrons and a troop of SBS made covert entry into Sierra Leone.

Meanwhile, the political and military activity upon which a successful rapid reaction to a crisis is founded moved on apace. On 7 May orders were sent from London to redeploy Royal Navy assets, to ensure ships 'were going in the right direction' if circumstances should make them necessary. Led by HMS *Ocean*, the Amphibious Ready Group (ARG), among whose particularly valuable attributes are littoral operations, received orders to sail from Marseilles, to make for Gibraltar and thence go south down the west African coast. The ARG spends up to six months of the year at sea in the Mediterranean with support ships. Embarked in HMS *Ocean* was the 600-strong 42 Royal Marine Commando Group with heavier weapon support than was available to the Spearhead battalion, the 1st Battalion The Parachute Regiment.[6] The battalion's A Company had been detached on a training exercise in Jamaica and had as its nominal replacement D Company of 3 Para. In the event of close air support being required, the carrier HMS *Illustrious* with seven Sea Harriers and six GR7 Harriers aboard was ordered to make for the west African coast from Lisbon.[7]

On Monday 8 May, Lungi Airport had been secured. 1 Para Group set about the domination of their tactical area of responsibility. Rapid reaction becomes progressively less relevant and effective the longer it takes ground forces to dominate the territory into which they have been inserted. 1 Para Group oversaw the evacuation of 299 expatriates in the first forty-eight hours but the calming influence brought about by the force's arrival stemmed the flow of civilians seeking repatriation. Brigadier Richards faced up to the fact that no sooner had he arrived than his mission was complete. Loath to offend his political masters by entering into a whole new regime of mission creep, the Brigadier nevertheless had to face the reality that his withdrawal would undermine the UN mission and possibly see the fall of the democratically elected government of Sierra Leone. The adoption of this pragmatic new approach was confirmed by Robin Cook: 'We must not allow a few thousand rebels to prevent an end to violence.' 'His judgement', commented *The Times*, 'may be unduly influenced by his earlier bruising over Sierra Leone.'[8]

Attention turned to the training and disciplining of Sierra Leone's three battalions with a view to reversing the RUF's advance. In this they were substantially successful in so far as they regained much of the strategic horseshoe route connecting Freetown to the airport. The role of the 250 trainers and approximately seventy advisers deployed from the UK alongside Operation Palliser was to maintain momentum and to build an army of nine battalions in three brigades with supporting arms and logistics from Sierra Leone nationals. The intention was that this national force would eventually take the battle to the RUF, defeating it in its heartland to the east. During the training phases, trained elements would maintain the military initiative and, in the event that the UN should go wobbly, secure key terrain. A principal component of the UK exit strategy, especially in information operation terms, was to keep Operation Palliser in being until the UN had been brought up to what was then its mandated strength with the capability of deploying into key terrain on the horseshoe.

The success of the British Operation Palliser was largely due to respective commanders at the tactical and operational levels being entirely focused upon their own responsibilities. At the tactical level, the Paras pressed on, keen to engage in the business for which they had been trained, until relieved by 42 Commando Royal Marines on 26 May 2000. 42 Commando withdrew on 15 June 2000, leaving behind a profoundly more confident UN, a bolstered president and a modest training team of Royal Irish at Benguema Camp 20 miles (32 kilometres) south-east of Freetown to expedite the training and confidence-building of the Sierra Leone Army. Sankoh was captured for a second time but on this occasion there would be no prospect of immunity. Britain 'restated her strategic priorities: to repel the rebels; to restore the peace and to rebuild Sierra Leone'.[9] Operation Palliser had made its own statement which the RUF could not ignore. The outlook appeared encouraging – a time for self-congratulation. This, however, would be premature. Having achieved a textbook rapid reaction with Operation Palliser, the UK now found itself, sooner than it would have wished, conducting another rapid reaction operation in Sierra Leone.

The Royal Irish Regiment were responsible for delivering short-term training to the Sierra Leone Armed Forces under the direction of Brigadier Gordon Hughes, Commander International Military Assistance and Training Team (IMATT) and Commander British Forces.[10] The West Side story began when, after a lunchtime plate of goat curry with UNAMSIL's Jordanian battalion, Major Alan Marshall, OC C Company, The 1st Battalion The Royal Irish Regiment, together with ten members of his regiment and one Sierra Leone regiment guide, drove northwards towards Laia in three Land Rovers. The three vehicles were open, the rear vehicle, Britain's 'technical', mounting a Weapons Mounted Installation Kit (WMIK), two machine guns – a 12.7-mm (0.5-inch) Browning and a 7.62-mm GPMG – in addition to the group's personal weapons. It was Friday, 25 August 2000. Then, unusually, the British patrol turned off the Masiaka–Freetown Highway. They drove down a narrow, potholed, 7-mile- (11-kilometre-) long, laterite road, heading for Magbeni in the Ocra Hills on the banks of Rokel Creek.

The shattered village of Magbeni formed part of the divided

base of a notoriously fickle and dangerous band of irregulars and bandits who terrorized the west side of Sierra Leone. The 600-strong group called themselves the West Side Soldiers but they were more usually described in the media as the West Side Boys (WSB). Their diminutive title belied just how dangerous was this group which had, until recently, supported the Government. Their unpredictability was fuelled by heroin, cocaine and alcohol. The effects of this cocktail reached an apogee in mid-afternoon, precisely the same time the group of twelve was about to make its courtesy call. To the WSB, murder, rape, torture and mutilation were common. They were led by 24-year-old, self-styled 'Brigadier' Foday Kallay, who had recently killed twenty-seven disenchanted followers. Below him in the pecking order were a number of colonels, each with his own adherents.

Kallay was not at Magbeni when the Royal Irish arrived and were surrounded by an indignant, armed mob. 'Who gave you permission to come here?' they demanded. The situation quickly became ugly. A former Sierra Leone Army Bedford 4-ton lorry mounting a twin ZPU-2 14.5-mm heavy machine gun came up behind them, blocking their avenue of escape. Outnumbered and outgunned, Marshall told his men to lay down their arms. The heavy machine gunner turned the gun's control mechanism to single shots before they were all beaten, bundled down to the riverside, put into canoes and taken over the creek to Kallay's headquarters in the village of Gberi Bana.

When the international media picked up the story, the Ministry of Defence could do little more than speculate why Marshall had made his unscheduled diversion. Why, it was asked, had this heavily armed patrol not fought back?[11] The irony of the humiliating situation into which the professional British patrol had voluntarily put itself was that only two months previously the British had spoken with contempt of UNAMSIL surrendering a large number of hostages. Now some sectors of the UN reverberated with a satisfying sense of *schadenfreude*. 'We asked the British what their men were doing,' said a senior UN military officer, 'but they have not told us. Perhaps the reason is that their commanders just don't know.' Which was true. Of all the reasons adduced, the most plausible was that this had been a case of 'military tourism'.[12] It happens.

Immediately, the British media roundly condemned the British Government's Sierra Leone policy. Of the hostages, *The Times* editorial thundered: 'They had better be rescued fast, by negotiation or by force, if the Government is not to be held culpably reckless for the safety of Britain's armed forces.'[13] The 'H' word, hostages, will always have the effect of pressurizing liberal Western democracies because of the implication of political and military failure. Tactical miscalculation had immediately become a strategic crisis. Almost all of the 5,000-strong Palliser assets had long gone, replaced by a 250-strong training team, the Military Assistance and Training Team (MATT)[14] with force protection. The British Government had made a strategic commitment to Sierra Leone but had resourced that commitment with sufficient force to achieve only local tactical success in an emergency.

Had not the Director Special Forces (DSF) in the rank of Brigadier found himself sent on an aircraft winging its way towards Sierra Leone, he would have been expected to be present at the Government high-level security committee, the Cabinet Office Briefing Room (COBRA). Common criticisms of past operations have been of weak or indecisive diplomacy and decision-making. That was not the case in Operation Barras. It had a sound, assured start from the beginning with reliable inter-agency linkages and it maintained that high standard through to completion.

Positioning DSF at the British High Commission formed part of a contingency plan. The Government had no intention of using military force as a reprisal, only if negotiations failed. Over the road from the Cabinet office, deep in the bowels of the Ministry of Defence at the Ministry's Crisis Management Centre, from where Palliser had been co-ordinated, staff settled down once again to co-ordinate Operation Barras. The intention to separate policy from operations, PJHQ's *raison d'être*, had therefore not entirely come to fruition. The forces required to effect a contested release of the hostages now had to be warned to make rendezvous in Sierra Leone.

There are four SAS squadrons (A, B, D and G) each with a strength of approximately fifty men. Squadrons are organized into four specialist troops – Mountain, Boat, Mobility and Air. B Squadron, the standby SAS Squadron, had more or less been firmed up for operations in Macedonia. A decision was accordingly made to recall an acclimatized D Squadron from a training exercise in Kenya.[15] With two village targets to pacify, the SAS would need reinforcement. Two dozen members of the SBS found themselves added to the Order of Battle as reinforcements to the SAS. The Spearhead battalion at that stage was The Grenadier Guards. Alternatively, The Royal Irish had only very recently completed a tour of duty in Sierra Leone. It was their own people in danger. Either of these battalions could have provided the reinforcing company but neither was asked.

DSF asked for an unspecified Parachute Regiment company to support Special Forces. 1 Para had recently returned from Operation Palliser. The Commanding Officer was asked to appoint a company to join Operation Barras. He nominated A Company which had not gone on Operation Palliser because the company had been on an intensive live-firing exercise in Jamaica. The choice did not impress the Field Army from where there were complaints of favouritism and of there being two armies.

Three Chinook of 7 Squadron RAF, Joint Special Forces Aviation Wing, dedicated to Special Forces support, were ordered to Sierra Leone. Ideally the number should have been four. Two army Lynx helicopters capable of firing machine guns and rockets, required in the fire support role, had been disassembled to fit inside a Hercules transport aircraft and consigned to Lungi airport. There they would be reassembled and made airworthy by HMS *Argyle*'s and REME artificers, and have an engine change.

Gberi Bana, where the hostages had been taken, was the more important of the two villages occupied by the West Side Boys. This was where Kallay, his colonels and families and 200 of their men lived, together with twenty to thirty slaves captured from local villages or plucked out of vehicles on the highway. They suffered terrible indignities, the men forced to fight for the bandits who executed or mutilated them on the slightest whim. The women became sex slaves, living out the atrocities of each day until out of boredom they would as likely as not be killed. The officers' and administrative quarters could be identified separately from the accommodation of the rank and file. The former, of which there were more than a dozen, were single-storey buildings with stained concrete walls, atop which lay rusty corrugated iron sheets forming the roofs. The junior members of the group had to be satisfied with thatched mud huts. Open to the riverside, the habitation might be described as fitting within a 1,000-yard-wide ((914-metre-wide) monster bite taken out of the primary jungle. There was an assembly area and a football pitch, both of which would be considered for use in a future attack.

The hostages had been taken across the 250-yard-wide (228-metre-wide) Rokel Creek, now in full spate at the height of the wet season, thus obscuring an intricate pattern of sandbars below its surface. The hostages' point of departure had been the village of Magbeni, the larger of the two garrison villages, with a population of 400. The villages could support each other with heavy firepower. The need therefore to neutralize Magbeni at the same time as the hostage release attempt was being made became a factor in a wider plan. In terms of the courses open to an attacker, the fact that the track the Irish had taken was the only way in and out tended to rule out a ground-launched attack through the jungle into a populated area. The proof of that particular pudding was assessed by inserting observation patrols along the river. Their report also led to that option being set aside. The sandbars, logistics and movement rendered a full-force water approach difficult. Moreover, if that option were taken, it might appear that this was an SBS-led operation. The argument in favour of an air-launched attack therefore appeared so strong as to suggest a formal Appreciation of the Situation or Estimate would prove nugatory.

The question uppermost in Kallay's mind was why the British had come. The suggestion that Marshall had come to his territory in an attempt to persuade him to join the SLA (Sierra Leone Army) training package appeared too implausible. What seemed likely was that this was a reconnaissance force, a preliminary to an attack. Corporal Mousa Bangura, the Sierra Leone Army guide, insisted that that which Marshall said was true. If that were indeed so, Kallay had no intention of looking a gift horse in the mouth. The increase of helicopter traffic passing above his headquarters confirmed the Boys' nervousness when aircraft were in their vicinity. An uncompromising message went back to the military authorities: stop the air traffic or the hostages would be killed.

It seems that Kallay decided to use the Irish to secure advantage in the negotiations which he knew would follow. He would endeavour to extract the most he could out of the British. That was his Plan A. His Plan B revised one of Sankoh's ideas, to achieve the 'Somalia Effect'. If the negotiations failed, he would initiate 'Operation Kill British', beginning with an attack on Benguema Training Camp, and the seizure of weapons and ammunition, followed by a march on Freetown where he would instal himself as president. To achieve the Somalia effect would require the killing of the hostages. In Somalia in 1993, eighteen US military fatalities was all that was required to force the withdrawal of the Americans and the corresponding collapse of the UN presence there. Kallay had eleven Britons whose deaths might well encourage a British withdrawal and the collapse of UNAM-SIL. Already in the UK the opposition Conservative Party was calling for withdrawal from Sierra Leone. Kallay felt confident that the British would not attack him, for that would most surely lead to the death of the hostages. Either way, the British hostages would be Kallay's means of securing his destiny. One hostage, however, was of no value to Kallay, the man whom Kallay blamed for bringing the British. He was of course Corporal Mousa Bangura.

While the British were roughed-up and subjected to mock execution, they would not be badly injured for as long as there remained a prospect of negotiations producing something of value. They were kept together, first in the home of a relatively benign colonel before being put under the care of one who was less so. Kallay kept Mousa away from the British, his arms and legs bound. He had as his prison a deep trench latrine from where he was brought up every now and again for a severe beating. The Boys regarded him as a traitor, insisting on his separation so that there was no interpreter available to prevent them talking freely among themselves. So consistent and violent were the beatings Mousa had to endure that it was only a matter of time before he died. Occasionally the Small Boys Unit was let loose upon him as a reward or treat.

Elsewhere, the wheels were in motion to plan and mount a hostage rescue operation – a process which took approximately ten days. In the British High Commission, the High Commissioner liaised with the Sierra Leone Government – President Kabbah's permission was required to initiate Operation Barras. DSF had responsibility for the operation. The DSF had his own dedicated secure means of communication while Brigadier Gordon Hughes, the public face of the British, took responsibility for the support of the operation. On 31 August, the sixth day of the crisis, having done a quick turnaround after arriving back from Kenya, the Special Forces advance party was on its way to Sierra Leone. They had been allocated the relatively obscure tented camp at remote Waterloo where the presence of military would not be seen as out of the ordinary. Operational security took precedence over everything. As ever, the media were alert for signs.

The SAS needed as much intelligence of the layout of the two villages as possible: where the people were, what weapons they had and where they were sited, their state of alert and when they would be at their most vulnerable. Now, with the arrival of the main body from the UK, a priority had to be the insertion of four-men observation teams at both Gberi Bana and Magbeni. A small group of SAS had remained in Sierra Leone after the Operation Palliser force withdrew. A unanimous view would be that the bandits were at their most vulnerable at first light, when the Boys would be suffering the effects of drugs and drink. It has been alleged that two insiders had been recruited to provide intelligence, but coming and going and making physical contact would have proved difficult. Nevertheless, it does seem that on at least two occasions the hostages were passed messages, one of reassurance and one telling them the attack would be the next day. Both could have come from the observation team. The SAS would also discover the significance of voodooism within the group. Both Sankoh's and Kallay's wives had been ju-ju priestesses. The foot soldiers were persuaded that they would be bullet-proof in conflict, allowing them to close with their enemy and throttle them. This meant that, as in Somalia, the warriors would press their attacks fearlessly. Every factor had to be carefully considered, analysed for risk, and preventative measures devised to ensure Operation Barras would not be remembered solely as a brave, forlorn hope.

Meanwhile, the negotiation process had begun, with a rendezvous at the top of the track on the Benguema–Masiako road. The fact that the British team leader was Lieutenant-Colonel Simon Fordham, a real colonel, impressed the Boys. No one envied him his task, nor the unenviable position in which he, as Commanding Officer of The 1st Battalion The Royal Irish, found himself. Over the days, there were incremental enhancements to the British unarmed negotiating team. Two Metropolitan Police negotiators arrived from England and two SAS men with negotiation skills, dressed in Royal Irish uniform, joined the team.[16] Occasionally the Boys brought selected hostages with them, not as participators but as proof of life. One of those hostages had been the regimental Signals Officer. As he bade a policeman goodbye, shaking his hand, the policeman's hand closed over an object which passed between them. When out of sight, the policeman unclenched his hand and found a biro top in which a map had been hidden and which revealed the hut occupied by the hostages, the village's defences and its geography.

Among the items on the West Side Boys' wish list were an outboard motor, a satellite radio, education in England and incorporation into the Army. So delighted was Kallay with the gifts that followed, including an outboard motor, that he agreed to the release of five hostages. Marshall originally decided that the five to be released would be the junior ranks and that is what he told them. Unfortunately for them, he changed his mind. The OC was a bachelor and, on reflection, Marshall thought it best to allow the five married men their liberty.[17] Ultimately that decision proved to be sound because the senior ranks were in a better, more informed position from which to brief the SAS. The change of heart, however, gave rise to some distress within the group.

After debriefing the five hostages, 'the conclusion was drawn that there was little prospect that the remaining seven hostages would be released unharmed. This military judgement was based largely on the breakdown of negotiations, the unpredictability and volatility of the WSB, and in particular the manner in which released hostages had been treated whilst in captivity.'[18]

The SAS wasted no time in getting down to rehearsals. At Waterloo, they laid out a model of Gberi Bana. After individuals had been allocated to the hostage rescue team and eight six-man fire teams, time and again they walked the course, applying risk management, remembering the outer limits of their arcs of fire so as to minimize the possibility of fratricide. On 5 September, four days after D Squadron's arrival, A Company 1 Para arrived.[19] They were collocated yet separate. OC A Company made no attempt to strengthen the three rifle platoons in his company group. A number had just arrived from the recruit training organization. There was no question of them being excluded. He did, however, add members from the battalion patrols platoon and support company which brought 81-mm mortars, all assets not integral to a rifle company. The SAS cast an eye over their partners in the enterprise. What struck them most was the youthfulness of the Paras. They had an average age of nineteen and no combat experience. On the other side of the coin there was an instinctive sense of hero worship. Many SAS had their origins in The Parachute Regiment. In that respect the example of the relationship between the Paras and SAS was identical to that seen between the Rangers and Delta Force in Mogadishu, 1993. The SAS had not worked so closely with The Parachute Regiment before. The success of Barras would contribute towards the decision that one of the three Parachute Regiment battalions would be assigned to Special Forces support.

The British Government's desire for a negotiated settlement remained Government policy. The negotiators increasingly had their impressions confirmed to the extent that the West Side Boys were merely going through the motions. They consistently arrived later and later after the appointed time and their accompanying armoury increased. Colonel Fordham's team reflected on the wisdom of their attending the meetings unarmed. Not only did it convey to the Boys a sense of weakness but also an encouragement to make the relatively straightforward move to top up the number of hostages. The six British hostages sensed a mood change in the camp, so much so that they seriously considered making their escape down the river when their escorts were inattentive.

The plan to rescue them moved on apace. Two of the three large Chinooks with their twin rotors would shoehorn themselves into the narrow confines of Gberi Bana, an armed enemy camp. The plan epitomized the SAS motto 'Who Dares

Wins' for, examined dispassionately, the concept seemed to invite disaster. The Chinook carrying the hostage rescue team would hover outside the hostages' hut while the SAS/SBS fast-roped down to secure them in their building. The principal role of the in-place observation team was to use their firepower to protect the Chinook. The task of the second Chinook was to land at the football pitch, from where the remaining fire teams would begin to attack in their assigned areas. The concept of operations was to inflict casualties on the enemy wherever presented with a view to forcing the Boys out to the jungle edge, from where the attack helicopters were authorized to engage them. There was no such sensitivity in the free-fire zone of Magbeni. While the Chinooks were offloading the Paras south of the village, the attack helicopters would rake the village and sites identified as being the locations of heavy weapons capable of putting supportive fire down on Gberi Bana.

For both these attacks, Gberi Bana and Magbeni, the attackers were to be self-sufficient, having to carry everything required – ammunition, food and water – with them. They also took night vision goggles. Their bergens weighed in excess of 100 lb (45 kg). For planning purposes, the Chinook will carry forty-five combat troops. On operations, risks are taken. In the Falklands, the Chinook Bravo November carried eighty members of 2 Para and their bergen rucksacks but the paras carried less per man than the Special Forces committed to Barras. Additional space also had to be found to accommodate the door-mounted 12.7-mm chain guns fitted for the operation. For the time being, the SAS/SBS and Paras continued with their preparations; they would carry on until the negotiations either succeeded or irretrievably collapsed.

On Thursday 7 September, two weeks into the hostage crisis, there occurred one of those serious operational breaches of security similar to the one which had caused so much consternation at Goose Green. The arrival of A Company 1 Para at Lungi airport had been witnessed by two reporters. The lid could not stay on the story, and it was released on Tuesday 5 September by the *Guardian*. In Freetown on Wednesday 6 September British Joint Public Relations admitted that Paras had arrived in Sierra Leone but merely as a contingency measure, keeping options open. The press were told it remained the military's hope that the problem could still be resolved peacefully through negotiation. The presence of the SAS/SBS had not been noticed.

The next day there was a serious escalation in the reporting of the event when the BBC World Service told of the Paras' deployment to Sierra Leone, suggesting that the purpose was to confront the West Side Boys. There was an outside possibility that the West Side Boys might not have seen the story in the press but as avid listeners, and more recently contributors, to the BBC World Service, the story was well and truly out. Operations in the Falklands, Kuwait, and now Sierra Leone, had all been compromised by the media. Kallay had to reconsider his conviction that there would be no attempt to rescue the hostages for fear of their being killed. The SAS, SBS and Paras cursed. The effect of the release of the news that the Paras were in-country – and their purpose did not need spelling out – was not to give the West Side Boys the jitters. Quite the contrary, their attitude being, 'bring them on'. They were absolutely confident in their own ability, certain that they would win, that they had all the advantages. They had *most* of the advantages.

The newspaper first to break the story gave 'unnamed military sources' as its informant. The leak was not part of a considered strategic concept but rather crass stupidity from within Headquarters Land Command, Wilton (HQLAND

Command), the designated support headquarters, which, according to an officer: 'started sending signals all over the place (many of them totally unnecessary) and so from the outset the deployment of the Paras was in the public domain'.[20] Barras would be a close call without the home team raising its degree of difficulty. At the negotiation venue, the signs of collapse became self-evident. The West Side Boys advised they would not release the seven hostages until a new interim government was formed. Surgeon Lieutenant Jon Carty of HMS *Argyle* received orders to report to the RFA *Sir Percivale* in Freetown harbour. *Sir Percivale* was to operate as a hospital ship in the probable event of there being an operation in the Ocra Hills.

The countdown for the extraction of the hostages had begun as Kallay hovered between switching from Plan A to Plan B. 'I was told', said Carty, 'that within the next forty-eight to seventy-two hours, an operation to extract the casualties would be initiated.'[21] A hollow array of sea containers had been arranged on the jetty opposite '*Percy*' allowing helicopters to land in the centre. Carty's triage centre, from where he could examine casualties as they came off the helicopters, was in one of the sea containers. Royal Marines from HMS *Argyle* took over responsibility for securing the area. The final indication of a change of direction within the insurgents' planning cycle came in the form of intelligence that the West Side Boys intended to apprehend the entire negotiating team at the next meeting. That particular trap was barely avoided but it meant an end to playtime. Negotiation had run its course; now was the time for action – almost.

On Friday 8 September, Geoff Hoon, Secretary of State for Defence, and the Chief of the Defence Staff, General Guthrie, sat down for a pre-COBRA briefing on the Barras situation. At that stage, Barras was to operate in tandem with Operation Amble, a plan to give the Sierra Leone forces a slice of the action, albeit on the fringe. Noble as that sentiment might have been, the question had to be asked, was it essential at this stage to take risks with operational security when there would be ample opportunity after Barras for the Sierra Leone Army to have its share of glory and prove the efficacy of British training? DSF's Chief of Staff outlined the plan, ending with the butcher's bill. 'We might lose a Chinook, up to sixty SAS and, in all likelihood the Royal Irish hostages as well. We probably won't get all the hostages out alive, and we're most unlikely to nail Kallay.' General Guthrie, to whom the plan had been rehearsed the day before, said he had no confidence in Operation Amble and thereupon had it cancelled. The Ministry of Defence people then moved off to COBRA to brief the agreed plan. A Special Forces officer picked up the designated telephone in the Special Forces booth and put a call through to DSF. 'It's on', he said, 'but we've lost the Sierra Leone Army bit.' 'Good. Great. Bugger,' came DSF's reply.[22] The attack to release the hostages was thereupon set for first light, Sunday 10 September.

After hearing confirmation on Saturday 9 September that the operation was definitely on, the SAS/SBS left their briefing to do one more rehearsal, to confirm each in their own minds their own particular role. Every day they had waited for news that the plug had been pulled, that the operation was off. Few betting men would have put money on Barras proceeding. The atmosphere that night among the Special Forces was electric with anticipation. On the other side of the camp, among the Paras, the situation has been described as tense. They had their mobile phones taken off them as they went into a state of enforced isolation. Each individual was uncertain as to how he would perform when first coming under

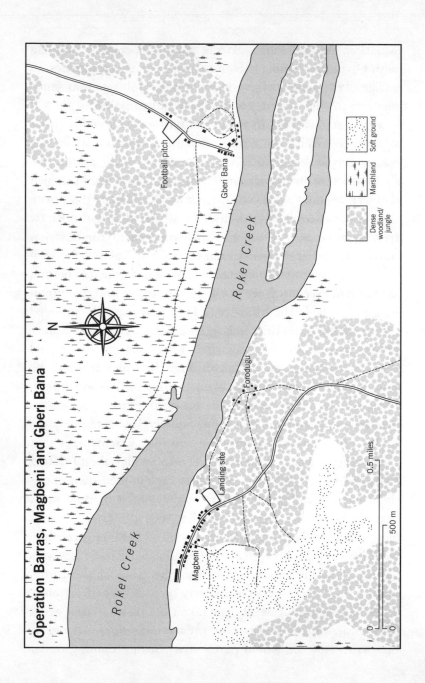

Operation Barras, Magbeni and Gberi Bana

Rokel Creek

Rokel Creek

Rokel Creek

N

Football pitch

Gberi Bana

Forodugu

Landing site

Magbeni

Soft ground

Marshland

Dense woodland/jungle

0   500 m

0   0.5 miles

fire. The common attitude in both groups was a philosophical recognition that now, with the decision made, the sooner it all began the better. The given mission was to defeat, not to destroy the enemy. This latitude allowed commanders to fight the battle in such a way as to permit the enemy to slip away if that were deemed necessary. Barras was not about settling scores but saving lives.

Shortly before 6 a.m. on the Sunday, an armada of helicopters assembled out at sea – three Chinook, two Army Lynx, one Royal Navy Lynx and a Mi-24 gunship of the Sierra Leone Air Force operated by its former Executive Outcomes crew. The Chinook destined to fast-rope Special Forces men outside the hostages' hut had solely Special Forces men aboard. The Chinook that was to land at the Gberi Bana football pitch had two-thirds Special Forces and one-third Paras on board. After dropping the Special Forces, the Chinook would hop over the river to the landing site used by the third Chinook, to disgorge its entire Para complement for the concurrent attack on Magbeni.

The Paras had to tailor their plan to the available resources. A Company comprised three rifle platoons, a patrol platoon of three patrols, signals group, two pairs of snipers, four heavy machine gun sections, a mortar section of three 81-mm mortars and a company aid post. While the attack helicopters attacked Magbeni, the plan provided for one platoon to advance to clear the village from east to west with one following in reserve, while the two Gberi Bana Chinooks made the thirty-minute round trip to Waterloo to bring the balance of A Company to the battle.

Those inside the Chinooks became aware that the manoeuvring out to sea had ended and they were now flying towards their target for an H-Hour at 6.15 a.m. They skimmed along Rokel Creek, the intention being that the trees along the bank would muffle the noise, but the West Side Boys would still have three to four minutes' warning that they were on the way. The Creek served as an essential boundary for the British to delineate different tasks, different styles and different skills.

As they arrived over Gberi Bana, the downdraught of the two Chinooks lifted the corrugated iron and thatched roofs off the Gberi Bana huts – a welcome distraction. The Chinooks came directly over their landing sites, hovering momentarily while the hostage rescue and fire teams fast-roped to the ground below. Two RPG-7 rockets in quick succession headed for one Chinook, the pilot apparently able to take evasive action. Drugged West Side Boys took advantage of the fleeting moment to engage – none too accurately – the two Chinooks, while SAS observation teams already on the ground began taking a toll of the West Side Boys from ranges as short as 54 yards (50 metres). The message had been conveyed to the slaves to remain in their accommodation – to lie low. One individual found the commotion too much. He fled from his sanctuary and died as a consequence.

The hostage rescue team went directly to the hut where they knew the hostages would be found. Within minutes of arrival, the British hostages had been shepherded out. The SAS radioed the news back to Freetown – the hostages were safe. That report had not included Mousa, found later in a hut known as the White House. The element of surprise had been total. Instinctively the befuddled minds of the West Side Boys said 'escape' but, as their minds cleared, they paused collectively and briefly. Had they not been persuaded bullets would run off them like rainwater? They turned and attacked the British soldiers, only to be struck down by the accurate fire of the SAS/SBS and the machine guns of the Lynx attack helicopters.

The Irish had no difficulty walking very fast to the rescue helicopter. Mousa was far less certain on his feet, his evil-smelling body being supported by two unfortunate SAS men. They were rightly proud of their achievement. Mission accomplished.

Sometimes operations intent upon saving lives lead to loss of life among the rescuers. That was the case here. SAS Trooper Brad Tinnion[23] took a 7.62-mm round in his lower body which tracked upward. A helicopter came in to casevac him but he had been mortally wounded. The 7.62-mm round which killed Trooper Tinnion is the calibre of bullet used in the self-loading rifle (SLR) issued to the British Army before the SA80. The West Side Boys had SLRs in large quantity. A Company 1 Para took two SLRs back to Dover as souvenirs from the operation. When the serial numbers were checked, it was discovered that one of them had previously belonged to 1 Para. The weapon had been used on 'Bloody Sunday' in Londonderry in 1972 when thirteen protesters were shot. When the Saville Inquiry asked for the rifle, the court was told it had been destroyed.[24]

What had been intended to be a short operation extended to over four hours of fire-fighting, at the end of which 10 per cent of the attackers had been wounded. Only twenty minutes had been required from crossing the start line to the release of the prisoners. A subsidiary aim had been to account for Kallay but he had not appeared at the head of his men. During the course of clearing the buildings the Special Forces found him hiding under a bed. His wife had been killed in action but the WSB leader proved to be a coward. The SAS pulled the hostages' rings off his fingers and took him unceremoniously to the waiting helicopter to begin a long period of loss of freedom.

The West Side Boys kept their vehicles at Magbeni; these

included a captured Bedford 4-ton vehicle with twin 14.5-mm machine guns, at least three technicals and pick-up trucks with heavy machine guns mounted on the rear. The Paras faced considerable firepower. They followed up the work of the attack helicopters, wading waist-deep in water towards their objective. 'This was the only fire fight I have been in,' said a Para corporal. 'It is the only experience I have had of a two-way, as they call it, when the rounds are coming towards you . . . it was scary. But when the battle started, training just took over.' 1 Para confirmed what 2 Para had learned at Goose Green: the value of the 66-mm light anti-tank weapon. The Paras had gone in light. The 66-mm was therefore a useful supplement, capable of penetrating the 18-inch (46-cm) walls of the village huts. As Company HQ advanced to liaise with the forward platoon, a mortar bomb landed among them. The West Side Boys were equipped with 2-inch, 60-mm and 81-mm mortars. The bomb removed the Officer Commanding and his signaller, the 2 platoon commander and three of his HQ, all suffering varying degrees of injury requiring casualty evacuation. 'The OC called me up and told me I was to take command of the company,' said the second-in-command.[25]

The change in command at a critical juncture caused no disruption in the attack as a result of careful preparations including rehearsals and the adoption of mission-oriented orders. The area around Magbeni was soon thick with flying ammunition fragments. The risk of fatalities and injuries had been reduced through wearing body armour and helmets. The mortar section was intentionally delayed in setting up for fire missions in order to avoid fratricide. When flown in to the landing site, it was discovered that they could not be set up because of the soft surface. Redeployed to the second landing site they had difficulty adjusting their fire on to their targets. The use of smoke also failed as the jungle canopy prevented the fall of rounds being observed. By 08.00, Magbeni was in Para hands. Chinooks lifted the Royal Irish Land Rovers out while the West Side Boys' surviving equipment, arms and ammunition were destroyed by plastic explosive, petrol or red phosphorous. The Chinook carrying the hostages made the slightest of diversions, collecting A Company's casualties, and took them all off to *Sir Percivale*. The butcher's bill there, though significant, was far less than forecast. The point was made that the British Government would not be found to be casualty-averse in those situations where there was a just cause.

Mopping up continued in Magbeni and Gberi Bana. There were bodies in the jungle and in the river. A member of the Small Boys Unit reported 'many corpses and wounded people lying on the ground moaning. One commander was standing and his friend was trying to remove a fragment from his shoulder. The rest of the people were on the ground.'[26] Those within the villages had to be tidied up and removed. The only item apparently to have been overlooked was body bags. To the dismay of the RAF's loadmasters, two dozen bodies were put on the floors of the Chinooks and delivered to the nearby Jordanian battalion, together with Kallay. The West Side Boys had taken a significant pasting in a demonstration of Britain's ability to plan and execute an operation few states would have attempted. It had been a joint operation in which all parties had done what was asked of them. The pilots had been outstanding and the Special Forces operation in Gberi Bana had been conducted professionally and with clinical effect. A Company 1 Para stood out, for not only had their command structure been disrupted at the outset but a unit which for a good part comprised teenage soldiers had attacked a numerically superior force and protected the

Special Forces' open flank. At the end of the day, the hostages had been released, Kallay arrested, Mousa saved and the slaves' liberty restored. Emotional men could be excused for pausing to reflect upon the scale of the achievement. They would have been quietly pleased with their own contribution to the impossible task they had been set.

The casualty figures had been lower than expected in an operation with 'lots of potential for things to go wrong'. The loss of a total airframe and passengers had been factored into the estimate. That did not arise. The strength, resilience and courage of the West Side Boys had, however, taken the Special Forces aback and herein the British had a problem that was also seen with the Americans in Mogadishu and Fallujah, namely, underestimating the enemy. Jason Burke, a veteran reporter for the *Observer* in Sierra Leone, wrote:

> It is the old problem. We just don't get it. We look at these irregular forces. We look at these kids and young women fighting in trainers and T-shirts. We laugh at the way they wear charms to ward off bullets. We look at their drunken and doped-up leaders and we cannot take them seriously. But these kids have grown up fighting and killing and committing atrocities. They also don't understand the rules. No one has ever told them that war is not like a *Rambo* video, about how soldiers should behave, when to be scared, so they will just stand there and blast away.[27]

That the Sierra Leone Army had two brigades with which to advance north, assisted by the British rather than the UN, was just the right leverage to apply during the November peace negotiations. In the days that followed Barras, 300 members of the dispersed West Side Boys surrendered to the Jordanian battalion and were redirected to a disarmament and reintegration centre, prompting Sierra Leone's information minister,

Julius Spencer, to declare that the West Side Boys 'were finished as a military threat'. Freetown's largest-selling daily came out with the screaming headline 'BRITS KICK ASS IN WEST SIDE'. The operation had done much to restore the confidence of the majority, pro-British Sierra Leoneans and the reputation of Britain's armed forces.

In Freetown, a *Sierra News* reporter commented upon the public face of the British command there, Brigadier Gordon Hughes. 'He was like a latter day Saladin with a relaxed ambience and like a rock star in a mosh pit who would smile gamely at the gaggle and ululation of greeters.' The Brigadier was less happy to read the findings of the inevitable inquiry, an inquiry apparently more concerned with finding a head to blame than in doing so convincingly. 'The Commander British Forces has been reminded that Sierra Leone remains an unstable and volatile environment, that the deployment of forces is to be strictly controlled; and that the Commander is to take all necessary measures to ensure that UK forces do not find themselves in a position that may lead to their capture.'[28] 'There had been no "reminding" by the chain of command,' said the Brigadier.[29] To suggest Gordon Hughes could have been in any way responsible for Major Marshall's whimsy is to enter the realm of unreality. *Julius Caesar* has it that the good that men do is oft interred with their bones.

The inquiry continued, 'the commander of the patrol, Major Alan Marshall, made an error of professional judgement in diverting from a planned and authorized journey so as to make an unauthorized visit to the village of Magbeni on the banks of Rokel Creek'.[30] His was not the first British patrol down the track to Forodugu. His timing could have been better. What cannot be criticized are his leadership, courage and fortitude during the period he and his men were held hostage. Major Marshall transferred from the Royal Irish to the Intelligence Corps.

On 20 September 2000, the Secretary of State for Defence, Geoff Hoon, called upon the 1 Para soldiers in their barracks in Dover to congratulate them on the success of Operation Barras. 'I have no doubt that many years from now, it will be held up as an example of how these things ought to be done. You should all be proud of your part in it.'[31] The lesson Operation Barras had once again emphasized was that of forces for courses or quality versus quantity. Half-hearted intervention will not succeed, more particularly in Africa than anywhere else. The decision has to be made on the optimum number, type and origin of armed forces to manage a volatile situation such as that in Sierra Leone. A simple quantitative approach is unlikely to succeed. Africans tend to be impressed by power and by those representative armed forces of former colonial powers prepared to demonstrate and use power. Operation Barras was a reprise of Executive Outcomes' earlier successes in Sierra Leone. It demonstrates how properly resourced, well-trained, fit and resolute armed forces are capable of achieving results disproportionate to their size.

The Rapid Reaction Operation Palliser addressed the insurrection in Sierra Leone. The stunning Rapid Reaction Operation Barras came about as a result of part of the solution to Sierra Leone's problems – the training of the military – inadvertently becoming part of the problem. The requirement for Barras, and its huge success, complemented the movement towards a military solution to Sierra Leone's problems, beginning with Palliser. Both operations had a huge impact on advancing the reputation of Britain's armed services throughout the world. Their highly successful Rapid Reaction operations and follow-on training package were studied, copied and implemented by those states with the capacity to do so. In the same way that the Falklands conflict and Grenada had enhanced the reputations of Mrs Thatcher and Ronald Reagan, so too did Sierra Leone assist the career and reputation of Tony Blair. He did not understand, however, that the special circumstances applicable to the intervention in Sierra Leone did not mean that military intervention was the panacea to cure all international ills. To pinpoint the genesis of British intervention in Iraq and Afghanistan there is no need to look beyond Sierra Leone.[32]

Barras worked because it employed well-trained, dedicated, military professionals. There was absolute unity of command and the two separate though complementary operations were tightly controlled so that neither interfered with the other. The entire intelligence picture will never be revealed but suffice it to say that there was little the Special Forces did not know about the enemy and the two locations. Operational security had been guaranteed. The British were able to conduct Palliser and Barras independently because they had all the requisite resources under national control. That is the point of separation between Sierra Leone and America's experience in Mogadishu, where America could not operate truly independently because she was not self-sufficient.

All that has been written of Palliser and Barras concerns military solutions but the military contribution is only part of the journey. The ultimate solution must be political, the responsibility of the people themselves, and it is here that seriously difficult, unanswered questions remain. Brigadier David Richards reported being taken aback when a Sierra Leonean told him the British should return and take charge. I heard something similar when I was told that the answer to Rwanda's problems was to invite the Belgians to return. When we bear in mind how bad the Belgians had been as colonial administrators, that is some request.

Brigadier Gordon Hughes postulated the outcome of a referendum by the Sierra Leoneans on the preferable outcome for their future. It 'would almost certainly indicate that British political and military leadership would be preferable to any fleeting benefits that Sierra Leoneans might have enjoyed since independence'. He said Sierra Leone had 'not made much progress over four decades in building its state institutions; indeed the opposite is true'.[33]

Interventionist states that invest blood and treasure for another state's benefit have a right to expect to see positive progress. Gordon Hughes explained:

> The educated elite (80 per cent of the population is illiterate) prosper through informal connections which bypass and infiltrate the state system of governance . . . On the surface, Sierra Leone appears to have a working set of democratic institutions but these are largely a façade . . . Business and politics are inextricably linked and corruption and bribery, in a wide variety of shades, are now part of the normative way of doing business, from the top of the state to local, routine business transactions . . . young people have built up a deep resentment against the 'Old Guard' and feel unable to make their voices heard.[34]

'Sierra Leone is not working,' wrote Mills and McNamee. 'According to some estimates, unemployment tops 90 per cent. Infant and maternal mortality rates are among the highest in the world. Poverty confronts you around every bend of this staggeringly beautiful country. Sierra Leoneans expected a lot more from peace and democracy.'[35] In the September 2007 elections, the people elected as president the former leader of the opposition, Ernest Bai Koroma. 'Sierra Leoneans are entitled to expect more from peace and democracy. They have chosen ballots over bullets. To ensure it stays that way, Sierra Leone now needs a New Deal to stimulate recovery, growth and prosperity. Koroma will be thankful for such an approach.'[36]

Eight years have passed since Barras to the time of writing. Post-conflict resolution has made no appreciable contribution to the health and wealth of Sierra Leone's people. In view of the importance of reconstruction towards the ultimate settlement in Iraq and Afghanistan, it behoves the parties responsible to examine those features shared with Sierra Leone with a view to determining why reconstruction has failed. After the the battles of Fallujah a glimmer of a possibility of eventual success was evident. Yet the lesson of Iraq for would-be interventionist states is that if the intention is to overthrow a state's leadership, interventionist states should be certain that there is a workable plan acceptable to the host state's people for an alternative leadership; otherwise, do not bother. The tragic outcome to be feared in Sierra Leone is that the considerable investment made in training the military and the police will be demonstrated through an efficiently executed *coup d'état*.

8

The Battles for Fallujah
2003–2004

'If I were treated like this, I'd be a terrorist.'

In late November [2004] a high ranking American General from Baghdad drove through the city, looking carefully to the left and to the right. After several minutes he told the driver to stop. He got out and looked up and down the devastated street, at the drooping telephone poles, gutted storefronts, heaps of concrete, twisted skeletons of burnt-out cars, demolished roofs and sagging walls. 'Holy Shit', he said.

Bing West, *No True Glory: A Front Line Account of the Battle for Fallujah* (Random House, New York, 2005)

The covert purpose of America's invasion of Iraq had been the unspoken promise of a violent reaction against any other state or organization attacking America or her interests. This response to 9/11 had been entirely emotional, tempered by the predictability of a violent reaction to any challenge made to America's status as the world's sole superpower. That Iraq had no involvement with 9/11 was a matter of little consequence. America could hardly attack Saudi Arabia for what her nationals had done. Fifteen of the nineteen hijackers had been Saudis. Besides, was not Iraq Arab and had not the dress rehearsal for an attack in 1990–1 suggested that an attack in 2003 would be 'do-able'? There were incentives, including oil reserves at least equal to those in Saudi Arabia[1] and the prospect of establishing garrisons in Iraq post-conflict. None of this, of course, could be declared as the *casus belli* for invading a sovereign state. The best of the reasons that could be conjured up as the underlying purpose of the mission was cast in the tradition of the American Way – namely the bringing of democracy to the unenfranchised of Iraq. This intense, evangelically driven delivery of democracy to Iraq was taken by President George W. Bush and his senior colleagues as a beneficial form of manifest destiny. The same formula had been applied to Palestine where the wrong people were democratically elected and accordingly were politically and economically ostracized.

The women's rights movement within the United States associated itself with the emancipation of Iraqi females, whereas theorists formulated a strategic rationale around an argument that history revealed democratic states did not war with one another. People gifted with 20:20 foresight wondered whether proponents of exporting democracy to Iraq were fully aware of the consequences of what they were doing. The liberal-Western democracy model of one man, one vote, if implemented, was obviously going to lead to a political and social, tectonic upheaval, possibly leading to the break-up of the state.

The Sunnis, approximately 20 per cent of the population – the Tutsis of Iraq – had ruled Iraq, just as Arab Sunnis ruled in eighteen out of twenty-one states in Arabia. The southern Shia, approximately 60 per cent of the population – the Hutus of Iraq – had not been represented in any number within the higher echelons of the armed forces or the Ba'ath administration. Following the first Iraq war, the Kurds in the north, approximately 20 per cent of the population, had secured virtual self-determination.[2] When democratic elections were held, however, the population either voted or refused to vote according to the sect to which they belonged. The polarization which flowed from the institution of democracy merely exacerbated internal disorder. 'To remove Arab Sunnis from their traditional positions of authority within the state will prove to be a burdensome task for whoever has to do it.'[3] The mass sacking of Ba'athist administrators, members of the armed forces and security men, affecting up to 7 million Iraqis, had a disproportionate effect upon the Sunnis.

Once the interim governmental arrangements were behind them, the Shia majority duly elected Nouri al-Maliki as the first Iraqi Prime Minister since the invasion. Unsurprisingly, accusations arose that Mr Maliki was favouring the Shia and not governing in the manner that President George W. Bush wished. Bush let it be known that, in his opinion, Maliki should be voted from office before the country's security situation deteriorated further. The Bush intervention represented an incomplete understanding of democracy. The matter was left to 'generals in the field [to suggest] that an effective government, which can provide services and security, is more important than a democratic one'.[4]

In cities where democracy threatened established theocracy, such as Fallujah, imams spoke out against the American belligerent occupation of their city. They told their congregations that Washington intended to remove their birthright. The imams, led by Abdullah al Janabi, raised the temperature. They broadcast a common message from their minarets: 'America is bringing in Jews from Israel and stealing Iraq's oil. Women, take your children into the streets to aid holy warriors. Bring them food, water and weapons. Do not fear death. It is your duty to protect Islam.'[5]

The Pentagon has divided the globe into areas of responsibility for the various American unified commands. Based in Tampa, Florida, US Central Command (USCENTCOM)'s military responsibilities included Iraq but also extended, among other states, to Afghanistan, Pakistan and Iran. General Tommy Franks, whose original plan for a heavy land force was thrown out by Secretary of Defense Rumsfeld and who had previously been Commander CENTCOM, left in July 2003. The conventional phase had ended symbolically with the toppling of Saddam Hussein's statue in Baghdad on 10 April and the fall of Tikrit, Saddam Hussein's home town, four days later. The four-star, Arabic-speaking General John Abizaid, who featured in the Grenada operation, relieved General Franks as Commander CENTCOM.

The Iraq war began on 20 March 2003 with a pre-emptive strike upon a bunker where Saddam Hussein was believed to be sheltering. On the twenty-second day of the war, Saddam Hussein's statue in Baghdad was toppled, signifying the fall of Baghdad. CENTCOM's Land Component had been based upon HQ 3rd US Army under Lieutenant-General David McKiernan, who departed Baghdad soon after the fall of the city. General McKiernan handed over to the relatively inexperienced Lieutenant-General Ricardo S. Sanchez, who would command the multinational Task Force of all American and coalition forces in Iraq but who was subordinate to Abizaid. General Abizaid did not establish his Advanced Headquarters in Baghdad but chose to do so 400 miles (644 kilometres) to the south, in Qatar. He could speak directly with President Bush without going through the Joint Chiefs of Staff. Understandably, there were unity of command problems, particularly after the civilian component took up its position in Baghdad.

In March 2004 when the Commander the 1st Marine Expeditionary Force, three-star Lieutenant-General James Conway, assumed responsibility for 6,178 square miles

296 of MODERN WARFARE

(16,000 square kilometres) of Anbar Province, he came under the command of General Sanchez but also had direct access to General Abizaid. At times, the Abizaid–Sanchez relationship appeared strained. However, General Abizaid wrote: 'General Sanchez deserves particular credit for dealing with multiple crises and his decisive use of the 1st Armored Division in the south at a time when the Spanish Brigade was pulled out of the region.'[6] It would be reassuring to believe that the concept of forces for courses was being applied in relation to tricky Anbar Province and that the relief of 82nd Airborne Division by the 1st Marine Division was not accidental. That it was, 82nd Airborne being obliged to return soon after departure, reveals an almost total absence of options as to who went where.

'The need for CENTCOM to serve as a theatre command was absolutely essential,' wrote General Abizaid:[7]

Twenty-seven countries in the area of operations, extensive naval, air and reconnaissance forces serving the theatre, protection of the oil lines of communication and a need to control land operations in the Horn of Africa and Afghanistan made CENTCOM's role as a joint force theatre HQ essential. The problem of the undermanning of the multinational Task Force in its early stages was immediately recognized and it began to expand from its Corps base as early as August 2003. However, it was not until later, under 4-star commander Casey [General George Casey, Commander of the Multinational Force], that the multinational Task Force became the robust Land HQ required for the complexities of Iraq.

There was a second, civilian command chain, one of two, based in Baghdad's heavily protected Green Zone, headed by Ambassador Paul Bremer, notionally equal in rank to

General Abizaid. Bremer directed the Coalition Provisional Authority (CPA), responsible for the development and return of Iraq to full sovereignty as a democratic state. The situation in Baghdad therefore was that the civilian Bremer outranked the soldier Sanchez. That was not the position at the outset when the CPA had been the responsibility of retired Lieutenant-General Jay Garner, reporting to Commander CENTCOM. The blame for the looting and disorder which followed the stunning *blitzkrieg* victory in Baghdad was placed firmly at Garner's feet. No such civil disorder occurred in Fallujah where a governing council had responsibility for maintaining utilities and security. President Bush relieved Garner on 10 May 2003, effectively splitting the chain of command by appointing Bremer, who had access to the President through Defense Secretary Donald Rumsfeld.

The third chain of command appeared five months after Bremer's appointment, in October 2003, and reflected the number of departments with competing interests in Washington – the White House, the State Department and the Pentagon. The Iraq Stabilization Group (ISG) represented the National Security Advisor's one-to-one ear to the ground in Iraq. Ambassador Robert Blackwill reported directly to Condoleezza Rice, Secretary of State, despite Bremer keeping the White House informed of developments. There appeared at times to be an overall lack of confidence among the hierarchy.

The poor, sometimes frigid relationship between the military and civilians was far from beneficial in the unequal struggle to reconstruct Iraq. The military interpreted CPA as 'Can't Plan Anything'. Speaking of the situation at that time, one senior military officer said: 'Bremer had little or no under-standing of military matters at all, and was advised by a group of politicos who thought all tactical level direction should come from civilians.' In reality Bremer and his civilian staff had no authority to indulge themselves in military matters. The tradition of civilian control had been set aside. The truth is that the military staff was more effective and more professional than a civilian counterpart starved of talent due to a reluctance if not refusal to serve in Iraq.

The trend towards military superiority had already been established prior to the invasion of Iraq. 'Because of Gold-water-Nichols, [the Goldwater-Nichols Department of Defense Reorganization Act 1986] the quality on the military side has gone up tremendously, where the reverse has happened on the civilian side. Revolving-door restrictions have made government service so unattractive that the pool from which you can pick political appointees is not as rich as it once was.'[8] One general said cynically, 'CPA was run by old, old men on 90-day tickets [three-month tours of duty], assisted by little girls from college, brought in to make coffee.'

What the Goldwater-Nichols Act could not do was prevent the establishment of a self-destruct mechanism in the joint command and control process. Nor, for that matter, could it guard against an irresistible tendency within the hierarchy to micromanage events at the tactical level, best left to warriors on the ground.

Fallujah is located within the so-called Sunni Triangle of Anbar Province 43 miles (69 kilometres) west of Baghdad on the east bank of the Euphrates. The city's population in April 2003 stood at 280,000 people, almost all of whom had fled the city prior to the November 2004 attack. Although not as large as Ramadi, with a population of 400,000, Fallujah's importance lies in its ranking as a growing centre of the Sunni Islam movement, as emphasized by the 200 or so mosques in this the 'city of mosques'. The imams provided the population with leadership, derived from their position as teachers of Islamic history, law and language. Early in 2003, the Wahabi sect established itself in Fallujah, introducing its own *madrasa*, or Islamic religious schools, teaching Wahabism, a particularly austere and rigid form of Islam originating from Saudi Arabia. Although the tribal structure was strong, many sheikhs allowed their influence to be diluted by the prospect of being awarded lucrative American government contracts. The local tribal leaders selected the staunchly pro-American Taha Bidaywi Hamed as the new mayor. There is no doubt, however, where their loyalty lay and they, the imams and redundant Ba'ath Party officials represented an active opposition from the moment paratroopers of 82nd Airborne Division entered the city on 23 April 2003.

In general, fundamentalist imams were not initially opposed to the removal of secular Saddam Hussein from power. They became virulently hostile to the Americans, however, after they had inflicted humiliating defeat upon a proud people. The insult was compounded when the Americans disbanded the ruling Ba'ath Party, whose stronghold was in Fallujah, their generals and their army. The selection of the former Ba'ath Party headquarters on the outskirts of the city as the American headquarters was probably not the smartest of moves. There is a difficult balance that has to be drawn here between the needs of force protection on the one hand and the reality that the source of human intelligence comes from patrol activity within the city. The balance would find itself. A senior officer observed that the army acted as they did 'as much owing to their presence as their actions' resembling 'fuel on a smouldering fire'.[9]

Al-Qa'eda, from as far afield as Chechnya, Afghanistan, Saudi Arabia, Syria and Egypt, made their way into Fallujah like bees to a honey pot, intent upon forcing the infidel to withdraw. This demonstration of Muslim solidarity is known as *Ummah*. The sacking of Iraq's security officials meant that the borders were left open for a ten-month period. The resistance comprised trained warriors, often dressed in black, who, rather like the militia in Mogadishu, attracted three times their number to the *intifadah* from among the Iraqi population. They operated as small groups with no hierarchy, impossible to penetrate. The battle lines were therefore drawn between, on the one side the Ali Babas insurgents and their Iraqi adherents content to die as martyrs for the cause, and those who would rather not.

Theatre-wide, 150,000 American soldiers endeavoured to close and destroy a few thousand insurgents able to hide themselves and their identities among 5 million provincial sympathizers. For an insurgency to be effective it requires no more than 2 per cent of the population to be actively committed.

There was no shortage of weapons available to the insurgents. Individuals had an entitlement to hold an AK-47 automatic rifle. There was a fair distribution of rocket-propelled grenades – RPG-7 – among the population, and there was also a cottage industry in the manufacture of improvised explosive devices (IEDs). The term IED came from Northern Ireland, normally referring to IRA bombs made from fertilizer and more commonly used in rural environments. Here in Iraq the IED presented a greater danger in urban areas, where they accounted for 68 per cent of American fatalities. The prevalence of the IED and other weapons was due to looting of former Iraqi ammunition depots left unguarded by coalition forces. Saddam Hussein was partly responsible for the number of arms in circulation, having distributed large quantities prior to the invasion. The insurgents made a number of their IEDs from 155-mm artillery rounds wired together with a detonator which would be activated remotely. Out in the bazaars, among the fruit and vegetables, clothing and hardware, there were outlets selling whatever arms and ammunition were required. Many more ammunition supplies would originate from official sources attempting to build the new army.

On 28 April, Ba'athists marked Saddam Hussein's birthday by taunting the paratroopers in their midst. Starting at the headquarters, 400 protesters, including women and children, toured the platoon areas shouting, some firing their AK-47s in the air. It was dark when the group arrived in the Nzal district, at the primary school which had been occupied by a platoon of paratroopers on 26 and 27 April. The protesters demanded the Americans leave immediately so that the dispossessed schoolchildren could resume their education in the morning. Activists in the background sought to provoke a reaction. Weapons were again fired in the air. Believing his command to be under attack, the local commander sought permission from his company commander to retaliate. The OC replied in the affirmative. The paratroopers opened fire, killing fifteen men, women and children. More were injured.

The incident at the al Qaid primary school became one of two catalysts to initiate the destruction of Fallujah. There was press coverage but in the context of the war recently fought, the killings did not attract the level of external attention they might have done. Facing a riot during a rebellion in Amritsar in the Punjab in 1919, Brigadier Reginald Dyer's men fired on an unarmed crowd; 379 were killed. Of similar proportions to the Fallujah incident, however, was the killing of fourteen civilians by British Paras in 1972 in Londonderry. Unlike the killings at the primary school, both the Amritsar and Londonderry killings attracted considerable international attention, the significance of the attacks upon civilians having long-term implications. Whereas memories may have been short elsewhere, the people of Fallujah did not forget what had happened to them and would wait a full year before setting in train their smouldering revenge, with terrible consequences for their city.

Meanwhile, the 3rd Infantry Division, the planned relief for 82nd Airborne Division in Anbar Province, engaged in its pre-deployment Stateside training. For neither their preparatory training nor on operations were any guidelines laid down as to how commanders were to train or operate. The 3rd Infantry Division chose to focus their attention upon conventional war at a time when the training priority would seem to have been counter-insurgency operations. Arguably, at this point in the Iraq Conflict, there were two further skills which the military required: 'It must be able to see issues and actions from the perspective of the domestic population, and it must understand the relative value of force and how easily excessive force, even when apparently justified, can undermine popular support.'[10]

Many American commanders eschew the idea of indulging in 'hearts and minds' campaigns. It is simply not warfighting. They will argue that 'hearts and minds' detract from the troops' central role of fighting the nation's wars and are best left as the province of the National Guard-run Civil Affairs. It is part of the American military mentality always to seek to rely upon specialists. Once the 2nd Brigade of the 3rd Infantry Division had relieved the 82nd Airborne battalion in Fallujah, they revealed, nevertheless, an understanding of the 'hearts and minds' dimension working in parallel with offensive operations. What the 3rd Infantry Division quickly learned was that 'hearts and minds' can operate only among a receptive, unintimidated population. The soldiers spent weeks providing Fallujah with a first-class soccer field, only to find that on completion their opponents wrecked the facility.[11]

The reception of the victorious coalition had not been the euphoric outpouring of welcome by a suppressed people that Rumsfeld had been promised by out of touch émigrés now struggling to form Iraq's first interim administration. What President Bush incautiously described as a 'crusade' immediately hit a discordant note with imams and redundant employees of the old regime, who saw the coalition as no better than the regime it had replaced. The infidels who had humiliated Iraq and entered the country illegally now took up the role of belligerent occupants among them. Iraqis who collaborated with the Americans risked severe punishment, even death, at the hands of the insurgent resistance. If the key assumption that the coalition would be welcomed with open arms proved false, it followed that everything which flowed from such a premise would also be wrong.

The reconstruction budget allocated 80 per cent towards social improvements and utilities and only 20 per cent on security. An adjustment might have been thought to be straightforward but that is not to comprehend the workings of Congress. The situation could have been different had Fallujah not been regarded as a poor relation and thus failed to attract the inflow of funds required to address the city's problems. Some money came through but nowhere near what was needed. The same problem had bedevilled reconstruction and development in Afghanistan. Fallujah was the home of an estimated 43,000 former Ba'ath Party members and military veterans. There were 70,000 unemployed: 140,000 idle hands, a good proportion of which were turned against the Americans. The going reward for an IED team was $50 for a lookout, $100 to dig the hole and $200 to trigger the device.[12]

It is true that one party cannot be well disposed to another party consistently committed to killing them. The ease of the coalition victory against the Iraqis served to set the Fallujans against them and this was also reflected in the coalition forces' attitudes and actions towards the local community. Some were certainly proper and positive: 'Examples are legion of the toughest US soldiers in Iraq exercising deeply moving levels of compassion in the face of civilian suffering and often under extreme provocation.'[13] But the majority were unhelpful: they entered homes invariably in darkness having first kicked the front door in. Residents would be wakened, orders shouted at them which none understood, requiring them to assemble in one room while the house was thoroughly searched, showing no respect for the householders' property. They arrested suspects, tying their hands behind their backs with flexicuffs, hooding them, and taking them away. Sometimes they arrested all adult males in the house, including the elderly, handicapped or sick. Treatment often included pushing people around, insulting them, taking aim with rifles, punching and kicking and striking with rifles.[14] The Americans consigned those arrested to nearby Abu Ghraib gaol, 10 miles (16 kilometres) to the east of Fallujah, where they stayed for an interminable period. What was happening to Iraq's population was commented upon anonymously by one senior coalition officer: 'If I were treated like this, I'd be a terrorist.'[15] What was clear for all to see were the actions of a party that had won the war but was in the process of losing the peace.

Comparisons arose between the American *modus operandi* in the north and the British 'softly, softly' approach in the south. It was an unfair comparison since the level of violence in the north was then infinitely more severe than the 5 per cent of the overall violence occurring in the south.

While the British wore berets, the Americans always wore combat helmets. The former had suffered only light casualties while the latter had heavy losses. The 1st Battalion The Black Watch battle group had the misfortune to prove the risk disparity between north and south on Operation Bracken, 3 November–4 December 2004, in what was seen as a deployment into the American area of operations with a political rather than a military rationale. The battle group's mission was to prevent the reinforcement of Fallujah by insurgents. Threats of inflicting heavy casualties against the British were borne out by what happened. In a fortnight they had lost five soldiers and an interpreter, which, putting a brave face on the situation, 'were proportionally less than those suffered by neighbouring units over the course of the month'.[16] The Black Watch was hit hard, not least because the media flagged up its every move. One observer in Baghdad said: 'The media are directly responsible for the death of those young men.'

To get an idea of Fallujah, imagine a square approximately 3 miles by 3 miles (5 kilometres by 5 kilometres). Through the centre, east to west, runs a six-lane dual carriageway, Highway 10. The Highway, entering the city from the east, takes the Main Bridge over the Euphrates river. Immediately to the north is a second river bridge, the so-called Brooklyn Bridge, reminiscent of a large bailey bridge. The smart side of the city lies to the north of Highway 10 in East Manhattan and Midtown, site of the Government Centre. 'Smart', however, is a relative term because Fallujah was not a smart city. It was a medieval place where not much worked. The old souk and market place are in the north-west Jolan district. Less salubrious is the area to the south of Highway 10 including a cluttered, ramshackle, industrial sector. The southern sector has narrow alleys, piles of rubbish, cheek-by-jowl concrete buildings and chicanes created by abandoned shells of motor vehicles.

The 82nd Airborne Division left Anbar in May, only to return in September, thereby emphasizing the severe manpower constraints under which the United States was working. The reinforced 505 Parachute Infantry Regiment comprised six battalions, of which Lieutenant-Colonel Brian Drinkwine's 900-strong 1st Battalion was assigned to Fallujah. These men were unfamiliar with the area. They had previously been in Afghanistan. No longer was the military deployed in the town to be baited by the insurgents for it had moved to a large camp 2 miles (3.2 kilometres) outside the city, from where regular, mounted patrols, rarely fewer than five vehicles, attempted to dominate their tactical area of responsibility. The acquisition of human intelligence was now much more difficult. In 2007 the British would make the same mistake in abandoning Basra city in favour of the airport 5 miles (8 kilometres) away.

Insurgents marked the end of the 1st Battalion's tour in Fallujah with an attack on the local police station, killing their own people – a warning to anyone who collaborated with the Americans. Twenty-three policemen died and seventy-five prisoners absconded. The two Iraqi National Guard battalions that arrived in February got the message and refused to fight. The end of the paratroopers' seven-month tour arrived with the appearance in March of the 1st Marine Division. The intensity of operations had increased. A new momentum was discernible. Drinkwine left Iraq having lost ninety-four killed and wounded from his battalion.

The Marines emphasized the operational, dominating their tactical area of responsibility, but they intended to show a human face in their dealings with the residents. The divisional commander, Major-General James Mattis, insisted there would be no kicking doors down, that the local people would be respected and that when it was necessary to fire, the norm would be a single, aimed shot, not a barrage from a multiplicity of automatic weapons. 'We are learning from what the army has done,' said Mattis's immediate superior, Lieutenant-General James Conway. 'We will achieve the level of fire superiority necessary to take care of each situation. But we need to be discerning in our fires to make sure we don't create enemies in the process.'[17] This declaration of a textbook 'hearts and minds' programme brought an immediate protest. The Marines were accused of criticizing what the Army had done. Ironically, and very unfortunately for the Marines, it transpired that what the Army had done in Fallujah on 28 April 2003, after a gestation period of almost a year, would have a dramatic effect on the Marines' best intentions. Lieutenant-Colonel Gregg Olson and his 2nd Battalion, the 1st Marine Regiment, drew the short straw that was Fallujah. There was another skeleton in the closet over which the Fallujah garrison had no control, but once it emerged it had a dramatic influence upon military operations: Abu Ghraib.

The Abu Ghraib prison, the Baghdad Correctional Facility built by British contractors in the 1960s, covers 280 acres (113 hectares). The Red Cross report of February 2004 reveals how suspected insurgents effectively disappeared into the prison 'for weeks even months until contact was finally made'. On entering the prison, prisoners faced enhanced interrogation techniques overseen by individuals such as Specialist Sabrina D. Harman from Alexandria, West Virginia. She was one of the individuals seen in the notorious photographs, stacking naked bodies in the process of breaking prisoners down for interrogation. 'They would bring in one to several prisoners at a time already hooded and cuffed,' wrote

Harman. 'The job of the MP [Military Police] was to keep them awake, make it hell so they would talk.'[18]

Abu Ghraib procedures had been prescribed by Major-General Geoffrey D. Miller, one of Rumsfeld's protégés, who moved from Guantánamo Bay to advise Brigadier General Janis Karpinski what best to do. She said he told her to treat the prisoners like dogs. 'If you allow them to believe at any time that they are more than a dog,' Miller allegedly said, 'then you've lost control of them.'[19] Former CIA agent Mike Baker admitted, 'Abu Ghraib was an abomination. With Abu Ghraib you had people running a correctional facility that were completely unprepared for that sort of function. Low-level individuals.'[20] The well-intentioned, just-arrived Marines could not avoid the local stigma, being tarred by the same brush, arising from the antics of these 'low-level individuals'. Arab revulsion to what was happening to their people remained temporarily contained and localized. When the lid came off in a big way, behaviour at Abu Ghraib led directly to the death of a number of high-level individuals who were just doing their jobs.

Insurgents marked the outgoing Paras and incoming Marines' courtesy call upon the city's elders at the Government Centre with a mortar attack on the civic building, wounding over thirty military and killing two civilians. The insurgents seemed intent upon giving the Marines a warm reception, there being in addition a number of attacks on or around Highway 10. The intensity of the local reaction to the Marines patrolling left few in doubt that they would never ever be welcomed here. Their tour of duty still had seven months to run.

What happened next on Highway 10 became a tipping point in Iraq. On 31 March 2004, a utility vehicle driven with some urgency towards the Brooklyn Bridge pulled into the side of the street, the passengers gesticulating to those with nothing better to do but stand in the street to go away. 'Americans coming!' they shouted, chivvying an otherwise docile collection of individuals by the use of a hand grenade rolled down the pavement where it exploded harmlessly to show they meant business. Shortly after the streets had cleared, two soft-skinned 4x4s travelling in the same direction came into view. The occupants had not heard the sound of the detonating grenade. There were two men in each vehicle; three were former servicemen, at least one or two of whom were Special Forces, attracted by the relatively high salaries available in the security and personal protection field. The Blackwater Security Consulting Company was one of a number of businesses giving the military cause for concern by persuading highly qualified servicemen to leave the forces.

The forewarning that these two vehicles were on their way was clearly the work of the civil police. Rarely could insurgents expect to be gifted this, the softest of soft targets. The contractors were taking a risk in travelling in just the two vehicles, something the military were forbidden to do. Arguably, they should have known better. As soon as they entered the killing zone, the insurgents riddled the unprotected vehicles with fire. One man got out of his vehicle but was soon dead. For all four, their lights had just gone out.

The authorities had paid blood money to the families of those killed at the school on 28 April. It had not been sufficient. Only an extreme act of revenge such as this could close this particular loop. The Iraqis were particularly resentful of Blackwater mercenaries, accusing them of arrogance and aggression. There were 40,000 'contractors' in Iraq who, among other logistic tasks, relieved the military of close protection and escort duties and were therefore an integral part of the security machinery. 'Security Contractor', wrote a manager, 'is just another name for paid mercenary, and [referring to the four men brutally murdered], the general feeling outside the United States is that they got what they deserved.'[21]

Children cheered and petrol was poured over the bodies, which were then set alight. The mob clapped, applauding while two bodies were dragged towards the nearby Brooklyn Bridge. When these images appeared on TV, viewers were immediately reminded of Mogadishu. But Mogadishu had been a disaster. Had not America won the war in Iraq? Did not the President on 1 May 2003, standing there in his flying gear (he had defended American air space during the Vietnam conflict) on board USS *Abraham Lincoln*, announce 'mission accomplished'? Clinton could, and did, sneak out of Mogadishu. So, for that matter, did Reagan withdraw from Lebanon and Ford from Vietnam. Such an option was unavailable in Iraq for the time being. Bush, or his successor, would withdraw from Iraq. The question was, when. The local people hanged two blackened bodies resembling severely overdone barbecue meat from the bridge's superstructure. The gauntlet had been thrown down. What would America do next?

The images particularly revolted America and Americans. 'They can't do that to Americans' represented the common view. The Joint Task Force told the Marines to do something. That was the opinion of Bremer as told to Sanchez and with which Abizaid agreed. The Marines, who were in the best position to decide the nature of an appropriate response, believed an immediate search for the insurgents unwise because it would lead to unnecessary loss of life and collateral damage, making their job in the city that much more difficult. The contractors were dead. Nothing was going to bring them back. Unmanned aerial reconnaissance drones – sophisticated model aircraft – had filmed the whole attack. The CIA had identified ringleaders, knew where they lived and could pull them in at a time of their choosing. The problem was that the international community had seen America attacked and humiliated. The President wanted a visible, dramatic response. No one told him the local view was that such a move was considered unwise. The insurgents knew the Americans would take up the challenge. Fallujah would be where America exacted her revenge and Iraqi fighters from around the country began to assemble in the city.

No attempt was made to try to understand why the four Blackwater men had been killed. Only later would a House of Representatives Committee investigate charges that Blackwater employees had been involved in the indiscriminate shooting of Iraqi civilians. A Committee report indicated that Blackwater's 861 employees in Iraq had been involved in 195 shooting incidents since 2005 and opened fire first 84 per cent of the time. The Committee Chairman, Congressman Henry Waxman, said, 'Privatizing is working exceptionally well for Blackwater. The question for this hearing is whether outsourcing to Blackwater is a good deal to the American taxpayer, whether it's a good deal for the military and whether it's serving our national interest.'

The incident nearly led to corporate breakdown in the relationship between the Americans and British in Baghdad. The British advised the Americans not to overreact: 'this is a come on'. An American general, reportedly normally sound and sensible, said: 'This is an outrage, something has to be done, we should raze the whole of Fallujah to a parking lot.' No proper estimate of the likely casualties was made at the planning stage, nor was there any underlying professional rigour invested into considering the plan and its possible response. The whole process continued, as would a funicular railway, climbing painfully every cog of rising gut reaction.

The idea that American might is right was responsible for a gross strategic misunderstanding that if the Fallujans were hit hard enough they would crumble. Fallujah, like Bloody Sunday in Londonderry, recharged insurgents' determination, leading to a long war.

America was supposed to come down on Fallujah, the centre of the Iraqi insurgency, with all her might. The problem was that the Marines' divisional area was too large for her to control. The force assembled to assault the city in order to arrest the perpetrators of the attack on the contractors was originally no more than two reinforced battalions. It says much for the Marines' WILCO attitude that they were content to set off on what they must have recognized to be an impossible mission. Instead of planning to storm through the city, the basic mission could have been achieved by a series of clinical strikes against the homes and businesses of the half-dozen men involved. The plan became complicated by virtue of becoming multi-missioned, with the additional requirements to open Highway 10 to military traffic, remove heavy weapons and arrest the Ali Babas.

On 2 April, the Marines partially secured the city by putting an earth barricade around it, ready for Olson's battalion to approach the centre from the north-west corner and the 1/5 battalion advancing from the south-east corner. Presentationally, an Iraqi presence in these coalition operations became increasingly important. Olson took an Iraqi company under command. The assault was always bound to fail because the objective area had not been invested, it had not been sealed off from reinforcement or escape.

Operation Vigilant Resolve employed leaflets and the radio to establish the ground rules. There was to be a curfew. There would be no random searches, no kicking down doors, but a lengthy targeting of known houses where it was believed weapons had been stashed or where insurgents were believed to be taking refuge. If American forces entered such a home, the occupants were required to assemble in one room.

Just as Vigilant Resolve took off, under the overall responsibility of General Abizaid and commanded by Marine divisional commander Major-General James Mattis, Ambassador Bremer ordered the arrest of the principal adviser of the radical Shi'ite cleric, Moqtada al Sadr. The cleric called his militia, the Mahdi Army, to mobilize. The timing could not have been worse. The Marines' progress through Fallujah ran into early difficulties as the opposition was far more competent than expected. Two more battalions were promised, one of which was the 2nd Iraqi Battalion from Baghdad. Already imbued with doubt as to what was being asked of them, fighting fellow Iraqis, the battalion ran into an ambush en route to Fallujah. As a result, the reluctant soldiers mutinied, voting with their feet. They were in good company at that time for the coalition troops assigned to the normally placid Shi'ite areas also panicked. 'The Bulgarian battalion in Karbala took shelter in its base and called for American soldiers. The Ukrainian battalion in the city of Kut came under siege and cracked. The Spanish soldiers in Najaf abandoned the streets. Sadr's militia – street gangs actually – was taking over city after city without a serious battle.'[22]

There were no coalition reserves with which to contain the situation. For political reasons, reinforcements were out of the question. The Joint Task Force took as their solution the apparently morale-deflating measure of extending 1st Armoured Division's tour of duty by three months. The division's advanced freight and vehicles had already been delivered to the port of embarkation in Kuwait. An appeal to their patriotism, duty, honour, country and a reminder of 9/11 appears to have sufficed to get the tankers to buckle down and raise their horizons for a later departure.

That would not have been the British soldier's reaction to the news. Although he does genuinely revel in taking part in military operations, there is a dichotomy at play here. On arrival in the theatre of operations the British soldier creates his or her *chuff* chart with each day-to-do carefully marked out in descending numerical order down to zero. Anything which arises to interrupt that which is theoretically pre-ordained can be guaranteed to lead to a severe sense of humour failure. It is important to recognize that the British and American soldier are separated more by what they do not have in common than united by the traits they share. The reason why there should be such a marked, different reaction is partly cultural and partly to do with the circumstances arising from the invasion of Iraq. The American military understood they were in Iraq to even scores resulting from the unprecedented, massive attacks on Washington and New York. By contrast, the 7 July 2005 terrorist attack on London was predicted, preventable and on a far smaller scale than 9/11. Besides, in their recent history, the cities of the UK had been the targets of attack of the Germans and the Irish to an extent never experienced in America.

In an attempt to keep a lid on Shia activity while the Sunni problem was being addressed in Fallujah, the 1st Armoured Division sent a Task Force into Najaf to quell the disturbance there. The Marines had need of additional manpower in Fallujah but with insurgents now running riot in Ramadi there was none. The chief executive of the main hospital in Fallujah was no friend of America. He favoured Al Jazeera, which syndicated images from the hospital to other television channels that had no access. Signals Intelligence indicated that the treatment of patients was not the only activity in the small, one-storey bungalow which served as the hospital. The terrorists recognized that the Americans were unlikely to bomb or shell a hospital deliberately. The images of dead and dying children, brought to the hospital after every case of collateral damage, were particularly harrowing and damaging to the coalition cause. No attempt was made to tell the public how the children had been killed or injured, the inference being that the Americans were to blame. The Sunnis were winning the information war hands down. Unspoken images of dead and dying civilians represented a powerful deterrent to any person seeking to justify what was happening. The inescapable truth was that, but for the invasion, these people would be alive.

The Fallujah battle required close air support to unblock the opposition. An AC-130 Spectre gunship, known as Slayer and later given the less aggressive name of Basher, cleared a group of insurgents assembled in a courtyard with one burst of its 20-mm guns. Jets fired rockets at four houses, allegedly killing twenty-six Iraqis and wounding thirty others. Jolan residents told Al Jazeera the US had used missiles and cluster bombs against them. 'This is not retribution. This is not vendetta,' insisted battalion commander Brennan Byrne. 'This is about making the city liveable so people don't have to live in fear of the thugs who have taken over the city . . . This city has long been a haven for smugglers and bandits, a dumping ground for foreign fighters and bad guys. No one ever took the time to clear it out properly.'[23]

By 9 April, the Marines had had an opportunity to assess their opposition. They found themselves pitted against trained insurgents as well as local people, all of whom wanted to kill an American in order to prove themselves. With the massive firepower available to them, the Americans had no difficulty, just knocking down any insurgent who stood out

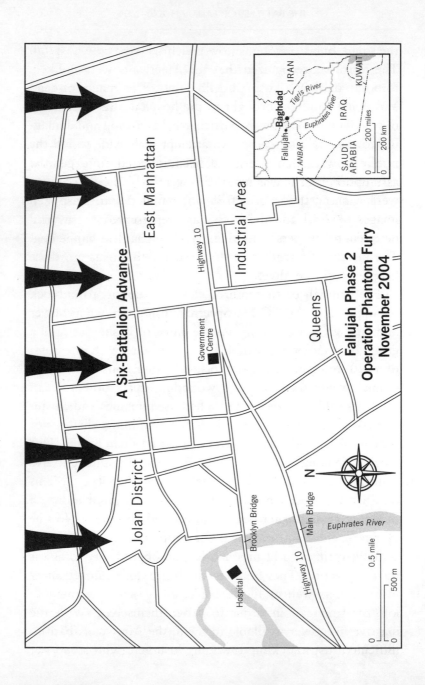

A Six-Battalion Advance

Jolan District

East Manhattan

Highway 10

Government Centre

Industrial Area

Queens

Brooklyn Bridge

Main Bridge

Highway 10

Euphrates River

Hospital

N

0.5 mile

500 m

0

0

Fallujah Phase 2
Operation Phantom Fury
November 2004

IRAN

Tigris River

Baghdad

Euphrates River

Fallujah

AL ANBAR

IRAQ

KUWAIT

SAUDI
ARABIA

200 miles

200 km

0

0

in front of them. Where insurgents had adopted good fire positions, however, collateral damage invariably occurred. The Marines lost five men at the first count but, according to hospital sources, approximately 600 Iraqis had died and that was with restrictive rules of engagement affecting the use of close air support and indirect fire. The 600 figure was never substantiated yet its frequent use led to a general assumption that it was true.

This, the first battle of Fallujah, revealed an urgent need for the Marines to review their attitude to the use of force multipliers in urban conflict. Their behaviour clearly indicated that they were in uncertain territory. They were a light division, light in manpower in relation to their task and light in medium and heavy weaponry. The first Gulf conflict underlined the importance to them of the 7th (UK) Armoured Brigade coming under their operational control to compensate for their natural shortage of armour. The whole United States Marine Corps had only 403 tanks on its inventory, only 16 of which they brought with them to Iraq.[24] The first Gulf conflict had been fought in the desert. In urban Mogadishu, General Hoar and other senior officers claimed that armour such as the Abrams main battle tank had no place. Non-combatants, however, had remained in Mogadishu, which was not the case in Fallujah. Armour, airpower and artillery were used against Fallujah.

What is true of armour is more true of the employment of artillery, which cannot be used so precisely. The oft-repeated quote that Hue in Vietnam had had to be destroyed in order to be saved is over-used. The example of Manila 1945 is apposite. There, the Americans used their artillery against the Japanese in the city. For each Japanese marine or soldier killed, more Manileños lost their lives. General MacArthur initially placed restrictions on close air support and the use of artillery against Manila. Major-General R.S. Beightler, Commander of the 37th Infantry Division, was not prepared to countenance the loss of a single American life through limiting the use of his artillery. He made his case to his superiors. 'As a result he was able to get "restrictions lifted to permit both direct and overhead or indirect fire. From then on, putting it crudely, we really went to town".'[25]

In Fallujah, the Marines continued making slow progress through the city's industrial and domestic sectors. They, rather more than the Army, chose to conduct a good proportion of their patrolling on foot. Their unprotected Humvees, highbacks, with a central bench down the middle, the troops facing outward, a machine-gunner standing between them and the vehicle commander, were not ideally suited to urban operations, particularly when struck by an IED or caught in an ambush.[26] Out on the streets there was freedom to move. There were snipers among the insurgents but, generally, those armed with the AK-47 and RPG-7 were indifferent shots. It was not unusual for insurgents to place themselves among women and children, from where they engaged the Americans. Body armour saved many American lives. The disadvantage inherent in its restriction of individual mobility was massively offset by the reassurance given to those wearing the kit. When the quality of medical support is added to the quality of the body armour, the overall effect was to establish a ratio of eleven wounded to each fatality, 'almost twice the survival rate of previous wars'.[27] Normal death rates arising from contact with insurgents can be expected to be around 0.3 per engagement. In the case of the IEDs, death rates are 1.1 per engagement.[28]

The insurgents would typically place themselves ahead of the American direction of movement. They used taxis, buses, ambulances and police cars to get to their killing zones and to get away soon after contact. While they knew the city well, they were rarely certain where precisely the Americans were. As a consequence, they often presented themselves as high-value targets when their vehicles turned a corner to come face-to-face with an American patrol. There was no hierarchy or central control but they did talk to one another, group to group, using mobile telephones. Employing intercept techniques and passage of translated information down to patrols on the ground, it was possible for the Americans to sense the mood and intentions of those who had, as their sole purpose, the killing of the Marines.

Unflattering images from the conflict in Fallujah were beamed across the world. There was insurrection in at least six Iraqi cities at the time, but it was the fighting in Fallujah which attracted attention and caught the imagination. The city had fast become the centre for Iraqi resistance against the infidel and a source, at last, of national pride. At his ranch in Crawford, Texas, President Bush became uncomfortable. His advisers insisted he remain strong. America had been challenged and had to see Fallujah through to victory. The Iraqi governing council was far less certain. They, being Iraqis and the intended foundation of the country's democracy, did not like what they saw. The CPA had been among those who opposed the Marines, who had not wished to be associated with the Fallujah undertaking. It now did an about-face. Members of the Iraqi governing council threatened resignation which, if carried out, would destroy all the best-laid plans for Iraq's future. The unavoidable fact had to be faced that the coalition had failed to win over the middle-class intelligentsia whose support was vital if Iraq was to be successfully rebuilt: '. . . their sense of kinship with Iraqis in Fallujah, Najaf and elsewhere runs deeper than any pull towards abstract notions of democracy offered by the Americans –

notions that to them appear increasingly hypocritical given the reliance of the occupiers on overwhelming force as a means to an end'. [29]

In the city, Lieutenant-Colonel Byrne's battalion had cleared through the industrial sector and was about to cross over Highway 10 to make rendezvous with Olson in the Jolan district. Attitudes were fast changing in relation to the use of force multipliers. When the overall shortage of manpower imposed delay, the way found to release the log-jam was to use smart bombs and Cobra attack helicopters. For the press, this was of course all grist to the mill. To work one of the two uncovered quadrants, General Mattis ordered Lieutenant-Colonel Brian McCoy's battalion to the north-east sector of the city. Mattis had the scent of victory – believing two to three more days would suffice. One question not adequately addressed was what the plans were to be once the Marines had swept the city of insurgents to stop other insurgents from taking their place.

Meanwhile, in Baghdad, Bremer called a conference to assess the situation. In attendance were three Sunni members from the governing council and Generals Abizaid and Sanchez. The Iraqi civilians spoke eloquently, insisting that a halt be called to the fighting in Fallujah. In reality, facing the threat of Government resignations, General Abizaid had little option but to tell General Sanchez to tell General Conway to cease operations there. On 9 April, Abizaid flew to Fallujah to explain the political facts of life to the unbelieving Marines. He told them he would reconsider the situation twenty-four hours later. Listening to the President's weekly radio broadcast, the Marines heard Bush tell the nation how they, the Marines, were taking control of the city block by block and that the offensive would continue 'in the weeks ahead'.[30] One of the former émigrés, now a member of the governing council, told the world in a television interview: 'We consider the action carried out by US forces as illegal and totally unacceptable. It is a form of mass punishment.'[31] Where people stand is where they sit. Prime Minister Blair agreed with that sentiment and told President Bush as much.

The insurgents preferred not to understand the meaning of ceasefire, attacking the Marines whenever the opportunity presented itself. Only after a mortar attack on McCoy's position did Mattis deem there to be sufficient justification for an act of self-defence. On 11 April the advance into Fallujah resumed, only to be halted again after McCoy had been making significant progress. With time on his hands, Mattis decided McCoy's battalion could be usefully used to turn over a group of insurgents in nearby Karma, where they had cut the highway through the town. The situation in the town became difficult, extraction being achieved by calling in tanks, which once again proved their worth.

While this stop-start business went on, there were discussions on the margins as to whether a complete Iraqi solution might not be the best answer to resolve the political impasse that was Fallujah. This was a military initiative driven by General Conway that specifically excluded the CPA. An option of last resort emerged among the parties engaged in Fallujah. The idea being teased out with the CIA envisaged the Iraqi Army taking responsibility for security in the city. On 28 April, the Marines planned concurrently to resume operations against the city from the lines where they had been stopped. They had not wanted to start this business at all, but now those who had overruled their advice were intent on reining them back. The Marines wanted to finish what they had started. Too many lives had been invested in the operation to walk away. Politics had, however, intervened.

General Abizaid reluctantly agreed with Bremer that to continue the advance could lead to the collapse of America's initiative to build a long-term government for Iraq.

The ceasefire was a sham. The Marines came under attack from the insurgents in the positions they now occupied in fortified properties. The Americans had every intention of resuming the momentum once the word was given. They knew Bremer was in Fallujah discussing that very subject. They were losing men while they simply sat where they were, awaiting a decision. Their snipers however remained active. The insurgents had not understood that to be seen in the city carrying an AK-47 qualified them as targets. Lieutenant-Colonel Gyles Kyser's battalion deployed to take the militarily vacant south-west quadrant. The plan was for Olson to hold Jolan in the north-west of the city, the centre of the insurgency, as a catcher while McCoy, Byrne and Kyser closed on Olsen's tactical area of responsibility in Jolan District, progressively squeezing the insurgents. Movement would have to be carefully co-ordinated to avoid fratricide. In the event, the concept died. There would be no advance; instead, the Americans were to begin a patrolling programme with the Iraqis. The presence of Iraqis among the Americans overcame the political difficulty of the role change of those who had first come to Iraq as liberators, became occupiers and who could now again be thought of as liberators.

The theory of joint patrols was sound enough as an idea. It failed in practice because the Iraqi military feared that being seen working with the Americans would bring fatal retribution down upon them. Four battalions of Marines, half the division, could not sit *ad infinitum* where they had stopped in the city, however. Something had to break the deadlock. The time had come to examine the option of last resort. Former Iraqi military leaders Major-General Jasim

Saleh and Colonel Muhammad Latif proposed to General Conway that they, together with former Ba'athists and soldiers resident in the city, would form a Fallujah brigade up to 500 strong[32] guaranteeing security and peace within the city. One condition was that the Marines keep out of Fallujah. General Conway put the proposal to Generals Abizaid and Sanchez, and was surprised by finding them in ready agreement. Middle-ranking commanders were less certain, pointing out that the Iraqi brigade plan meant turning the city over to their opponents. 'Once we are out, we will never be able to get back. The *muj* will use Fallujah as a firm base from which they will hit us.'

Major-General Saleh was probably genuine. He meant well and wished to do the best for his battered city. The trouble is that he had a parochial view of the city as opposed to the *muj* who saw Fallujah as the centre of the entire insurgency, a safe haven and focus of the opposition against foreign occupation. Baghdad remained oblivious to Saleh's immediate assumption of command in Fallujah until the newspapers informed their disbelieving readership. Bremer had not been involved in an agreement. His own people in Anwar pleaded that he overturn Conway's verbal arrangement, pointing out that his own subordinates criticized the agreement. Incensed that they had been marginalized in determining policy in an area rightfully theirs, the CPA's relationship with the military became intensely frigid. The increasingly vocal Government appointees complained of appeasement and Shi'ites questioned the nature of this form of democracy. Imams in Fallujah celebrated the victory. Before the situation could be reviewed by the appropriate authority intent upon identifying precisely what had been agreed, a major political scandal erupted, relegating everything to the backburner.

There were so many officers of the rank of general in Iraq

at the time that one extra could quite comfortably be at work within the theatre without drawing attention to himself. General Antonio Taguba began his investigation into alleged abuses at Abu Ghraib gaol in January 2004. His terms of reference were limited – only to investigate the behaviour of junior Military Police (MP), principally those who had appeared in photographs or on video. Politicians and senior military were therefore acutely aware of what had happened. They were also aware of the damage the release of the news of the systematic abuse would have. Such was the risk of serious repercussions that had this material surfaced earlier it is unimaginable that the Fallujah Brigade initiative would have gone ahead.

General Taguba reported that the MPs who had abused the prisoners had done so with the encouragement of military intelligence. General Taguba subsequently stated his belief that General Sanchez was aware of the abuse conducted between October and December 2003. Secretary Rumsfeld told the Congressional Armed Services Committee how it 'broke his heart'. He had not been aware of this institutional abuse earlier. He said he saw the photographs for the first time the night before they were released. General Taguba told the *New Yorker* that his report had gone up the chain of command. The impact the revelation of the Abu Ghraib abuses had upon the prospect of establishing a proper form of government in Iraq was incalculable. 'Whatever dubious intelligence may have been obtained by abusing prisoners, those photographs were responsible for attracting hundreds of horrified Muslims to fight alongside insurgents in Iraq, each intent on driving the American infidels from the Middle East.'[33]

The American military hierarchy had the unreasonable expectation that Fallujah's Sunnis would wish to demonstrate their own form of sovereignty and self-determination by opposing the intervention of the jihadists. The truth was that every interest group shared the common aim of keeping the Americans out of Fallujah. General Miles, Chairman of the Joint Chiefs of Staff, went so far as to express the hope that the Fallujah Brigade would forcibly expel the foreign fighters, trace those responsible for the murder of the contractors – still an emotional subject – and disarm the insurgents of heavy weapons. Light weapons had not been included. A contributory factor towards the folly and fiasco of the creation of the Fallujah Brigade had been the issue of American vehicles, radios and assault rifles, many of which ended up in the hands of the insurgents.

No one really understood that the Fallujah Brigade could do only what the imams allowed them to do. It was the imams' intention that Fallujah would be run as an Islamic city in accordance with Sharia law. They supported and sponsored those who had come into their communities to foment resistance, even at the expense of their own misguided people in the Fallujah Brigade. The American generals remained positively robust in their defence of the way in which the brigade had come into being. It was, they insisted, a precedent for the time when the Iraqis would decide their own future. Arguably they could have found a more appropriate setting for this important social engineering.

The brigade's beginning had been none too auspicious. General Myers publicly announced the sacking of the brigade commander, General Saleh, on a Washington television chat show. Thereafter, visitors to Fallujah reported seeing the insurgents controlling the checkpoints, with brigade members acting as passive onlookers. Officers, men of the new brigade and public officials who sought to play a leadership role in the city or gave the slightest impression of an affinity with the despised Americans, often suffered cruel intimidation or kidnapping. They had homes. The insurgents knew where they lived. After being given the sign, the wise sought refuge in another province or another country while the brave or misguided who stayed suffered torture and often death.

The members of the Fallujah Brigade were first and foremost Iraqis and were pleased to see those who had so conclusively beaten and humiliated them in battle leave their city. American-inspired development projects were not permitted to proceed. The local people were encouraged to reject help – even help in repairing damaged houses. Of the 2,300 capital projects approved and budgeted by the CPA throughout Iraq, only 140 came to fruition.[34]

Before the time came for Fallujah's final act to be played out, a number of principal actors left the show. The purpose for which the CPA had been assembled came to an end in June when an Iraqi interim Government took charge. No representatives from Anbar Province had been included in the new Government. Ambassador Bremer took a flight home having handed over to a seasoned diplomat, Ambassador Negroponte. The three-star Lieutenant-General Sanchez moved on to Germany, being replaced in Baghdad by the new Task Force commander, Lieutenant-General Thomas Metz. The Marine Major-General James Mattis returned to the USA on promotion, handing the 1st Marine Division over to Major-General Richard Natonski. The new commander would not have the benefit of seasoned troops to command. The battalions' seven months' tours had come to an end and, short of being extended, as 1st Armoured Division's had been, they were on their way home. In September, Mattis's superior, Lieutenant-General Conway, departed Iraq, handing over to Lieutenant-General John Sattler. Above him, General George Casey came to fill the new post of Commander of the Multinational Force. Prime Minister Iyad Allawi and General Casey operated a dual key in so far as operational-level initiatives could only be taken with the approval of both men. This meant there could be no attack on Fallujah without Allawi's agreement.

While politicians talked of their intentions towards Fallujah and discussed options with the parties concerned, the insurgents continued their favourite pastime of killing Marines. Allawi decided to take control of Fallujah. The Marines had, of course, planned for such a contingency. To them, the tragedy was that on the previous occasion they believed they had been within two to three days of success. In April they had faced perhaps five hundred dedicated terrorists supported by a thousand sympathizers. The Abu Ghraib effect had served to double those figures and, to make matters worse, the Marines had to begin clearing the city from square one. General Sattler was an exponent of the Powell doctrine of using overwhelming force. The heavy forces he needed were not on the Marines' inventory. He recognized that if Fallujah were to fall it would require a joint Marines–Army force to do so. Marines and Army had rarely worked together but this time both sides were determined to set aside inter-service rivalries. According to Natonski, Sattler was well aware military protocol meant he could only ask the Army for the capabilities he required, not the specific units whose services he preferred. Sattler met Casey and Metz: 'He asked for capabilities, for example "mech armour" for the assault into the city and then went on to mention specific Army units 2-7 CAV and 2-2 INF . . . I knew those were the two units he wanted but he was astute enough not to blatantly ask for them by name, only mentioning that they were good units and we had worked with them before.'[35] And then, for good measure, he requested the Blackjack

Brigade from the 1st Cavalry Division, to seal off the city from the east and south.

The Army assets joined the Marines' Regimental Combat Teams 1 and 7. Presentationally, the presence of Iraqi ground forces was of vital importance. They would, however, deliver more than presentation, in part due to the small band of attached American advisers who were never far from the thick of it, giving the Iraqis continuous guidance and support. Sadly, only half the intended number of Iraqis had been recruited into the new army. Bush and Rumsfeld recognized that military advisers were central to the plans to hand over security duties to the Iraqis but it took three years to implement the programme.[36]

The attack force comprising nine Army and Marine battalions and six Iraqi battalions numbered 12,000 out of an overall strength, including logistics and support, of 45,000. The final component to add to this particular order of battle was the British Black Watch battle group, brought in to assist with blocking insurgents' escape routes through the Euphrates river. Whether they were called up from Basra to satisfy either a military or political rationale is academic. There is no doubt, however, that on the previous occasion a request was made for this battalion the intention was indisputably political. President Johnson saw the Black Watch pipe band at John F. Kennedy's funeral. He asked Downing Street for 'just a few bagpipers' to go to Vietnam. The answer was in the negative, as most certainly it should have been with regard to a British presence in Iraq this time round.[37]

On 8 November, Prime Minister Allawi duly authorized the attack upon Fallujah, Operation Al-Fajr, the Dawn, one of the most telegraphed military operations in history. It had originally been named Operation Phantom Fury but General Sir John Kiszely, a Briton and General Casey's deputy commander, thought this might not be the most tactful of names and proposed that the operation should have an Arab name. Nevertheless, Phantom Fury became the unofficial name for the operation, an apposite term reflecting the mood of the Marines keen to re-engage in battle.

Politicians and the military had spoken of the imminence of an attack. The city had been under exclusive insurgent control since April with no American presence since April. Psychological operations began a whisper campaign encouraging residents to leave the city. Secretary of Defense Rumsfeld made his own contribution, assuring all parties that this time there would be no ceasefire. Operations against or near Fallujah began two to three months before the Americans crossed their line of departure. An attempt to place informers inside the city failed, yet the large amount of artillery employed on preliminary fire missions had a positive effect. It is unclear whether this was intended as a tactical or strategic level measure to drive the population out of Fallujah. At the daily briefing, those present might be told that 115 155-mm rounds had fallen on Fallujah – every day large numbers of rounds were fired into the city. The upshot was that the population left, meaning that when the forces engaged it was as near to warfighting as could be imagined with no requirement for rules of engagement. The battle for Fallujah therefore resembled the invasion battle in so far as the lessons learned related to combat rather than counter-insurgency.

In the mass exodus that followed, the population fell from 280,000 to fewer than 500 civilians,[38] in effect giving a virtual green light to declaring Fallujah a free fire zone. In the meantime the insurgents strengthened their positions. Coalition intelligence identified 306 well-prepared positions. The layout of these defences suggested the insurgents were anticipating an attack into the south-east quadrant, through the industrial area. Almost half the mosques in Fallujah were in some way connected to the insurgency and as a result they lost their protected status. IEDs had been set out, some in series, holes knocked through walls of safe houses, tunnels and trenches dug and barriers erected across the obvious through-routes. The insurgents were, however, not natural night-fighters and could not compete against the advantages the Americans derived from their night observation devices.

The Prime Minister addressed the problem of the information war when in August he banned Al Jazeera. General Casey's staff instituted a media pool. At the height of Al-Fajr, there were ninety-one embedded correspondents representing sixty media outlets.[39] The problem of Fallujah hospital, source of so much propaganda, was addressed on D-Day, 7 November 2004. A light armoured reconnaissance battalion sealed the western side of Fallujah, including the capture of two bridges, and went on to take the hospital from a small group of insurgents. Iraqi sources reported fifteen Iraqis killed and twenty wounded. The insurgents stood-to in vain to await the main attack but, unknown to them, this was not scheduled until 19.00 hours on 8 November 2004. The Iraqi interim Government announced a sixty-day state of emergency in preparation for the assault, including closing the Syrian border and banning all vehicular traffic in the vicinity of Fallujah.

On 7 November all was ready for the main attack. 'Iron mountains' of supplies had been assembled forward to give the attacking force a self-sufficiency of fifteen days, enabling them not to be dependent upon convoys susceptible to IEDs. The Army's armoured battalions, one to each Regimental Combat Team, were to be used as penetration forces to dominate and control the routes through the city. Artillery was available to fire into the city. An executive decision placed

Marine helicopters on casevac duties rather than being detailed as attack helicopters. There was no sense in risking vulnerable helicopters in an urban environment when a surfeit of fixed-wing aircraft was available from airfields or a nearby carrier. The trusted Basher AC-130 gunship, the armoury in the sky, would superimpose its own deadly firepower over that of the other weapon systems.

In the afternoon of 8 November, A-Day – A for attack – battalions manoeuvred from their assembly areas towards their line of departure. The ground assault plan was simplicity itself, as all good plans should be. Regimental Combat Team 1 was on the right, Regimental Combat Team 7 on the left, their start line the northern perimeter of Fallujah. The plan was tweaked during the course of the attack, with the effect that both Regimental Combat Teams headed due south until reaching the outer perimeter of the city. As each component in the attack came forward to adopt its pre-determined position, they paused momentarily until at 19.00 hours a hypothetical 3-mile-long (4.8-kilometre-long) tape was raised and they were off. The key to a successful operation would be command, control and information, in support of which the joint force had a single chain of command. Ahead of them lay 29,000 houses to clear. The counter-insurgency principle pertaining to this situation is unequivocal. 'There is only one means of defeating an insurgent people who will not surrender, and that is extermination. There is only one way to control a territory that harbours resistance and that is to turn it into a desert. Where these means cannot, for whatever reason, be used, the war is lost.'[40]

Once two breaching operations had overcome their difficulties, the steamroller made its inexorable progress southward. The number of artillery rounds fired is classified: the number of bombs dropped is not. In this early stage of the operation, over 200 500-lb bombs, 10 1000-lb bombs and 10 2000-lb bombs were dropped on Fallujah. When the infantry went in they used their firepower unconcerned by matters of collateral damage. The insurgents had no answer. They fought in small, unco-ordinated groups, continually being reduced through attrition. Some chose to make a stand in a house, to fight there until killed, in the hope of taking a number of the attackers with them. Others moved ahead of the bow wave, sniping, dodging, with the apparent intention of slipping away to fight another day. The clever ones could find their way through and around the blocking positions, the most likely escape route being west along the Euphrates river. Lieutenant-Colonel P. Newell, Commander Task Force 2-2, US Army, told his men what he expected of them:

> Keep hammering targets and if you see a guy with an AK-47, I expect you to hose him with a .50 calibre machine gun. If firing is identified from a house, then artillery fire should be called in to pancake the building because there is not a building in this city worth one of our soldiers' lives.[41]

There is an interesting comparison with what General Beightler said in Manila in 1945. 'To me,' he wrote, 'the loss of a single American life to save a building was unthinkable.'[42] The difference between the former and the latter is that in the latter case, the buildings destroyed often housed non-combatants.

In Fallujah, the Army showed themselves more inclined to use extreme force than the Marines in bloody, house-to-house, Stalingrad-type fighting. The Marines maintained their habit of moving on foot, only to be perplexed to find how far ahead the mechanized Army units had gone ahead of them. They had fewer tanks available to them than the Army:

'. . . it may be argued they lacked enough tanks to support most of their infantry during the fierce house-to-house clearing operations. This concern was voiced by a few Army officers, many of whom felt frustrated as they watched Marines sustain heavy and perhaps avoidable casualties.'[43]

Notwithstanding doctrinal and operating differences, the two Regimental Combat Teams exceeded best expectations in their speed of advance. Planners had assessed the assault reaching Main Supply Route Michigan, their name for Highway 10, as between seventy-two and ninety-six hours. Regimental Combat Team 7 was over Highway 10 in fourteen hours. Regimental Combat Team 1, which had the tough nut of Jolan district to crack, reached the highway in forty-three hours.[44] As in Gorazde, where the youngest Royal Welch soldier had the privilege of eating a leek on Saint David's Day, the Marines marked their 229th birthday on 10 November by giving their youngest member a slice of cake. The 10 November was a day of consolidation prior to the advance being resumed the following day. By day's end, the forward elements had reached the southernmost extremity of the city.

Planners divided the city into six sectors to which the clearing force returned to winkle out bypassed insurgents and collect arms caches[45] which had been identified on the way through. Concurrently, the humanitarian and reconstruction programme kicked off, proving that lessons had been learned from 2003. Six sectors became four and then exploded into eighty-six, all of which were meticulously cleared until they appeared on the master map coloured green. Prime Minister Allawi pressed for the return of the inhabitants to their homes, something which could not be hurried. Bodies were still being found. Imams had been flown in from Baghdad to conduct religious ceremonies for the deceased, including burial according to the custom.[46] The military re-opened Fallujah to its residents on 23 December 2004.

Operation Al-Fajr had been a rare but successful joint operation. The rivalry between the Army and the Marines had not entirely dispersed. 'In the midst of all the success and camaraderie achieved during Operation Al-Fajr, a degree of parochialism and animosity undoubtedly remains. As with any urban fight, the battle of Fallujah was won at the squad level. In the end, however, the success of the joint operation rests on the shoulders of exceptional leaders.'[47] 'The real key to this tactical victory rested in the spirit of the warriors who courageously fought the battle,' said General Sattler. There have been claims that it was willpower which won Goose Green, spirit which won Fallujah.

Any assessment of civilian casualties, including insurgents, arising from the battle of Fallujah is bound to carry political baggage. An 18 November 2004 Department of Defense news report stated that as many as 1,350 insurgents had been killed and approximately 1,000 captured. The actual numbers killed, which may have included non-combatants, was 2,300. From 10 November to 31 December, 85 Americans died and 737 were wounded. America had achieved her victory with relatively few casualties. Supporting Iraqi forces lost 11 killed, 43 wounded. On 23 March 2005, the Chairman of the Fallujah Compensation Committee, Hafid al-Dulaimy, gave an official estimate of the extent of the damage suffered by Fallujah:

Almost thirty-six thousand houses have been demolished,[48] nine thousand shops, sixty-five mosques, sixty schools, the very valuable heritage library and most of the government offices. The American forces destroyed one of the two bridges in the city, both train stations, the two electricity stations and three water treatment plants. They also blew up the whole sanitation system and the communication network.

While the coalition went home, many of the residents of Fallujah had no home to go to.

In Jolan District the Americans found Abu Musab Al-Zarqawi's film studio, where his terrorist gang had filmed the emotive pleas of those they had kidnapped. On the floor was a large, dried bloodstain from Zarqawi's beheading on video of Nicholas Berg in May. Al-Zarqawi and others in the leadership had heeded the warnings of the coalition attack, leaving beforehand to fight and die at a different time in a different place. The final stages of the battle were essentially fought by Iraqi volunteers from Anbar and Baghdad. Again, in a situation such as this there are guiding principles, this time written by C.E. Callwell in *Small Wars, Their Principles and Practice* in 1899. 'To avoid desultory warfare the enemy must be brought to battle, and in such a manner as to make his defeat decisive, but he should sometimes be left a golden bridge of eventual escape from the field.'

The analogy of the golden bridge could equally have been a drain, a drain down to the Euphrates, because this had been the preferred escape route. From the local commander's point of view, that may not have been undesirable; it depended upon his mission. Was he to take Fallujah, or kill all insurgents therein, or both? From the broader picture, allowing terrorists to escape was undesirable. Not long after the fall of Fallujah, apart from the city itself, the whole of Anwar Province was in insurgents' hands.

There can be little doubt that the 'Holy Shit' general referred to in the quote at the beginning of this chapter was General Casey. He had taken Lieutenant-General Kiszely along with him to inspect the damage. Some might consider it ironic making the British Lieutenant-General Kiszely responsible for Phase IV post-Conflict Resolution. As they both surveyed the scene, there was an enormous explosion in the next block and both ducked instinctively, while the Marines all around them continued working as though nothing had happened. As they drove around that day, they must have seen two thousand buildings. Although they were not all destroyed, the number of buildings not bearing some form of damage was in single figures. As they passed the market they saw that every steel roller-blind had a Bradley round through its centre.

A massive operation swung into action involving hundreds of engineers and infanteers with orders to clean up the city. Within two weeks, Fallujah underwent a remarkable transformation. There was no working infrastructure in a city unable to receive back its quarter of a million-strong population. One of the most immediate tasks for the Americans was to locate the city's internally displaced. Wide-ranging reconnaissance revealed a gathering of no more than a few hundred. With winter on its way, the military were extremely sensitive lest images of a second Kosovo be generated, but the residents had averted humanitarian disaster by their own actions. Almost all had been absorbed into nearby towns and villages, had gone to their families or to nearby Baghdad.

Health checks mattered, but central government was not functioning. The state of the hospital was described as 'dirty, scruffy, absolutely filthy . . . all the staff had gone bar a number of janitors'.[49] Interested parties set up a number of clinics throughout the city: the Jordanians brought a hospital. There were very few competent people around, the middle class had gone and officials worked five ranks above their level of competence. The population remained content to bide their time until the schools reopened. The Americans brought in large quantities of ration packs and bottled water and were followed by entrepreneurs offering a choice of goods.

There were two compensation schemes: one Iraqi, the other American. The Americans paid householders a lump sum; the Iraqi system somehow never got off the ground. The fact that there were many claimants, that al-Qa'eda had gone, that payment centres had been carefully sited, meant the funds were readily and gratefully received. Every inhabitant had a biometric identity check and obligatory identity card, which meant that the dispensation of funds did not encounter the difficulty experienced in Helmand.

Ten per cent of the inhabitants who fled Fallujah had returned to the city by January, 30 per cent by the end of March. Six months after returning, approximately 100,000 were still displaced, unable to return to homes which, for a large part, no longer existed. 'Roughly 60 per cent of the houses and buildings inside the city sustained enough damage to make them uninhabitable. Most people continue to live in tents, or amid the rubble of their homes.'[50] It had been a strange way to hope to win friends and influence people. Which leads to one last question: who won the battle for Fallujah?

Unfolding events in Anbar Province rendered redundant whichever answer applied. In September 2006, Sheikh Abdul Sittar Bezea al-Rishawi, thirty-six, responded to the killing of his father and four brothers by forming Anbar Awakening, a coalition between the Sunnis and the Americans, to rid Anbar of al-Qa'eda and their Taliban brand of terror. Anbar Awakening proved hugely successful, transforming the formerly violent province into one of the safest in Iraq. Al-Qa'eda shot themselves in the foot when they killed one of al-Rishawi's associate sheikhs, then refused to return the body so that it could be buried immediately, as required by convention. 'We began to see what they were actually doing in Anbar Province. They were not respecting us or honouring us in any way,' he said. With the support of other sheikhs, readily available human intelligence and the American military, the Ali Baba and al-Qa'eda extremists had been virtually removed from Anbar's principal cities including Fallujah and Ramadi, where al-Rishawi lived. The measure of the Sunnis' rejection of al-Qa'eda could be seen in the statistics. Monthly attacks in Anbar had fallen from 1,350 in October 2006 to somewhat over 200 in October 2007.[51]

President George W. Bush came to Anbar Province in September 2007, immediately prior to outlining plans to Congress for a limited reduction of force levels in Iraq. In the full blaze of the international media, he inadvertently put the spotlight on Sheikh al-Rishawi, eulogizing him for having rejected 'murder and violence in return for moderation and peace'. There had been many previous attempts on the sheikh's life but shortly after meeting Bush, the assassins' persistence was rewarded. They killed him with a roadside bomb and then used a car bomb for good measure. Of this loss, General Petraeus, architect of the surge, the reinforcement of Iraq in 2007, and responsible for its evaluation with Ambassador Crocker said: 'This is a tragic loss. He was an organizing force who helped to keep the various tribes together.' His fellow sheikhs promised to press ahead with the reforms. Islamist websites applauded the death 'of one of the biggest pigs of the Crusaders'. They showed themselves to be utterly ruthless in their determination to prevail.

Conduct of Fallujah's two battles was significantly

different. For the second battle, the city had been cleared of non-combatants. The attacking force allocated for the first battle became established through incremental reinforcement rather than having been properly resourced at the outset. Moreover, the city had not been effectively contained. Ultimately, it was the fact of the presence of large numbers of non-combatants in the city which influenced the decision of Iraqi politicians to bring a halt to military operations in the first battle of Fallujah. Nevertheless, as General Abizaid told me, the Fallujah fight was 'one long battle in two pieces':

> The key difference in piece one versus piece two is that the political preconditions for victory were set in the second piece while they were very nearly lost in the first. Iraqi government support was essential for the final assault and that was assured by very agile preparatory work done by General Casey. By contrast, the first battle was hampered by constant threats of the Sunni Iraqis to wreck the fragile government that Ambassador Bremer had tried to form. You are correct to note the assault was stopped for political not military reasons in the first piece of the campaign. In the end, Iraqi support for the second piece of the battle was essential. This came about both politically and militarily.
>
> One point that is almost never discussed is that between the two pieces of the battle there was a very extensive targeting of extremist elements by our special operations that paid very high dividends. We learned how to focus our intelligence and more ably use our special operations capabilities in conjunction with our more conventional activities. The number of enemy casualties suffered in that interim phase was quite significant and ours quite low.[52]

With the city cleared for the second battle, the force multipliers, tanks and howitzers trundled out while fighters, bombers and Spectre AC-130Hs were on call to eliminate hotspots in the city as soon as they became identified. Such an array of options had not been available in southern Mogadishu for no other reason than the city remained populated. In Manila in 1945 artillery was freely used to eliminate the Japanese, who had taken up positions among the inhabitants, and thousands of them died. It was not least due to the presence of the media and the UN that Mogadishu did not become a Manila. Neither would be present in Sangin, in Helmand Province, Afghanistan.

9

Helmand
2006–2007

'If we are not to repeat the bloody mistakes of the past
in Afghanistan, then we must learn about its history.'

Following the January 2006 London Conference, British
Secretary of State for Defence John Reid announced the
deployment of 16 Air Assault Brigade, to Helmand Province,
Afghanistan. The capped Task Force comprised 3,300 British
military supported by Estonian and Danish contingents. The
brigade had as its mission the establishment of security so
as to allow reconstruction, the extension of political control
and the containment of the opium industry within Helmand
Province. Conceptually and unrealistically the *raison d'être*
revolved around peace-support, assuming with stunning
optimism that the brigade would be able to set the agenda
on the ground. Nothing had been learned from the Gorazde
experience. John Reid emphasized to the men going into
Helmand that they were on a peace-building mission 'to help
and protect the Afghan people construct their own democracy.
. . . We would be perfectly happy to leave in three years and
without firing one shot because our job is to protect the
reconstruction.'[1] The recent history of military intervention
is replete with examples where interventionists have set out
with a clean piece of paper, as though there is nothing to be
learned from history. Five years prior to the Reid statement,
General Sir Michael Rose wrote: 'If we are not to repeat the

bloody mistakes of the past in Afghanistan, then we must learn about its history.'[2]

The Great Game, the world's longest-established imperial rivalry between Britain and Russia, took place in Afghanistan during the nineteenth and twentieth centuries. The Afghans used their guile to set one side against the other. The British entered Afghanistan in 1839 at the outset of the First Afghan War. Squeezed out of the country in 1842 and granted safe passage back to India, the British force of 16,500 soldiers and refugees was slaughtered in the Khyber Pass when the Afghan commander had an apparent change of mind. The East India Company returned, exacted their revenge and in December 1842 evacuated Afghanistan.

The Second Afghan War, 1878–80, arose through a change in Afghan leadership, the new leader favouring the Russians. General Sir Frederick Roberts led three columns out of India, installing a British Resident in Kabul. The Resident survived four months. Ayub Khan of Herat marched on British-held Kandahar with a 25,000-strong army, meeting a 2,500-strong Anglo-Indian brigade at Maiwand, 50 miles (80 kilometres) north-west of Kandahar on 27 July 1880. The British lost 43 per cent of their number, Khan losing approximately 3,000 killed and wounded.[3] Roberts set out from Kabul with an avenging army, routing Khan at the Battle of Kandahar on 1 September 1880. After installing a pro-British government, the British again withdrew from Afghanistan in 1881.

While in Kabul, Roberts discovered the town to be 'much more Russian than English', concluding that there was no obvious advantage in maintaining close proximity with the Afghans. 'I feel sure I am right when I say the less the Afghans see of us, the less they dislike us. Should the Russians attempt to conquer Afghanistan, we should have a better chance of

attaching the Afghans to our interest if we avoid all interference with them.'[4]

In 1893 the Durand Line, named after Sir Mortimer
Durand, established Afghanistan's eastern border, bisecting
the Pashtuns, 28 million of whom live in Pakistan's North
West Frontier Province, representing 15 per cent of present-
day Pakistan's population. The Durand Line cut through
the homeland of a dozen significant Pashtun tribes. Future
military operations in the east and south would be affected
by Pashtuns on either side of the Durand Line acting as
though there were no border, a 1,355-mile (2,180-kilometres)
border recognized by neither Afghanistan nor Pakistan.
Afghanistan's borders are all potentially volatile. They are
with the former Soviet Union, Turkmenistan, Uzbekistan
and Tajikistan (1,481 miles; 2,384 kilometres), China (47
miles; 75 kilometres), India (75 miles; 120 kilometres) and
Iran (510 miles; 820 kilometres).

On 3 May 1919, the Russians capitalized on a jihad
declared against Britain, the prelude to the Third Afghan
War.[5] The timing could not have been worse for Britain,
there being few regular battalions in India. Nevertheless, with
air support, there were sufficient to force the Afghans back
into Afghanistan, thereby rubbishing the canard that the
Afghans had always defeated the British. Agreed, battles had
been lost, but the wars were always won. India's and
Pakistan's Independence in 1947 effectively concluded
Britain's territorial adventures in Afghanistan. The same was
not true of Russia.

In December 1979, justifying their action as military
intervention by invitation, the Soviets established a force of
115,000 men in eighteen garrisons and 170 military bases
in Afghanistan.[6] The USA's provision of substantial support
to the Mujahidin set in train a superpower proxy war. Afghan

battle tactics wore down the Soviets, 60 per cent of whom were conscripts, imposing upon them comprehensive defeat, precisely as they had upon the British in a number of set battles. They had 'no tradition of waging conventional war and no shame about preferring irregular tactics of which they are masters'.[7] Mohammed Yousaf, Head of the Afghan bureau of Pakistan's Inter-Service Intelligence – in effect the Mujahidin's commander-in-chief, wrote:

> At no time during the war were the communists able to do other than hold the towns and the bases, try to secure their lines of communications and carry out a series of search and destroy operations of varying sizes. By and large, the Soviet soldier fought poorly as he lacked motivation. He was frightened of night operations, he seldom pressed home attacks, he was casualty shy and kept behind his armour plate on the roads instead of deploying into the hills . . . to win in the field would have meant a vast escalation of men, money and equipment.[8]

When the Soviets left Afghanistan, the Mujahidin lost the enemy that had kept them up to the mark. The picture to emerge was 'one of reactionaries fighting among themselves and unable to form a government'.[9] The departure of the Soviets also resulted in the West's interest in Afghanistan dissipating, leaving a vacuum for terrorists, warlords and religious fanatics to fill. The strong martial tendency is particularly strong among the Pashtun people, driven by rivalry and bitter feuding. They are committed to the sixth pillar of Islam – Jihad or Holy War. 'Islam has always been forceful and uncompromising,'[10] wrote Charles Allen. Taliban means 'religious students' whose actions are guided by a social code known as *Pashtunwali*, the way of the Pashtuns. Here, issues of honour and revenge are set out in a blood code. The

Pashtuns respond to killing by revenge killing, a significant consideration when facing an insurgency.

The overwhelmingly Pashtun Taliban emerged from the shadows in the autumn of 1994 led by Mullah Mohammed Omar, who had lost his right eye fighting the Soviets. They established as their mission the end of domestic squabbling between tribes, the restoration of peace and security and the universal introduction of Sharia law. Approximately 99 per cent of Afghanistan's 28.6 million population profess to be Muslim. The Pashtun comprise 42 per cent of the population. The Tajiks and Uzbeks are Sunni Muslim. The Hazara are Shia Muslim. It was against the Hazara that the Taliban exerted the worst of their excesses. The Taliban derived popular support for securing the lines of communication, acting against corruption and reintroducing law and order, albeit *their* law and order. Murderers were executed in public, those who stole suffered amputation and hard-line regulations controlled many aspects of Afghan life. The broadcaster John Simpson, who encountered the Taliban in their capital Kandahar, wrote: 'They were alarming indeed. Kandahar is famous for its homosexuality, and it was commonplace to find Taliban soldiers with mascara'd eyes, painted finger and toenails, and high-heeled gold sandals. Also the AK-47.'[11]

Following the al-Qa'eda attack on 11 September 2001, the US demanded the Taliban hand over Osama bin Laden for trial. They refused. The United Nations Security Council made an enabling Resolution, number 1373 (12 September 2001), which contains the first reference to Chapter VII enforcement authorization in Afghanistan. The US and UK envisaged 'a lengthy engagement in Afghanistan . . . into the summer of 2002 at the very least'. The King of Jordan warned the UN not to expand its campaign beyond Afghanistan into Iraq.[12]

In October 2001, a US-led international coalition operation, Enduring Freedom, supported by Iraq's Northern Alliance, attacked al-Qa'eda training camps and Taliban compounds in Afghanistan. Both organizations collapsed under a welter of Tomahawk missiles and laser-guided bombs, the majority of their people withdrawing from southern Afghanistan by December 2001 into the anonymity to be found in the tribal areas of Pakistan. For al-Qa'eda therefore, 9/11 had proved to be counter-productive. The United States had cooperated with a number of tribal leaders to achieve a successful, swift campaign against the people and the territory where terrorists had formerly been trained.

The reason why Helmand became necessary was because the initial victory was not consolidated – Special Forces were withdrawn to prepare for the invasion of Iraq and the reconstruction efforts were feeble. The Taliban realized it had a chance to exploit the vacuum and also learned from its mistakes. The unanswered question is whether history is in the process of being repeated.

The United Kingdom had four principal aims for Operation Veritas, its version of the 'war on terror'. These were to deny al-Qa'eda its Afghan base, to deny it an alternative base beyond Afghanistan, to attack al-Qa'eda internationally and to support other states in their efforts against al-Qa'eda. The aims of the Taliban are synonymous with al-Qa'eda – a marriage of convenience between a militant political organization intent upon establishing a revolutionary new regime in Afghanistan and a terrorist organization. The heart of Taliban territory is around Quetta, while al-Qa'eda is based in the far north of Pakistan's North West Frontier. There is therefore no requirement to 'deny al-Qa'eda its Afghan base'. The Taliban is known to be cooperating with Pakistan's Army in its own counter-insurgency against Baluchi rebels. Many of the Afghans who joined the Taliban are former students of Pakistan's *madrassas*. Radicalized, home-grown, European terrorists have not been trained in Afghanistan but, almost without exception, in Pakistan where they were safe from NATO intervention.

The British first deployed into Afghanistan in 2001 to assist in the rolling back of the Taliban, withdrawing in July 2002. UN Security Council Resolution 1386 and successive resolutions sanctioned NATO's International Security Assistance Force (ISAF) to maintain security in Afghanistan and support reconstruction following the removal of the Taliban. Assistance was rendered to the Afghan Transitory Authority to create and maintain a safe and secure environment in Kabul. Presidential elections followed in October 2004, the Bonn process being finalized with universal, democratic, Parliamentary elections. Once the thirty-seven national representatives supporting ISAF had taken up secure residence in Kabul, they had unintentionally replicated Baghdad's Green Zone.

No one ever doubted that the solution to Afghanistan's problems lay in the hands of the Afghans themselves. From March 2003, the UK proceeded to train Afghanistan's junior NCOs and create an officer training programme based upon the Sandhurst model. The UK set up two Provincial Reconstruction Teams (PRTs) – one in northern Afghanistan and the other in Meymaneh. Civilian organizations insisted upon acceptable levels of security before they would assist with the reconstruction work. The British handed over their PRTs to NATO in 2006 to enable the UK to consolidate its forces in Helmand, one of thirty-four provinces in the country and an unpopular area with a number of ISAF members and NGOs. To paraphrase Smith Hempstone, however, for the British, 'If they enjoyed Dhofar they will love Helmand'.

Helmand was the quintessential British fighting environment; so different from what the British had seen of NATO headquarters in Kabul, replete with national representatives. 'There were lots of people with red tabs in Kabul, bored silly and not doing a great deal, acting out a First World War analogy in so far as the difference between Kabul and the operations in front line Helmand was the biggest I have seen. The Commander had to play the hand he had been dealt. He and his dedicated immediate staff were decidedly not numbered among the chateaux generals.'[13]

A Royal Marine officer described his deployment to the NATO four-star headquarters in Kabul:

> The working environment in ISAF HQ is somewhat surreal, especially for those used to operating at the tactical level. In excess of 1,000 staff are squeezed in a compound no more than 500 metres square [598 square yards]. The Headquarters staff is drawn from 37 different nations, ensuring that communications and work ethic can never be taken for granted. Many nations have left a lasting influence here including coffee bars and a garden – the location of choice for many meetings.[14]

Each military representative of the thirty-seven states carried a red card which he would use if the HQ attempted to task his national representatives for any mission either he or his country opposed. Many NATO states maintained caveats forbidding their men's assignment to the dangerous south. Among these were France, Germany, Italy and Spain. Collocated in Kabul are representatives of the EU and UN, resulting in Afghanistan representing 'the largest multinational intervention of its genre . . . Yet some international organizations, donors and military missions work against each other in pursuit of their own self interests.'[15] The British in Helmand faced the possibility of achieving tactical victory yet suffering strategic defeat because they were part of an unwieldy organization.

While the Helmand Task Force was deploying into the south of Afghanistan, the UK was also deploying its principal operational (or theatre level) headquarters to Kabul in order to exercise command over the whole NATO/ISAF operation. Headquarters Allied Rapid Reaction Corps had a short but distinguished history, having run NATO's operations in Bosnia and Kosovo at critical junctures in the 1990s. Now commanded by Lieutenant-General David Richards, the headquarters was once again working under NATO. Adopting the name HQ ISAF and augmented by officers from most ISAF contributing nations, the headquarters was charged specifically with ensuring the smooth expansion of the NATO-controlled ISAF operation from the relatively quiet north and west of Afghanistan to include the much more troublesome south and east.

Taking over from the US-led HQ Combined Forces Command Afghanistan, and much to the credit of both headquarters, HQ ISAF achieved its narrow military task with singular efficiency and skill. Its principal role thereafter was to set the conditions for success at the lower tactical level. Not well understood by some military pundits, nor by many front-line soldiers who perhaps naturally view such apparently non-military activity with some suspicion, this is nevertheless a key task that links strategic direction with traditional tactical activity. Without it one can win battles but will never win wars. It involves much interaction with government and civilian agencies as well with key international leaders. By early October therefore, Lieutenant-General Richards was responsible for NATO's first 'war fighting' operation, commanding 35,000 troops in five regions each with its

own regional headquarters, while conducting complex negotiations on the wider campaign with a host of other military and
non-military actors, including some in Pakistan. About 10,000
troops were deployed in the south. Drawn principally from
the UK, USA, Canada, Netherlands, Romania and Denmark,
these forces were initially under a Canadian- and then Dutch-
led headquarters based in Kandahar.[16]

Creating a secure environment and development and
reconstruction were vital if progress was to be made. The
training of the civil police has been described as a 'farce'.
That was also the term used in Kosovo where EU states all
wanted visibility through sharing the tasks. Chaos ensued.
The tragedy is that nothing is being learned. 'We have a
multiplicity of trainers committed to police training.
Everything has to be first translated into English before being
translated into Arabic. The only effective ANP [Afghanistan
National Police] I have encountered throughout Afghanistan,
strangely enough, was half a dozen in Sangin of all places.'[17]
In provinces such as Helmand, the military's association with
the ANP, universally loathed by the local population and
viewed as 'corrupt to the core', was counter-productive,
handing to the Taliban a very useful propaganda tool. The
Afghan National Army (ANA) is relatively better than the
Iraqi Army. They enjoy fighting, will go into action and will
not run away, although it has to be said that they do not
fight too well.

39 Regiment Royal Engineers, with a protection force
provided by 42 Commando Royal Marines, had the task of
building a fort in the desert to accommodate a below-strength
brigade and all the paraphernalia associated with its support,
including C-130 fixed-wing aircraft. They had four months
to build Camp Bastion – so called after the proprietary name

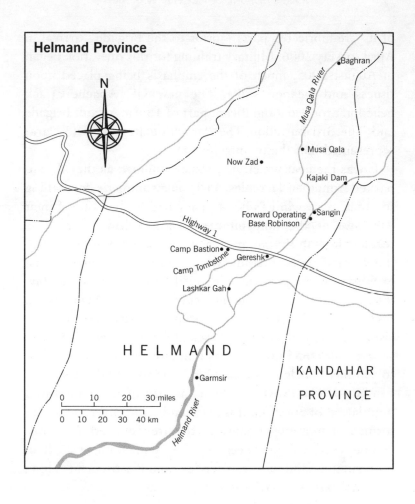

of its pre-fabricated parts – prior to the brigade's arrival in April to May 2006. Military training for this operation began in August 2005, much of the emphasis being placed upon fitness and weapon skills. The new UK Apache attack helicopter formed a significant part of 16 Air Assault Brigade and The 3rd Battalion The Parachute Regiment (3 Para) represented half the infantry.

It was the heat which first struck the men as they disembarked from their Hercules, 45°C on a summer's day, falling to -15°C on a winter's night. They had looked out of their windows at the inhospitable terrain below them. One recalled how in the summer the scene had reminded him of the *bocage* in Normandy where, instead of wheat, vast expanses of poppies were in full bloom. Understandably, the men adopted a Helmand-centric view of Afghanistan, the province having a different personality to provinces elsewhere in a massive land-locked state covering 252,900 square miles (655,000 square kilometres), almost equivalent to France, Belgium, the Netherlands and Denmark combined. The Province is half the size of England with a population of 300,000. It is bisected by the River Helmand, formed of multiple streams up to three-quarters of a mile (1 kilometre) wide between the river banks, an obstacle in both summer and winter. There are small settlements along its green banks, known as the 'green zone'.

Sixty per cent of the population live in the provincial capital, Lashkar Gah. The other strategically important towns are Now Zad, Sangin, Musa Qala and Kajaki. At Kajaki there is an iconic dam set in beautifully rugged country, a smaller version of the Grand Canyon, which regulates the flow of the river and supplies hydro-electricity to southern Afghanistan. Behind it lies a 32-mile-long (52-kilometre-long) reservoir containing 1.85 million cubic metres of water. Route

One is the only tarmac road worthy of the description. Off-road travel is dangerous because of randomly strewn mines, thus adding to the importance of air for travel and resupply.

Brigade Commander, Brigadier Ed Butler, established his headquarters in Kandahar[18] where there were two squadrons of RAF Harriers and the ISAF southern regional headquarters commanded by a Canadian Brigade Commander. Add to this complication of a one-on-one (British and Canadian brigadiers) the presence of independent, itinerant Americans looking for al-Qa'eda leaders and we have the usual chain of command glitch. A Dutch Commander said that if it were necessary for the Americans to hunt for terrorists in an area, they should discuss their intentions with the NATO Commander. 'There must not be a situation', he said, 'in which we work on reconstruction one day and the bulldozers flatten everything again the next.'[19] What the General complained of was the undesirable consequence of mixed missions, the bulk of ISAF being committed to counter-insurgency whereas large elements of the American presence had been committed to counter-terror operations.

The Ministry of Defence describes Helmand as 'a province where security is "less benign" than in the north'. The soldiers called the place Hell Land. The Commanding Officer 3 Para, Lieutenant-Colonel Stuart Tootal, waited impatiently for all his infantry to assemble at Camp Bastion, something which took over a month to complete. Serendipitously the Taliban had a ceasefire in place to allow the uninterrupted collection of opium. The time was not wasted. The Commanding Officer's concept of operations could be described as essentially manoeuvrist, within a triangular tactical area of operations between Camp Bastion, Lashkar Gah and Gereshk. He was utterly opposed to his battle group becoming bogged down in defensive locations along the Helmand River. That judgement was based upon a number of factors: the roads were always susceptible to ambush and there were countless Soviet-era, unmarked minefields off the roads. This meant heavy demands being placed upon the helicopter fleet for the movement of personnel, casualty evacuation and resupply. The central problem lay in the force having only seven twin-rotor Chinooks (that is five normally available at any one time) and eight Apache attack helicopters making their debut appearance.

3 Para battle group had no control over the tasks placed upon them. The Commanding Officer was ordered where he had to go. The Taliban held the initiative and the Afghan political elite let their requirements be known. This meant 3 Para being drawn principally into the extremities of a box up to 50 miles (80 kilometres) from Bastion as the crow flies, with Sangin, the Kajaki Dam, Musa Qala and Now Zad at each corner. Taliban attacks upon the Kajaki Dam could not be tolerated. The dam had to be secured in order to be serviced and repaired. It thus represented a key component in the reconstruction plan for southern Afghanistan. The Soviets had come here in 1955 to build the 300-foot- (91-metre-) high, 900-feet- (274-metre-) long dam in the expectation of gaining political influence. In 1973 the United States, also intending to achieve political influence, rebuilt the dam as a hydro-electric facility. There is a hope that outstanding repairs on the dam and electric transmission lines will bring power to 2 million people in southern Afghanistan. Water supplied for irrigation allows a million people to be fed and wheat to be grown throughout the year.[20] It is difficult to imagine what the Taliban hope to gain by the obstruction of a reconstruction project promising huge benefit for the population of southern Afghanistan. The fact remains that the Paras were obliged to put a fire support team into Kajaki.

On 6 September 2006 a Para sniper group descended the ridge they occupied towards the road below, where the Taliban could be seen interrupting traffic. On the way down, one of the group trod on an anti-personnel mine, sustaining severe injuries. Corporal Mark Wright led a group of Paras down towards the casualty. Wright knew that if he took time to clear the minefield the casualty would die. He took a calculated risk. He called for a helicopter for casualty evacuation and told one of his men to clear the route through the minefield from the casualty to the landing site. Unfortunately the soldier overlooked a mine which detonated, causing a traumatic amputation. Wright moved through the minefield to treat and reassure this, the second casualty, until a medic arrived. The helicopter came but had no winch with which to lift the casualties out of the minefield. On standing up, Wright detonated a third mine, seriously injuring himself and the medical orderly.

Another medical orderly moved forward to treat Wright but detonated another mine, wounding himself and others around him, including intensifying Wright's injuries. There were now seven casualties in the minefield, three of whom had lost limbs. Wright maintained command of the group in the minefield, 'shouting encouragement to those around him, maintaining morale and calm among the many wounded men'. He died of his wounds aboard the rescue helicopter. The citation for his brave conduct read: 'His supreme courage and outstanding leadership were an inspiration to his men. For acts of the greatest gallantry and complete disregard for his own safety in striving to save others, Corporal Wright is awarded the George Cross.'[21]

Lieutenant-Colonel Tootal, who had set out intending to hold back resources so as to manoeuvre to emerging crises, had no option but to occupy Kajaki, Now Zad, Forward

Operating Base Robinson (covering Sangin), Sangin and Musa
Qala. Visibility in and around the settlements was often no
more than 50 yards (46 metres) as the buildings were in close
proximity. Buildings in Afghanistan are stoutly made of thick,
baked stone, barely penetrable except by barmines. The high,
broad, mud walls and ditches draw foot soldiers into places
they instinctively know they should not be going. Immediately
beyond the settlements intensive farming and irrigation posed
numerous challenges once patrols had left the District Centres,
referred to as Platoon Houses. That was a misnomer. Sangin's
'Platoon House' was a company-size commitment.

The District Centres which the Paras requisitioned
comprised a cluster of low buildings inside a compound with
walls so high it was often not possible to see over. They were
all much the same. The important difference was the proximity
of other buildings. At Musa Qala, for example, the town's
buildings adjoined the District Centre so that there was little
time to react or respond to attacks. Sangin was set apart so
there the defenders were in a better position to respond to
direct attack, but all District Centres became shell traps for
indirect fire such as mortar rounds. The population who had
homes near to District Centres had long gone. Preparing and
repairing defences became an endless occupation. The District
Centres suffered continual attacks day and night. There was
no respite, but out in the country there was a different regime.
The battle group equipped with night vision devices conveyed
to the Taliban the subliminal message 'if you move at night
you die'.

The clinging brown dust of talcum powder consistency
got everywhere, bringing with it enhanced maintenance
problems. That was particularly undesirable given the totally
inadequate number of helicopters to bring in food, ammunition and personnel. Water could be found in wells. It needed

purifying. Food could sometimes be purchased locally, but the extraordinary expenditure of ammunition had to be made good.

The helicopter pilots were extremely brave. The 100-foot (30-metre), twin-rotor Chinook presented a particularly large target. Its armour protection ran only along the bottom of its fuselage. Nevertheless, these were superb, rugged machines, which also included among their number call-sign Bravo November, the solitary helicopter which had worked continuously throughout the Falkland Campaign twenty-five years earlier. The arrival of a Chinook at a District Centre attracted Taliban intent upon shooting it down and required a manpower-intensive commitment by the Paras to prevent them doing so.

The force multiplier which gave 3 Para any hope of compensating for their acute shortage of manpower and difficult mission was the close air support sorties flown principally – over 80 per cent – by Americans with RAF support. Among the aircraft committed to their round-the-clock protection were RAF Harriers and USAF A-10 tank-busters, Spectre gunships and B1 bombers. A second lieutenant therefore had the firepower available at his disposal which in 1944 would have been the preserve of a brigade commander. Having a communications system that worked not only facilitated mission-oriented orders but allowed hugely professional fire support teams to bring down fire on to a given point from the air and ground simultaneously. The Paras had their own 81- and 51-mm mortars. Sangin and its immediate area also had cover from Forward Operating Base Robinson supplied by their own support artillery.

The surprise of the adaptability and courage of 3 Para, no less heroic than their fathers and grandfathers, is that when their unashamed arrogance – part of the Paras' self-pumping mechanism so good-naturedly tolerated by those not of the maroon machine – is set aside, there is no history of battle experience upon which to claim this position of excellence. 2 Para fought Goose Green with perhaps three of their number having had previous combat experience. 1 and 3 Para were only lightly committed in Iraq in 2003. Yet, having said that, the Toms and those who followed them performed as veterans. How could that be? 'It is not a natural thing to move towards something that will kill you,' said a 3 Para lance-corporal. 'Not doing it, however, would mean jacking on your mates and that will never happen so you just push on through.' There is also something to do with receiving a dividend on investments in training. 'There was an explosion behind us, and rounds started coming in and around the wagons,' explained a 3 Para private. 'I wasn't even thinking about being scared, we all just got straight into the drills we had been taught.'[22]

The story of Musa Qala became the most controversial event of the Paras' tour. The District Centre there was virtually indefensible and it seemed that in time it would be overrun by the confident Taliban, an action which might have endangered the British Government. 'With the governmental and service infrastructure in a state of collapse and the economy at an extremely basic level it has created a situation in which it [the Taliban] has very little to lose from military action from external powers.'[23] Sergeant Brangan of the Royal Irish described the mortar attack which killed Lance-Corporal Muirhead and Ranger Draiva:

> The fridge door used to bang, and it was like a pop in the distance of a mortar round being fired. So you didn't know if someone was opening the door or not. 30 seconds before the rounds landed, we heard this pop, which used to send me mad,

because people used to react to the pops and used to shout 'Stand to, stand to' and you were up and out of your bed more times than, I don't know what. So anyway this time, I was sitting having a cigarette and a brew with Boyley at the back door. And heard a pop, and I said 'Who the fuck's at the fucking fridge'. And then obviously, lo and behold, them rounds started to land in the compound and the first one obviously landed where Cpl Muirhead and Ranger Draiva were on stag [sentry].[24]

Major Wright-Boycott of 3 Para's Pathfinders described an attack on Musa Qala from another perspective:

After about ten days of attacks, you know RPGs, small arms, they then launched a full-on attack on us, where they destroyed our outpost position. At that stage, I saw the outpost position destroyed and it was quite heart rending just watching this thing get wiped out by two RPGs. I thought 'Nobody is going to live in that'. And I was up on the roof of the building I was on, controlling the fire-fight. It was the most intense fire-fight I've ever been in in my life, there was fire coming from 360 degrees around the compound, into it, you know we reckon there was at least six or seven different positions, potentially 150 to 200 fighters trying to take it on. Just the . . . the noise, it was no use using a radio because you couldn't speak on the radio so we were just shouting, you know to link them [the positions]. I remember crawling to the corner of a building to look down and as I shouted down to my link man so he could basically run off and tell the other people what to do to make sure that the security was in place . . . The [sic] whole bit that I was looking through basically erupted in a cloud of mud as the AK rounds landed, they'd basically seen me and fired at me and then an RPG round basically came straight across my head and there was a bamboo pole. . . I didn't realize it was there, but the bamboo pole had taken the RPG, the

RPG clipped it . . . I was well below it and I was in hard cover, but [I] looked around and my whole body was covered in bamboo splinters, so it was quite close.[25]

The British thought long and hard as to how they might be able to resolve the problem of Musa Qala without appearing to be running away. The solution came to them from the town's head man, representing the elders. Fed up with the fighting, damage and interruption to life in the town, it was proposed to the British and the Taliban that they both go, leaving the management of the town's security to the town's elders. The Taliban would not have known of the British difficulties but they did know that they had suffered substantial casualties. Both sides had fought themselves to a standstill. A meeting was duly held, after which the British and the Taliban withdrew from Musa Qala. Britain would have been satisfied with the deal, having separated the townspeople from the Taliban. That was the theory. With Government support, the Musa Qala deal prospered and survived into January 2007. It was al-Qa'eda who intervened to change the arrangement. There is a principle here: in war, do not expect your enemy to do what they promise. The Taliban returned, killed the head man and established the town as a logistics base for further operations against the towns to the south. By 11 December 2007 a combined British, American and Afghan force had retaken Musa Qala.

What Sangin, 'the heart of darkness', told of 3 Para's tour is that there had been no reconstruction, only destruction. The security environment did not allow for reconstruction and development. Allegedly, the British Department of International Development's representative did not wish to be seen to be associated with the military, henceforth known as DfID's diffidence.

The war would never be fought and won simply by sitting in defended bases, however. The province had to be dominated by a military presence; easy to say, difficult to achieve. Three divisions might have been successful. The initial rules of engagement proved to be remarkably stringent. The reason was understandable; the military and civil authorities wanted no collateral damage anywhere. The British rules of engagement allowed them to shoot only when their lives became obviously threatened. There was the case where a truckful of Taliban drove past a Para patrol unchallenged. The terrorists had been so close that the patrol leader reported: 'They had black beards and were wearing eyeliner – why I don't know.'[26]

Sangin would normally have had a population of 2–3,000. That it was now virtually empty of non-combatants explains how it was that the two sides exchanged such heavy firepower. Sangin resembled a knocked-about film set for a spaghetti western. The British had no intention of allowing the Taliban a free run there. As 29-year-old Corporal Bryan Budd's section advanced with the platoon down the dusty road towards the market, all was eerily silent. As in so many other counter-insurgency operations, Afghanistan proved once again to be a section commander's war. Two gunmen moving from their firing point to improve their position were engaged by the Paras who, almost immediately, came under fire from behind. Taliban marksmanship is not normally of a high standard. On this occasion, one of Budd's men took two rounds in his leg, collapsing in the street, rounds continuing to fall around him. Aware that he had to create space to allow Private Edwards to be evacuated, Budd attacked the building from where the fire was heaviest, driving the enemy out into open ground 'where they were successfully engaged'.

A month later, on 20 August, Budd's company, A Company, was out on patrol with engineers to improve visibility from the District Centre and create new routes by blowing holes in nearby walls with barmines. The barmines were used for tasks more heavy duty than those for which mousehole charges would have been appropriate. Budd's section had a screening role. He led his section through a field of maize with the other sections in his platoon in mutually supporting positions including a WMIK Land Rover mounting the weapon the Taliban most feared, the .50-inch machine gun. Ahead of him, Budd saw a group of Taliban and motioned to the rest of his section to go firm while he himself went forward to engage them. They, in the meantime, had seen the Land Rover with the .50 machine gun and fired at it. With the element of surprise gone, Budd led his section towards the sound of gunfire. Immediately, they could hear the sounds of the withering fire aimed at them of 'Afghan bees', bullets passing all around them and at them, three men falling wounded, three of eight down. Budd responded by charging the Taliban, at which point the engineers detonated the barmine, thereby obscuring the view.

The platoon commander set out to locate Budd but found the area alive with Taliban. His company commander at the District Centre called Bastion for air support, receiving two Harriers almost immediately with Apaches to follow. No one knew precisely where Budd was or whether he was dead or alive. When one of their own is out, lost in hostile territory, all stops are pulled out to locate him and return him to base. The manning problem continued to make life difficult. Major Loden found no shortage of volunteers. An ad hoc platoon, 'very much a ragtag bunch of soldiers', including Household Cavalry Regiment, Royal Engineers and Military Police under Lieutenant Andy Mallet, set off towards where Budd had last been seen. 'I then moved around with this makeshift platoon around to the left-hand side and basically fought our way through and over to the position where Bryan had fallen.'[27] The Harriers appeared but could not be directed on to the enemy in the maize. The Apaches fared better, clearing through the maize and thereby allowing A Company to conduct the search for Budd.

An hour after losing contact they found his body. He had been killed in crossfire. Four of his friends laid him in the quad bike for the return to the District Centre while desultory, harassing fire continued from the Taliban. He had been an excellent, humorous, first-class NCO, a soldier's man and a family man. His platoon commander remembers how Budd would

> Every now and then come up to me with pictures in his hand of his family and would say, 'Boss, this is my little girl (Isabella), this is my wife (Lorena), we are expecting another baby'. Wherever he put his bed down he would put up pictures of his family. No one else did that . . . he would have a nice neat bed space and a picture of his family, and that is what he wanted to talk about most.[28]

They rewarded his courage. His citation read:

> Corporal Budd's conspicuous gallantry during these two engagements saved the lives of many of his colleagues. He acted in the full knowledge that the rest of his men had either been struck down or had been forced to go to ground. His determination to press home a single-handed assault against a superior enemy force despite his wounds stands out as a premeditated act of inspirational leadership and supreme valour. In recognition of this, Corporal Budd is awarded the Victoria Cross.[29]

It was the first posthumous award of a Victoria Cross since the Falklands Campaign. The next day, the British public would hear on the six o'clock news that 'another British soldier has died in southern Afghanistan' and that 'next of kin have been informed'. The following day his photograph appears. 'How sad' think the public, until their minds are taken away by the next item of news. Sara Jones, widow of 'H' Jones, wrote of her own situation: 'To the world he was a soldier, to us he was the world.'

An under-strength 3 Commando Brigade relieved the under-strength, under-equipped 16 Air Assault Brigade. Eighteen members of the returning brigade, including some from The Parachute Regiment, were lost – the same number as died at Goose Green, Grenada and Mogadishu. This had been the mission from which they were told they would probably return home 'without firing one shot'. They knew their history.

On 12 October 2006, 3 Commando Brigade, Royal Marines, under command of Brigadier Jerry Thomas, assumed command of UK Task Force, Helmand, from Brigadier Ed Butler's 16 Air Assault Brigade. This book began with 3 Commando Brigade's involvement in the Falklands conflict a quarter of a century earlier. In the Falklands, Brigadier Julian Thompson complained of the paucity of helicopters having had a debilitating effect upon his ability to conduct operations as he would have wished. He would not have wanted to be in either Basra or Helmand. On occasions, the number of Chinooks available to Brigadier Thomas fell to two or three.

Helicopters were available in the arms bazaar. A number of companies could have hired to the UK sufficient helicopters to overcome the tactical restraints being imposed upon military operations. Iranian vehicles smuggling IEDs into Afghanistan had been intercepted. The effects of these roadside bombs placed greater demands upon air support. Security Support Solutions Limited, for example, offered to hire

Ministry of Defence UK four Soviet-era Mi17 Hip helicopters and an Mi26 Halo transporter flown by former British and European Special Forces pilots. It also offered a maintenance package. The helicopters had been fully tested in an Afghanistan environment. The Ministry of Defence preferred to accept the tactical risks rather than have British troops travel in Soviet-era helicopters.[30] The rather obvious question, why not use NATO helicopters, is the source of anger among states whose men are committed to the dangerous south. States such as France, Germany, Greece, Spain and Turkey have sheltered behind caveats to restrict their support of NATO.

The problem with the intervening period between the Falklands conflict and operations in Iraq and Afghanistan is that the transition from Cold War to Hot War had not been accompanied by adequate changes and supplies of equipment. The lack of helicopters was a classic example. 'The shortage of helicopters in both Iraq and Afghanistan is nothing short of a disgrace. [Half the allocated Apache helicopters were unserviceable, as were a third of Chinook transport helicopters. Of the venerable Sea King and its replacement Merlin Mark 3 Support helicopters, only half were available.] The current total in Afghanistan is 20 and rather fewer in Iraq. The US Army owns 485 helicopters in the 101st Airborne Division alone.'[31] The procurement book is full of large, capital projects involving British jobs in Government constituencies, none of which would make a significant impact upon the type of conflict seen in Iraq and Afghanistan. There were, for example, two £4 billion aircraft-carriers on the books. One option considered to fund the carriers was to shed 6,000 Army jobs, a proposal put on the table at a time when the overcommitted regular forces were already 7,000 under-strength.

In October 2006, 42 Commando Battle Group commanded by Lieutenant-Colonel Matt Holmes relieved 3 Para battle group. The Marines inherited the obligation to man the fixed positions at Gereshk, Sangin, Now Zad, Robinson and Kajaki. In Gereshk, the Taliban had taken to coming down river to attack the security forces and the small dam there. The Marines established a buffer between north-east Gereshk and the Sangin valley. Gereshk is second in size to Lashkar Gah, its importance being as the gateway into the Afghan Development Zone. The allocation of troops to task became complicated because of a manpower cap allowing the Marines seventy-five fewer men than the Paras, although with subsequent task organizing at times the 42 Commando battle group comprised up to 1,500 personnel and eleven companies. Nevertheless, allocating troops to essential tasks meant fielding six- rather than eight-man sections. On relieving the paratroopers in Fallujah, the US Marines presented their own concept of operations in such a way as to appear to be obliquely criticizing the paratroopers. That did not happen here, where it was possible to observe not revolution but evolution. Similarly, manoeuvrist ideas were in place but the wherewithal to put these ideas into effect came to the Marines six weeks into their tour. The requirement for a protected, all-terrain vehicle had been identified during the Balkan campaign. The Viking, a very manoeuvrable, tracked, armoured personnel carrier with crew-served weapons, came out of the naval procurement system. The value of the Viking was not simply as a capable platform from which to fight; its ability to manoeuvre also enabled enemy lines of communication to be cut and equally for embarked troops to access and reach out to dispersed villages to conduct *shuras* (meetings with the elders) and communicate with local elders. A rebalancing of manpower in fixed locations according to threat meant 42 Commando could take risks in generating manpower for specific operations to exploit its capability further. When 42 Commando returned to the United Kingdom, the Vikings remained in Afghanistan.

These developments allowed the Marines' Commanding Officer to form a Mobile Operations Group based upon J Company, introducing unpredictable ground manoeuvres and surprise as a means of disrupting and defeating the Taliban. The Taliban never knew where the Mobile Operations Group had gone, or where it would appear. The Marines had produced an ideal unit with which to exercise Mission Oriented Orders. In an attack which began at dawn on Monday 15 January 2007 on the Taliban base of Jugroom Fort to the south of Garmsir, Viking-mounted Z Company, 45 Commando, supported by C Squadron The Light Dragoons, crossed the Helmand River prior to making a dismounted attack on the fort. Z Company had the support of engineers, artillery, attack helicopters and other close air support. The weight of Taliban fire was described as 'ferocious'. After an engagement lasting five hours, the Marines withdrew over the river, having satisfactorily completed their mission. 'Our intention', explained Lieutenant-Colonel Rory Bruce, 'was to show the insurgents that they are not safe anywhere, that we are able to reach out to them and attack whenever and wherever we choose, even where they think they are at their safest.'

On regrouping, Lance-Corporal Mathew Ford was found to be unaccounted for. He had to be found and brought back. Time was of the essence. The answer to the problem was to use three of the Apache WAH-64 attack helicopters, the cabins of which have room only for the crew. Two soldiers were strapped to each of the two small side wings of two helicopters. A third Apache provided aerial cover from supporting fire which came down during the search in hostile territory. 'It was', continued Lieutenant-Colonel Bruce, 'an extraordinary tale of heroism and bravery of our airmen, soldiers and marines who were all prepared to put themselves back into the line of fire to rescue a fallen comrade.' The rescuers found Ford had been killed and returned to base with his body on the wing of an Apache.[32] It was a selfless act such as this, by Special Forces and Rangers in Mogadishu, determined that none of theirs, dead or alive, would be abandoned, that contributed to the complication of that mission. The question to be asked is why were there no utility helicopters available with which to carry out casualty evacuation.

A continuation of the evolutionary process saw the Task Force or Brigade Headquarters move into the provincial capital of Lashkah Gah so as to be in the best position to focus upon the Afghan Development Zone and Helmand Executive Group[33] in collaboration with a Danish reconstruction group. 'Hearts and minds' projects were started, flowed outward, and the majority completed. Over fifty such projects were commenced in Gereshk. Circumstances meant 3 Para had been unable to complete a single civil project.

A 200-strong detachment from 45 Commando had the task of forming the nucleus of the Operational and Mentoring Team, the type of work undertaken by American 'advisers' in Fallujah. Their job was to provide advice and support to the Afghan National Army, conduct cross-coalition liaison and ensure effective co-ordination with other friendly forces on operations and to enable Afghan National Army training. The new role required some adjustments in the way the Marines behaved. 'The Commanding Officer suffered his own personal battles when much to his discomfort, he found himself walking hand in hand with the ANA Brigade commander to lunch.'[34]

Captain Matt Williams, second-in-command of Mentoring Team A (there was also B) brought the 3rd Kandak of the 3rd Brigade, 205 Corps, down to Camp Tombstone, alongside Bastion, they having passed off the square the previous day – i.e. completed their training in Kabul. This would be a new experience for all the assigned Marines, having to face 'the management of our own expectations'. The Afghan soldiers were a vital part of the preparation of Afghanistan to be responsible for its own security. Having an Afghan face on operations was deemed essential. The Marines went a step further and partnered the Afghans. In view of their poor administration and poor logistics they were not employed above platoon level. There was never any question of them being political adjuncts. They had a military purpose, being the fourth component in some of the British Marine rifle companies. Each Afghan platoon commander was covered by a mentor who had two others acting as his force protectors. These early beginnings represented real ink spots. As can be imagined, the time required to join the ink spots would be very long. Looking into a crystal ball, one could imagine the future of Afghanistan formed around a Kemal Atatürk solution of a strong army consolidating security across the country. The ultimate political solution might be based upon a loose confederation, acknowledging the power and interests of the major warlords in their own mini client states.

A 'stay put' policy had applied to Now Zad, a settlement which was not part of the main effort. After 42 Commando had moved in and K Company began patrolling, a good rapport became established with the elders and the Taliban lost ground. They would call unofficial ceasefires for ten to twelve days, which gave the Marines the opportunity to bring in engineer plant to clear rubble and garner local support. The programme became so effective that the Taliban broke the ceasefire.

The Marines aimed to make the Taliban irrelevant by separating them from the people. That implied an appropriate use of force, meaning there was to be no engagement if there was an unacceptable risk of collateral damage. The inability to fight discriminately would lead only to strategic defeat. The Taliban had been graded into two tiers. Those in tier one were deemed to be irreconcilable and had to be defeated; in the second tier were those identified as potentially capable of being won over. A wedge had to be driven between tiers one and two to split the Taliban in order to concentrate upon their leadership and military experts. The number of contacts increased, their nature becoming more offensive than defensive as the initiative was seized. For example, as a result of fighting patrols and deliberate, offensive operations to defeat the Taliban, the number of attacks upon the Kajaki dam fell from five to one a day.

In an environment such as Afghanistan's, intimidation is rife and intelligence takes time to mature. 3 Para described intelligence as 'at best incomplete and complex'. Time spent in *shuras* talking to headmen to gain their confidence and trust is one of the initial steps leading towards the isolation of the Taliban. General Dannatt, Chief of the General Staff, warned that bringing an end to terrorism would take a generation. The British Army's commitments since 1945 span the generations, claiming 16,000 lives. One revelation arising from the year under examination in Helmand, tragic as it is, is the high-tech investment being put into the support of tactical operations. That was evident when, on 2 September 2006, an RAF Nimrod MR2 came down near Kandahar with the loss of fourteen lives.

At the time of writing in early 2008, it is possible to look back upon the media coverage of operations in Afghanistan and conclude it has been the best seen over this quarter of

a century. Reporting has been responsible, objective, inform-
ative, well written, individualistic, well illustrated and told
straight, free of gimmicks. Why should that be? The answer
would appear to lie in the way the story is gathered. Reporters
in Helmand go out with the boys, face the same risks – they
are shot at – and put their lives in the hands of those around
them. Commanding Officer 42 Commando embraced and
welcomed the media but emphasized to those who came into
his bailiwick that the anxious families of his men would read
every single word they wrote.

The first chapter on Goose Green included discussion of
the emotive subject of honours. It is a relevant topic to examine here too. Some Commanding Officers do their utmost to
do their very best for their men, aware that if successful the
unit basks in reflected glory – there might be a battle honour
in it. One aspect of honours management which does not sit
at all well with what seems to be right is the advanced
advertising in newspapers of candidates for awards before
the committee could possibly have come to a decision. There
was Nurse A who we were told was going to be awarded
an MC and Sergeant B and Officer C who were both going
to be awarded a VC. It is an insidious business, unfair to
those nominated and unfair to the deserving whose
F/HONS/776 applications state their cases fairly, *sans*
embellishment.

At Goose Green, the intermediate awards for bravery were
the Military Cross for officers and the Military Medal for
the non-commissioned ranks. Former Prime Minister John
Major decided to take the egalitarian step to scrap the Military
Medal, retaining the Military Cross for all ranks. Of the
thirteen Military Crosses awarded to 3 Commando Brigade
at the end of their tour in Helmand, every one was awarded
to non-commissioned ranks. That reflects the nature of the

conflict and the reality that this was a section commander's war, except that only three corporals were among those to be recognized. Egalitarianism is all very well but a one-size-fits-all at this level appears to favour the non-commissioned ranks. Had the system prevailing at Goose Green been in operation in Helmand, the officers would have been examined as a separate group, befitting their rather different functions in conflict.

Does it matter? Napoleon thought so. Having engaged and beaten the Ancien Régime, he reinstituted the Légion d'Honneur. Those who knew him well enough complained, 'We have just gone through a revolution to do away with honours and privilege, why are you doing this?' He replied, 'It is with baubles that men are led.'

The subject is unfamiliar territory to those not within the system. I spoke to 42 Commando's Commanding Officer, Lieutenant-Colonel Matt Holmes.

'Who was 42 Commando's bravest of the brave?'

'That accolade goes to Corporal John Thompson. He performed a key role within Juliet Company Group in over thirty fierce fire-fights with the Taliban. He manned the unprotected WMIK Land Rover armed with a .50 machine gun and general purpose machine gun.'

'So, it was obviously a target of the Taliban?'

'Yes, on numerous occasions his vehicle was hit by small arms fire and shrapnel.'

'It is often the case that individuals are consistently brave with perhaps one particular incident which stands out above the others.'

'That would have been during Operation Bauxite on 10 January 2007 when we had as one of our tasks the reconnoitring deep into Taliban held territory 5 kilometres [3 miles] to the

east of Gereshk. The Company Group proceeded to enter the
Taliban stronghold of Habibollah Kalay to search a known safe
house and clear it of Taliban and their weapons. There had been
a number of earlier engagements against this position so, unsurprisingly, it was well prepared for a return visit. The place was
groaning with Taliban glad of the opportunity to take Juliet
Company on.'

'How therefore were you able to maintain the element of
surprise?'

'The truth is we did not, for as Corporal Thompson led the
Company Group towards the target house, his vehicle came
under fire on three sides from a heavy weight of fire from mortars,
RPG and AK-47 fire. The situation therefore had Thompson
isolated out front with the remainder of the company in a
vulnerable position behind him. He engaged five separate firing
points from his exposed position, becoming, as a consequence,
the focus of the enemy attention pumping out withering fire for
almost twenty minutes. So effective did his targeting prove in
keeping Taliban heads down that the company was able to take
advantage of the lull in fire coming their way to dismount from
their Vikings . . . and move forward to assault the enemy
position.'

'The Taliban have a reputation for being poor shots but
Corporal Thompson must have enjoyed a charmed life.'

'He did. His sole injury had been a burst eardrum from the
detonations of RPGs and heavy machine gun fire. By this time the
vehicle was badly shot up, only one gun functioning and 80 per
cent of his ammunition gone. He held his ground fully conscious
of the vulnerability of his own people, putting fire into the Taliban
at a distance of only 50 metres [55 yards]. His steadfastness and
courage enabled the company to win the fire-fight.'

'Did he then come out of the firing line?'

'Yes, but only to restock with ammunition and change his

defective machine gun, after which he returned to continue from where he had left off. He made a major contribution through his bravery fighting from an exposed position to defeat an overwhelming number of the Taliban. That had been the fiercest contact the company experienced throughout the six-month tour, lasting over four hours. The fact that we suffered no casualties is due to a considerable degree to Corporal Thompson's gallantry, determination and outstanding professionalism.'

'In the citation, what did you recommend him for?'

'I recommended him for the highest public recognition.'

'And what was that?'

'He was awarded the Conspicuous Gallantry Cross.'

This falls between a Victoria Cross and a Military Cross. Speaking on 22 March 1944, Winston Churchill said:

The object of shiny medals, stars and ribbons is to give pride and pleasure to those who deserve them. At the same time, a distinction is something which everybody does not possess. If all have it, it is of less value. There must therefore be heart burnings and disappointment on the border line. A medal glitters but it also casts a shadow. The task of drawing up regulations for such awards is one that does not admit of a perfect solution. It is not possible to satisfy everybody without running the risk of satisfying nobody. All that is possible is to give the greatest satisfaction to the greatest number and to hurt the feelings of the fewest.[35]

The last hurrah of 42 Commando on this tour occurred the week before they were relieved by 12 Mechanized Brigade. Sangin had been quiet for much of the time, a cessation of hostilities having been agreed by the provincial governor, elders and Taliban. It did not necessarily suit the Marines.

A wave of Taliban attacks began in early March 2007 at the end of a negotiated ceasefire, during which three soldiers were killed in the district compound. Operation Silver, to clear Sangin of Taliban, arose through the insistence of Major-General Van Loon, the new regional commander south based in Kandahar. The timing was far from ideal, a brigade relief was in progress and it coincided with poppy planting and the possibility of alienating the local population. The attack on Sangin became a combined operation, Brigadier Jerry Thomas being given a battalion from the US 82nd Airborne. 42 Commando's mission initially involved a feint to distract the Taliban before disruption and interdiction of lines of communication to the north to enable the 82nd to seize Sangin. The paratroopers had their line of departure to the south between Robinson and Sangin and aimed to fight through the close country of the green zone before breaking into the town. The Taliban had had all winter in which to prepare defences.

The 42 Commando positioning operation commenced on 3 April with J Company Group departing Gereshk and executing a bold right hook which took them on to Route 611, a dirt track to the north of Sangin. They sat there to draw the Taliban's attention and disrupt the lines of communication to facilitate the paratroopers' insertion on 4 April and their subsequent advance towards Sangin. L Company Group deployed to the east of Sangin to increase the pressure on the enemy. The operation encapsulated the audacious offensive spirit for which 42 Commando had rightly become highly regarded. Operation Silver had all the essential hallmarks of shock, surprise and deception. On 6 April Sangin came under pressure from all sides. With K Company having flown into the district compound in preparation for the assault, the Marines' main effort thrust down from the north along 3.8

miles (6 kilometres) of a single dirt track, highly vulnerable to ambush, to effect break-in while the paratroopers continued to advance steadily from the south. Within six hours, prior to the assault, 42 Commando suffered casualties from three separate mine strikes but proceeded to seize and clear Sangin of Taliban, leaving a sanitized town for 82nd Airborne who arrived to relieve them and subsequently for the incoming 12 Mechanized Brigade with its additional battle group to develop and further exploit from the town centre.

The operation concluded on 8 April and advance parties, including the Commanding Officer, flew back to the United Kingdom the following day. Of those who had set out with 42 Commando Group on Operation Herrick 5, eight had been killed. It had been a job exceptionally well done but for which there would be no immediate public recognition. To the disbelief of 42 Commando returning home, the headlines had been monopolized by the more newsworthy apprehension by Iranians of an ad hoc boarding party from HMS *Cornwall* in the Shatt-al-Arab.[36]

Asked for his assessment of progress with development, an Afghan Government official said: 'What the Russians built is still here to be seen. They were here for eight years. You have been here for five. What have you done?' It is the usual problem. Money was promised and rarely came. When it did it was wrapped in so many conditions that it was not reaching where it was needed to make a difference and initiate change. Tribesmen claiming compensation were expected to produce the kind of documentation which would not be out of place in a London solicitor's office. Many who qualified for compensation were unable to reach Sangin and those who did very often found the office unmanned. Government and humanitarian officials stressed their duty of care and were often unwilling to fund the £15,000 a trip required to pay for the protection of their representatives. The health and safety culture meant that the Taliban had succeeded in separating Government departments and the non-governmental organizations from the people they should have been support- ing. Korean Christian missionaries and Italians who blundered around were rounded up by the Taliban. Their Governments paid enormous ransoms with the result that progress was simply not being made.

There is a slow-moving strategy in place. Where there is no governance the plan is to initiate a governance zone or ink spot. In time these ink spots would merge, once recon- struction and development had been introduced and was up and running. The overall plan is co-ordinated by President Hamid Karzai's Policy Action Group or development war cabinet, an initiative identified with General Richards. The strategy is seen to be in Afghan hands, for were that not the case there would be a strong domestic reaction against the interventionists.

The problems with the multiplicity of national forces supporting ISAF was that they had neither a common idea how long they would remain deployed nor was there a common level of risk. The first fissures in the coalition's effort were likely to appear in the south where a number of NATO states refused to deploy – 'too dangerous' – and where the existence of a bolt-hole into Pakistan led observers to contemplate the nature of the exit strategy. How would the conflict end and when? A ten-to-one rule has been suggested: for successful military intervention akin to Iraq and Afghanistan, planners should assess the duration of the conflict in years, then multiply that figure by ten. For example, the Defence Secretary quoted three years which, under this rule, translates into thirty. In reality, the intervenors will be long gone without having achieved success. Certainly the

Taliban had been defeated but they returned. 'The increasing number of rocket attacks targeting coalition bases was a testimony to the support for the Afghan resistance from the pro-Taliban administration in the North West Frontier Province and Baluchistan. For the first time since their ousting, some key former Taliban leaders resurfaced and openly operated from inside Pakistan.'[37] Encouragingly, there appeared to be no attempt to maintain a body count – irrelevant when the presence of NATO, combined with casualties inflicted upon the Taliban, would merely generate replacements tenfold to ensure that ultimately the enemy would have their way.

The Taliban had the luxury of numbers and time on their hands. Moreover, it is the poppy fields of Helmand which generate the funding for the Taliban's war in Afghanistan and the wider 'war on terror'. The poppies will not be given up lightly. Poppy eradication had been one of 16 Air Assault Brigade's roles. No orders to enact the policy were ever forthcoming, nor were NATO troops involved in poppy eradication. Arguably the military task had been invented to satisfy the Cabinet but it made no sense on the ground. How could the British work a 'hearts and minds' campaign by removing from the local farmers their wherewithal to generate a living? The system of land ownership is medieval. Women inherit land. This means fields are constantly being sub-divided. A small field which is too small to produce a crop of wheat can produce a bankable crop of poppies. A hectare (2.5 acres) of wheat is valued at £264 while a hectare of opium fetches £2,300. In this global village of ours, the Taliban became aware of the poppy eradication task given to the British military by their Government; moreover they made especially sure that Helmand farmers also knew.

The 2007 United Nations *Annual Opium Survey* shows Afghanistan's opium crop to have doubled in two years to

8,000 tons, or 93 per cent of the world's total. Whereas the number of provinces now declared to be drug-free has risen from six to ten out of thirty-four, Helmand's production has increased by 34 per cent in the year. The increase is mostly the result of favourable growing conditions. However, to put Helmand's drug trade in perspective, it is the world's largest source of illicit drugs, surpassing the output of recognized drug-producing countries such as Morocco and Colombia. This trade is valued at £1.5 billion or 40 per cent of Afghanistan's economy. Approximately 95 per cent of the heroin which arrives in Britain has been produced in Afghanistan. The United States favours an agent orange type solution, spraying poppy fields with glyphosate. Other states believe such a proposal to be too indiscriminate and would gift the Taliban a substantial propaganda opportunity. We have here a revisitation of the logic of Bosnia whereby the Americans, under their Kabul ambassador William B. Wood,[38] are blinded to the effect spraying poppies with herbicide will have on the battle against the Helmand Taliban. It is predictable that Britain and other NATO countries will be expected to take a more active role in opium eradication in the future.

The problem in ultimately concluding the conflict in Afghanistan is that armistices are normally struck between the combatant states. There is very little experience of making lasting peace with terrorist organizations such as al-Qa'eda and the Taliban. An intermediary state will have to be co-opted. For the time being, the emphasis in Afghanistan rests upon a military solution. Such a course of action can only be temporary as a preliminary to achieving a political solution. Secretary of State for Defence John Reid's misconception[39] as to what the Afghanistan intervention involved meant that, once again, the long-suffering British soldier had been put in a position of danger with an insufficiency of men and equipment to deal with the threat. An officer who had seen service in Helmand said the British approach had been 'a textbook case of how to screw up an insurgency', with commanders 'sucked into a problem unsolvable by military means. The ground has been lost and all we are doing is surviving. It's completely barking mad.' With the right number of troops, such a picture might yet be proven to have been too dismal.

There is a psychological war being lost in the UK through inactivity. The manner in which al-Qa'eda can be defeated is to deprive the organization of its oxygen. That involves winning over the minds of young, potentially radical Muslims who are otherwise swayed by extremist ideology because they identify what they hear from the unscrupulous with what they see on the ground. That includes the continuing war in Iraq, the detention of terror suspects and sending suspects to another country for interrogation. NATO's presence in Afghanistan is not dissimilar from the coalition's situation in Iraq in so far as it supports the extreme Muslim conviction that they are victims of Western aggression. The United States and the United Kingdom initiated the global 'war on terror' against Iraq and in Afghanistan and have been very successful in bringing all the world's terrorists together against them. Put quite simply therefore, NATO's presence in Afghanistan is more likely to exacerbate than defeat terrorism. Some say, however, that this is part of a clever NATO ruse, leaving the initiative in NATO's hands through having contained the enemy in a relatively small part of the world. The route to the cessation of international, Islamist-inspired terrorism is not to be found in either Iraq or Afghanistan but through Palestine.

There is an argument that the Afghan crisis will end once all foreign forces have left. NATO, however, is somewhat hoist by its own petard. NATO withdrawal, whenever it occurs, will provide Islamist extremists with immense satisfaction and encouragement. There is then the poppy eradication issue which makes a significant yet rarely admitted contribution to the overall reason for NATO being there. The departure of the foreign military will be signified by the return of acres of blooming, previously eradicated poppies. For the moment, NATO has 50,000 men deployed but not necessarily where NATO would wish them to be deployed. A recent US troops-to-tasks assessment reported that under the present conditions a force of between 400,000 and 600,000 is required to pacify Afghanistan sufficiently to provide the essential environment for reconstruction to take place.

A writer responded to the question as to whether he had seen anything near as bad in Helmand as he had witnessed in Fallujah. He had visited Fallujah after the rubble had been removed but the damage to buildings was clearly visible. 'The damage is more concentrated in Sangin but it is worse than I saw in Fallujah.'[40] Serious damage to NATO's best efforts has derived from the collateral killing of non-combatants such that President Karzai felt it necessary to intercede and complain. It is understood that NATO Secretary-General Jan de Hoop Scheffer appealed directly to President George W. Bush to rein his people in.

The nub of the problem lies again in a failure to adopt unity of command. While it is true that 15,000 US troops are under the tactical control of NATO, it is also true that 12,000 American troops, predominantly Special Forces, are entirely under US command. There were two independent Task Forces roaming around Helmand Province. It is groups such as these which have been principally responsible for non-combatant death and injury in Afghanistan. 'The purpose of extending NATO command across the country [in 2006] was to ensure unity of effort and the proportionate use of force,' said a senior diplomat in Kabul. 'We don't have unity of effort. It has taken until now to realize that there are Special Forces and other agencies[41] acting independently. It doesn't work. You are getting small forces operating outside NATO getting into big fights and making a big mess.'[42] General Richards recognized this to have been a key issue from the very beginning: 'Greater unity of effort did follow; the situation was never totally out of control.'[43] It is military groups either small or inadequate for the task that most consistently require close air support. It is in such situations that innocent civilians are killed and blue on blue events occur.[44]

This book began with the story of Goose Green, the opening battle in the Falklands War. Two hundred and fifty-five servicemen and three Falkland Islanders were killed in the conflict. Since 1982, over 300 Falklands veterans have taken their own lives, more than were killed in the Falkland Islands during the campaign, the majority having suffered Post Traumatic Stress Disorder (PTSD).[45] Twenty-five years on, the services are very much aware of the vulnerability of their people to PTSD and have put safety nets in place at the outset of any potential future difficulties. The Royal Navy has adopted a trauma management initiative to ensure that the tragedy following the Falkland conflict is not repeated. 'We employed a trauma management process in Helmand,' explained Lieutenant-Colonel Matt Holmes, 'whereby we identified individuals who had been exposed to particularly horrific or stressful circumstances, counselled them periodically and, by keeping a register, were able to monitor their dispositions, as well as support them on return to UK.'[46] There were 121 American combat-related suicides in 2007.

The counter-insurgency campaign in Afghanistan continues. The warriors for whom the time has come to return to the country will want to see that progress has been made during their absence.

10

Reflection

'Whoever does not have the stomach
for this fight, let him depart'

Having discussed eight significant conflicts among many to have taken place over the past twenty-five years, it might seem to be a relatively simple task to trace the evolution of modern warfare from Goose Green to Helmand. Unfortunately it is not. The problem lies not least in the diversity and variation in environment, conditions, scale, effectiveness of the antagonists, numbers involved and the quality of political direction. We have visited islands, urban areas, deserts, European temperate terrain and high mountain ranges. The surprise is the adaptability and speed at which some nations' forces adjusted to what had to be done.

At the core of these battles lies the schism that is so obviously apparent, separating traditional, conventional war from what the Americans describe as Operations Other Than War, or irregular warfare. The invasion of Iraq, 2003, illustrated both types. It was conventional warfare which took the coalition into Baghdad, where Saddam Hussein's statue was unceremoniously pulled down. By the time President George W. Bush declared 'mission accomplished' the irregular phase of the war was already well established.

The requirement to address conventional conflict with the whole panoply of maritime forces, armour, fighter aircraft and bombers has not gone away. Nevertheless, what we have seen over the past twenty-five years is a decided shift away from conventional warfare towards irregular conflict involving light or medium forces. In close-quarter psychological conflict, often with an Islamic connection, there will almost certainly be asymmetric threads present in the response – roadside bombs are but one of the most common examples. In circumstances such as this, the equipment associated with conventional warfare will often be found to be wanting, to such an extent that more appropriate equipment is having to be designed and procured at short notice. The United States, for example, has produced a Humvee vehicle replacement better able to survive the effects of roadside bombs or IEDs. Similarly, the United Kingdom has reworked and upgraded its Cold War, lightly armoured equipment, the 430 series armoured taxis. During the course of many miles driven across NATO's Central Region, not one 432 was destroyed in action. The new generation of the vehicle, the Bulldog, represents a reaction to today's realities. The equipment we send out for mid-level armed conflict has to be up to standard. Given the current preoccupation with medium forces, gaps in capabilities – generally manpower – require compensation with appropriate force-multiplying equipment. More artillery is a sensible answer; a less than sensible response to balancing the battlefield is the unwise and incoherent cancellation of the procurement of a lightweight 155-mm howitzer.

States have been obliged to widen their approach to modern conflict, changing culture even. All this comes at a price. Politicians will protest that they have increased defence spending, without having the worldliness to comprehend that the new environment to which they have committed their military requires a totally new investment. Lord Robertson, Secretary of State for Defence 1997–9, admitted British defence expenditure should increase from 2.3 per cent of GDP to 3 per cent to cover additional costs. There are, however, no votes in defence. Extra money allocated to it is reluctantly made available at the expense of important domestic social programmes popular with the electorate. The identifiable reluctance among some politicians to do the best for their armed forces is therefore readily explained.

At the heart of the equipment problem is the fact that one size does not fit all. For example, the £4 billion invested in two new aircraft-carriers makes sense in some circumstances, but they would be totally irrelevant for the land-centric Afghanistan conflict. In some areas there have been consistent shortages. In the Falkland Islands there was an acute shortage of support helicopters. Twenty-five years on, in Afghanistan, there is still a serious shortage of British support helicopters.

Both Goose Green, 1982, and Afghanistan, 2006–7, revealed a requirement to provide for dismounted close combat. In 1993, there was a programme described as the Future Integrated Soldier Technology, forecasting the need for future infantry equipment. No one was prepared to procure this equipment until there was a proven requirement. When such a contingency arose, the appropriate equipment was not there and lives were lost. Urgent operational requirement applications had to be made to match equipment to the conflict. A parsimonious Treasury insisted that any emergency equipment programmes which exceeded its estimate would have half the excess cost set against the defence budget.

Gradually equipment the infantry required began to come on-stream, including a light support weapon, night vision goggles, personal role radios, the Minimi light machine gun, the underslung grenade launcher, the exceptional WMIK 0.50 heavy machine gun and urgent reliability modifications made to the SA-80 standard rifle raising its performance from 20 per cent to 97 per cent. 'It is unfortunate', wrote former

Chief of the Defence Staff General the Lord Guthrie, 'that too many people were killed and lives were lost through its late arrival; the equipment could have been made available earlier if adequate funding had been found sooner, when the requirement was known about.'[1]

Still to appear is an identification system to offset risks to men and vehicles on the ground from being targeted by coalition fighter and fighter bombers. The technical problems involved in introducing an IFF system should not be minimized. As an interim measure, however, there has to be greater investment in pilot training, particularly of the National Guard, and better situation awareness. Over one-third of British deaths and injuries in Iraq and Afghanistan have been avoidable. Another embarrassing, related statistic is that the number of British suicides attributable to the Iraq and Afghanistan conflicts now exceeds 10 per cent of those thus far killed on operations.

There have been two major changes affecting the way the British in particular operate in conflicts. We are now having to engage in counter-insurgency situations outside areas familiar with United Kingdom law and administration. That separation, having to work in unfamiliar territory, has proved to have made a significant difference. The second major change relates to the nature of the enemy. He is more irrational, regards dying for the cause as the ultimate sacrifice and is not susceptible to the usual deterrent strategies.

In two out of eight stories the United Kingdom took unilateral action. The Falklands was a case of assisted unilateralism and Operation Barras was a very small operation, albeit with significant though as yet not fully realized consequences. Rapid and Quick Reaction capabilities are essential components for a modern military force to enact the glass of water strategy – to put the fire out with minimal fuss before it has a chance to spread. Barras underlined the problems arising from the taking of hostages, something repeated in Mogadishu and Gorazde. The taking of hostages is politically sensitive, not so much because it represents fallibility, but because it represents the loss of initiative.

What is apparent, particularly from the Gorazde study, is the decline of the United Nations as a meaningful collective security organization. If the UN is to have any bite, it has to attract the professional battalions such as those of a some-times ambivalent United States.

Those responsible for garnering American lessons learned from the 1990–91 Gulf conflict were in agreement with Sir Anthony Parsons's assessment in Chapter 4 that the battle had been so unique as probably to be unrepeatable. 'Whether any major, long-term lessons can be drawn at all from the Gulf War is in fact questionable.'[2] Arguably, there were two important lessons which had been learned. The first was that investment in high technology had produced valuable force multipliers. The revolution in information technology and its integration into command, control and information systems and advanced military capabilities proved so beneficial as to justify budgets which would serve to maintain the momentum. The availability of American smart weapons on call in quantity did much to enable British forces to hold their own in Helmand Province.

The second lesson confirmed that, for the United States, the option of going it alone in future did not exist. Immedi-ately, the presence of a dichotomy becomes apparent due to the conflicting national interests within a coalition between the lead or framework state – invariably the United States – and lesser, supporting states. It could be argued that the wars in Iraq and Afghanistan were not, for the United States, wars of obligation, but it cannot be argued that those wars did not, for the United States, resemble wars of obligation. In both conflicts, the United States did not allow herself to become restricted by the usual factors affecting the presence of lesser states engaged in wars of choice: low cost, low risk, short duration. That this model works can be seen in 2008 Iraq where almost all lesser states have left the scene, leaving the United States still in place. Organizationally, where we go from here remains to be seen.

While UN deployments are, in spring 2008, at historically high levels, the same cannot be said of NATO, which is an organization in decline. Its experience in Afghanistan, where America's presence and national association with 9/11 categorizes this conflict as close to a war of obligation, which is not the case with any other coalition state. The application of national caveats is an obvious example of a number of NATO states limiting the risks to their nationals. NATO had to go way, way out of area to fight in Afghanistan, leaving an unfortunate analogy of an end of career actor having to travel far to play what could be a final role.

There are exceptions to every rule but the overall impression of a dutiful United Kingdom acting out the part of a warrior satellite of the United States is valid. Claims have been made that supporting the United States is in the British national interest, not that the United Kingdom has influence over the United States when the latter is determined to do what she wants. While the jury remains out on Afghanistan, despite strongly held, opposing British views, the United States acted independently in Grenada, Bosnia and Iraq.

The political difficulties of states pursuing their own interests unilaterally and the decline of the effectiveness of both the UN and NATO as plausible collective security organizations prompt some urgent thinking outside the box. Action leads to reaction. Violent reaction invariably targets a state, its people and its interests. The ideal solution is to minimize such risks by moving away from the vulnerable fabric of a state towards more evasive targets such as those represented by non-state actors. The barest hint of such a possibility can be seen in the exponential rise of contractors acting as agents in conflict, invariably to plug gaps. 'Contractors' fulfil a whole range of activities – as advisers, in logistics, close protection and offensive operations. The activities of Executive Outcomes and Sandline International in Sierra Leone, while not altruistic, were hugely more cost-effective when compared with the costs of the deployed UN force. There will be occasions, admittedly rare, when the military functions in support of a crisis could be contracted out. Needless to say, the levels of command and control to be expected of contractors operating in support of international law and order should not be less than that expected of the armed forces of intervening states.

At the beginning of this study it was evident that a number of states appeared to want to abide by international law. They were, however, never entirely confident of acting out that desire. It depended whether action would run contrary to their state sovereignty. The longevity and anarchic status of UN Charter law is obvious, yet it is the best, indeed all that is available. The UN was ignored when NATO entered Kosovo in 1999 but due to the prevailing special circumstances, there was a general agreement to condone what NATO had done to relieve the undoubted suffering of the Kosovan people. There was no such generosity of spirit when George W. Bush and Tony Blair invaded Iraq illegally. Many had difficulty observing two leaders committed to the global 'war on terror' taking action guaranteed to encourage the very terrorism they insisted they opposed. By the same token, it would have appeared obvious to many that taking Western liberal democracy into Iraq's theocracy was bound to encourage the majority Shia, confound the experienced governors among the Sunni sect and inevitably lead to civil conflict. The anarchic status of international law represents an almost insurmountable challenge. The Charter will not be amended. States will have the option of obeying international law in its imperfect state, as it is; taking action in accordance with the spirit of the law; or, taking illegal action and facing whatever consequences arise.

The insufficiency of provision for human intelligence has been a frequent problem. It is a fact that patrolling, developing a good relationship and adopting confidence-building measures with local people is vital. No two environments are the same, some are more fertile than others. The relationship between non-combatants and the military is bound to be fragile and can be ruined, for example, by some form of near or distant collateral damage inflicted upon non-combatants.

Media relations have also consistently produced problems. The media plan has to be fashioned to the environment and due regard paid to the numbers of media representatives seeking accreditation. Today, media operations require a huge investment of time, manpower and facilities. The evidence is that it is better to assist the media with their despatches rather than risk loss of operational security through correspondents roaming outside the pool. Fortunately, one reason reporters are amenable to being embedded is because it is too dangerous not to be.

The giving of orders by the commander is the start point for any operation. At the extremes of this study we have the examples of two types of orders. At Goose Green there were 'H' Jones's formal orders – laborious and which put a successful outcome of the battle at risk. Twenty-five years on, in 42

Commando's final battle in Helmand in 2007, there was reassuring evidence of beneficial change. These were not identical situations. An absolute comparison is not possible. It would be reassuring to think that the reason no direct comparison is possible is that the Goose Green lessons had been learned. Operation Silver was an all-arms, well-supported, combined battle. Goose Green had been 2 Para's first battle, and one in which it was desperately short of support. 42 Commando's generously supported Operation Silver came at the end of their six-month tour, by which time their battle skills had been finely honed. Their orders were mission-oriented and driven by such principles as shock action, surprise, deception and, of course, aggression. Rather than have six restrictive, pre-planned phases, as was the case at Goose Green, for Operation Silver the Commanding Officer gave his subordinate commanders a manoeuvrist, phase-free concept of operations. Facilitated by mobility within the group and excellent communications, this allowed sub-units to keep the Commanding Officer informed of their action and intentions. 'Companies were allocated initial areas of Sangin to clear once in, and secondary areas on my order, so I had control and flexibility within the plan should I need to react to something and redeploy forces accordingly.'[3] The key to success is command and control.

Problems with command and control have been a feature in two-thirds of the battles examined. In industry, the level of latitude seen on most operations here would never have been permitted. The warning is real. In the Second World War, General Omar Bradley insisted that professionals talked logistics followed by tactics. We have moved on from there. With his nine-month tour in Afghanistan in mind, General Sir David Richards said, from his experience, 'Professionals talk command and control, followed by logistics (I mean force ratios as well as logistics) followed by tactics.'[4] If we bear in mind the truth that logistics wins wars, this new pecking-order takes on great significance. US Special Forces' insistence, for example, that they be free to operate outside the chain of command has generated recurring command and control problems. Special Forces' operations in Afghanistan have increasingly targeted the Taliban leadership, decapitating the head from the body.

With the exceptions of Grenada and Barras, all other operations have been endangered through under-resourcing and a failure to commit sufficient troops to undertake tasks. The most glaring economies made in force levels were in Iraq and Afghanistan.

There was a sea-change in the public's attitude towards the armed forces between the Falklands in 1982 and their return from Iraq and Afghanistan in 2007.[5] The timespan of this fall from grace was, however, not twenty-five years but a much shorter, more recent period, 2003–8. The cause of this change of fortune was the war in Iraq, which had little popular support, and the little understood conflict in Afghanistan. The American military returning from Vietnam also suffered not so much public hostility as public indifference. The returning British soldiers could reluctantly abide public indifference but even the returning Vietnam warriors did not also have to suffer the indifference of their Government.

No Government relishes the charge of indifference towards its own armed forces put in positions of danger in support of Government policy. In one week in November 2007 five former Chiefs of the Defence Staff in the House of Lords, a leaked report from the Chief of the Defence Staff fresh from a tour of the battlefronts and a critical, leaked report written by the Chief of the General Staff, all chastized the Government for its lack of support. The Chiefs of Staff within the Ministry of Defence must therefore at some point have attempted to advise Blair and Brown on the military realities of their desired Iraq and Afghanistan policies.

Strategic military estimates are made to validate operational deployments. One wonders how, in a changing world, a military estimate can be used in an effective manner so as to influence a dogmatic politician. Generals have to thump tables to attract attention. The Chief of the Defence Staff checked on the legality of the war in Iraq. It had been my letter to *The Times* which prompted such action. Faced with a large element of the armed forces still stuck in the quagmire of Iraq, it did not seem the best of times to volunteer for a concurrent operation in Afghanistan. Sources within the Ministry of Defence stress that they were caught off balance by planning assumptions that later proved to be wishful thinking. First, they assumed that Britain's involvement in the Iraq Conflict would have ended prior to commitment to Afghanistan and that support there would be forthcoming from NATO allies.

What these back-to-back commitments did, in the words of Chief of the General Staff, General Dannatt, was to put the military covenant 'out of kilter'. The military covenant has as one of its aims the safeguarding of family life. Ideally, the infantry should have two years' grace between operations. That period has fallen to fifteen months and when pre-operational training is taken into account the interval falls to less than a year. Operational over-stretch means that long-planned leave can be cancelled at short notice.

There are other factors which link in here. There is the dilapidation of the military estate. Paras for operations in Afghanistan in April 2008 had only six of the 110 WMIK Land Rovers that should have been in their training package.

For many, the situation has gone beyond tolerance. At the end of 2007, the outflow of trained officers doubled in six months. Among those who had had enough was 3 Para's Lieutenant-Colonel Stuart Tootal, who allegedly complained that his men were poorly treated, poorly paid, shoddily handled within the medical system and under-equipped in Afghanistan – he had had to borrow heavy machine gun and mortar rounds from the Americans and Canadians.[6] Overall, logistics does not appear to have been a significant problem. There were local difficulties, such as those that 3 Para faced, but it was not a major issue. According to a military source, the problem was more than that. 'It was as much the perceived apathy in government and their sheer indifference.'

This charge of Government indifference is not about scoring political points. The Conservative Government grossly underfunded the military during the Cold War and was about to make critical cuts to the RN surface fleet just before the Falklands campaign. A Potemkin Village is low maintenance. They took risks and got away with it. The difference today is that we have two ongoing military operations where indifference kills.

Shortly after becoming Prime Minister, Gordon Brown insisted that he had nothing but praise for the military and that defence spending had continued to increase, which was true. The problem was it had a long way to catch up if the armed forces were to carry out the Government's military ambitions. What has sustained the accusation of Brown's indifference more than any other act was his decision, in June 2007, to give the Secretary of State for Defence additional responsibility for Scotland.

The writing is on the wall. General Sir Richard Dannatt, Chief of the General Staff, said that years of Government indifference had left the Army 'devalued, angry and suffering from fatigue'. The Easter 2008 strength forecast put the Army 11 per cent short of trained recruits, the Royal Navy 10 per cent short and the Royal Air Force 14 per cent short. The real problem is that of retention. The Army strength should be 107,500. At the end of 2007 it was 99,300. Forty-two per cent of the Army suffered from critical to severe weaknesses in their ability to be ready to deploy. Today, the Royal Navy, with twenty-two major ships, is under half the size it was at the time of the Falklands Campaign (when it had forty-two ships with eight in reserve). 'Is it not immoral', asked Marshal of the Royal Air Force Lord Craig, 'to commit forces that are under-prepared and ill-equipped for their task?' Flight XV230, a Royal Air Force Nimrod on intelligence-gathering, blew up in the air near Kandahar, killing all fourteen on board. Safety warnings had been ignored by the Ministry of Defence. Men need to be confident in what they are expected to do and with what they are given to do it. If a failure of confidence arises, those concerned will vote with their feet. What is true of the British Army is equally true of other forces.

Sir Lawrence Freedman, Professor of War Studies at King's College, wrote, 'if the Government wants to avoid, not so much criticism from former officers, but disillusion and demoralization among those on the front line, it needs to find some way to show that it cares'.[7]

Two themes have dominated this examination of eight modern battles. The first theme we set out with was the assertion that the greatness of a battle is not determined by its size or by the numbers involved but rather by its effect and influence upon future events. The second theme adopted a comment by Sir Francis Tuker, that the battles worthy of study are not the bloody ones but those that lead to victory with few casualties. So what, in the final analysis, is the one common denominator present in these great or worthy battles? The answer comes down to an individual's self-belief and strength of character, whether he be a British or American warrior. This is not a matter of quantity but of the quality of military personnel. I have long been impressed by a maxim which General Douglas MacArthur required no encouragement to proclaim and which had so impressed him at West Point as setting a standard to live by: Duty, Honour, Country. It is an individual's willpower, courage and stamina that provides the strength to overcome primordial fear. This was evident at Goose Green where each motivated, well-trained soldier was part of a unit, a fighting force, convinced that he could not, would not be beaten. Something of that same spirit of grim determination was evident at a memorial service held in Mogadishu immediately after the Special Forces' and Rangers' mission and before the inevitable questions, inquisition and Senate Committee hearings. General Garrison simply gathered his warriors around him and 'captured their feelings of sadness, fear and resolve'[8] by quoting a modernized and abridged passage from Shakespeare's *Henry V* before Agincourt:

Whoever does not have the stomach for this fight, let him depart. Give him money to speed his departure since we wish not to die in that man's company. Whoever lives past today and comes home safely will rouse himself every year on this day, show his neighbour his scars, and tell embellished stories of all their great feats of battle. These stories he will teach his son and from this day until the end of the world we shall be remembered. We few, we happy few, we band of brothers; for whoever has shed his blood with me shall be my brother. And those men afraid to go will think themselves lesser men as they hear of how we fought and died together.

ABBREVIATIONS

AFRC	Armed Forces Revolutionary Council
ANA	Afghan National Army
ANP	Afghanistan National Police
APC	armoured personnel carrier
ARG	Amphibious Ready Group
CARICOM	Caribbean Community
COBRA	Cabinet Office Briefing Room
Coy	Company
CPA	Coalition Provisional Authority
DfID	Department of International Development
DPKO	Department of Peacekeeping Operations
DSF	Director Special Forces
EC	European Community
ECOMOG	Economic Community of West African States Ceasefire Monitoring Group
ECOWAS	Economic Community of West African States
EO	Executive Outcomes
EU	European Union (from 1993)

FIBUA	Fighting in Built-up Areas
GOC	General Officer Commanding
GPMG	General Purpose Machine Gun
humint	human intelligence
ICC	International Criminal Court
IED	Improvised Explosive Device
IFF	Identification Friend or Foe
IMATT	International Military Assistance and Training Team
ISA	Intelligence Support Activity
ISAF	International Security Assistance Force
ISG	Iraq Stabilization Group
JSOC	Joint Special Operations Command
MAU	Marine Amphibious Unit
MLRS	Multiple Launched Rocket System
MOOTW	Military Operations Other Than War
MOUT	Military Operations in Urban Terrain
MP	Military Police
NBC	Nuclear, Biological, Chemical
NCO	non-commissioned officer
NEO	Non-Combat Evacuation Operation
NGO	non-governmental organization
OAU	Organization of African Unity
OC	Officer-in-Command
OECS	Organization of East Caribbean States
OOTW	Operations Other Than War
OP	observation post
PJHQ	Permanent Joint Headquarters, Northwood
PRA	People's Revolutionary Army
PRAF	People's Revolutionary Armed Forces
PRG	People's Revolutionary Government
PRM	People's Revolutionary Militia
PRT	Provincial Reconstruction Team

PWGF	Prisoner of War Guard Force
QRF	Quick Reaction Force
RAP	Regimental Aid Post
RMC	Revolutionary Military Council
ROE	rules of engagement
RPG	rocket-propelled grenade
RSM	Regimental Sergeant-Major
RUF	Revolutionary United Front (Sierra Leone)
SBS	Special Boat Service
SEAL	Sea, Air, Land
SIGINT	Signals Intelligence
SITREP	situation report
SLA	Sierra Leone Army
SLR	self-loading rifle
SMG	sub machine gun
STUFT	ships taken up from the trade
TEZ	total exclusion zone
UN	United Nations
UNAMSIL	UN Mission in Sierra Leone
UNDP	UN Development Programme
UNFICYP	UN Force in Cyprus
UNHCR	United Nations High Commissioner for Refugees
UNITAF	United Task Force, Somalia
UNOMSIL	United Nations Observer Mission in Sierra Leone (UNOMSIL)
UNOSOM	United Nations Operation in Somalia
UNPAs	UN Protected Areas
UNPROFOR	UN Protection Force
USCENTCOM	US Central Command
WMIK	Weapons Mounted Installation Kit
WSB	West Side Boys

NOTES

1 Introduction

1. Carl von Clausewitz, *Vom Kriege,* Vol. 1 (Bonn, 1952), 2.
2. Robert Thompson, *Defeating Communist Insurgency: Experiences from Malaya and Vietnam* (London, 1966).
3. Ibid, 52.
4. Ibid, 171.
5. Brian Urquhart, *A Life in Peace and War* (London, 1987), 93.
6. 'The British Military Doctrine', *Design for Military Operations,* (1989).
7. US Army War College Strategic Study Institute, Figure 3 in Don M. Snider, John A. Nagl and Tony Pfaff, *Army Professionalism, the Military Ethic and Officers in the Twenty First Century* (Carlisle, December 1999), 18.
8. Benjamin Schwarz and Christopher Loyne, 'NATO at 50. It's Time to Quit', *The Nation,* 10 May 1999, 17; Colonel Gregory C. Kraak, 'NATO. Still Relevant After All These Years', in Williamson Murray (ed.), *Strategic Challenges for Counterinsurgency and the Global War on Terrorism* (Carlisle, 2006), 139–59.

9. Margaret Thatcher, *The Downing Street Years* (London, 1993), 828.

10. Interview with the author, The Hague, 22 March 1995.

11. As told to the author by a British Army brigadier present in Baghdad.

12. General Sir Michael Rose, *Fighting for Peace: Lessons from Bosnia* (London, 1998), xxi.

13. General Wesley K. Clark, *Waging Modern War* (New York, 2001), 404–5.

14. Richard Connaughton, *Military Intervention and Peacekeeping: The Reality* (Aldershot, 2001), 225.

15. Ibid, 212.

16. Oxfam spokeswoman in discussion with the author, Kigali, 27 April 1995.

17. Memo from Brigadier Gordon Hughes, former British military commander in Sierra Leone.

18. *The Times,* 30 November 2006.

19. Geoff Hoon, the *Daily Telegraph*, 9 December 2006.

20. Kendall Myers, *The Times*, 30 November 2006.

21. I asked Dr Reid what he meant. He told me to contact the Ministry of Defence. I wrote to the Secretary of State at the House of Commons. He did not deign to reply.

22. Mention is made throughout this book of Joint and Combined Operations. The understandings applicable here are that a Joint Operation involves two or more services (Army, Navy, Air Force, Coast Guard) of the same state while Combined Operations involves two or more services of two or more states.

2 Goose Green

1. Letter to the editor, *Daily Telegraph*, 15 June 2007.

2. Margaret Thatcher, commentary, *25th Anniversary, the Falklands Conflict 1982–2007* (Rock Ferry, 2007), 12.

3. Lawrence Freedman, *The Official History of the Falklands Campaign, Vol. II: War and Diplomacy* (London, 2005), 3.

4. Ibid, *Vol. I: The Origins of the Falklands War*, 207.

5. Ibid, 208.

6. E-mail, Major-General Julian Thompson to author, 9 May 2007.

7. Margaret Thatcher, *The Downing Street Years* (London, 1993), 179.

8. The two green lights inviting intervention were seen to be Britain's relative passivity in connection with the landing of Argentinian scrap metal workers in South Georgia, and their raising of the Argentinian flag there, in March 1982, and the British Government's decision to withdraw the ice patrol vessel *Endurance*.

9. Thatcher, 173. This idea that international law should prevail over the use of force was not an idea with which Mrs Thatcher was consistently identified. Had Mr Blair been of similar persuasion, Britain would not have joined the invasion of Iraq in 2003.

10. The Darwin Line did not feature in H's orders.

11. Major Richard Rockett, quoted in General Sir John Wilsey, *H Jones VC: The Life and Death of an Unusual Hero* (London, 2002), 124.

12. Ibid, 129–31.

13. Major-General Julian Thompson, *No Picnic* (London, 1985), 18.

14. Michael Bilton and Peter Kominsky, *Speaking Out* (1989), quoted in Mark Adkin, *Goose Green* (Barnsley, 1992), 16.

15. Mark Adkin, *Goose Green*, 17.

16. Discussion between the author, John Crosland, David Benest and John Wilson, editor of *British Army Review*, over dinner, 21 March 2007.

17. 'Toms' is a derivative of Tommy Atkins, immortalized in the writings of Rudyard Kipling.
18. As expressed to the author, 21 March 2007.
19. Max Arthur, *Above All, Courage* (London, 1985), 185.
20. Commentary on author's first draft by John Crosland, Darwin/Goose Green and 'H', nd.
21. Gordon Smith, *Battles of the Falklands War* (London, 1989), 83.
22. Thompson, 68–9.
23. The Pucara was an Argentinian, Falkland-based, twin-propeller aircraft armed with a machine gun and capable of carrying bombs and napalm.
24. HMS *Ardent*, HMS *Antelope* and HMS *Coventry*.
25. A regiment in Argentinian terminology equated to an infantry battalion of approximately 750 all ranks.
26. Two Argentinian subalterns, Estoban and Estevez, were exceptions to the general rule of indifferent officers.
27. John Frost, *2 Para Falkland: The Battalion at War* (London, 1983), 100.
28. Ibid, 159.
29. The enemy force included the 12th Infantry Regiment, C Company of the 25th (Special) Commando-trained Regiment and 25th Signals Company. There were a number of accomplished snipers among them.
30. N. Van der Bijl, *Nine Battles to Stanley* (London, 1999), 82.
31. D. George Boyce, *The Falklands War* (London, 2005), 126.
32. Hugh Bicheno, *Razor's Edge* (London, 2006), 157.
33. Max Hastings and Simon Jenkins, *The Battle for the Falklands* (London, 1983), 236.
34. Thompson, 74.
35. Adkin, 68.
36. Thompson, 43.
37. Boyce, 127.

38. Ibid.

39. Brian Hanrahan and Robert Fox, *I Counted Them All Out and I Counted Them All Back: The Battle for the Falklands* (London, 1982), 55–6.

40. General von Moltke would have known. He inherited the existing German Schlieffen Plan for the 1914 attack on France. He had no combat experience and his direction of the German Army proved catastrophic.

41. E-mail, David Benest to author, 28 February 2007.

42. As related to the author by David Benest, 28 February 2007. The battalion was in Camilla Creek House when the news came through. The outcome was the immediate dispersal of the companies away from the buildings. Later in the campaign, on 4 June 1983, Brigadier Julian Thompson wrote: 'Have just heard that BBC World Service reported that, "Teal Inlet is HQ of Force attacking Stanley". I am absolutely fed up with hearing my plans broadcast on BBC News.' The United States studied the operational–media relationship, applying a number of lessons learned to Operation Urgent Fury, Grenada, 1983.

43. Michael Nicholson, 'A Day of Extraordinary Heroism', *Daily Telegraph*, 13 April 2007.

44. General Sir Anthony Farrar-Hockley's synopsis of the Falkland Campaign, RUSI Library, London, nd.

45. Adkin, 122.

46. Commentary on author's first draft by John Crosland, Darwin/Goose Green and 'H', nd.

47. When asked the question, an officer present insisted there was nothing strange about the fact that nobody criticized 'H''s plan. 'Few understood it fully and who would have dared to say so, even had the mistake been spotted?'

48. E-mail, Dair Farrar-Hockley to author, 3 May 2007.

49. Author interview with Benest. 'I personally sought 'H''s agreement

to slim the radio scales back to a single command net and he
agreed prior to departing Sussex Mountain.'

50. Max Arthur, 189.
51. Dair Farrar-Hockley to author.   Defence Academy, March
    2007.
52. Adkin, 178.
53. Spencer Fitz-Gibbon, *The History and Mythology of the Battle
    of Goose Green* (London, 1995), 79.
54. Ibid, 81.
55. Wilsey, 279.
56. Michael Bilton and Peter Kosminsky, *Speaking Out* (London,
    1989), quoted in Mark Adkin, *Goose Green*, 31.
57. Hastings and Jenkins, 245.
58. The shooting down of Lieutenant Richard Nunn was the only
    confirmed Pucara success of the campaign.
59. Michael Bilton and Peter Kosminsky, *Speaking Out* (London,
    1989), 136.
60. Max Arthur, 144.
61. Ibid., 192.
62. Farrar-Hockley synopsis, 37.
63. 'Flak' is a Second World War term, an abbreviation of the
    German *Flugzeugabwehrkanone* or anti-aircraft gun. It refers
    not to the weapon but to its fire.
64. Jerry Pook, *RAF Harrier Ground Attack – Falklands* (Barnsley,
    2007), ix. The RAF began with six Harrier GR3s. Four more
    replacements were flown direct from Ascension to *Hermes*, a
    4,500-mile air-refuelled sortie with no diversions available en
    route.
65. Fox, one of 2 Para's embedded newsmen, was awarded an MBE.
66. Hastings and Jenkins, 250.
67. Thompson, 98.
68. Max Arthur, 144.
69. Hastings and Jenkins, 252.

70. Thompson, 98.
71. The Falklands victory established the foundation for Mrs Thatcher's re-election, changed the nation's perception of itself and defined what the eighties represented.
72. Michael Nicholson, 'A Day of Extraordinary Heroism', *Daily Telegraph*, 13 April 2007.
73. E-mail, David Benest to author, 20 February 2007.
74. Boyce, 127.
75. The Parachute Regiment set up the Battle School at Brecon before handing the establishment to HQ Infantry in 1974.
76. I have included the Argentinian air force personnel in this equation.
77. Wilsey, 290.
78. Commentary on author's first draft by John Crosland, Darwin/Goose Green and 'H', nd.
79. Discussion of author, Dair Farrar-Hockley, Philip Neame, David Benest at the Defence Academy, March 2007; Adkin, 118.
80. Commentary on author's first draft by John Crosland, Darwin/Goose Green and 'H', nd.
81. E-mail, Neame to author, 6 May 2007.
82. Regimental Headquarters and the Military Secretary overruled Brigadier Thompson's recommendation that Chris Keeble remain in command of 2 Para after the battle for Goose Green. A replacement CO was accordingly sent out as 'H' Jones's replacement, parachuting into the sea from where he caught up with operations, fighting the battle of Wireless Ridge with flair, skill and success.
83. 'Crosland and Farrar-Hockley received the MC but Neame . . . unconscionably received no recognition'. Bicheno, 312.
84. E-mail, Major-General Julian Thompson to author, 10 May 2007.

3 Grenada

1. General H. Norman Schwarzkopf, *It Doesn't Take a Hero* (London, 1992), 244–5.

2. Author interview with Leslie Pierre, Calabash Hotel, St George's, Grenada, 3 November 2007, an opinion corroborated by Gregory Sandford and Richard Vigilante, *Grenada: The Untold Story* (New York, 1984): 'Unbeknownst to the Grenadian people, Bishop and his New Jewel Movement had harbored a secret Communist agenda since the NJM's inception in the early 1970s. Elaborate and rhetorical posturing had succeeded in concealing the movement's true colors from political observers in the West. In the meantime, Grenada was well on its way to becoming a Soviet puppet state in a strategically vital region (for the USA) of the eastern Caribbean.'

3. Despite his culpability in bringing revolution to Grenada, even today the lionization of Bishop continues. He had the Maurice Bishop Highway named after him and there have been substantive discussions to name the Point Salines Airport the Maurice Bishop International Airport.

4. Winston Whyte went to Trinidad early in the troubles to address a convention of the ruling party. 'There, I voiced again my total abhorrence over the suspension of our constitution and the very distinct probability that what was euphemistically termed *protective custody* would turn into permanent incarceration for those being arrested willy nilly. The way in which to promote greater freedom was to obey the constitution and abide by its regulations. They did not like what I said, so on my return they put me where they thought I belonged, to still my voice.' He would spend over four years in prison, sharing a cell at the end of his term with Leslie Pierre. Winston Whyte to author, Calabash Hotel, Grenada, 11 November 2007.

5. Author interview with Bernard Coard, Richmond Hill Prison,

7 November 2007. This interview required the permission of the Prime Minister.

6. Coard had been one of Sir Paul's students at secondary school.

7. Author interview with Coard, 7 November 2007.

8. Mark Adkin, *Urgent Fury* (London, 1989), 24.

9. The desire for a territorial *cordon sanitaire* overseen by the United States was first postulated on 2 December 1823 by President James Monroe at a time when the United States lacked the power of enforcement.

10. Author interview with Leslie Pierre, Calabash Hotel, Grenada, 3 November 2007.

11. Adkin, 48.

12. Author interview with Coard, 7 November 2007.

13. Margaret Thatcher, *The Downing Street Years* (London, 1993), 329.

14. Telephone conversation, representative of St George's University to author, True Blue, 2 November 2007. She was at the medical school at the time but does not wish to be identified.

15. Lee E. Russell and M. Albert Mendez, *Grenada 1983* (London, 1985), 11.

16. As advised, Adkin to author.

17. *New York Times,* 30 October 1983.

18. Hugh O'Shaughnessy, *Grenada* (London, 1984), 156.

19. Adkin, 131.

20. Ibid, 126.

21. Schwarzkopf, 245–6.

22. The Joint Chiefs responded strongly to any attempt to compare Grenada to the Falklands. 'It is inappropriate to compare Grenada with the Falklands operation due to differences in mission, enemy, troops available, terrain, time available and rules of engagement.'

23. Schwarzkopf, 245–6.

24. Adkin, 123.

25. O'Shaughnessy, 206.
26. Schwarzkopf, 247.
27. Correspondence, General John Abizaid to author, 12 November 2007.
28. Adkin, 130.
29. Schwarzkopf, 246.
30. When the prison was taken the next day, it was found to have been abandoned.
31. Adkin, 175.
32. G. Hopple and C. Gilley, *Policy without Intelligence* (New York, 1983), 55.
33. Schwarzkopf, 247–8.
34. The Americans did not confide in Adams their intentions to intervene in Grenada until twenty-four hours after the decision had been made. Criticism of Britain for not intervening was misconstrued since Grenada did not invite the UK to intervene in its sovereign territory.
35. O'Shaughnessy, 171.
36. Ibid, 170–1.
37. Thatcher, 331–2.
38. Schwarzkopf, 249.
39. Adkin, 161.
40. Ibid, 157.
41. Finance Minister Bernard Coard had recently increased the Armed Forces' pay scales.
42. O'Shaughnessy, 216.
43. Ibid, 175.
44. Schwarzkopf, 249–50.
45. Correspondence, General Abizaid to author, 12 November 2007.
46. Adkin, 186.
47. Ibid, 188.
48. Ibid, 190.

49. Schwarzkopf, 250.

50. The shortage of pilots trained in night-flying restricted the strength of 1st/75th Rangers to 350. 2nd/75th Rangers had fewer men.

51. Correspondence, General Abizaid to author, 12 November 2007.

52. Ibid.

53. Adkin, 213.

54. Schwarzkopf, 252.

55. Russell and Mendez, 20.

56. Schwarzkopf, 253.

57. Those who had were mostly Marines.

58. Captain T.A. Dennis, 'The Military and the Media: The Way Forward', course paper, April 1985, 8.

59. Michael Massing, 'Grenada, We Will Never Know', in *Index on Censorship*, Vol. 13, No. 2, April 1984, 15, quoted in Captain T.A. Dennis, 'The Military and the Media: The Way Forward'.

60. Winant Sidle, 'A Battle Behind the Scenes: The Gulf Reheats Military–Media Controversy', *Military Review*, September 1991, 52–63.

61. Russell and Mendez, 22.

62. Schwarzkopf, 254–5.

63. Russell and Mendez, 23.

64. During clearance operations on the fourth day, a further 202 American students were discovered at Lance Aux Epines.

65. The number of helicopters lost throughout the operation is disputed but a figure of 10 per cent would be close.

66. Quoted in Captain William C. Mayville, 'A Soldier's Load', *Infantry*, January–February 1987, 26.

67. Adkin, 264.

68. Brian Crozier, *The Grenada Documents* (London, 1987), 16.

69. Schwarzkopf, 256.

70. Approximately 500 artillery rounds were fired at the camp. Only one hit.

71. Schwarzkopf, 256.

72. Adkin, 309.

73. Author interview with Leslie Pierre, Calabash Hotel, Grenada, 3 November 2007.

74. Sir Paul Scoon, *Survival for Service* (Oxford, 2003), 160.

75. According to Adkin, 99. 'The State Department obliged by drawing up a draft of the sort of letter it would like to receive and sent it to Barbados, unsigned and undated.' Local British diplomats were more closely identified with the support of the intervention initiative than their Government might have wished. 'I helped', said Grenada-based John Kelly, 'because I had what was best for the future of Grenada in mind.' Kelly to author, St Paul's, Grenada, 10 November 2007.

76. One external copy each for Tom Adams, Jamaican Prime Minister Edward Seaga, Eugenia Charles and Ronald Reagan.

77. Interview, Sir Paul Scoon with author, 8 November 2007.

78. Correspondence, General Abizaid to author, 12 November 2007.

79. Schwarzkopf, 256.

4 Iraq

1. *The Times*, 3 August 1990.

2. *Tales of the Foreign Service: In Defence of April Glaspie*, Washington Report on Middle East Affairs, August 2002.

3. Author's italics.

4. Anthony Parsons, *From Cold War to Hot Peace* (London, 1995), 58.

5. Lady Meyer, wife of the then British Ambassador, observed from Washington how 'Blair started talking about getting rid of Saddam Hussein way before September 11 . . . in 1998. So I think that on Iraq he was more ready than Bush, who only

really came into this conversation after 9/11.' *Independent,* 20 March 2007.

6. Margaret Thatcher, *The Downing Street Years* (London, 1993), 817.

7. Ibid, 819.

8. Other contributory factors were the sanction regime imposed against Iraq and the Israel–Palestine conflict.

9. Thatcher, 821.

10. Ibid, 828.

11. General H. Norman Schwarzkopf, *It Doesn't Take a Hero* (London, 1992), 301.

12. Margaret Thatcher required of the manufacturers, Vickers, a minimum availability of 80 per cent.

13. There were no anti-tank helicopters.

14. Thatcher, 826.

15. Major-General Patrick Cordingley, *In the Eye of the Storm* (London, 1996), 27.

16. Ibid.

17. Ibid, 38.

18. Ibid, 34.

19. General Sir Peter de la Billière, *Storm Command* (London, 1992), 26–7.

20. De la Billière, 65.

21. Schwarzkopf, 376.

22. Cordingley, 63.

23. The rat is in fact a jerboah.

24. Winant Sidle, 'A Battle Behind the Scenes: The Gulf War Reheats Military–Media Controversy', *Military Review,* September 1991, 63.

25. Despite the Iraqis occupying defensive positions, the basis for that assumption was drawn from their poor state of training, poor equipment, the resources available and low morale.

26. Cordingley, 131–3.

27. Ibid, 147.
28. Hansard, column 167, 4 December 1990.
29. Cordingley, 140–1.
30. Ibid, 111.
31. The Americans describe their brigadiers as brigadier-generals, hence General Cordingley.
32. Cordingley, 115.
33. Ibid, 128.
34. Parsons, 63.
35. Ibid, 72.
36. AWACS – Airborne Warning and Control System. JSTARS – Joint Surveillance Target Attack Radar System.
37. Schwarzkopf, 417.
38. Ibid, 418.
39. De la Billière, 191.
40. Schwarzkopf, 394–5, 432, 439.
41. Ibid, 433.
42. Ibid, 384.
43. Major-General Rupert Smith, Operation Granby, Directive 1/90, 30 November 1990.
44. General Sir Rupert Smith, *The Utility of Force: The Art of War in the Modern World* (London, 2005), 155.
45. 1st (British) Armoured Division Post Operation Report.
46. Major-General Rupert Smith, 'The Gulf War: The Land Battle', *RUSI Journal*, Vol. 137, No. 1, February 1993.
47. On the first day the Marines had one fatal casualty.
48. Schwarzkopf, 462.
49. Fewer than 250 of the coalition's men were killed in action.
50. Cordingley, 288.
51. Ibid, 293.
52. Ibid, 294. 1st Armoured Division had a total of 233 Challenger main battle tanks in the desert, representing over 50 per cent of the Challenger stock.

53. Robert Fisk, *The Great War for Civilisation* (London, 2005), 787. This event was revealed by Seymour Hersh.

54. *Operation Granby: An Account of the Gulf Crisis 1990–91* (Ministry of Defence, 1991), 5–21.

55. Cordingley, 297.

56. Fisk, 790.

57. Thatcher, 828.

58. Christopher Greenwood, 'Command and the Laws of Armed Conflict', Strategic and Combat Studies Institute Occasional, No. 4, 1993.

59. Fisk, 791.

60. De la Billière, 311.

61. Schwarzkopf, 498.

62. Ibid, 421.

5 Mogadishu

1. Elizabeth Drew, *On the Edge: The Clinton Presidency* (New York, 1994), 319, 326.

2. Ibid, 326.

3. Anthony Parsons, *From Cold War to Hot Peace* (London, 1995), 198.

4. Keith B. Richburg, *Out of America* (New York, 1997), 74.

5. Ibid, 59.

6. *Washington Times*, 1 December 1992.

7. Richburg, 52.

8. Parsons, 201. In view of the experience of the Iraq War, it is of interest that in 1992 the requirement for post-conflict peace-building had been registered.

9. *Washington Post*, 2 December 1992.

10. Parsons, 201.

11. *Independent*, 30 June 1993.

12. Ibid, 28 November 1992.

13. Boutros Boutros-Ghali, *Unvanquished* (London, 1999), 60.

14. Ibid, 60.
15. John Drysdale, *Whatever Happened to Somalia?* (London, 1999), 1.
16. Parsons, 203.
17. Daniel P. Bolger, *Savage Peace* (Novato, 1995), 296.
18. Farer produced a report for the Secretary-General on the killing of Pakistani soldiers on 5 June 1993.
19. Reported in the *Independent*, 22 September 1993.
20. Boutros Boutros-Ghali, 92.
21. Drysdale, 8.
22. Ibid, 10.
23. T.W. Lippman and B. Gellman, 'A Humanitarian Gesture Turns Deadly', *Washington Post*, 10 October 1993.
24. Chris Seiple, *The US Military/NGO Relationship in Humanitarian Interventions* (Carlisle, 1996), 126.
25. *Independent*, 22 September 1993.
26. Drysdale to author, Staff College, Camberley, May 1994.
27. Ibid.
28. Drysdale, 181.
29. Report pursuant to para 5 of Security Council Resolution 837 (1993) on the investigation into the 5 June 1993 attack on UN forces in Somalia conducted on behalf of the Secretary-General, S/26351, 24 August 1993.
30. Richburg, 64.
31. Françoise Bouchet-Saulnier, *Life, Death and Aid*, Médécins Sans Frontières Report on World Crisis Intervention, 22 November 1993.
32. Professor Farer appeared before the Senate's Committee on Armed Services. Highly critical of the UN, he said: 'They made the UN a player rather than an honest broker in the country's unruly political life, and thus they set the stage for confrontation.'
33. Bolger, 301.
34. Richburg, 76.

35. Ibid, 80.

36. United States Senate, Review Document, 29 September 1995, 48.

37. Drew, 322.

38. United States Senate Committee on Armed Services, 'Review of the Circumstances Surrounding the Ranger Raid on October 3–4, 1993 in Mogadishu', 29 September 1995, 6.

39. Final draft FM 100–5, Operations, 19 January 1993, 2–9.

40. Bolger, 308.

41. *Independent on Sunday*, 17 October 1993.

42. Mark Bowden, *Black Hawk Down* (London, 1999), 50.

43. Bolger, 313.

44. Boutros Boutros-Ghali, 96.

45. Drew, 323.

46. Boutros Boutros-Ghali, 96.

47. General Hoar, in evidence to United States Senate Committee on Armed Services Report, 29 September 1995, 28. Note Chapter 8 and their employment in the civilian populated areas of Fallujah. The Spectre had been employed earlier in Somalia.

48. Bolger, 317.

49. Bowden, 41.

50. Drug usage among Muslim militias is common; others also take alcohol. *Khat* resembles watercress except that its effect is to generate a powerful high. Chewing the amphetamine usually begins at midday so that crucially by mid-afternoon the militia was fired up and ready for the fight. Ibid.

51. Bolger, 319.

52. Drew, 335.

53. Bowden, 499.

54. Seiple, 163. In Afghanistan, in 2007, German pilots refused to fly at night, quoting health and safety regulations.

55. Boutros Boutros-Ghali, 134.

56. Ibid, 135.

57. Drysdale, 14.

58. Drew, 326.

59. Lieutenant-Colonel Larry Joyce US Army (Retd), father of Sergeant James Casey Joyce, killed in Somalia, in testimony before the Senate Committee on Armed Services, 12 May 1994.

60. *Time International*, 18 October 1993.

61. Ibid.

62. Joseph Verner Reed, in Boutros Boutros-Ghali, *Unvanquished*, 304.

63. *International Herald Tribune*, 25 May 1999.

64. Democratic National Convention, August 1996.

65. Drew, 335.

66. General Sir Michael Rose, *Fighting for Peace: Lessons from Bosnia* (London, 1998), 186.

6 Gorazde

1. Anthony Parsons, *From Cold War to Hot Peace* (London, 1995), 220.

2. Lieutenant-General Dick Applegate aide-memoire.

3. Parsons, 223.

4. Ibid, 228.

5. Boutros Boutros-Ghali, *Unvanquished* (London, 1999), 51.

6. UNPA West was ethnically cleansed in May 1995 and the two UNPAs that were the Krajinas were cleansed by the Croats in July 1995.

7. UNPROFOR had other regional commands in Zagreb, Croatia and Skopje, Macedonia (including a US presence).

8. Rose, 186.

9. Boutros Boutros-Ghali, 45.

10. Misha Glenny, *New York Review of Books*, 27 May 1993.

11. Boutros Boutros-Ghali, 49.

12. Frank van Kappen, 'Intelligence and the United Nations', in

Ben de Jong (ed.) *et al*, *Peacekeeping Intelligence* (Oakton, VA, April 2003), 7.

13. Patrick Cammaert, 'Intelligence in Peacekeeping Operations: Lessons for the Future', in de Jong, 14.

14. Jonathon Riley reported having seen mujahidin in Croatia in 1992. During a visit by Douglas Hogg, he also saw Iranian 747s delivering cargoes of weapons to Tirana, Albania to destabilize Kosovo.

15. Cees Wiebes, *Intelligence and the War in Bosnia, 1992–1995* (Lit Verlag, 2003), 159–62.

16. Wiebes, 167.

17. Confidential source.

18. 'The Clinton Administrations's "wink and nod" to allow Iran into Bosnia', House Republican Policy Committee, 26 April 1996.

19. Wiebes, 167.

20. Ibid, 176.

21. My italics.

22. General Sir Michael Rose, *Fighting for Peace: Lessons from Bosnia* (London, 1998), 360.

23. Ibid, 162.

24. Ibid, 169.

25. Ibid, 324.

26. The Saxon had been a private development intended to exploit a gap in the APC market. The British Army purchased the vehicle off the shelf. The Saxon did have one saving grace. It had good levels of protection provided by its armour.

27. Tim Ripley, *Operation Deliberate Force* (Lancaster, 1999), 28.

28. Ibid, 53.

29. Draft, 1RWF Records, undated, 4.

30. Ibid, 5.

31. The numbers exceed 500 if every individual is present on the

base. Every 1RWF soldier took two weeks' home leave during their deployment.

32. The established war role of the Corps of Drums is to act as stretcher-bearers. In Gorazde's particular circumstances, where 1RWF had dedicated medical cover provided by the Norwegians, the Drums were available to take on other tasks.

33. There was a national chain which ran to the UK brigade commander in Gornji Vakuf and then on to C-in-C Land Command, the Joint Commander at Wilton near Salisbury. This arrangement preceded the establishment of PJHQ. 'The chain should have kept us supplied and informed, especially on strategic developments that would have strengthened my hand,' said Jonathon Riley.

34. 1RWF Presentation, *Gorazde – When Peacekeeping Fails*, 5.

35. Ibid, 4.

36. Lieutenant-Colonel Jonathon Riley (ed.), *White Dragon: The Royal Welch Fusiliers in Bosnia* (Wrexham, 1995), 9.

37. Ibid, 40.

38. Draft, 1RWF Records, 7.

39. Riley, 20.

40. Draft, 1RWF Records, 9.

41. Ibid.

42. British Air Commodore Mike Rudd, NATO LO to UN Zagreb, in Ripley, 57.

43. Ripley, 57.

44. Riley, 23.

45. Ibid, 44.

46. Ibid, 45.

47. 'Jones the Jammer foils Serbs', *The Times*, 24 March 1995.

48. Interview with Major-General Jonathon Riley, Caernarfon, 12 April 2007.

49. Ibid.

50. Ripley, 115.

51. The Netherlands Institute for War Documentation, *Srebrenica*, Part 4, Chapter 9, Section 8 (2002).

52. Draft, 1RWF Records, 21.

53. Ibid; Riley, 48.

54. Ripley, 117.

55. Riley, 57.

56. Ripley, 142.

57. Richard Connaughton, 'Talking to Serbs', *The Officer*, Jan/Feb 1997.

58. Ibid.

59. Correspondence, General Smith to author, 6 October 2007.

60. General Rose wrote in a note to the author: 'Air strikes *could* be authorised – even if only civilians at risk.'

61. Ripley, 145.

62. Ibid, 103

63. Ibid, 148.

64. Ibid.

65. Author interview with Riley, Caernarfon, 12 April 2007.

66. Riley, 61, 65.

67. Ripley, 153.

68. Field Marshal Sir Dick Vincent, quoted in ibid, 25.

69. Correspondence, General Smith to author, 6 October 2007: 'The delay in the deployment of the Rapid Reaction Force was caused by the Federation and the Croats in particular, who thought it might be used against them; critically, the essential artillery elements had yet to be fully deployed. There were constraints on its use: the French would only allow their elements to be used within the range of French forces. There were limits to what could be done in terms of reach and sustainment with, in effect, a weak armoured infantry brigade, an airmobile brigade, an artillery group, and lacking engineer

support, even if you have on-call and under your direction 5 ATAFs' weighty air assets. Additionally, I was trying to conceal the Rapid Reaction Force's potential until it was fully available.'

70. Draft, 1RWF Records, undated, 27.

71. Discussion, General Smith with author, 6 October 2007.

72. Riley, 66.

73. Rose, 179.

74. Author interview with Riley, Caernarfon, 12 April 2007.

75. Riley, 67.

76. Ibid.

77. C.J. Francis, 'C Troop Summary', *GTR Journal*, 1995.

78. Author interview with Riley, Caernarfon, 12 April 2007; Smith, 365.

79. Riley, 69.

80. General Sir Rupert Smith, *The Utility of Force: The Art of War in the Modern World* (London, 2005), 365.

81. Riley, 69.

82. Smith, 365.

83. A recent EU Chaillot Paper, No. 101, dated May 2007, by Johanna Valenius, *Gender Mainstreaming in ESDP Missions*, defined peacekeeping in an entirely different way: 'Peacekeeping operations have become more complex because conflicts – or at least our understanding of them – have become more complex, and we have started to talk about crisis management.'

84. Author interview with Riley, Caernarfon, 12 April 2007.

85. The other principles are: The selection and maintenance of the aim; Operate within the law; Maintain consensus; Establish, as required, an effective *cordon sanitaire* around the target area; Military Intervention is the last resort of a collective security machine; Know your enemy; Win the Information War. From Richard Connaughton, *Military Intervention and Peacekeeping – The Reality* (Aldershot, 2001), 80.

86. Marcel de Haas, 'Dutch Military Power: From Srebrenica to Uruzgan', *The Officer*, July/August 2007.

7 Operation Barras – Sierra Leone

1. The editor neglected to acknowledge the significant contribution of the Special Boat Service.
2. The *Economist*, 13 May 2000.
3. Damien Lewis, *Operation Certain Death* (London, 2004), 613.
4. Ibid, 625.
5. 'Somalia Revisited', *The Times*, 9 May 2000.
6. This battalion had led the advance into Kosovo when it was part of the now disbanded 5 Airborne Brigade. Quite by chance, it was the duty Spearhead battalion at the time the Sierra Leone crisis broke.
7. HMS *Illustrious* was taking part in Exercise Linked Seas off the Iberian Peninsula, so she was closer to Freetown than the HMS *Ocean* Group which had to re-victual at Gibraltar. *Illustrious* arrived off Freetown on 11 May and the HMS *Ocean* Group on 14 May.
8. *The Times*, 10 May 2000.
9. Gordon Hughes, 'The West Side Story: Reflections – Sierra Leone and Operation Barras', unpublished paper, October 2007.
10. Brigadier Hughes relieved Brigadier Richards after Operation Palliser.
11. That same question would be asked in March 2007 when a motley boarding party from HMS *Cornwall* was taken hostage in the Shatt-al-Arab by Iranian gunboats.
12. Military tourism was the view of the then senior military officer in Sierra Leone, Brigadier Gordon Hughes, as expressed in an interview with the author on 22 March 2007.
13. *The Times*, 28 August 2000.
14. Soon after, MATT became partially internationalized, hence IMATT.

15. During the recovery, two SAS men were killed in a road traffic accident. The casualty account had thus opened before a foot could be put in the country.

16. Lewis, 254; William Fowler, *Operation Barras* (London, 2004), 130.

17. The conscience of one of the married men got the better of him. He made way for a junior rank.

18. Hughes, 22 March 2007.

19. A new anti-malaria drug, larium, provided immediate protection.

20. Fowler, 122.

21. Ibid, 134.

22. Tim Collins, *Rules of Engagement: A Life in Conflict* (London, 2005), 15–16.

23. Tinnion had lived with his partner Anna Homsi. She was seven months pregnant with their first child. Anna was denied a war widow's pension because they were not married. Following understandable protest, the Ministry of Defence relented, extending the qualification for a war widow's pension to partners – including homosexuals and lesbians.

24. Collins, 17.

25. Fowler, 145.

26. Ibid, 152–3.

27. Ibid, 148.

28. Ministry of Defence Press Release 236/00, 14 September 2000.

29. Interview with author, 22 March 2007.

30. Ministry of Defence Press Release 236/00, 14 September 2000.

31. Ministry of Defence Press Release 245/00, 20 September 2000.

32. Blair's father was for a long time external examiner of Sierra Leone's Fourah College.

33. Author interview with Brigadier Gordon Hughes, Shrivenham, 9 May 2007.

34. Gordon Hughes, 'The West Side Story: Reflections – Sierra Leone and Op Barras', unpublished paper, October 2007.

35. Greg Mills and Terence McNamee, 'Sierra Leone Poised to Stand Alone', *Business Day Weekender*, 8–9 September 2007.

36. Greg Mills and Terence McNamee, 'A New Democracy Spinning Its Wheels', *The Star*, 3 October 2007.

8 Fallujah

1. In his book *The Age of Turbulence: Adventures in a New World* (London, 2007), Alan Greenspan, the former Chairman of the US Federal Reserve, writes, 'I am saddened that it is politically inconvenient to acknowledge what everyone knows: the Iraq war is largely about oil.'

2. The Kurds' intention through self-determination was to annexe the oilfields of Kirkuk.

3. Gareth R.V. Stansfield, 'Politics and Governance in the New Iraq: Reconstruction of the New versus Resurrection of the Old', in Jonathon Eyal (ed.), *War in Iraq*, Whitehall Paper No. 59 (Royal United Services Institute, London, 2003), 82.

4. Editorial, *Daily Telegraph*, 24 August 2007.

5. Bing West, *No True Glory: A Front Line Account of the Battle for Fallujah* (New York, 2005), 173.

6. This comment refers to activity at the time of the first phase of the Battle of Fallujah. Correspondence, General John Abizaid to author, April 2008.

7. Ibid.

8. James Kitfield, 'Pentagon Power Shift', in Christopher M. Bourne, 'Unintended Consequences of the Goldwater-Nichols Act', *Joint Force Quarterly*, Spring 1998, 103.

9. Major-General A.J.N. Graham, Deputy Commanding General, Multi-National Corps Iraq, speaking to Brigadier Nigel Aylwin-Foster in 'Changing the (US) Army for Counter-Insurgency Operations', *British Army Review*, Number 140, Autumn 2006.

10. Brigadier Nigel Aylwin-Foster, 'Changing the (US) Army for Counterinsurgency Operations', *British Army Review*, Number 140, Autumn 2006, 7.

11. West, 16.

12. Ibid, 30.

13. Aylwin-Foster, 7.

14. *On the Treatment by the Coalition Forces of Prisoners of War and Other Protected Persons by Geneva Conventions in Iraq during Arrest, Internment and Interrogation*, International Committee of the Red Cross, Geneva, February 2004.

15. An anonymous US Army Colonel, Baghdad, September 2004, quoted in Aylwin-Foster, 6.

16. 1BW Post Operation Report – Operation Bracken, 9 December 2004.

17. West, 51.

18. Clive Stafford Smith, *Bad Men* (London, 2007), 34.

19. Ibid, 185.

20. Ibid, 46.

21. Gerry Schumacher, *A Bloody Business: America's War Zone Contractors and the Occupation of Iraq* (St Paul's, 2006), 45.

22. West, 61.

23. *Learning from Fallujah: Lessons Identified 2003–2005*, Peace Direct and Oxford Research Group, 12.

24. David Wood, 'Lack of Heavy Armor Constrains Urban Options in Iraq', New House News Service, 27 April 2004, quoted in Matt M. Mathews, 'Operation Al Fajr: A Study in Army and Marine Corps Joint Operations', *Global War on Terrorism*, Occasional Paper No. 20, CSI Press, Fort Leavenworth.

25. Richard Connaughton, John Pimlott and Duncan Anderson, *The Battle for Manila* (London and Novato, 1995), 175–6.

26. On 6 April, a Marine Humvee caught in an ambush near Ramadi lost nine men, bringing the Ramadi dead that day to twelve.

27. West, 266.

28. Author interview with Major-General Jonathon Riley, 2 September 2007.

29. Edward Wong, *New York Times*, 22 April 2004.

30. West, 122.

31. Ibid, 123.

32. The Fallujah brigade was self-evidently not a brigade, having a strength less than a battalion.

33. Stafford Smith, 279.

34. West, 236.

35. Matthews, 15.

36. 'Army is Training Advisors for Iraq', *Los Angeles Times*, 25 October 2006.

37. Jim Garamone, AFPS (Washington, 8 November 2004).

38. Lieutenant-General John Sattler and Lieutenant-Colonel Daniel Wilson, 'Operation ALFAJR: The Battle of Fallujah – Part II', *Marine Corps Gazette*, July 2005, 12–24.

39. Ibid, 16.

40. Robert Taber, *The War of the Flea: A Study of Guerrilla Warfare, Theory and Practice* (London, 1965), 11.

41. Matthews, 40.

42. Connaughton, Pimlott, Anderson, 175.

43. Matthews, 81.

44. Sattler and Wilson, 21.

45. By the end of March 2005, 629 arms caches had been recovered.

46. Sattler and Wilson, 23.

47. Matthews, 83.

48. Although this is an official estimate, figures from elsewhere suggest that the number of buildings in Fallujah totalled no more than 39,000. To say therefore that 36,000 were demolished introduces a strong element of doubt as to the veracity of these figures.

49. Author interview with General Kiszely, 19 September 2007.
50. Dahr Jamail, *Asia Times*, 3 June 2005.
51. Martin Fletcher, 'Peace Hopes are Shaken as Bush's Champion Dies in Roadside Attack', *The Times*, 14 September 2007.
52. Correspondence, General Abizaid to author, April 2008.

9 Helmand

1. Story from BBC News, 24 April 2006.
2. General Sir Michael Rose in his Foreword to Patrick Macrory, *Kabul Catastrophe* (London, 2001). General Rose was born in Quetta, 5 January 1940.
3. Brian Robson, *The Road to Kabul: The Second Afghan War 1878–1881* (Staplehurst, 2003), 239.
4. Anthony Hyman, *Afghanistan Under Soviet Domination 1964–91*, third edition (London, 1992), x.
5. Afghan forces crossed into India, occupying a number of Indian towns. British and Indian forces responded by reclaiming the occupied villages and launching a land and air campaign against Afghanistan. http://www.regiments.org/wars/20thcent/19afghan.htm
6. Hyman, 252.
7. John Keegan, 'The Ordeal of Afghanistan', *Atlantic Monthly*, Vol. 256, No.5, 95, quoted in Amalendu Misra, *Afghanistan* (Cambridge, 2004), 51.
8. Mohammed Yousaf and Mark Adkin, *Afghanistan, The Bear Trap: The Defeat of a Superpower* (Barnsley, 2001), 216.
9. Peter Marsden, *The Taliban: War, Religion and the New Order in Afghanistan* (London, 1999), 114.
10. Charles Allen, *Soldier Sahibs. The Men Who Made the North West Frontier* (London, 2000), 13.
11. John Simpson, *Strange Places, Questionable People* (London, 1998), 501.
12. Harvey Langholtz *et al.*, *International Peacekeeping: The*

Yearbook of International Peace Operations, Vol. 8 (Leiden, 2004), 437–44.

13. Military historian to author.

14. Major Rich Howard, 'Warfighting at the Operational Level', *The Globe and Laurel*, May/June 2007, 180.

15. Greg Mills, *Business Day*, 29 January 2007.

16. Much of this detail has been extracted from the National Army Museum's Helmand Exhibition, 2007.

17. Sandhurst academic.

18. The British Brigade Headquarters later moved to Lashkar Gah, where it was in a better position to manage a counter-insurgency campaign and the reconstruction programme.

19. General Dick Berlijn, *Daily Telegraph*, 20 January 2006.

20. *The Times*, 14 February 2007.

21. *British Army Review*, No. 141, Winter 2006/07, 6.

22. Helmand Oral History Records Extracts, National Army Museum.

23. Peter Marsden, *The Taliban* (London, 2002), 153.

24. Helmand Oral History Records Extracts, National Army Museum.

25. Ibid.

26. Patrick Bishop, *3 Para: Afghanistan, Summer 2006* (London, 2006), 40.

27. Helmand Oral History Records Extracts, National Army Museum.

28. Bishop, 221.

29. *British Army Review*, No. 141, Winter 2006/07, 5.

30. Thomas Harding, 'MoD Shunned Chance to Hire More Helicopters', *Daily Telegraph*, 18 June 2007.

31. Colonel Michael Dewar, *Officer*, July/August 2007, 4.

32. 'Apache Rescue Mission', *The Globe and Laurel*, January/February 2007, 18.

33. A grouping of common interest parties in developing the security and reconstruction of Helmand.

34. *The Globe and Laurel*, March/April 2007, 96.

35. Quote given to me by Lieutenant-Colonel Matt Holmes, CO 42 Cdo RM.

36. The *Daily Telegraph* had one embedded reporter with 42 Commando which captured Operation Silver.

37. Zahid Hussain, *Front Line Pakistan* (London, 2007), 180.

38. Wood, known as 'Chemical Bill', had formerly been US ambassador to Colombia, where he was actively engaged in the spraying campaign against cocaine.

39. What matters is what sound bites are thought newsworthy. It is true that Reid knew the Afghan situation could turn nasty and said as much. It was an ambiguous situation. However, to have sent a one-battle group brigade into an Afghanistan he truly thought might turn nasty was the height of irresponsibility.

40. Correspondence with a Sandhurst academic.

41. This includes armed poppy eradication agencies.

42. Tom Coghlan, 'NATO Presses US to Curb Special Forces in Afghanistan', *Daily Telegraph*, 22 May 2007.

43. Author discussion with General Richards, 31 October 2007.

44. Blue on blue, friendly fire or fratricide occurs when allied forces are hit by their own side. Coalition air forces, however, save many more allied lives than they take. Close air support is an essential force multiplier. Blue on blue can occur in cases involving aircraft where the margin of safety is tight or through human error.

45. The Falklands Veterans Association, *25th Anniversary: The Falklands Conflict 1982–2007* (Rock Ferry, 2007), 29.

46. Correspondence with author, 22 September 2007.

10 Reflection

1. General the Lord Guthrie, 'Our Defence has been Underfunded for Years', *Daily Telegraph*, 24 November 2007.

2. *Army Research, Development and Acquisition Bulletin*, November/December 1991.

3. Author interview with Commanding Officer, 42 Commando Royal Marines, 26 November 2007.

4. Discussion with author, 10 November 2007.

5. A number of newspapers stirred the conscience of the nation. As a result, some city and town councils made special efforts to invite returning military with a local connection to march through the streets, colours flying, bayonets fixed and band and drums playing. *Sunday Telegraph*, 18 November 2007.

6. Ibid.

7. *The Times*, 24 November 2007.

8. Mark Bowden, *Black Hawk Down* (London, 1999), 472.

SELECT BIBLIOGRAPHY

Place of publication London unless otherwise stated.

Adkin, Mark, *Goose Green* (Barnsley, 1992).

Adkin, Mark, *Urgent Fury* (1989).

Allen, Charles, *Soldier Sahibs: The Men Who Made the North West Frontier* (2000).

Arthur, Max, *Above All, Courage* (1985).

Bicheno, Hugh, *Razor's Edge* (2006).

Bilton, Michael and Kominsky, Peter, *Speaking Out* (1989).

Bishop, Patrick, *3 Para: Afghanistan, Summer 2006* (2006).

Bolger, Daniel P., *Savage Peace* (Novato, 1995).

Boutros-Ghali, Boutros, *Unvanquished* (1999).

Bowden, Mark, *Black Hawk Down* (1999).

Boyce, D. George, *The Falklands War* (2005).

Clark, General Wesley K., *Waging Modern War* (New York, 2001).

Clausewitz, Carl von, *Vom Kriege* (Bonn, 1952).

Collins, Tim, *Rules of Engagement: A Life in Conflict* (2005).

Connaughton, Richard, Pimlott, John and Anderson, Duncan, *The Battle for Manila* (London and Novato, 1995).

Cordingley, Major-General Patrick, *In the Eye of the Storm* (1996).

Crozier, Brian, *The Grenada Documents* (1987).

De Jong, Ben (ed.) *et al.*, *Peacekeeping Intelligence: Emerging Concepts for the Future* (Oakton, VA, 2003).

De la Billière, General Sir Peter, *Storm Command* (1992).

Drew, Elizabeth, *On the Edge: The Clinton Presidency* (New York, 1994).

Drysdale, John, *Whatever Happened to Somalia?* (1999).

Fisk, Robert, *The Great War for Civilisation* (2005).

Fitz-Gibbon, Spencer, *Not Mentioned in Despatches: The History and Mythology of the Battle of Goose Green* (Cambridge, 1995).

Fowler, William, *Operation Barras* (2004).

Freedman, Lawrence, *The Official History of the Falklands Campaign, Volume II: War and Diplomacy* (2005).

Frost, John, *2 Para Falklands: The Battalion at War* (1988).

Greenspan, Alan, *The Age of Turbulence: Adventures in a New World* (2007).

Hanrahan, Brian and Fox, Robert, *I Counted Them All Out and I Counted Them All Back: The Battle for the Falklands* (1982).

Hastings, Max and Jenkins, Simon, *The Battle for the Falklands* (1983).

Hopple, G. and Gilley, C., *Policy without Intelligence* (New York, 1983).

Hussain, Zahid, *Front Line Pakistan* (2007).

Hyman, Anthony, *Afghanistan Under Soviet Domination 1964–91*, third edition (1992).

Lewis, Damien, *Operation Certain Death* (2004).

Macrory, Patrick, *Kabul Catastrophe* (2001).

Marsden, Peter, *The Taliban: War, Religion and the New Order in Afghanistan* (1999).

Marsden, Peter, *The Taliban* (2002).

Meyer, Karl E. and Brysac, Shareen Blair, *Tournament of Shadows: The Great Game and the Race for Empire in Asia* (1999).

O'Shaughnessy, Hugh, *Grenada* (1984).

Parsons, Anthony, *From Cold War to Hot Peace* (1995).

Pook, Jerry, *RAF Harrier Ground Attack – Falklands* (Barnsley, 2007).

Richburg, Keith B., *Out of America* (New York, 1997).

Riley, Lieutenant-Colonel Jonathon (ed.), *White Dragon: The Royal Welch Fusiliers in Bosnia* (Wrexham, 1995).

Ripley, Tim, *Operation Deliberate Force* (Lancaster, 1999).

Robson, Brian, *The Road to Kabul: The Second Afghan War 1878–1881* (Staplehurst, 2003).

Rose, General Sir Michael, *Fighting for Peace: Lessons from Bosnia* (1998).

Russell, Lee E. and Mendez, Albert M., *Grenada 1983* (1985).

Sandford, Gregory and Vigilante, Richard, *Grenada: The Untold Story* (1984).

Schumacher, Gerry, *A Bloody Business: America's War Zone Contractors and the Occupation of Iraq* (St Paul's, 2006).

Schwarzkopf, General H. Norman, *It Doesn't Take a Hero* (1992).

Scoon, Sir Paul, *Survival for Service* (Oxford, 2003).

Seiple, Chris, *The US Military/NGO Relationship in Humanitarian Interventions* (Carlisle, 1996).

Simpson, John, *Strange Places, Questionable People* (1998).

Smith, General Sir Rupert, *The Utility of Force: The Art of War in the Modern World* (2005).

Smith, Gordon, *Battles of the Falklands War* (1982).

Stafford Smith, Clive, *Bad Men* (2007).

Stewart, Rory, *The Places in Between* (2004).

Taber, Robert, *The War of the Flea: A Study of Guerilla Warfare, Theory and Practice* (1965).

Thatcher, Margaret, *The Downing Street Years* (1993).

Thompson, Major-General Julian, *No Picnic* (1985).

Thompson, Robert, *Defeating Communist Insurgency: Experiences from Malaya and Vietnam* (1966).

Urban, Mark, *War in Afghanistan* (1988).

Urquhart, Brian, *A Life in Peace and War* (1987).

Van der Bijl, N., *Nine Battles to Stanley* (1999).

Van Kappen, Frank, 'Intelligence and the United Nations', in Ben de Jong (ed.) *et al.*, *Peacekeeping Intelligence* (Oakton, VA, April 2003).

Wiebes, Cees, *Intelligence and War in Bosnia, 1992–1995* (Lit Verlag, 2003).

Wilsey, General Sir John, *H. Jones VC: The Life and Death of an Unusual Hero* (2002).

Yousaf, Mohammed and Adkin, Mark, *Afghanistan, The Bear Trap: The Defeat of a Superpower* (Barnsley, 2001).

INDEX

Abizaid, General John 26, 90, 98,
    103, 104, 105–6, 107, 122, 166,
    295, 310, 313, 320, 322, 339
Abols, Corporal David 59
Abu Ghraib prison 304, 307–8, 327
AC-130 Spectre 98
Adams, Tom 84, 85, 94
Adkin, Mark 114
Afghan National Army (ANA) 350,
    368
Afghan Transitory Authority 347
Afghan War
  First 342
  Second (1878–80) 342
  Third 343
Afghanistan 3, 5, 26–7, 347–83, 394
  attacks on al-Qa'eda training camps
    and Taliban compounds by
    coalition forces (2001) 346
  borders 343
  disunity of command 381–2
  equipment shortages and lack of
    helicopters 386, 394–5
  and Helmand province see Helmand
  history 342–3
  invasion of by Soviet Union (1979)
    343–4
  and media coverage 370–1

and NATO 8, 9, 20, 26, 380–1, 389
  NATO HQ in Kabul 348–9
  opium crop and eradication issue
    378–9, 381
  reconstruction efforts after removal
    of Taliban 27, 347–50
  role of HQ ISAF 349
  and Taliban 344–5
Afghanistan National Police (ANP)
    350
Aideed, General Farah 17, 18, 163–4,
    167, 169, 171, 172–3, 176, 177,
    181, 185, 193, 197–8
Air Assault Brigade (16) 341, 352,
    364, 378
Airborne Division (82nd) 87, 296,
    299, 302, 306
Airmobile Brigade (24) 229
Akashi, Yasushi 215, 225, 241
Al Jazeera 314, 330
Al Jubayl 131–2
Al-Fajr Operation (Fallujah) 327–34
al-Qa'eda 299–300, 337, 338, 346,
    360, 380
Albright, Madeleine 185, 197, 199,
    209, 225, 229, 234, 237, 257
Allawi, Prime Minister Iyad 327,
    328, 333

Allen, Charles   344
Amble Operation (Sierra Leone)   279
Amphibious Ready Group (ARG)
   263
Amritsar massacre (1919)   301
Anbar Awakening   337–8
Annan, Kofi   257, 260
Apache helicopters   352, 354, 365,
   367
APCs (armoured personnel carrier)
   194, 217, 366
Arab League   127
Argentina, invasion of Falklands by
   see Falklands
Argentine Air Force   41
Argyle, HMS   269, 278
Armed Forces Revolutionary Council
   (AFRC) 255
Armoured Brigade (4th)   138, 139,
   152
Armoured Brigade (7th)   130–1,
   133–9, 151, 158, 317
Armoured Brigade (11th)   208
Armoured Division (1st)   138, 139–40,
   150, 153, 296, 313–14
Armoured Infantry Division (24th) (US)
   147, 154
armoured taxis   385
Arrow, HMS   46
Aspin, Les   177, 197, 199
Atlantic Charter (1941)   15
Ato, Osman   183
Austin, General Hudson   81
AWACS   142

Ba'ath Party   299
Bahto, Brigadier Hamid   221, 229,
   235
Baidoa (Somalia)   163
Baker, Mike   308
Baker, Secretary of State   126, 129
Barras Operation (Sierra Leone) (2000)
   21–2, 186, 248–9, 250–2, 265–91,
   387, 388
   attack on Magbeni and engagement
      with West Side Boys   284–5
   capture of Kallay   283
   casualties   283, 286
   censorship over   251–2
   forces and resources deployed
      268–9
   high standard of   21–2, 267
   inquiry into   287–8
   and intelligence   272–3, 289

landing of forces at Gberi Bana and
   rescue of hostages   282–3
negotiation process with West Side
   Boys and collapse   273–4, 275,
   278
plan of attack and preparations
   270, 274–6, 278, 279
relationship between Paras and SAS
   275
security breach due to media leak
   276–9
setting in motion   272
success of and reasons   285–6, 288,
   289
underestimating of enemy   286
Barre, Siad   163, 164
Barry, Lieutenant Jim   62, 63
Basher AC-130 gunship   331
Basra   9, 201
Bauxite Operation (Helmand)   372–3
Bazoft, Farzad   124
Beightler, General R.S.   318, 332
Beirut, truck bomb attack on
   American Marines (1983)   162
Beloff, Nora   207
Benest, David   36, 47, 48
Beresford, Lance-Corporal   59
Berg, Nicholas   335
Bihac   213, 237
bin Laden, Osama   124, 129, 211,
   345
Bir, General Cevik   172, 180
Bish, Ambassador Milan   84
Bishop, Maurice   77–8, 80–1, 82, 96
Black Watch battle group   305, 328
Blackhawks
   loss of in Mogadishu   188–94
   shooting down of in Grenada   100–3,
      116
Blackwater Security Consulting
   Company   309, 311
Blackwill, Robert   297
Blair, Tony   22, 24, 289, 390
Boca House (Falklands)   61–2
Boomer, General Walt   132, 137,
   139, 151
Bosnian conflict   18, 203, 203–4,
   205, 206–7
   arming of Bosniacs by Iran   211–12
   and battle for Gorazde see Gorazde
   Bosniac attack on UN Ukrainians in
      Zepa   235
   Cessation of Hostilities Agreement
      216–17, 222, 224

and Dayton Peace Agreement 18, 19, 244, 245
declaration of 'safe areas' by UN 213
and intelligence 210–11, 232, 248
mortar attack on Markale Market (Sarajevo) 214, 241, 243
and NATO 205, 210, 215, 244
people killed and refugees 208
refusal by United States to deploy ground troops 196, 205, 210
and Russia 208
search for peace and agreement 213–14
shooting down of NATO aircraft 215–16
and Srebrenica massacre (1995) 203, 211, 233
support of Bosniacs by United States 200, 202
UNPROFOR mission 202, 207–8, 210, 244, 245
see also Gorazde
Boutros-Ghali, Boutros 164, 165, 169, 171–2, 175, 185, 196, 197, 199, 208
Bracken Operation (Helmand) 305
Bradley, General Omar 392
Bramall, Field Marshal Lord 29
Brangan, Sergeant 358–9
Bremer, L. Paul 'Jerry' 24, 296–8, 310, 313, 320, 322, 323, 326
Britain
command and control of joint forces arrangement 261
defence expenditure 385–6
dilapidation of military estate 394–6
and Falklands War *see* Falklands War
forces deployed in Iraq conflict (1990–91) 16, 130–1
lack of government support for armed forces 393–4, 395–7
supporting of United States 389
system of responding to crises 261–2
British Army 11, 12–13, 395–6
British Army of the Rhine (BAOR) 133
Brown, Gordon 395
Bruce, Lieutenant-Colonel 367, 368
Bubiyan Islands 123, 126
Budd, Corporal Bryan 361–3

Bullard, Giles 94
Bulldog vehicle 385
Burke, Jason 286
Burnham, Forbes 85
Bush, George (Sr) 127, 165–6
Bush, President George W. 24, 293, 294, 319, 338, 390
Butler, Brigadier Ed 353, 364
Byrne, Lieutenant-Colonel 320

Calwell, C.E., *Small Wars* 335
Cambridge Principles 246
Camp Bastion (Helmand) 350, 352
Canberra, SS 33, 41
Caribbean Community (CARICOM) 84–5
Carter, Jimmy 216–17
Carty, Surgeon Lieutenant Jon 278
Casey, General George 326–7, 335–6, 339
Cassells, Major-General James 170
Castro, Fidel 78, 83, 96
CENTCOM 295, 296
Chalabi, Ahmad 23
Chapter VII (UN Charter) 3, 6, 15, 17, 20, 207, 258, 259, 345
Cheney, Dick 128, 146
Chester, John 44
Chinooks
in Afghanistan 354, 357, 364
deployed in Operation Barras 269, 275–6, 281–2, 285
in Sierra Leone 262
Chirac, President 230
Christopher, Warren 209
Churchill, Winston 29, 374
Churkin, Vitaly 216
CIA 211
Clark, General Wesley 19
Clausewitz, Carl von, *Vom Kriege* (*On War*) 2
Clinton, President Bill 24
and Bosnian conflict 208, 209–10, 212
and Kosovo 19
and Mogadishu 18, 161, 176, 195–6, 198–9, 212
Coalition Provisional Authority *see* CPA
Coard, Bernard 78, 79, 80, 81
COBRA (Cabinet Office Briefing Room) 267
Coe, Second Lieutenant 56
Coiffet, Colonel Phillippe 232

Cold War 6, 12, 14
Comas, Pedro Totolo 89
command and control 392–3
Commando Brigade (3) (UK)
 in Falklands 33, 34, 37, 42, 364
Commando Royal Marines (42) (UK)
 in Helmand 350, 352, 366–7,
 368–9, 372–6
 in Sierra Leone 263, 264
Commando Royal Marines (45) 368–9
conflicts of choice 8–9
conflicts of obligation 8–9
Congo 7
Connaughton, Richard 250
Connor, Lieutenant C.S. 71
contractors 257, 309–10, 390
conventional warfare 11–13
Conway, General James 26, 295–6,
 307, 321, 323
Cook, Robin 256, 257–8, 260, 264
Cooper, David 39
Cordingley, Brigadier 131–2, 135–9,
 153, 155
counter-insurgency, principles of 4–6
CPA (Coalition Provisional Authority)
 297, 319, 323, 326
Craig, Sir David 135, 396
Croatia 203, 206, 207, 209
Crosland, Major John 36, 38, 39,
 43, 51, 69–70, 71
Cuba 80, 83
Cuban Military Mission 88
Cuéllar, Pérez de 164

Dannatt, General Sir Richard 370,
 394, 395–6
Darwin (Falklands) 34, 38, 50, 51,
 54–60, 71, 74
David, Lieutenant-Colonel William
 187, 191, 192
Davidson-Houston, Lieutenant-Colonel
 Patrick 217
Dayton Peace Settlement 18, 19, 244,
 245
de Haas, Lieutenant-Colonel Dr
 Marcel 246–7
de la Billière, Lieutenant-General Sir
 Peter 131, 132, 133, 134, 137,
 138, 145, 157
defence expenditure 385–6
Delta Force 100, 170, 178, 179, 186,
 275
Department of Peacekeeping
 Operations (DPKO) 7

Desert Storm Operation see Iraq
 conflict (1990–91)
Dhofar 74
di Mello, Sergio 239
domino theory 81
Downing, General Wayne 145
Draiva, Ranger 358–9
Drinkwine, Lieutenant-Colonel Brian
 306
Drysdale, John 169, 172, 173, 174
Dual Key system 210
Dugan, General 146
Duke of Wellington's Regiment 216,
 217
al-Dulaimy, Hafid 334
Durand Line 343
Durant, Warrant Officer 192–3, 197
Dutch battalion 233, 246–7
Dyer, Brigadier Reginald 301

Eagleburger, Lawrence 86
Economic Community of West African
 States Ceasefire Monitoring
 Group (ECOMOG) 257
ECOWAS (Economic Community of
 West African States) 259
Elizabeth II, Queen 230
Enduring Freedom 346
equipment 385–7
 and infantry 386–7
Ernst, Major-General Carl 198
Estevez, Lieutenant 59–60
ethnic cleansing 205, 206
Executive Outcomes (EO) 255, 256,
 257, 288, 390

Fahd, King 128–9
Falklands War 29–30, 125, 387
 air–sea battle 41
 and Argentine army 41–2
 deployment of Task Force 32–3,
 38–9
 and Goose Green see Goose Green
 invasion by Argentineans 31, 32,
 33
 landing of infantry 39–40
 and media 47–8, 76
 shortage of helicopters 40–1, 386
Fallujah (Iraq) (2003–4) 2, 11–12,
 17, 18, 23, 25, 201, 292–340,
 298–9, 381
 al Qaid primary school killings 301,
 309
 al-Qa'eda in 299–300

assigning of Para 1 to and replacement by Marines 306–7
attitudes towards local community by US soldiers 304
casualties and damage inflicted after second battle 334–5, 336
creation of Fallujah Brigade 323, 325–6
deployment of Marines in 306–7
described 305–6
establishment of Wahabi sect in 299
exodus of population before second battle 329
'hearts and minds' campaign 302–3
and imams 298–9, 325
impact of de-Ba'athification on 24–5
insurgents and weapons available to 300–1
joint patrols between Americans and Iraqis 322
killing of Blackwater contractors by insurgents 309–11
and media 330
and Operation Bracken 305
and Operation Phantom Fury (Al-Fajr) 328–35, 339–40
and Operation Vigilant Resolve 313–21, 339
opposition to American occupation 294, 299, 303–4
propaganda war by Sunnis 314–15
reconstruction of after second battle and compensation schemes 336–7
reconstruction budget 303
Fallujah Brigade 325–6
Farer, Professor Tom 171, 175
Farrar-Hockley, Major Dair 38, 52, 54, 57, 60, 65, 70, 71
Fearless 32, 33
Fieldhouse, Admiral 33, 45, 48
Fighting in Built-up Areas (FIBUA) 201
Ford, Lance-Corporal Mathew 367–8
Fordham, Lieutenant-Colonel Simon 273, 275
Forward Operating Base Robinson (Helmand) 356, 357
Fox, Robert 45, 66
France
and Bosnian conflict 208
and Iraq conflict (1990–91) 130
Franks, General Tommy 295
Freedman, Sir Lawrence 396

Freetown (Sierra Leone) 252
Frost, John 42
Furth, Leon 209
Future Integrated Soldier Technology 386

Gairy, Eric 77
Galbraith, Peter 212
Galtieri, General Leopoldo 33
Garner, Lieutenant-General Jay 24, 297
Garrison, General William F. 179–80, 181, 182, 188, 189, 397
Gaylord, Joseph 105
Gberi Bana (Sierra Leone) 269, 272, 274, 275, 276, 282–3
General Purpose Machine Gun (GPMG) 40
Gereshk (Helmand) 366
Gergen, David 162
Gile, Brigadier Greg 187, 193
Glaspie, April 125–6, 171, 172, 174
Glenny, Misha 209
global positioning systems 159
Goldsmith, Lord 4
Goldwater-Nichols Department of Defense Reorganization Act (1986) 298
Goose Green (Falklands) (1982) 1, 9–10, 29–76, 247, 391–2, 397
advance on settlement of 62–6
Argentine defence 41–2
attack on Boca House and surrender of 61–2
cancellation of initial raid 44–5
casualties 38, 53, 55, 58, 59, 63, 67, 68, 382
command and leadership at battle group level 73–4
communications problems 52
engagement with Argentineans around Darwin ridge and surrendering of 54–60, 71, 74
first night assault 50–4
headlong attack by 'H' Jones and death of 59, 60, 70, 75
honours and awards given 70–2, 371
lack of fire support 47, 56
and media 47–8, 75
orders to Paras to conduct attack 43–5, 74–5
RAF attack 64–5
similarities to Grenada 106
six-phase plan of battle 45–6, 48–50, 74

surrender of Argentineans 66–8
undersourcing of 10, 46–7
use of MILAN missile 73
Gorazde (Bosnia) (1995) 2, 6, 18, 200, 202, 214–49, 388
agreement to stop fighting by Serbs and TEZ agreement 216, 219
attacks on by Serbs and fighting of by RWF 222–3, 224, 225, 228–9
Bosniac attack on Ukrainians in 235–6
Bosniac troops in 221
declared 'safe area' 213
entering of by Royal Welch Fusiliers (RWF) and missions 217–18
manning of observation posts by RWF 220
NATO ultimatum to Mladic 237–8
obstruction of UN relief convoys by Serbs and rationing enforced 218–19, 225, 226–7, 231–2
opening of Serb offensive against 215
Serb army besieging 221–2
stress management regime 234–5
sub-units allocated to 220
withdrawal of RWF from and Bosniac attacks on 238, 239–43, 245
Gorbachev, Mikhail 13
Gore, Al 209
Gosende, Robert 171, 197
Graves, Major-General Dick 77, 87
Great Game 342
Grenada (1983) 1, 77–122, 88, 178, 179
America's justification of action in 119
body count issue 108–9
bombing of forts and killing of mental patients 107–8
and Castro 96
criticism of invasion 97–8
death toll 117
decision to intervene militarily and reluctance of CARICOM states to intervene 84–6
deployment of Navy Task Forces 87–8
detaining of American medical students as hostages 83, 87, 89–90
diplomatic activity 94–5

encounters with Cuban fighting force 106–7
ending of Cuban resistance 115
failure of attack on Richmond Hill Prison by Special Forces 100–3, 108
goal of operation 86–7
Grenadian army and resource 88, 97
history and events leading up to 77–82
importance of operational security 86
landing of Marines at Pearls and taking of town and Grenville 98–9
legality of invasion question 118–20
lessons taken from 122
and media 10, 76, 109–11
mission to clear Point Salines runway by Rangers 103–6, 107
operation to take Calivigny and death of soldiers 116–17
operational plan 90–3
poor intelligence 93–4, 98, 100, 107, 115
rescue of Scoon 99–100, 108, 111
rescuing of students from Grand Anse 111–15
resources and manpower 87–8
SEAL teams' attack on Beauséjour transmitting station and taking of 99
seen as liberation by Grenadians 118
shooting down of Blackhawks 100–3, 116
and Soviet Union 115
Grenadier Guards 268
Guam 87
Guantánamo Bay 4
Gulf conflict (1990-91) *see* Iraq conflict (1990–91)
Gurkha Transport Regiment 241
Gurung, Lance-Corporal Ganeshbahdur 241
Guthrie, General 278–9, 387
Guyana 84–5

Hamas 212
Hamed, Taha Bidaywi 299
Hammarskjöld, Dag 170
Hammerbeck, Brigadier Christopher 152

Harding, Lord 29
Harley, Corporal 62
Harman, Sabina D. 307–8
Hastings, Max 67
Headquarters Allied Rapid Reaction Corps 349
Headquarters Land Command, Wilton (HQLAND Command) 277–8
'hearts and minds' campaigns 302–3, 368
helicopters
  shortage of in Falklands 40–1, 386
  shortage of in Iraq and Afghanistan 364–5, 386
Helmand (Afghanistan) (2006–7) 2, 347–83, 392
  air support for Paras 357
  assessment of progress with development 376–7
  attempt to split and isolate Taliban by Marines 370
  awards given 371–4
  building of Camp Bastion 350, 352
  casualties 364
  deployment of 16 Air Assault Brigade to and mission 341
  description 352–3
  drugs trade 379
  employment of trauma management process in 382
  engagement between Marines and Taliban at Jugroom Fort 367
  engagement with Taliban by Paras 361, 362–3
  killing of Budd 363–4
  lack of helicopters 364–5, 386
  and media 75, 370–1
  minefield casualties 355
  occupation of settlements mission 355–6, 369
  and Operation Bauxite 372–3
  and Operation Silver 375–6, 392
  poppy eradication task 378, 379
  relieving of Paras by Marines 366
  rules of engagement 361
  securing of Kajaki Dam by Paras 354
  support and advice given to Afghan National Army by Marines 368–9
  Taliban attack on Musa Qala and deal over 358–60
Hempstone, Smith 167, 347
Hermes 33
Hezbollah 212

Hoar, General Joseph 172, 178, 180, 317
Holbrooke, Richard 216
Holmes, Lieutenant-Colonel Matt 366, 372–3, 382
honours 72, 371
  and Goose Green 70–2
  and Helmand 371–4
Hoon, Geoff 25, 278–9, 288
Horner, General Chuck 143, 160
hostage-taking 388 see also Barras operation
Howe, Sir Geoffrey 94–5, 98
Howe, Admiral Jonathan 171–2, 176–7, 197
howitzer 385
HQ ISAF 349
Hudson, General 97
Hughes, Brigadier Gordon 265, 272, 287, 290
Humvee vehicle replacement 385
Hunt, Rex 30
Hunter, Colonel Hugh 105
Hurd, Douglas 157
Hussein of Jordan, King 127

Identification Friend or Foe (IFF) 159–60, 387
IEDs (improvised explosive devices) 25, 300–1, 330, 385
Illustrious, HMS 263
Independence, USS 88
Infantry Division (3rd) (US) 302–3
information technology 388
intelligence 391
  and Barras operation 273–3, 289
  and Bosnian conflict 210–11, 232, 248
  and Grenada 93–4, 98, 100, 107, 115
Intelligence Support Activity (ISA) 179
International Criminal Court (ICC) 4
International Security Assistance Force see ISAF
Intrepid 32, 33, 39
Invincible 33
IRA 201
Iran
  and Bosnian conflict 211–12
  war with Iraq 123
Iraq
  British occupation after First World War 26

chemical attack on Kurds (1988)
124
post-war relations with Britain 124
war with Iran 123
Iraq conflict (1990–91) 1, 7, 15–16,
122, 123–60
adoption of UN Resolution (678)
140–1
air war 141–2, 147, 160
and Arab League 127, 128
arrival of 7th Armoured Brigade in
Al Jubayl and joining up with
American Marines 131–9, 317
beginning of land campaign 150–1
casualties 152, 155
chemical weapons issue 133–4
contrast with 2003 conflict 159
deployment of US forces in Saudi
Arabia 128–30, 160
destruction of Scud sites 144–5
failure to disarm Saddam Hussein
155–7
first-phase advance of Marines
towards Kuwait City 150–1
initial appeasement of Saddam
Hussein 125–6
invasion of Kuwait by Iraq 126–7
Iraqi raids into Al Wafra and Khafji
143
keeping Israel out of war aim by
coalition 144
launching of Scud missiles against
Israel by Iraqis 143–4
lessons to be learned from 388–9
and media 134, 136–7, 145–7
operational plan for ground force
attack 147–9
prediction of casualties 136–7
preparatory 'artillery raids' 150
reassigning of 1st Armoured
Division to VII Corps main attack
138–9, 140
Schwarzkopf's deception plan 132,
142, 150
second-phase attack and advance on
Kuwait 151–3
success of 159
and Thatcher 127–8, 129, 130–1,
155–6
ultimatum issued to Saddam Hussein
150
and United Nations 129
US coalition forces and resources
135

Iraq conflict (2003) 4, 8, 15, 22–3,
128, 158, 292–3, 295, 384, 390–1,
393, 394
Iraq, post-war 23–4, 293–4, 295–7
Abu Ghraib abuses and impact of
307–8, 324, 327
battle against insurgents and
weapons used by 300–1
and battle for Fallujah see Fallujah
British approach in south 304–5
chains of command 295–7
'contractors' in 309–10
and CPA 297–8, 319
de-Ba'athification and disbanding of
Iraqi Army 24–5, 299
election of al-Maliki as Prime
Minister 294
formation of Anbar Awakening
337–8
formation of new Iraqi interim
government 326
insurgency in 23, 25
looting and disorder 297
rejection of al-Qa'eda by Sunnis
337–8
Iraq Stabilization Group (ISG) 297
Iraqi Air Force 141–2
Iraqi Battalion (2nd) 313
Isa, Sheikh 131
ISAF (International Security Assistance
Force) 347, 348, 349, 353
Israel, and Iraq conflict (1990–91)
143–4
Izetbegovic, President Alia 206, 215,
217

Jackson, General Mike 19, 170
al-Janabi, Abdullah 294
Janvier, Major-General Bernard 140,
234
Jilao, General 182–3
Johnson, President 328
Johnston, Marine General Robert
168, 172–3
Joint Rapid Reaction Force 261
Joint Special Operations Command
179
Jones, Lieutenant-Colonel 'H'
(Herbert) 34–8, 44, 45–6, 47,
50–1, 53, 54, 56–60, 69–70, 71,
73, 74
Joulwan, General George 225
JSTARS 142
Junor, John 137

Kabbah, Ahmed Tejan 255, 256, 257–8, 272
Kabul (Afghanistan) 342, 347, 348
Kajaki Dam (Afghanistan) 354–5
Kallay, 'Brigadier' Foday 266, 269, 270–1, 274, 277, 283, 286
Kamajors 255
Kandahar, Battle of (1880) 342
Karadzic, Radovan 216, 217
Karremans, Lieutenant-Colonel Thom 233
Karzai, President Hamid 377, 381
Keeble, Major Chris 35, 38, 60–1, 65, 66–7, 68, 70, 71
Kelly, John 89, 125
Khomeini, Ayatollah 123
King, Tom 131, 137, 138
Kiszely, General Sir John 328–9, 335–6
Kloske, Dennis 125
Kopaci (Bosnia) 239
Korbelova, Marie 209
Korean War 125
Koroma, Ernest Bai 290, 291
Koroma, Johnny Paul 255
Kosovo 19–20, 390
Kouyate, Lansana 172, 259
Krajina (Bosnia) 238
Kurdistan 26
Kurds 124, 293
Kusic, Major 222–3
Kuwait
    invasion of by Iraq (1990) see Iraq conflict (1990-91)
    threat of Iraq invasion (1961) 123–4
Kwai, River 58
Kyser, Lieutenant-Colonel Gyles 322

Lake, Anthony 212
Lashkar Gah (Helmand Province) 352, 368
Latif, Colonel Muhammad 323
Leach, Admiral Sir Henry 31, 32
League of Nations 6
Lewis, Damien, Operation Certain Death 250
Lomé Peace Agreement (1999) 258
London, July bombings (2005) 314
London Conference
    (1992) 207
    (1995) 237
    (2006) 342
Londonderry 201, 301

Lucas, Captain Keith 102
Lynx helicopters 269

MacArthur, General Douglas 159, 317–18, 397
McCaffrey, Lieutenant-General Barry 147, 154, 210
McCoy, Brian 320, 321
McDonald, Admiral Wesley L. 86, 90, 93–4
McKiernan, Lieutenant-General David 295
McKnight, Lieutenant-Colonel Danny 187, 188, 189–90
Magbeni (Sierra Leone) 265–6, 270, 272, 276, 287
Major, John 225–6, 231, 246, 371
Malaya emergency 4, 5
al-Maliki, Nouri 294
Mallet, Lieutenant Andy 362
Manila 317–18, 332, 340
Mao Zedong, On Guerrilla Warfare 2
Marine Amphibious Unit (MAU) (22) 87–8
Marines (UK)
    in Helmand 350, 352, 366–7, 368–9, 372–6
    in Sierra Leone 263, 264
Marines (US)
    in Fallujah 306–7, 308–9, 310–13, 315, 317, 318, 320–1, 327–8, 332–3
    and Iraq conflict 132, 140, 143, 154
    rivalry between Army and 113, 334
    and Somalia 168
Marshall, Major Alan 265, 266, 270, 274, 287, 287–8
Mattis, Major-General James 306–7, 313, 320, 321, 326
Mechanized Brigade (12) 374
medals see honours
Médécins Sans Frontières 175
media 75–6, 391
    adverse influence on warfare 47–8
    and Afghanistan 370–1
    and Barras Operation 277
    and Falklands/Goose Green 47–8, 75
    and Fallujah 330
    and Grenada 10, 76, 109–11
    and Helmand 75, 370–1

and Iraq conflict (1990–91) 134,
   136–7, 145–7
and Sidle Report 111
and Sierra Leone 267
Melia, Corporal 55
Menendez, Brigadier 41, 66
Menzies, John 236–7
mercenaries 257 *see also* contractors
Meredith, Sergeant 62–3
Merlin Mark 3 Support helicopters
   365
Mesopotamia 26
Metcalf, Admiral Joseph 90, 94, 96,
   98, 107, 108–9, 117
Metz, Lieutenant-General Thomas 326
MILAN missile 73
Miles, General 325
Military Assistance and Training Team
   (MATT) 267
Military Cross 371
military estimates 394
Military Medal 371
Military Operations Other Than War
   (MOOTW) 12, 247, 284
Military Operations in Urban Terrain
   (MOUT) 201
Miller, Major-General Geoffrey D.
   308
Milosevic, Slobodan 209, 232
Ministry of Defence 251–2
Mission Command 73, 247–8
mission-oriented orders 75, 357, 392
Mitterand, President François 216
Mladic, General Ratko 207, 211,
   215, 227, 230, 232, 237, 238–9,
   240, 242, 243
Mogadishu (1992–3) 2, 16–18, 26,
   161–202, 212, 317, 368
   air and ground attacks and engage-
      ment with Aideed's men 176
   American casualties 193, 196, 198
   attack on Qaaybdid's house 177
   attack on UN Pakistani troops and
      reaction to 171, 174–6
   attempt at gaining control of radio
      173–4
   deployment of Task Force Ranger to
      capture Aideed 178–85
   disunity of command 201
   Jilao mission 182–3
   men and aircraft allocated to Aideed
      mission 185–7
   personnel blamed for disaster
      196–7
      raid on UNDP HQ debacle 181–2
   relationship between Rangers and
      Delta Force 275
   shooting down of Blackhawks and
      operations to rescue men from
      crash site 161, 188–94
   tit for tat killing 177
   underestimating of enemy 198,
      201, 286
   and United Nations 17, 199–200
Mogadishu Line 207
Moltke, Helmuth von 46
Momoh, Major-General Joseph Saidu
   254–5
Monk, Roy 155
Monroe Doctrine 81
Montgomery, Corporal J. 64
Montgomery, David 120
Montgomery, Major-General Thomas
   171, 172, 173–4, 180, 193
Moore, Major-General Jeremy 42, 44
Motorman Operation (Londonderry)
   201
Mountain Division (10th) 170
Mousa, Corporal 270, 271–2, 282,
   283, 286
Mozambique 261
Mubarak, President Hosni 126, 127
Muirhead, Lance-Corporal 358–9
Musa Qala 356, 358–60
Myers, General 325
Myers, Kendall 24

Najaf 314
Napoleon 372
National Guard 387
NATO 7, 10–11, 200
   and Afghanistan 8, 9, 20, 26,
      380–1, 389
   and Bosnian conflict 205, 210,
      215, 244
   decline of effectiveness 389
   enlargement of 14
   and Kosovo 19–20, 390
   and United States 14
Natonski, Major-General Richard
   326
Neame, Major Philip 38, 43, 45, 53,
   56, 61, 62, 64, 67, 71, 72
Negroponte, Ambassador 326
Nelson, Second Lieutenant 97
Newell, Lieutenant-Colonel P. 332
Nicholson, Michael 48, 67–8
Nigeria 57

night vision 159
Nimrod 396
9/11 9, 292, 314, 345
Non-Combat Evacuation Operation
    (NEO) 262
Noriega, General Manuel 124, 178
Norland 38
Norman, Sergeant 59, 60
Northern Alliance 346
Northern Ireland 38
Nott, John 31, 32
Now Zad (Helmand) 352, 369
Nunn, Lieutenant Richard 60
Nye, Andrew 155

Oakley, Robert 172–3, 197
Ocean, HMS 263
Ocean Venture (81) 83–4
OECS (Organization of East
    Caribbean States) 84, 85, 95,
    119, 120
Ollala, Lieutenant-Colonel David
    Santa 216
Olson, Lieutenant-Colonel Gregg
    307, 312
Omar, Mullah Mohammed 345
orders 391–2
    formal 392
    mission-oriented 62, 75, 247, 357,
        392
Organization of African Unity (OAU)
    164
Organization of East Caribbean States
    see OECS
Owen, David 207

Pacific Settlement of Disputes 6
Pakistan 346–7
Pale (Bosnia) 227
Palliser Operation (Sierra Leone) 21,
    248, 262–7, 288, 289
Para (1) (Parachute Regiment)
    and Barras Operation 251, 263,
        264, 268–9, 274–5, 279–81, 284,
        285, 285–6, 288
    in Iraq/Fallujah 306, 358
Para (2)
    and Falklands War 37–40, 69–70
        see also Goose Green
    Northern Ireland tour 38
    training of under 'H' 35–7
Para (3) 37
    in Helmand 352, 353, 354–8
    in Iraq 358

Parsons, Sir Anthony 141, 203, 206,
    388
Pashtuns 343, 344
Pathfinders 103–4
peacekeeping 6–7, 16, 78, 245–6
Pedroza, Vice-Commodore Wilson 66,
    67
People's Revolutionary Armed Forces
    (PRAF) 81
People's Revolutionary Army (PRA)
    84, 97, 115
People's Revolutionary Government
    (PRG) 77
People's Revolutionary Militia (PRM)
    81
Permanent Joint Headquarters (PJHQ)
    (Northwood) 260, 261
Petraeus, General 338
Phantom Fury Operation (Fallujah)
    328–34
Pierre, Leslie 78, 81, 118
Pike, Otis 110
pilot training 387
Pioggi, Lieutenant-Colonel 67
Pook, Squadron Leader Jerry 64–5
Popovic, Colonel 240
Post Traumatic Stress Disorder (PTSD)
    382
Powell, General Colin 135, 146, 178
Presidential Decision Document (25)
    (PDD 25) 196
Price, Paul 102
Principals Group 208, 209
Prisoner of War Guard Force (PWGF)
    152
Provide Comfort Operation 166
Provincial Reconstruction Teams
    (PRTs) 347

Qaaybdid, Colonel Abdi 174, 177
Queen's Own Highlanders 37
Quick Reaction Force (QRF) 170,
    172, 187–8, 189, 191, 195

Ranger Battalion (1st) 87, 89, 91,
    93, 103–4, 275
Rapid and Quick Reaction capabilities
    387–8
Reagan, Ronald 162
    and Grenada 78, 83, 86, 95
Reid, John 27, 341, 379
Republican Guard 147
Restore Hope Operation (Somalia)
    163, 166

Revolutionary United Front *see* RUF
Rice, Condoleezza 297
Richards, General Sir David 262,
    289, 349, 377, 382, 392–3
Richburg, Keith 163–4, 165
Riley, Colonel Jonathon 217, 218,
    221, 224, 226, 227, 231, 236,
    239, 241–2, 243, 245–6, 247, 248
al-Rishawi, Sheikh Abdul Sittar Bezea
    337, 338
Roberts, General Sir Frederick 342–3
Robertson, Lord 385
Rogatica Brigade (Serbian) 222–3
Roquejeoffre, Lieutenant-General
    Michel 130
Rose, General Sir Michael 169, 341–2
    and Bosnian conflict 19, 202,
    207–8, 213–14, 215, 216
Royal Air Force 396
Royal Engineers 350
Royal Gloucestershire, Berkshire and
    Wiltshire Regiment 217
Royal Irish Regiment 265, 266, 268
Royal Navy 12, 31–2, 33, 142, 396
Royal Welch Fusiliers (1st Battalion)
    (RWF) 211, 212, 217–30, 234–6,
    239–43, 245, 248
RPGs
    use of by insurgents in Iraq 300
    use of by Somalis 188, 190, 191,
    192
    use of by Taliban 359
Rubin, James 199
RUF (Revolutionary United Front)
    20, 21, 254–5, 257, 259, 260–1,
    265
Rumsfeld, Donald 23, 295, 297, 303,
    324, 329
Russia, and Bosnian conflict 208
Rwanda 18, 196
Ryan, Major 36

Saddam Hussein 25, 123, 125–7,
    142, 295
al-Sadr, Moqtada 313
'safe areas' in Bosnia 213, 244
Saleh, Major-General Jasim 322–3,
    325
Sanchez, Lieutenant-General Ricardo S.
    295, 296, 297, 310, 320, 324, 326
Sandline International 256, 257, 390
Sangin (Helmand province) 356, 361,
    374–6, 381
Sankoh, Foday 254, 257, 258, 265

Sarajevo 203, 207, 209, 213, 237
    mortar attack on Markale Market
    (1994) 214, 241, 243
SAS (Special Air Service Regiment)
    42, 100, 251
    and Barras Operation 268, 272–3,
    274–7, 279–86
Sattler, Lieutenant-General John 326,
    327, 334
Al-Saud, Prince Khalid bin Sultan bin
    Abdul Aziz 130
Saudi Arabia 128–9, 141, 160
SBS (Special Boat Service) 39–40,
    100, 251, 268, 276–7
Scheffer, Jan de Hoop 381
Scholtes, Major-General Dick 90,
    93, 104
Schwarzkopf, Major-General Norman
    and Grenada 89, 90, 96, 103, 107,
    109, 112–13, 115–18, 122
    and Iraq conflict (1990-91) 122,
    129–30, 132, 135, 140, 144, 145,
    146, 154, 159, 160
Scoon, Sir Paul 79, 84, 93, 108, 111,
    118, 119, 120–1
Scud missiles 141, 143–4
Sea Kings 40, 365
SEAL team 98, 99–100
Second World War 130, 392
Security Support Solutions Limited
    364–5
Serbia 206
Serbs 205 *see also* Gorazde
Sheffield, HMS 41
Shia 293, 294, 391
Shughart, Sergeant Randy 196
Sidle Report 111
Sierra Leone 18, 20–2, 248, 290, 390
    attempt to overthrow government by
    RUF 254–5, 260–1
    backtracking on Lomé agreement by
    Sankoh and taking of UN
    hostages 259–60
    and Barras Operation *see* Barras
    Operation
    capture of hostages by West Side
    Boys 266–7, 270
    and diamonds 252–3
    elections (2007) 290–1
    employment of Executive Outcomes
    to fight RUF 255
    history 252
    Lomé Peace Agreement (1999) and
    monitoring of process 258–9

and Operation Amble 279
and Operation Palliser 21, 248, 262–7, 288, 289
problems in 290
Sandline initiative and return of Kabbah to power 256
training of Sierra Leone's army in battle against RUF 264, 265
use of amputation 253–4
Silajdzic, Haris 215
Silver Operation (Helmand) 375–6, 392
Simpson, John 345
Sir Percivale, RFA 278
Slinger, Paul 117
Slovenia 203, 205, 206
SLRs (self-loading rifles) 283
Small Boys Units 253–4
smart weapons 14, 22
Smith, General Rupert 149–50, 153, 217, 219–20, 221, 236, 237, 238, 241, 242, 244
Somalia 26, 161–202, 271
agreement to ccascfire by Aideed 197–8
agreement on US-led humanitarian intervention 166–7
command and control arrangements for UNOSOM II 170
establishment of UNSCOM I and failure to control situation 164–5
independence of 162
overthrow of Barre 163–4
passing of UN Resolution (794) 166
starvation in 165
transition from UNITAF to UNOSOM II 169–70
UNITAF's humanitarian operation 168–9
US/UN attitude towards Aideed 171
see also Mogadishu
'Somalia Effect' 271
South Georgia 31
Soviet Union 13
and Grenada 97–8, 115
reaction to Iraq's invasion of Kuwait 124
war in Afghanistan 343–4
Special Air Service Regiment *see* SAS
Special Boat Service *see* SBS
Spencer, Julius 287

Spicer, Lieutenant-Colonel Tim 256
Srebrenica 214–15, 217
declared 'safe area' 213
massacre (1995) 203, 211, 232–3
Stanley (Falklands) 30, 31
Strasser, Captain Valentine 255
suicide bomber 26
suicides 387
Sunnis 293, 294, 391

Taguba, General Antonio 324
Talbott, Strobe 212
Taliban 27, 274–5, 344–56, 360, 366, 369, 370, 377, 378
Task Force Ranger 185–91, 193
Taylor, Lieutenant-Colonel Wes 104, 105
Taylor, President Charles 254, 258
Taylor, Sergeant Wayne 231
technology 14–15
Tehran hostage crisis 85–6
Thatcher, Margaret 10, 15, 24
and Falklands 29–30, 31, 32, 44–5, 74–5
and Grenada 95–6
and Iraq conflict (1990–91) 127–8, 129, 130–1, 155–6
sacking of 138
Thomas, Brigadier Jerry 364, 375
Thompson, Brigadier Julian 34–5, 40–1, 43, 44–5, 68, 364
Thompson, Corporal John 372–4
Thompson, Sir Robert 4–5, 13
Tiger Brigade 140
Tinnion, Brad 283
Tito, President 205
Toole, Lance-Corporal 58
Tootal, Lieutenant-Colonel Stuart 353, 355–6, 395
Tortolo, Colonel 96, 106
Travers, General Sir Paul 73
Trident 32
Trobaugh, Major-General Edward 90, 107
Truman, President Harry 113
Tucker, Sir Francis 1, 396
Tudjman, Franjo 209
Tuzla (Bosnia) 213, 215, 237

UN Charter (1945) 3, 6, 119, 390
see also Chapter VII
UN Force in Cyprus (UNFICYP) 7
UN Protected Areas (UNPAs) 207
UN Secretary-General 7

UN Security Council 3, 6, 15
  Resolution (660) 127, 129
  Resolution (661) 127
  Resolution (678) 140, 156–7, 166
  Resolution (713) 206
  Resolution (751) 164
  Resolution (752) 207
  Resolution (770) 207
  Resolution (776) 207
  Resolution (794) 166
  Resolution (824) 213
  Resolution (836) 213
  Resolution (837) 175–6
  Resolution (1132) 256
  Resolution (1270) 20, 258, 258–9
  Resolution (1373) (2001) 345
  Resolution (1386) 347
  and Somalia 164
UNAMSIL (United Nations Mission in
  Sierra Leone) 20, 21, 258, 259,
  262, 267
United Nations
  and Bosnian conflict 207
  decline in effectiveness 388, 389
  and Iraq conflict (1990–91) 129
  and Mogadishu 17–18, 199–200
United Nations High Commissioner
  for Refugees (UNHCR) 218
United Nations Mission in Sierra
  Leone see UNAMSIL
United Nations Observer Mission in
  Sierra Leone (UNOMSIL) 257
United States 388–9
  and Bosnian conflict 200, 208–10,
  211–12, 244
  casualty-aversion in operations after
  Mogadishu 196
  and NATO 14
  relations with UN in Mogadishu
  17–18
  rivalry between Army and Marines
  334
United Task Force, Somalia (UNITAF)
  168
UNOSOM I (United Nations Operation
  in Somalia I) 64–5
UNOSOM II 169–70, 202
UNPROFOR 202, 207–8, 210, 244,
  245
Urquhart, Sir Brian 6, 16
US Army 11, 12

  reduction in 14
  rivalry between Marines and 113,
  334
US Central Command (USCENTCOM)
  295

Van Loon, Major-General 375
Vance, Cyrus 207
Védrine, Hubert 20
Veritas Operation (Afghanistan) 346
Vessey, General 110, 111
Victoria Cross 70
Vietnam 85, 109, 317, 393
Vigilant Resolve Operation (Fallujah)
  313–21, 339
VII Corps 147, 150, 151, 153, 154
Viking (armoured personnel carrier)
  366

Wahabi sect 299
Waller, General Cal 146
war crimes 4
'war on terror' 4, 16, 380, 390
Warba 123, 126
Warner, Senator John 178–9
Warsaw Pact 8, 9, 10–11, 13–14
Waxman, Henry 311
Weinberger, Caspar 110
West, Bing, No True Glory 292
West Side Boys 21, 252, 256, 266,
  269, 273–4, 275, 277, 278,
  282–4, 286–7
Wharton, Clifton 197
Whyte, Winston 78
'Wider Peacekeeping' doctrine 16
Wiebes, Professor Cees, Intelligence
  and the War in Bosnia 211
Wilkes, Lieutenant-General 138
Williams, Captain Matt 69
Wood, William B. 379
Wright, Corporal Mark 355
Wright-Boycott, Major 359–60

Yeltsin, Boris 161
Yemen 140
Yousaf, Mohammed 344
Yugoslav Federal Army (JNA) 206
Yugoslavia, former 203, 204, 205

Al-Zarqawi, Abu Musab 335
Zepa 213, 217, 235